GOD'S LONG SUMMER

• C H A R L E S   M A R S H •

GOD'S
LONG
SUMMER

STORIES OF FAITH
AND CIVIL RIGHTS

• PRINCETON UNIVERSITY PRESS • PRINCETON, NEW JERSEY •

Copyright © 1997 by Princeton University Press
Published by Princeton University Press, 41 William Street,
Princeton, New Jersey 08540
In the United Kingdom: Princeton University Press,
Chichester, West Sussex
All Rights Reserved

Second printing, and first paperback printing, 1999
Paperback ISBN 0-691-02940-7

The Library of Congress has cataloged the cloth edition of this book as follows
Marsh, Charles, 1958–
God's long summer : stories of faith and civil rights / Charles Marsh
p.   cm.
Includes bibliographical references and index.
ISBN 0-691-02134-1 (cloth : alk. paper)
1. Afro-Americans—Civil rights—Mississippi—History—
20th century. 2. Civil rights movements—Mississippi—History—
20th century. 3. Civil rights—Mississippi—Religious aspects—
Christianity. 4. Civil rights workers—Religious life—
Mississippi—History—20th century. 5. Mississippi—
Race relations. 6. Mississippi—Church history—
20th century. I. Title.
E185.93.M6M26 1997   97-10668
305.896'0730762—dc21

Elizabeth Sewell, "Ballad," from "Five Mississippi Poems," reprinted
from *Signs and Cities* (Chapel Hill, University of
North Carolina Press, 1968).

This book has been composed in Berkeley Book

The paper used in this publication meets the
minimum requirements of ANSI/NISO Z39.48-1992
(R1997) (*Permanence of Paper*)

http://pup.princeton.edu

Printed in the United States of America

5   7   9   10   8   6

To

JOE PORTER,

JEROME JOHNSON,

TERRY CAVES,

WALTER CHANDLER,

JOEY ROBERTS,

and all my other classmates

in the first integrated school

in Laurel, Mississippi

———

You can sense it where you're lying, open-eyed, upon your beds,
  O the iron and the weeping such as loving eyes afford,
Where the tigerish divisions tear God's body into shreds,
  O the iron and the weeping where the grapes of wrath are stored,
Through the worship, through the concert, through the phalanx of police,
Where merely to be Coloured is disturbance-of-the-peace,
And you begin to wonder if this sound will ever cease—
  O the iron, O the weeping, O inexorable Lord!

  Elizabeth Sewell, from "Five Mississippi Poems" (1968)

CONTENTS

ABBREVIATIONS

Amistad	Amistad Research Center, Tulane University, New Orleans
CNAC	Cambridge Nonviolent Action Committee
COFO	Council of Federated Organizations
CORE	Congress of Racial Equality
LCFO	Lowndes County Freedom Organization
MFDP	Mississippi Freedom Democratic Party
NAACP	National Association for the Advancement of Colored People
NAG	Nonviolent Action Group, Cambridge, Maryland
SCLC	Southern Christian Leadership Conference
SNCC	Student Nonviolent Coordinating Committee

GOD'S LONG SUMMER

INTRODUCTION

With God on Our Side:
Faiths in Conflict

THE THEOLOGIAN Karl Barth once said that when God enters history,
something wholly different and new begins, "a history with its own dis-
tinct grounds, possibilities and hypotheses." The paramount question,
if this proposition be granted, is whether we have the good will to medi-
tate and enter upon this new world inwardly.[1] How would the world look
if we let ourselves be led far beyond what is elsewhere called history—into
a new way of seeing, into the world of God?

This book invites the reader to revisit the tumultuous landscape of the
American civil rights movement in Mississippi: to look again at some familiar stories (and to look for the first time at many unfamiliar ones) in
light of the hypothesis that God was—in some perplexing and hitherto un-
delineated way—present there. Of course, both the civil rights and the
anti-civil rights movements were saturated with religion; in every mass
meeting, church service, and Klan rally, God's name was invoked and his
power claimed. White conservatives and civil rights activists, black militants and white liberals, black moderates and klansmen, all staked their
particular claims for racial justice and social order on the premise that God
was on their side. Undoubtedly, religion played an instrumental role in
giving these claims authorization. Yet I ask the reader to consider how the
movement may appear anew if its complex and often cacophonous religious convictions are taken seriously—if the content of such language is
not dismissed as smooth justifications of cruelty or dissent, pragmatic tools
in the service of political ends, or opiates of the status quo. How do ordinary southern towns become theaters of complex theological drama?[2]

I tell the story of what happened when differing images of God inter-
sected, and then clashed, in one violent period of the black struggle for freedom and equality under the law. Yet I do not provide a systematic analysis
of how religion shaped the civil rights movement, which would encompass
not only Protestant and Catholic influences but Jewish and Hindu—and to
a lesser extent Islamic and Buddhist—as well. Nor do I provide an institutional history such as James F. Findlay, Jr.'s splendid *Church People in the*

Struggle.[3] Rather, I tell the story, or the interwoven stories, of certain individuals whose lives converged in Mississippi, sometimes with devastating consequences, during the long, hot summer of 1964, when civil rights activists in the Congress of Racial Equality (CORE) and the Student Nonviolent Coordinating Committee (SNCC), working under the auspices of the Council of Federated Organizations (COFO), turned their energies not only toward defeating Jim Crow on his own turf but toward transforming the country as well.[4] In the "Christ-haunted" south, and even more in Mississippi, "the most race-haunted of all American states," one finds an intensification of a religious conflict that existed throughout the civil rights movement (and exists, though perhaps with less intensity, in the American Protestant church as a whole).[5] The commitment to a brutal pigmentocracy was matched only by a fervent belief in Jesus Christ; and the fear of change (rendered "impurity") strained this fragile dialectic toward an inescapable apotheosis of violence.

I follow the lives of five religious persons from the experience of their "calling" through their spiritual and social formation to the turbulent season of their convergence in Mississippi—and in one case, to life beyond Mississippi. I try to reckon with the complexity of the story (or stories), and with the varied theological sources that configure these individuals' responses to black suffering and disenfranchisement. Although the lives of these five persons may be construed as types of responses, I wish to grant maximum appreciation to the particularity of their stories. Obviously, an accurate picture of how religion shaped the civil rights movement cannot be drawn from a crude juxtaposition of good social gospel guys on the one hand and bible-thumping racists on the other. Over the course of the movement, some bible-thumpers appeared as social progressives, and some who were weaned on liberal theology championed segregation.[6] There are no easy patterns for predicting the way religious ideas govern particular courses of action. Yet there is in each case a theological sense or inner logic in these embodied theologies, and thus there exist patterns specific to the complex interaction of faith and lived experience. I invite the reader to contemplate the inner sense of these religious worlds, to seek an understanding of how the social order looks from the various perspectives of faith, both to broaden our knowledge of the civil rights movement and better to discern how images of God continue to inform differing visions of civic life and responsibility. It is thus my hope that the book will appeal not only to scholars of religion but to the larger number of people interested in the public debate about race, character, and the common good.[7]

The book opens with Fannie Lou Hamer of Ruleville, Mississippi, leaving the cotton fields of the Delta in 1962 to "work for Jesus" in civil rights activism. In 1964 Mrs. Hamer burst onto the national scene as the commanding voice of the Mississippi Freedom Democratic party (MFDP) in its bold attempt to unseat the all-white state delegation at the National Democratic Convention in Atlantic City. As a member of the Student Nonviolent Coordinating Committee and a courageous leader in voter registration and grass-roots political organizing, Mrs. Hamer gave eloquent witness to a liberating, reconciling faith, shaped by a skillful blending of African American hymnody and spirituality, prophetic religion, and an indefatigable belief in Jesus as friend and deliverer of the poor.[8] Strangely, much historical literature has obscured her deep religious convictions, presenting instead the picture of a freedom fighter and political organizer whose faith seems, if not incidental to her movement life, at best peripheral.[9] I am heartened by James M. Washington's comment that the spirituality of the civil rights movement "begs for our attention."[10] Following Professor Washington's lead, I wish to describe Fannie Lou Hamer not only as the prophetic voice of Mississippi's "local people" but as one of America's most innovative religious imaginations.[11]

Sam Holloway Bowers, Jr., the high priest of white Christian militancy, considered Mrs. Hamer and her fellow travelers betrayers of "Jesus the Galilean." Elected in 1964 as Imperial Wizard of the White Knights of the Ku Klux Klan of Mississippi, Bowers ruled over a four-year campaign of white terrorism, and is alleged to have orchestrated at least nine murders, seventy-five bombings of black churches, and three hundred assaults, bombings, and beatings. Until my interviews with Bowers (the only interviews he has ever granted), it was the conventional wisdom among scholars and journalists that his convoluted theological promulgations were either shrewd covers for his criminal rage, used to rally angry, uneducated white men around the cause of white supremacy, or something akin to psychotic rambling. Yet the picture of Bowers that develops upon closer scrutiny of his life and vocation, and in light of new information regarding his biography and religious self-understanding, is that of a man with exceedingly clear ideas about his divine priestly calling—a man convinced of his own world-historical consequence.[12] Bowers once described his calling by distinguishing between a preacher and a priest. A preacher, he said, points people toward the truth, pleading with the sinner to seek forgiveness. But the priest searches out the heretic with deadly intent—"this is what makes him powerful like a warrior." And the heretic—who for Bowers takes the form of civil rights activists, "liberal media whores," and "pagan academics"—cannot be forgiven. He can only be "eliminated."[13] Bowers's sinister vocation, his central role in the murders of civil rights workers Michael Schwerner, James Chaney, and Andrew Goodman, paints a harrowing portrait of the violent extremities of Christian nationalist zeal, authorized by the empowering convictions of faith.

Of the images of God coming into conflict in the civil rights movement, none seems more replete with contradiction than that of white mainline Protestantism. In most cases, the Southern white Protestant adheres to an evangelical belief, the heart of which is the confession of "a personal Lord and Savior" who has atoned for the sins of humanity. Yet in most cases, the confession remains disconnected from race relations—and often from social existence altogether. A white conservative minister could stand at the pulpit of any Baptist church in any hamlet of the deep South and preach from Paul's letter to the Corinthians that Jesus Christ reconciles all people to God and each other, and he would undoubtedly receive an enthusiastic chorus of "Amen" from the congregation; yet if the minister proceeded to explain that the Gospel message requires brotherhood with black people, and justice and mercy toward them, he would be run out of town by sundown.[14] My narrative of the state's preeminent Southern Baptist minister, William Douglas Hudgins of the First Baptist Church of Jackson, illustrates this religious sensibility—the bifurcation between proclamation and practice—and its evolution from a serene, deracinated piety. Hudgins's preaching, with its unmistakable blend of traditional Southern Baptist theology, anti-modernist fundamentalism, and civil religion, was put in the service of his singular emphasis on personal and spiritual purity. The important matters of faith were found in the interior dimensions of the soul's journey to God, or in the soul's "competency" before God. In a sermon at the beginning of the civil rights years, Hudgins proclaimed, "Now is the time to move the emphasis from the material to the spiritual."[15] Social existence becomes secondary, inconsequential to the real intent of faith. In the final analysis, concern for black suffering has nothing to do with following Jesus.

How then can we understand the theological shifts that inspired a handful of Southern white Christians to condemn Jim Crow for the sake of a desegregated South—indeed for sake of the "beloved community"—and ultimately for the sake of the Gospel? I address the question by looking at the civil rights life of the Reverend Edwin King, who as the white chaplain of black Tougaloo College in Jackson and the National Committeeman of the Mississipppi Freedom Democratic party and its candidate for lieutenant governor, performed the roles of church reformer, theological prankster, and pastor of his "movement congregation." My narrative of this renegade Methodist minister highlights the sometimes comic, sometimes tragic story of the church visits campaign, which attempted to desegregate and agitate white conservative and moderate churches. Under Ed King's direction, these confrontations between integrated groups of church visitors and white church leaders created a space (usually on the front steps of the church) where previously unspoken ideas on religion and race dramatically came to the light of day. The church visits campaign enacted time and again spectacular scenarios, teasing out of the various antagonists darkly comic and ironic assertions about faith and social existence. King's driving conviction was simple at its heart, though costly in its demands. If people took seriously their identities as Christians, they had no choice but to give up the practices of white supremacy—and not only white supremacy, but also class privilege, resentment, the concession to violence, anything that kept one from sacrificing all for the beloved community, for that interracial fellowship witnessing to the redemptive possibilities of reconciling love. However, from King's perspective, the failure of the church visits campaign, or rather the failure of the white church to open its doors and to preach racial justice, signaled the need for broader, more aggressive civil rights activism. In 1964, Ed King became one of the leaders of the Mississippi Freedom Democratic party and an active player in the massive initiative in voter registration and political empowerment that was the Summer Project.

Yet by summer's end in 1964 a growing number of African Americans in the civil rights movement, in particular younger members of the Student Nonviolent Coordinating Committee had become disenchanted with the pursuit and vision of a reconciled brotherhood and sisterhood. A contingent of more militant activists appeared eager to put reconciliation (or its all-too-rough legal equivalent of integration) on the back burner. Cleveland Sellers, who in 1964 had worked as a SNCC staff member in Mississippi, emerged in 1965 and 1966, along with his close friend and SNCC comrade, Stokely Carmichael, as an earlier champion of the new racial spirituality and nationalistic consciousness called Black Power.[16] As Sellers explained, "Black babies are not dying of malnutrition because their parents do not own homes in white communities. Black men and women are not being forced to pick cotton for three dollars a day because of segregation."[17] The real issue was power, these activists claimed. "Integration has little or no effect on such problems," Sellers said. In terms now resonant in our cultural repertoire, Black Power sought black liberation from white oppression "by any means necessary." Yet the construction of a rigid racial orthodoxy led, in turn, to narrowing standards of toleration. Despite its celebration of the ethnic, cultural, religious, and biological particularities of Americans of sub-Saharan African descent, Black Power did more tearing down than building up—though such iconoclasm no doubt accounted for much of its rhetorical appeal. In 1966, after interracialists like John Lewis had been made unwelcome and Fannie Lou Hamer was rendered "no longer relevant," the new SNCC vanguard began purging the organization of its white members.[18] Sellers's courageous, frenetic, and ultimately cataclysmic life in the movement offers a complex narrative of an African

American student activist whose Christian faith was profoundly changed by the spirituality of black nationalism.

The story does not have a happy ending. Despite the impressive slate of civil rights legislation enacted in the wake of the Summer Project—the Civil Rights Act of 1964 and the Voting Rights Act of 1965—the movement began to fragment in ways that continue even now to polarize blacks and whites. What began with Fannie Lou Hamer's spirited devotion to the God who was liberating blacks and whites from bondage ended with the collapse of the beloved community. Many whites in the movement, like Jeannette and Ed King or SNCC activists Bob and Dorothy Zellner, were ostracized by black nationalists, their hopes for racial healing and reconciliation deemed quaint and even annoying. White Christian conservatives, in turn, remained largely indifferent to black suffering, preoccupied instead with evangelism and church growth, and with personal vices like drinking, dancing, and "heavy petting." Of course, the White Knights of Ku Klux Klan were the screaming exception to such moralism, preferring concealment, calculated harassment, and acts of sabotage to deal with those "atheists and mongrels" who promoted "BI-RACISM, CHAOS AND DEATH."[19] However, by the late 1960s, the white militant organization had begun to disintegrate; the Klan's extremist views, its demonization of the outsider, its paranoid theories about Jewish world domination, and its dreams of a Christian nation were left for the fundamentalist mainstream to assimilate in more polite forms.[20]

Yet I do not entirely despair. In the conclusion to the book I suggest that it may be possible, if only with the most modest of results, to sift among these narratives and find ways to discriminate among the differing, often conflicting images of God. Whether such work helps us overcome the racial misreadings of the past or lays the groundwork for a new thinking about reconciliation and beloved community remains uncertain. There is no obvious reason to think that a wider knowledge of past failures will inspire Christian communities to act more responsibly in the future. However, quite apart from concrete proposals for reconciliation, these narratives do give us clarity for the difficult work ahead. In Mississippi, there is a farming term that may illuminate the point. In late winter when the land is cleared for plowing, many farmers burn their fields so they can see the ground for what it is—to see what's there, the bottles, cans, dried roots, the detritus of winter. This is "clearburning," burning clear the fields to prepare for a new planting and harvest.

This book is a kind of clearburning, a preparation for a time when white Christians will not have to be reminded by the accusing evidence of history that their proclamation has too often served cruel purposes; and when African American Christians will not have to be chided by Fannie Lou

Hamer with the sober judgment that problems will not be solved by hating whites; preparation for a time when whites and blacks together will reckon with their common humanity, keeping in mind the difficult wisdom of James Baldwin's remark that "to accept one's past—one's history—is not the same thing as drowning in it; it is learning how to use it."[21]

ONE

"I'm on My Way, Praise God":
Mrs. Hamer's Fight
for Freedom

Sticking with Civil Rights

ON A NIGHT in August of 1962, Fannie Lou Hamer attended a mass meeting at the Williams Chapel Church in Ruleville, Mississippi. A handful of civil rights workers from the Southern Christian Leadership Conference (SCLC) and the Student Nonviolent Coordinating Committee (SNCC) were in Sunflower County spreading the news of voter registration. Sunflower County, in the heart of that "most southern place on earth," the Mississippi Delta, was perhaps the most solid core of the iceberg of southern segregation. Appropriately, SNCC had recently selected the Delta as one of the strategic points of its voter registration initiative. If the movement could crack the Delta, the reasoning went, it would send unsettling reverberations through the state's recalcitrant white majority.[1]

There was great excitement in the chapel as James Bevel, one of Martin Luther King, Jr.'s, young colleagues in the SCLC, stood to address the people. His short sermon was taken from the sixteenth chapter of the Gospel of Matthew. He asked the congregation—mainly black men and women who worked on the nearby cotton plantations—to consider the words of the Lord when he rebuked the Pharisees and Sadducees. He read the Scripture: "Jesus answered and said unto them, When it is evening, ye say, It will be fair weather, for the sky is red. And in the morning, It will be foul weather today; for the sky is red and lowering. O ye hypocrites, ye can discern the face of the sky; but can ye not discern the signs of the times?" How can we discern the signs of the times, Bevel asked. How can we not recognize that the hour has arrived for black men and women to claim what is rightfully their own—indeed the right to vote? To be sure, most folk are not trained to discern the weather nor to forecast the future. But that is not our demand, Bevel told the people. Our demand is that we not ignore the clear signs before our eyes. God's time is upon us; let us not back down from the challenge.

Bevel's words stirred Mrs. Hamer's tired spirit. She had endured the burdens of white racism for forty-four years, living the hard life of a field hand on the Marlowe cotton plantation near Ruleville, a small town in the Delta. The youngest child born to Ella and Jim Townsend, by the age of seven Fannie Lou Hamer was in the fields picking cotton with her fourteen brothers and five sisters, the family working long days together and still not making "enough money to live on."[2] "My parents moved to Sunflower County when I was two years old," Mrs. Hamer recalled. "I will never forget, one day [when I] was six years old and I was playing beside the road and this plantation owner drove up to me and stopped and asked me, 'could I pick cotton.' I told him I didn't know and he said, 'Yes, you can. I will give you things that you want from the commissary store,' and he named things like crackerjacks and sardines—and it was a huge list that he called off. So I picked the 30 pounds of cotton that week, but I found out what actually happened was he was trapping me into beginning the work I was to keep doing and I never did get out of his debt again. My parents tried so hard to do what they could to keep us in school, but school didn't last four months out of the year and most of the time we didn't have clothes to wear."[3]

Fannie Lou Hamer's mother, with her "poor, ragged, rough black hands," raised her children "to be decent" and respect themselves.[4] Still the family's crushing poverty made her task's every detail an uphill battle:

> I used to watch my mother try and keep her family going after we didn't get enough money out of the cotton crop. To feed us during the winter months mama would go round from plantation to plantation and would ask the landowners if she could have the cotton that had been left, which was called scrappin' cotton. When they would tell her that we could have the cotton, we would walk for miles and miles and miles in the run of a week. We wouldn't have on shoes or anything because we didn't have them. She would always tie our feet up with rags because the ground would be froze real hard. We would walk from field to field until we had scrapped a bale of cotton. Then she'd take that bale of cotton and sell it and that would give us some of the food that we would need.
>
> Then she would go from house to house and she would help kill hogs. They would give her the intestines and sometimes the feet and the head and things like that and that would help to keep us going. So many times for dinner we would have greens with no seasoning and flour gravy. Sometimes there'd be nothing but bread and onions.[5]

Her mother's sight was irreparably damaged when an object struck her eye as she was swinging an axe to clear away roots and weeds from the ground. Unable to receive adequate medical attention, Ella Townsend suffered permanent damage to her eyes and would eventually become blind.[6]

Fannie Lou Hamer's father was a resourceful and hard-working plantation hand. But in Mississippi these virtues did not translate into a better life for his family. His agricultural skills and success with his own small farming ventures threatened the cruel and unyielding economic arrangements of white supremacy. In the middle 1940s, Jim Townsend "cleared some money" and bought some wagons, cultivators, plow tools and mules, with the hope of renting a plot of land the following year. But just about the time the family began to see the rewards of the father's labors—when they had "started to fix up the house real nice and had bought a car"—a white man stole one night into the trough where the mules fed and stirred a gallon of Paris Green into the animals' food. "It killed everything we had," Mrs. Hamer recalls. "When we got there, one mule was already dead. The other two mules and the cow had their stomachs all swelled up. It was too late to save them. That poisoning knocked us right back down flat. We never did get back up again. That white man did it just because we were getting somewhere."[7]

Fannie Lou Hamer knew something was wrong with the world she inherited, yet on that night in August 1962, she had not even heard about her civil rights. "We hadn't heard anything about registering to vote because when you see this flat land in here, when the people would get out of the fields, if they had a radio, they'd be too tired to play it. So we didn't know what was going on in the rest of the state even; much less in other places."[8] But Bevel's sermon, followed by SNCC member James Forman's talk on the constitutional right to vote, spoke deeply to Mrs. Hamer's longing for justice. Her imagination was charged by new moral and spiritual energies; she felt empowered to discern the signs of the time. And with more certainty than a red sky presages a fair tomorrow or a red sunrise stormy weather, Mrs. Hamer understood that her life would be very different from this point on. "When they asked for those to raise their hands who'd go down to the courthouse the next day, I raised mine. Had it up as high as I could get it. I guess if I'd had any sense I'd a-been a little scared, but what was the point of being scared. The only thing [the whites] could do was kill me and it seemed like they'd been trying to do that a little bit at a time since I could remember."[9] She heard the call of Jesus—and James Bevel— a call demanding sacrifice, but a call also promising freedom and empowerment. She was excited by the speakers' description of the power of the vote. "It made so much sense to me," she said."[10] These very women and men gathered at Williams Chapel Church—dirt-poor sharecroppers, field hands, and domestics—could force out of office the hateful politicians and sheriffs who had controlled the oppressive social order for as long as anyone could remember.

The call also made sense because the faith of the black church had prepared Mrs. Hamer for this moment. The church had sustained her wearied spirit when all other institutions had served contrary purposes. While Jim Crow society was designed to convince blacks they were nobodies, the black churches—even those that remained quiet on civil rights—preached a gospel that embraced the longings and desires of a disenfranchised people. A new social space took shape, offering an alternative to the social world of Jim Crow—a "nation within a nation," as E. Franklin Frazier once wrote—a world displaying the very reversal of the racist patterns embedded in the segregated South.[11] After enduring the indignities of demeaning jobs and discriminatory practices six days a week, black people could experience on Sunday mornings a rare though passionate affirmation of their humanity.[12] The last could become first; a field hand or a janitor could become a deacon, the maid or the cook a leader in the women's union.[13] Moreover, as a "nation within a nation," the black church not only awakened spiritual energies but also inspired the exercise of political ownership through such practices as electing officers and organizing church programs.[14] Thus, by the time James Bevel delivered his testimony in Ruleville, Mississippi, in August of 1962, Mrs. Hamer had been made ready by her involvement in church life to "step out on God's word of promise"—to put her faith into action.[15] She was ready to move, and did the next week when she joined a busload of people heading to the county courthouse to register to vote.

On August 31, Fannie Lou Hamer and seventeen other people boarded a beat-up bus and rode the thirty miles to the county seat of Indianola. No vehicle deserved the honor more. Owned by a black man from a neighboring county, the bus had been used in summers to haul cotton pickers and choppers to the plantations, and in winters to carry the same people to vegetable and fruit farms in Florida because there was not sufficient work in Mississippi to keep food on the table.[16] Yet when the eighteen passengers arrived in front of the courthouse in the sobering light of a midmorning sun, most of the enthusiasm aroused in the mass meetings and in the bus ride over had disappeared. Everyone on the bus took note of the situation; and nobody moved toward the door. Charles McLaurin, the SNCC worker who had come to Ruleville earlier in the year to coordinate voter registration activities in Sunflower County, described the moment: "[When] we got there most of the people were afraid to get off the bus. Then this one little stocky lady just stepped off the bus and went right on up to the courthouse and into the circuit clerk's office."[17] The others on the

bus slowly followed Mrs. Hamer to the voter registration desk in the court-
house, where they were asked by the circuit clerk to state their business.
Mrs. Hamer explained that they had come to the courthouse to register.
The clerk replied that all but two of the group would have to leave. Mrs.
Hamer and a young man named Ernest Davis remained in the office to
complete the application.

The "literacy test," as the registration application was officially called,
consisted of twenty-one questions, beginning with such seemingly straightforward queries as "What is your full name?" and "What is the date?"[18] The
most trivial of errors—like the absence of a comma in the date or a dis-
crepancy in punctuation—would often result in an immediate failure. The
registration form also included the question, "By whom are you employed?"—a question certain to send chills down the spine of all who
sought to register. "This meant that you would be fired by the time you got
back home," Mrs. Hamer explained.[19] In any case, the local newspapers
routinely published the names of the people who had completed an application.[20] Even more intimidating to many people seeking to register was the
question, "Where is your place of residence in the district?" It was feared—
for good reason—that the white Citizens' Council or the Ku Klux Klan
would have the applicant's home address by the end of the day. But whenever the literacy test was completed, the clerk would produce a text of the
state constitution and select a passage to be copied and given a "reasonable
interpretation"—which was to say, interpreted to the satisfaction of the
clerk. On the morning she tried to register in August of 1962, Mrs. Hamer
realized for the first time in her life—at the age of forty-four—that the state
of Mississippi had a constitution![21]

The day was long and exhausting. She was assigned a passage from the
state constitution dealing with de facto laws. In addition to the stressful
demands of the exam, the constant flow of white people through the registrar's office heightened her anxiety. Mrs. Hamer described the scene:
"People came in and out of the Courthouse with cowboy boots on, and
with rifles and with dogs—some of them looked like Jed Clampett of
the 'Beverly Hillbillies,' but these men weren't kidding."[22] She worked on
the answer throughout the afternoon until the office closed at 4:30. "I
knowed as much about a facto law as a horse knows about Christmas
Day," Mrs. Hamer said.[23] Of course, her knowledge of de facto law—or
lack of it—had nothing to do with her failing the exam. Had she been
white, she would have been excused from the impossible requirement of
providing an exegesis of the state constitution.[24]

On the ride back to Ruleville at the end of the day, just two miles beyond the city limits of Indianola, an approaching highway patrolman sig-
nalled the bus to a stop. The driver was arrested on the charge of operating a bus that too closely resembled a school bus, and he was taken to jail,

leaving the rest of the people alone to contemplate their prospects for a safe return home. Everyone became frightened, McLaurin recalls. "They didn't know whether they were going to have to sit out there on the road or whether in a few minutes the police were going to come back and put everybody in jail." Then Fannie Lou Hamer, standing toward the back of the bus, started to hum, then sing,

> Have a little talk with Jesus
> Tell him all about our troubles,
> Hear our feeble cry,
> Answer by and by,
> Feel the little prayer wheel turning,
> Feel a fire a burning,
> Just a little talk with Jesus makes it right.

Soon the others followed the lead of her deep, strong voice, and the group sang through their fears. They sang other songs as well; "This Little Light of Mine," "Freedom's Coming and It Won't Be Long," "Down by the Riverside." Someone shouted with delight, "That's Fannie Lou, she know how to sing."[25]

In the end, the driver was fined $100 for the misdemeanor of driving a bus that was "too yellow" (as the citation stated). Though only $30 could be scraped together, the officers reluctantly agreed to a lower fine and permitted the bus to carry the tired men and women back home to Ruleville. But Mrs. Hamer's day was far from over. She later remembered that before leaving home that morning, she had had a feeling that "something might happen." She had even packed a pair of shoes and a small bag of clothes just in case. "If I'm arrested or anything I'll have some extra shoes to put on," she said.[26] Her intimations proved accurate. When she returned in the late afternoon to her small house near the cotton fields, her daughter rushed out to meet her, explaining that the man she worked for was "blazing mad" and had been "raisin Cain" since she left home that morning.[27] Mrs. Hamer's husband "Pap" soon confirmed that an angry B. D. Marlowe was on his way over to talk about her trip to the county seat.

Perry ("Pap") and Fannie Lou Hamer had worked for eighteen years on the Marlowe plantation, mostly as sharecroppers, though in recent years Mrs. Hamer had been given the job of timekeeper. The fields on the Marlowe plantation were rich with cotton. From the first days of planting in early April to the chopping of weeds under the hot suns of June and July to the picking of the completed harvest in the frosty mornings of October and November, Mrs. Hamer and the other field hands had worked from the gray hour before sunrise until long after darkness had descended. "Cain't to cain't," as one local person described; "cain't see in the mornin' 'cause it's too early, cain't see at night 'cause it's too late."[28] The work was monotonous and humiliating. "Oh Lord, you know just how I feel," Mrs. Hamer might drag out as she slowly walked a long row of cotton, filling her sack for what seemed the thousandth time:[29]

> Oh Lord, they said you'd answer prayer,
> Oh Lord, we sure do need you now,
> Oh Lord, you know just how I feel.

Mrs. Hamer, like her mother and father before her, and her slave ancestors, had looked on the long rows of cotton as the only future white Mississippi would afford black folks in the Delta.

Marlowe arrived at the Hamers' home as expected. The Circuit Clerk had already called him on the telephone with a report of Mrs. Hamer's activities in Indianola. By the time Marlowe pulled his pick-up truck into the dirt road leading to the Hamers' place, he was not only angry but also nervous about the consequences he might face himself for failing to keep his help in order. Mrs. Hamer, who had been resting in bed after the exhausting day, slowly got up and walked to the front porch. "Did Pap tell you what I said about all this?" Marlowe asked. "Yessir," she replied. "Well, you'll have to go back down there and withdraw that thing, or you'll have to leave," he said. Mrs. Hamer's response must have seemed incredible to her white overseer of eighteen years. "Mr. Dee, I didn't go down there to register for you. I went down there to register for myself."[30] Marlowe told Mrs. Hamer that she had until morning to decide whether to withdraw her name from the application form. If she did not, she would have to leave the plantation immediately. Mrs. Hamer knew then exactly what she must do. She picked up her bag and departed that night, leaving her husband and two adopted daughters behind. The long road to freedom lay ahead, but there would be no turning back from the journey. Mrs. Hamer said, "I had been workin' at Marlowe's for eighteen years. I had baked cakes and sent them overseas to him during the war; I had nursed his family, cleaned his house, stayed with his kids. I had handled his time book and his payroll. Yet he wanted me out. I made up my mind I was grown, and I was tired. I wouldn't go back."[31]

Mrs. Hamer remained with friends in Ruleville for a few days. One friend, Mary Tucker, insisted that she spend the night with her. "Don't say you ain't got nowhere to stay as long as I got a shelter," Tucker consoled Mrs. Hamer. "If I ain't got but one plank, you stick your head under there, too."[32] But Pap Hamer was worried about violent attacks from the Klan, so a few days later Fannie Lou moved from the Tuckers' to a relatives' home in neighboring Tallahatchie County. The next week nightriders driving by the Tuckers opened fire on the bedroom where Mrs. Hamer had slept, spraying the room with sixteen bullets.

Death threats or not, she had said "yes" to the call; what the Lord required, she was now willing to give. And it was not long before the Lord, and Bob Moses, asked for more. Moses, the Harvard-trained philosophy student who a year earlier had launched the first SNCC projects in Mississippi, sent instructions to Charles McLaurin to go find the "lady who sings the hymns." McLaurin had been captivated by Mrs. Hamer's courage during their trip to the county courthouse in Indianola. Moses wanted Mrs. Hamer to attend SNCC's annual conference in Nashville and to consider working full time for the organization in voter registration. On a stormy night in the late fall of 1962, McLaurin went in search of the woman who would soon become the prophetic voice of the civil rights movement in Mississippi. He described the search:

> That evening it was raining like hell. Thundering and lightning and raining, and I was out there searching. Finally, though a few miles out of the way, I was told that I would find a little cabin at the top of a hill in Cascilla, just off the road and that the house would have two sides with a corridor running right down the middle. After driving in the pouring rain for hours, I finally located the little house on the side of the hill right by the road with smoke coming out of the chimney and the two sides as I was told and the corridor right down the middle.
>
> I knocked on the first door to the left and someone said come in. I walked into the building. There was a woman with her back to the door putting wood in this little pot-bellied stove. It was red hot. I never will forget it because it was raining and it was a little bit cool. And I said, "I'm looking for Fannie Lou Hamer." And she turned around and said, "I'm Fannie Lou Hamer."
>
> I told her that Bob Moses and the people at SNCC asked me to pick her up and take her on to the Nashville conference. And she got up and went to getting her stuff. . . . She couldn't have known whether I was kidnapping her or what. But she just got right up and came.[33]

Soon after her trip to Nashville, Mrs. Hamer returned to the Tuckers' place, full of the conviction that she must remain with the people who knew her best—the poor people of Sunflower County who looked to her for strength. "She didn't stay gone long before she come back," Mrs. Tucker recalled, "and when she come back, she said, 'Well, killing or no killing, I'm going to stick with civil rights.'"[34] By the end of the year, Mrs. Hamer was determined to take the literacy test again. She told the clerk in the Indianola courthouse point blank, "Now, you cain't have me fired 'cause I'm already fired, and I won't have to move now, because I'm not livin' in no white man's house. I'll be back here every thirty days until I become a registered voter."[35] She was refused a test on her second effort, but registered successfully on her third attempt. Her success meant further hardships. Pap Hamer was fired from his job at the Marlowe plantation and his car seized. Both Pap and Fannie Lou were now jobless. With their resources exhausted, and facing a new level of impoverishment, they rented a small house in Ruleville. "That was a rough winter. I hadn't had a chance to do any canning before I got kicked off, so didn't have hardly anything. I always can more than my family can use 'cause there's always people who don't have enough. That winter was bad, though."[36]

Rough times would not end with the coming of warm weather. In the summer of 1963, Mrs. Hamer was invited by Annelle Ponder, the SCLC field secretary in the Delta town of Greenwood, to attend the organization's citizenship school in South Carolina. Seven black Mississippians were chosen for the long bus ride to Charleston, where they were led by well-known civil rights activist Septima Clark in training sessions on voter registration. A week later, on June 9, near the end of the all-night ride home from South Carolina, the Continental Trailways bus stopped in Winona, Mississippi. When members of the group sat down at the lunch counter and asked to be served, several Winona policemen and highway patrolmen entered the station and forced them to leave. (As in much of the South, town officials had not accepted the ruling of the Interstate Commerce Commission outlawing segregated transportation facilities.)[37] Once outside, Annelle Ponder made a point of writing down the license number of one of the patrol cars, so infuriating a police officer that he began arresting everyone in sight. Mrs. Hamer had returned to the bus because her left leg, disfigured from polio as a child, was sore from the strenuous week. But when she saw the officers herding her companions into police cars, she came out and asked Ponder what the folks left on the bus should do. Should they drive on to Greenwood or wait at the station? Before her friend could answer, an officer in one of the police cars noticed Mrs. Hamer and shouted to a colleague, "Get that one there, bring her on down in the other car!" Mrs. Hamer was then shoved into the back seat, kicked in the thigh, and cursed repeatedly on the drive to the jail. "They carried us on to the county jail. It wasn't the city jail, [but] the county jail, so we could be far enough out. [They] didn't care how loud we hollered, wasn't nobody gon' hear us. . . . When we got to the jail they started beatin' the man—his name was James West—and they put us in cells, two to a cell, and I could hear all this hollerin' and goin' on. Then they took Miss Ponder. I could hear these awful sounds and licks and screams, hear her body hit the concrete, and this man was yellin', 'Cain't you say yes sir, you nigger bitch?'"

Each time that Annelle Ponder refused to say "yes sir" to the police officers, the swing of the blackjack was harder. Mrs. Hamer heard the sounds from her cell down the hall. "She kept screamin', and they kept beatin' on her, and finally she started prayin' for 'em, and she asked God to have mercy on 'em, because they didn't know what they was doin'. . . . I don't know how long it lasted before I saw Annelle Ponder passing the cell with both her hands up. Her eyes looked like blood, and her mouth was swollen. Her clothes were torn. It was horrifying."[38]

June Johnson, a fifteen-year-old black teenager who had attended the voter registration workshop, was the next person led by Mrs. Hamer's cell in this grim parade of tortured bodies. "The blood was runnin' down in her face, and they put her in another cell."[39] In the booking room, whence Johnson was coming, the sheriff had pulled the young girl aside for his own personal whipping. He asked her whether she was a member of the NAACP. She told him yes. Then he hit her on the cheek and chin, and when she raised her arms to protect herself, he hit her on the stomach. He continued to ask her questions about the NAACP—"who runs that thing?" "do you know Martin Luther King?" Soon the four men in the room—the sheriff, the chief of police, the highway patrolman, and another white man—threw Johnson onto the floor, beat her, and stomped on her body in concert. The men ripped Johnson's dress and tore her slip off; blood soaked her tattered clothes.

The men came next for Mrs. Hamer. "Get up from there, fatso," one of the policemen barked. When the officers confirmed that this was Fannie Lou Hamer from Ruleville—the same woman stirring up trouble in the Delta—they began to revile her with insulting words. "I have never heard that many names called a human in my life," she said later. "You, bitch, we gon' make you wish you was dead," an officer said, as he brought two black inmates into the bullpen to carry out his ghastly design for torture. Mrs. Hamer asked them, "You mean you would do this to your own race?" But an officer quickly warned the men, "If you don't beat her, you know what we'll do to you." Mrs. Hamer recalled, "So they had me lay down on my face, and they beat with a thick leather thing that was wide. And it had sumpin' in it *heavy*. I don't know what that was, rocks or lead. But everytime they hit me, I got just as hard, and I put my hands behind my back, and they beat me in my hands 'til my hands . . . was as navy blue as anything you ever seen." She tried to put her hands over the leg that was damaged from polio, but this only made her hands vulnerable to the beating. When the first inmate grew exhausted, the blackjack was passed to the second inmate. "That's when I started screaming and working my feet 'cause I couldn't help it." One of the white officers became so enraged when he heard Mrs. Hamer's cries that "he just run there and started hittin' me on the back of my head." The torture became more brutal. "I remember I tried to smooth my dress which was working up from all the beating. One of the white officers pushed my dress up. I was screaming and going on—and the young officer with the crew cut began to beat me about [the] head and told me to stop my screaming. I then began to bury my head in the mattress and hugged it to kill out the sound of my screams." By the end, the flesh of her beaten body was hard, one of her kidneys was permanently damaged, and a blood clot that formed over her left eye threatened her vision. "They finally told me to get up, and I just couldn't hardly get up, and they kept on tellin' me to get up. I finally could get up, but when I got back to my cell bed, I couldn't set down. I would *scream*. It hurted me to set down."[40] Back in her dark cell, Mrs. Hamer was left alone to bear the physical and spiritual effects of torture.

The experience in the Winona jail proved to be a kind of Golgotha for Mrs. Hamer, an experience of intense physical pain and humiliation. Her world was unmade, stripped of inner security, "uncreated" (to borrow from writer Elaine Scarry's austere analysis of torture). Objects, places or situations associated with nurturing or pleasure became brutal and mocking.[41] In the bullpen, Mrs. Hamer was made to lie down on a bed (most jail beds were dark and rusty metal frames covered by a thin, filthy mattress), flat on her stomach, where she received blow upon blow of the hard instrument against her back, making it difficult, if not impossible, to sit normally or sleep afterward since her back was covered with welts and lacerations. "I been sleepin' on my face because I was just as hard as bone," she said.[42] In the bullpen, she was ordered not to scream, to allow herself that most elemental response to pain. Instead, her voice was muted by the mattress, her protests silenced. Not only was language destroyed for her in this annihilating moment, even the sounds anterior to language were quashed. Mrs. Hamer, "the lady who know how to sing," became voiceless.

The designers of Mrs. Hamer's beating introduced one particular component that deepened the level of degradation, exposing her to the most intimate humiliation. Unlike the beatings of the other civil rights workers in the Winona jail, Mrs. Hamer's torture was not performed by a white police officer, but by two black prisoners who worked in shifts. The black inmates wielded a large blackjack wrapped in black leather with the command to beat the prisoner until she was spent. The police officers stood in a semicircle, watching the hideous pantomime of racial and sexual stereotyping: a black man stinking of whisky (supplied by the white sheriff) abusing a black woman ("bitch," "fatso," "whore," the officers continued to shout) with a large, black iron phallus in the room set aside for interrogations, the "bullpen," conjuring an image of brute energy and enforced sterility. The significance of the pantomime could not have been lost on Mrs. Hamer. In 1961, she had been sterilized by the state of Mississippi without her knowledge. She had gone into the hospital to have a small uterine tumor removed—"a knot on my stomach," she said—when a doctor proceeded to give her a hysterectomy. Mrs. Hamer was in her early forties at the time; she and her husband had adopted two girls. Two earlier pregnancies had ended in stillbirths, but she still hoped to give birth to a child of her own. "If [the doctor] was going to give that sort of operation, then he should have told me. I would have loved to have children. I went to the doctor who did that to me and I asked him, Why? Why had he done that to me? He didn't have to say nothing—and he didn't."[43]

Now in 1963, in the bullpen of the Winona jail, the state was recreating

a savage mockery of her sexual barrenness. "What was so sad about the situation was that they had made two black inmates beat her," June Johnson
said. "The police made them take her legs and pull her dress up, then one
of the inmates sat on her feet while the other just constantly beat her. After
the beating she couldn't walk that whole time she was in the jailhouse."[44]
The pain engendered no life or rebirth. Rather, the pain invited an anger
that could neither be fixed solely on the white police officer—who was not
the immediate agent of torture—nor on the black inmates—who were
pawns in a hideous game; the pain invited an anger that could too readily
be turned against herself. "A person don't know what can happen to they
body if they beat like I was beat," Mrs. Hamer said. Mrs. Hamer's body became itself an instrument of torture. "I had been beat 'til I was real hard,
just hard like a piece of wood or somethin'."[45]

The fact that there was no confession to elicit from Mrs. Hamer and her
colleagues further displayed the sinister design in Winona. The few questions hurriedly addressed to her in the interrogation preceding the beating
held no urgency and were quickly dropped. "They came into my cell and
asked me why was I demonstrating—and said that they were not going to
have such carryings on in Mississippi. They asked me if I had seen Martin
Luther King, Jr. I said I could not be demonstrating—I had just got off the
bus—and denied that I have seen Martin Luther King. They said 'shut up'
and always cut me off."[46] Mrs. Hamer had nothing to confess; she harbored
no information needed by the torturers. She was not abused for the secrets
she kept. She was abused, it seems, for *being*—for being a black woman
with a voice.

Mrs. Hamer's beating illustrated what Scarry calls a "mimetic of death";
forced to participate in this obscene conflation of sexual and racial tragedy,
her body became "emphatically, crushingly *present*," her voice emphatically and crushingly *absent*.[47] Mrs. Hamer said to a pair of indifferent FBI
agents who visited her in jail two days after the beating: "Well, I can tell
you one thing: I want to get out of here now! Because this is just a death
cell." And later: "That was a death place down there. I don't see how . . .
under the sun that a people could do human beins like they're doin' them.
It's just a death trap."[48] ("Characteristic of the Mississippi jails is that you
sit and rot," Bob Moses once said.)[49] The torture of Mrs. Hamer might very
well have ended in death had not an unidentified white man come into the
bullpen and announced, "That's enough." No one else was beaten that
night, even though hours later Mrs. Hamer could hear the police officers
in the booking room planning her murder. "They said, 'We could put them
son of bitches in Big Black [River], and nobody would never find them.'"[50]
Mrs. Hamer's suffering and humiliation left her with the certainty that
death was imminent. There was no singing at this nightfall.

But then the next day something happened that slowly transformed the killing despair of the jail and dispersed the power of death. "When you're in a brick cell, locked up, and haven't done anything to anybody but still you're locked up there, well sometimes words just begin to come to you and you begin to sing," she said. Song broke free. Mrs. Hamer sang:

> Paul and Silas was bound in jail, let my people go.
> Had no money for to go their bail, let my people go.
>
> Paul and Silas began to shout, let my people go.
> Jail doors open and they walked out, let my people go

"Singing brings out the soul," she said.[51] And at Winona, singing brought out the soul of the black struggle for freedom, for Mrs. Hamer did not sing alone. Sitting in their cells down the hall, June Johnson, Annelle Ponder, Euvester Simpson, and Lawrence Guyot joined her in song. Church broke out, empowering them to "stay on 'the Gospel train' until it reaches the Kingdom."[52]

Mrs. Hamer "really suffered in that jail from that beating," June Johnson said.[53] The physical and psychological effects of Winona stayed with her for a long time—she almost never talked about her life without talking about Winona. Even so, her songs of freedom gave voice to her suffering and the suffering she shared with her friends. Their singing did not remove their suffering or the particularities of their humiliation; rather, it embraced the suffering, named it, and emplotted it in a cosmic story of hope and deliverance. At first tentatively, and then with growing confidence, their song floated freely throughout the jail, exploding the death grip of the cell. "Jail doors open and they walked out, let my people go." Despair turned into a steady resoluteness to keep on going. A miracle happened. And at least for Mrs. Hamer, a peaceable composure, incomprehensible apart from a deep river of faith, transformed not only her diminished self-perception but the perception of her torturers. She said astonishingly, "It wouldn't solve any problem for me to hate whites just because they hate me. Oh, there's so much hate, only God has kept the Negro sane."[54]

During the days in jail that followed Mrs. Hamer's beating, she pondered once again the familiar paradox of white Christians who hate and mistreat black people. She even struck up a conversation with the jailer's wife about the life of faith. When the white woman showed some kindness to the prisoners by offering them cold water, Mrs. Hamer thanked her and remarked that she "must be Christian people." The jailer's wife picked up on Mrs. Hamer's remark, telling her that she really tried her best to live right and to please God. She tried to follow Jesus, she said; she certainly believed in him, and had been baptized as a child. Mrs. Hamer assumed the role of counselor and spiritual gadfly in her response. She told the jailer's wife to get out her Bible and read the verses in Proverbs 26:26 and Acts 17:26.

Mrs. Hamer's counsel, spoken in the spirit of gentleness and edification, offered at the same time an effective one-two punch of divine judgment and costly forgiveness. There is nothing sanguine about reconciliation in these passages. The jailer's wife could not have missed the barbed irony of Mrs. Hamer's devotional suggestions. The first verse speaks of those "whose hatred is covered by deceit," avowing that they will be brought down by divine wrath and "shall be shewed before the whole congregation." The entire twenty-sixth chapter of Proverbs is a litany of warnings for fools, transgressors, sluggards, and hateful men. "Whoso diggeth a pit shall fall therein: and he that rolleth a stone, it will return upon him," verse 27 adds. The New Testament passage came from St. Paul's address to the Athenians at Mars Hill. Before a people who took great pride in its collective piety—in this respect, a people much like the Mississippi's faithful white churchgoers—the apostle Paul had said, "I perceive that in all things ye are too superstitious" (Acts 17:22). He intended to make clear to the congregation at Athens, as Mrs. Hamer did to the jailer's wife, that the gods they "ignorantly worship" were idols. They must confess their sin of idolatry and worship instead the one true God, the one of whom it may be said, "made the world and all things therein, seeing that he is Lord of heaven and earth, dwelleth not in temples made with hands; neither is worshipped with men's hands, as though he needed any thing, seeing he giveth to all life, and breath, and all things" (Acts 17:24–25). In other words, if you are going to be religious, then you need to understand the rich diversity of God's creation.[55] Of course, this particular point may have been lost on the white woman in Winona—as it seems to have been lost on the Athenians. What would have hit hard was precisely the verse Mrs. Hamer singled out: "[God] hath made of one blood all nations of men for to dwell on all the face of the earth." Indeed, all races are as one in God's sight. Mrs. Hamer said of the white woman's response, "She's taken that down, but she never come back after then. I don't know what happened."[56]

Later, when Mrs. Hamer was escorted by the jailer himself to her trial, she put the question to the very man who had helped carry out her beating just a few days earlier, "Do you people ever think or wonder how you'll feel when the time comes you'll have to meet God?" His response was full of embarrassment and vigorous denial. "Who you talking about?" he mumbled.[57] In fact, Mrs. Hamer knew all too well what had happened. "I hit them with the truth, and it hurts them," she said.[58]

In the short term, nothing changed as a result of her beating and incarceration. The cases brought by the Justice Department against the City of Winona would come to a dismal end. June Johnson explained, "They picked an all-white jury to try the policemen, and there were lots of white students from Ole Miss in the courtroom with Confederate flags."[59] Both civil and criminal charges filed by the Justice Department were decided in favor of local law officials. The defendants—the City of Winona in the civil suit, and officers Patridge, Herrod, Surrell, Basinger and Perkins in the criminal suit—were found not guilty. But even more disheartening news awaited Mrs. Hamer and her friends when they were released on the afternoon of June 12. They learned that civil rights leader Medgar Evers had been gunned down the night before in front of his own home—just seconds after his wife Myrlie and their three children had walked out into their carport to welcome home the weary traveler. The news of the murder was heavily felt. Evers stood as the animating center of the burgeoning Jackson movement, leading sit-ins and church visits, and organizing a wide range of strategic attacks on the city's segregated institutions. More than ever it seemed that the call to freedom was a call that might very well lead to death.

The torture left Mrs. Hamer in considerable pain. "I wouldn't let my husband see me for a month, I was in such bad shape."[60] In fact, after her release from jail, she stayed away from her family for six or seven weeks, traveling back and forth to Atlanta, Washington, and New York. Nonetheless, Mrs. Hamer emerged, as the ancient Christian theologian Athanasius wrote of Antony after his years in desert isolation, "with utter equilibrium, like one guided by reason and steadfast in that which accords with nature."[61] Or as she explained with an earthier candor, "If them crackers in Winona thought they'd discouraged me from fighting, I guess they found out different. I'm going to stay in Mississippi and if they shoot me down, I'll be buried here."[62] The experience brought her face to face with her worst fears about white racist violence, civil rights activism, and herself, but empowered by freedom songs and "the truth" she emerged full of courage and righteous anger. She said, "I'm never sure any more when I leave home whether I'll get back or not. Sometimes it seem like to tell the truth today is to run the risk of being killed. But if I fall, I'll fall five feet four inches forward in the fight for freedom. I'm not backing off."[63] Her determination was strong and sure, measured with a boundless generosity.

Mrs. Hamer emerged as the pillar of strength to local people in the struggle. As one of her fellow activists in the Mississippi movement, Mrs. Annie Devine, said, "Myself with others realized that there is a woman that can do all these things. And when she got herself beat in Winona, there was a greater woman. Why not follow somebody like that? Why not just reach out with one hand and say, just take me along?"[64]

The Beginning of a New Kingdom

Despite the threatening climate of violence, a tenacious band of local blacks and SNCC workers continued to plug away in the recalcitrant Delta throughout the summer and fall of 1963. After the Winona jailing, Mrs. Hamer returned to voter registration and organizing in her native Sunflower County, employed by SNCC at the rate of ten dollars a week—"if they had the money," she added. As the field secretary for Sunflower County, Mrs. Hamer visited cotton fields by day to encourage workers and solicit voters, and black churches by night to rally men and women with freedom songs and speeches. The mass meetings, with their mixture of freedom singing, strategy making, and testifying, became the religious center of the movement.

In his absorbing narrative of the civil rights movement in the Delta, Charles Payne recounts Mrs. Hamer's electrifying presence in one such meeting at Tougaloo College. Following the singing of Hollis Watkins, a native Mississippian, SNCC worker, and melodious tenor, Mrs. Hamer took the pulpit by storm. She gave a testimony of her involvement in the movement, including a darkly comic description of the various kinds of harassment she had faced. The most recent, she told the congregation, took the form of late-night visits from policemen and their barking dogs, an occurrence so regular she had grown accustomed to it. "Look like now the dogs help me to get to sleep," she exclaimed.[65] Then her thoughts became more sobering, and more evangelistic. People need to be serious about their faith in the Lord; it's all too easy to say, "Sure, 'I'm a Christian,' and talk a big game. But if you are not putting that claim to the test, where the rubber meets the road, then it's high time to stop talking about being a Christian. You can pray until you faint," she said, "but if you're not gonna get up and do something, God is not gonna put it in your lap."[66] Never would Mrs. Hamer back away from addressing both whites and blacks with salvation's hard demands. As she would say on another occasion in strikingly less pastoral terms, "Sometimes I get so disgusted I feel like getting my gun after some of these chicken eatin' preachers. I know these Baptist ministers. . . . I'm not anti-church and I'm not anti-religious, but if you go down Highway 49 all the way into Jackson, going through Drew, Ruleville, Blaine, Indianola, Moorhead, all over, you'll see just how many churches are selling out to the white power structure."[67] (Mrs. Hamer knew all too well that "most black preachers had to be dragged kicking and screaming into supporting the movement.")[68] In the Tougaloo meeting, however, she took a more upbeat approach, testifying instead of the wonderfully diverse ways movement people had witnessed to their faith, and concluded with the song:

> I'm on my way to the freedom land
> If you don't go, don't hinder me
> I'm on my way, praise God, I'm on my way.[69]

Combining praise and prophetic provocation, Mrs. Hamer set her eyes on the freedom land. If you were not going, you'd better get out of the way.

Although these mass meetings certainly provided a forum for organizational planning and strategy making, their spiritually and psychologically transformative power left the deepest impression on those gathered in the rural churches throughout the Delta. The language of the Gospel gave the local movement an indefatigable urgency and depth by placing black people's struggle for justice in a familiar and beloved narrative. And in Mrs. Hamer's hands, the meetings helped move the goal of the long journey from the life hereafter to the struggle here and now. As SNCC staff member Jean Wheeler Smith described the effect of the meetings on her own nascent activism, "The religious, the spiritual was like an explosion to me, an emotional explosion. . . . It just lit up my mind."[70] Through the mass meetings, Mrs. Hamer helped create a great reservoir of energy for all her brothers and sisters in the movement; experiences of sheer joy, as well as the dark nights of the soul when glad emotions were spent, were sustained by the spiritual energy radiating outward. There was, thus, much more to the resiliency they imparted than psychological empowerment. Lamentably, some historians have trivialized the meetings' complex theological character, describing it in terms resembling Alcoholics Anonymous or Weight Watchers—groups that try to change the behavior of their members "by offering a supportive social environment."[71] It ought not to slight the important work of twelve-step groups to insist that Mrs. Hamer's utterly serious devotion to Jesus not be regarded solely as a motivational tool.

What is further lost in such assessments is not only the particularity of Mrs. Hamer's vision of the movement but the shared theological perception of those very social realities local black people sought to change—indeed that they believed God wanted to change. Faith played an important role in motivating social protest, of course, and the meetings unquestionably solidified a sense of community that could not have been so readily formed elsewhere. But Mrs. Hamer's faith was far greater and infinitely more complex than the utility it offered, which was itself indisputably great. For though her faith was certainly inspired by the liberating energies of the mass meetings, it was—much more—charged by all the literal and exquisite detail of the Gospel story. In Mrs. Hamer's mind, the black struggle for justice received its inner sense from the dramatic imagery of the biblical narrative. She said, "We have to realize just how grave the problem is in the United States today, and I think the sixth chapter of Ephesians, the eleventh and twelfth verses helps us to know . . . what it is we are up against. It says, 'Put on the whole armor of God, that we may be able to stand against the wiles of the devil. For we wrestle not against flesh and blood but against principalities, against powers, against the rulers of this world, against spiritual wickedness in high places.' This is what I think about when I think of my own work in the fight for freedom."[72] The meetings were not simply pep rallies for wearied foot soldiers—"but a very powerful social ritual."[73] As one of Mrs. Hamer's movement colleagues put

it, "These meetings were *church*, and for some who had grown disillusioned with Christian otherworldliness, they were better than church."[74]
Only in church could one apprehend with such intensity both the theological expression of society's wrongs and the hope for decisive change;
only there were the memories of the people and the promises of the future
secured by trust in God.[75]

Yet hard times lay ahead. During that fall of 1963, financial support and
local registrants seemed to have dried up. Mrs. Hamer and her colleagues
encountered a series of setbacks. "Too little money was coming in for
voter-registration work," biographer Kay Mills explains, "and too many
sharecroppers were out of work."[76] SNCC had been a presence in Mississippi for two years without making great progress either in voter registration or in stirring the conscience of whites outside the South. At the same
time, white racist violence against both local black people and civil rights
workers surged to a new level of intensity. Laurel businessman Sam Bowers began forming the White Knights of the Ku Klux Klan, with the intention of opposing what he would call "the forces of Satan on this earth,"
waging a campaign of violence against civil rights activists and anyone who
appeared to give ground to their progress.[77] Beatings and jailings, death
threats and murders, church burnings and the constant fear of bombings
configured the state's threatening terrain. Although Mrs. Hamer might
speak humorously, especially with people who shared her fears, of the
daily barking of police dogs at her house, there was nothing funny about
the pervasive anti-black violence burgeoning throughout the region. She
lamented the constant harassment by automobiles "passing the house
loaded with white men, and trucks . . . with guns hanging up in the back"
and the threatening phone calls and letters.[78] Yet white extremists and terrorists were not the only ones busy with the business of massive resistance:
conservative whites pursued more insidious forms of retaliation, like with-
drawing food and medical supplies from black communities and tighten-
ing Jim Crow laws across the board. In any case, both forms of reprisal—
extremist and moderate—went largely unchecked by Justice Department
officials. To disconcerted civil rights activists who sought greater federal
protection against pervasive harassment and criminal assaults, the FBI repeated like a mantra: "We are an investigative not a law-enforcing agency."
"The Old Mississippi seemed to be winning," Mills writes.[79]

Movement organizers began to discuss the possibility of a more dramatic
form of protest—an event that would shake the foundations of the white
power structure and direct the national spotlight on Mississippi, "the middle of the iceberg," as Bob Moses called it. In November of 1963, the
Council of Federated Organizations (COFO) inaugurated the "Freedom
Ballot Campaign," a mock election aimed to empower black voters and
thus exhibit black Mississippians' determination to vote under less restric-

tive conditions. At its convention in Jackson, COFO nominated the respected Clarksdale pharmacist and state representative of the NAACP, Aaron Henry, as its gubernatorial candidate and Reverend Edwin King, the white Mississippi Methodist minister who served as the chaplain at historically black Tougaloo College, as its lieutenant governor. On election day, 83,000 blacks (and a few whites like Ole Miss historian James Silver, who is said to have voted several times) cast their ballots for Henry and King.[80] Although the number fell short of COFO's goal of 200,000, the turnout of 83,000 voters gave credibility to the claim that blacks were ready to move in large numbers to the polls. Mississippi "nigras" were not content after all, as white politicians had been nervously telling the media, their constituents, and themselves.

The strong turnout invigorated the movement like a shot of adrenaline, demonstrating the effectiveness of extensive grassroots organizing by the various civil rights groups in the state. As activists Lawrence Guyot and Mike Thelwell later concluded, the experience "took the Movement, for the first time, beyond activities affecting a single town, county, municipality, or electoral district, and placed us in the area of state-wide organization."[81] An often contentious relationship between SNCC and the NAACP had even been cast aside for the moment. (Student-based SNCC, along with the Congress of Racial Equality, commonly regarded the National Association for the Advancement of Colored People as overly cautious and fearful of direct acts of social protest.) The strong vote was also a credit to the small cadre of white student volunteers that had been recruited to assist the registration campaign. This inspired Bob Moses to discern in the Freedom Vote the outlines of a much more ambitious voter-registration initiative—one that would connect local activists with a larger group of student volunteers in a comprehensive civil rights campaign. In partnership with activist lawyer and teacher Allard Lowenstein, Moses began to think in more detail of the initiative that would be called the "Mississippi Summer Project," and later more popularly rendered as "Freedom Summer."[82] But there were controversial issues to iron out. Above all, many SNCC staffers raised the question of what would happen to indigenous black activism when white college students, most of whom were financially and educationally privileged, inundated the state. Would it not be difficult to keep the fragile balance of the various black coalitions with "a bunch of Yalies running around in their Triumphs," as one person worried.[83]

Numerous concerns surfaced in the subsequent debate about white involvement in the Summer Project. Some SNCC members argued that white college students would be reluctant to take orders from local black men and women. Did not the invitation to northern students only perpetuate the presumption that blacks needed whites to solve their problems? Local activist Willie Peacock tapped into the deepest source of concern when he explained, "If you bring white people to Mississippi and say, 'Negro, go and vote,' they will say, 'Yassah, we'll go and try to register and vote.'" But when the oppressor tells the oppressed to do something, Peacock said, that's not commitment or movement toward liberation; it is "the same slavery mentality." "I know that's not permanent," he added.[84]

However, John Lewis and Bob Moses argued tirelessly for a highly visible interracial initiative. Lewis, who worked with SNCC in Greenwood, believed that the time had come "to take Mississippi to the nation."[85] The state was in a crisis situation at every level, with nearly 450,000 blacks of voting age living in a constant state of oppression, and with fewer than 7,000 blacks registered to vote in early 1964.[86] Lewis said, "We had to find a way to dramatize the crisis and the best way to do this was not only to organize black people but to bring a large number of young whites to the state, and let people live alongside each other, and in the process, educate not only ourselves and the volunteers, but, perhaps more importantly, the whole nation about Mississippi. It was a very dangerous effort but it was something that had to be done."[87]

Moses reminded his fellow staffers (who included several white women and men) that the one thing SNCC could do for the country that no one else could was "be above the race issue."[88] He said, "I am concerned that we do integrate, because otherwise we'll grow up and have a racist movement. And if the white people don't stand with the Negroes as they go out now, then there will be a danger that after the Negroes get something they'll say, 'Okay, we got this by ourselves.' And the only way you can break that down is to have white people working alongside of you—so then it changes the whole complexion of what you're doing, so it isn't any longer Negro fighting white, it's a question of rational people against irrational people."[89] The civil rights movement needed to foster this new reality, to seek, as Moses said, a "broader identification, identification with individuals that are going through the same kind of struggle, so that the struggle doesn't remain just a question of racial struggle." Moses also invoked the vision of the beloved community, the ideal of a universal brotherhood and sisterhood of humankind, which Martin Luther King, Jr. had eloquently proclaimed in his recent sermons.[90] Moses's position was principled and philosophical and ultimately more persuasive.

Although for SNCC as an organization the controversy regarding white involvement was anything but resolved—it would resurface in following years with increasingly devastating intensity—organizers proceeded to make plans for the Summer Project, and Mrs. Hamer's dictum became the rule of thumb. "If we're trying to break down this barrier of segregation, we can't segregate ourselves," she said.[91] Others argued on more pragmatic grounds that white volunteers would bring with them "channels of publicity and communication."[92] They would surely generate widespread interest—publicity essential for awakening the nation's conscience—and help create a climate conducive to greater federal involvement in civil rights.

By April of 1964, SNCC had drafted a proposal—a manifesto of sorts—that was posted on campus kiosks and bulletin boards throughout the nation. The document announced a program "planned for this summer" and solicited "the massive participation of Americans dedicated to the elimination of racial oppression." Stated like this, the invitation to white student volunteers was no failure of nerve on the part of local blacks but a cooperative effort appealing to the "the country as a whole, backed by the power and authority of the federal government."[93]

In June, a training session for the volunteers was held at the Western College for Women in Oxford, Ohio. Several hundred students, with little understanding of life in Mississippi, gathered for an orientation to the summer that would bring them face to face with hatred, violence, and death—very possibly their own. The volunteer Sally Belfrage described the mood in Oxford: "No one seems quite certain what to do but the singing fills the gaps. They are all very young, very defenseless in all but the purity of their purpose, which connects them in a bond of immediate friendship."[94] Belfrage remembered their first anxious hours together: "Out on the lawn again afterwards, [the students] formed in haphazard circles around the guitars, looking at each other self-consciously as they sang the words they scarcely knew. Then there was a change: a woman whose badge read 'Mrs. Fannie Lou Hamer' was suddenly leading them, molding their noise into music.

> If you miss me from the back of the bus,
> You can't find me nowhere,
>
> Come on up to the front of the bus,
> I'll be ridin' up there . . .

Her voice gave everything she had, and her circle soon incorporated the others, expanding first in size and in volume and then something else—it gained passion. Few of them knew who she was. . . . But here was clearly someone with force enough for all of them, who knew the meaning of 'Oh Freedom' and 'We Shall Not Be Moved' in her flesh and spirit as they never would. They lost their shyness and began to sing the choruses with abandon, though their voices all together dimmed beside hers."[95] Although a well-known cast of speakers had been organized for the week, and the daily schedule offered a full slate of lectures and workshops, it was Fannie Lou Hamer whose indomitable presence was everywhere felt by those in attendance and who brought the purpose to focus.

In Oxford, as throughout the summer of 1964, Mrs. Hamer bore witness to her faith in a way that both inspired and disarmed the students, many of whom had long grown suspicious of the religious traditions of their parents.[96] With a pastoral gentleness, she explained the harsh realities for black people in Mississippi. She cautioned against sarcasm and cynicism. She admonished love and nonviolence as the only adequate response to white oppression. She insisted that the volunteers not stereotype Mississippi whites: they should look deeper and try to discern the good that is in them. "Regardless of what they act like, there's some good there," she insisted. At the same time, she put Christian love in the service of a new revolutionary framework, appearing radical and subversive in ways that jarred liberal sensibilities. To wit: "There is so much hypocrisy in America. The land of the free and the home of the brave is all on paper. It doesn't mean anything to us. The only way we can make this thing a reality in America is to do all we can to destroy this system and bring this thing out to the light that has been under the cover all these years. The scriptures have said, 'The things that have been done in the dark will be known on the house tops.' "[97] In the same breath, she could dismay the summer volunteers by her unwavering moral convictions, especially her traditional sexual ethics, and by her motherly fussiness toward social etiquette and sartorial propriety. "Mrs. Hamer was our moma in the movement," Curtis Hayes confirmed.[98] She disapproved of interracial dating and overly familiar gestures of affection between men and women in the Summer Project. When she saw the white female volunteers at the Freedom School in Ruleville sitting "out under the trees in the back yard playin' cards with the Negro boys," or standing around in the front yard "chattin' and laughin'," or (she could not believe her eyes!) waving at cars when they drove by, she exclaimed, "They're good kids, and they seemed to understand [in the training session in Ohio]. But they get down here and nobody's settin' their house on fire, so they act like they're visitin' their boyfriends on college week end!" She concluded irritably, "If they cain't obey the rules, call their mothers and tell them to send down their sons instead."[99]

Mrs. Hamer's irrepressible energy was put to the test during Freedom Summer. Aside from "mothering her brood of teachers" for the Freedom School,[100] traveling on behalf of the Mississippi Freedom Democratic Party, and keeping order in the Hamer home, she carried her voter-registration activities to a new level of intensity. Tracy Sugarman, a white New Englander who traveled to Ruleville for the summer wearing the two hats of journalist and volunteer, noted the powerful effect of Mrs. Hamer's relentless solicitations—often dreaded by fellow black Mississippians. On a "furiously hot Sunday morning" in July, Sugarman accompanied Mrs. Hamer to a worship service at a local black church. Mrs. Hamer had expressed no small frustration with the timid, albeit good-hearted minister of the small rural chapel. His continued balking at voter-registration efforts could no longer be ignored. Sugarman tells the story:

Our entry was about as unobtrusive as a platoon of tanks. One look at Fannie Lou's purposeful mien must have convinced the young country pastor that he was in for a trying morning. He paused, smiled tentatively, and then plunged ahead in his reading from Exodus. "And I will dwell among the children of Israel, and will be their God. And they shall know that I am the Lord their God that brought them forth out of the land of Egypt, that I may dwell among them: I am the Lord their God."

His voice dropped, and he closed the book. "This ends our readin' from Chapter Twenty-nine." His eyes lifted and he smiled at us. "I'm right pleased that Mrs. Fannie Lou Hamer has joined our service this mownin'. We are all happy to see you, Mrs. Hamer, and your friend. Would you like to say a few words to the congregation?"

Mrs. Hamer rose majestically to her feet. Her magnificent voice rolled through the chapel as she enlisted the Biblical ranks of martyrs and heroes to summon these folk to the Freedom banner. Her mounting, rolling battery of quotations and allusions from the Old and New Testaments stunned the audience with its thunder. "Pharaoh was in Sunflower County! Israel's children were building bricks without straw—at three dollars a day!" Her voice broke, and tears stood in her eyes. "They're tired! And they're tired of being tired."

Suddenly the rhetoric ceased, and a silence rushed into the room. Her finger trembled as she pointed to the shaken minister, and every eye fastened on the man in the pulpit. Fannie Lou's voice was commanding, but its passion came pure from her committed heart. "And you, Reverend Tyler, must be Moses! Leadin' your flock out of the chains and fetters of Egypt—takin' them yourself to register—*tomorra*—in Indianola!"[101]

God was leading black men and women to freedom in Sunflower County, and Mrs. Hamer was determined to gather as many people as she could for the great journey. The black clergy should help lead the way; but if it did not, God would find leaders from other places—as God always had.

In spite of numerous setbacks in voter registration and increased anti-civil rights violence, Freedom Summer was an exhilarating celebration of this promise to bless—a converging of divine deliverance with human readiness. But since human readiness required ultimate honesty about the Christian faith's capacity to change the South, the summer signaled a decisive transformation in the spiritual outlook of Mrs. Hamer and many of her local fellow travelers in the movement. In face of massive white resistance, black people could no longer assume that the faithful exhibition of Christian virtues would convict white Southerners of their social sins and overhaul Jim Crow's mean rule. Mrs. Hamer had learned all too well the unbending resolve of white racism. Christian love alone could not cure the sickness in Mississippi, she explained. If it could, then Mississippi would be the most just and decent state in America, considering that "[ninety] per cent of the Negro people in Mississippi have gone to church all their lives.

They have lived with the hope that if they kept 'standing up' in a Christian manner, things would change."[102] Instead, Christian love must shape concrete solutions and new visions for the disenfranchised and the poor. Mrs. Hamer said, "Christianity is being concerned about [others], not building a million-dollar church while people are starving right around the corner. Christ was a revolutionary person, out there where it was happening. That's what God is all about, and that's where I get my strength."[103]

And importantly, out there where it's happening, Mrs. Hamer learned that actions themselves can sometimes display the inner sense of faith and thereby witness to God's great goodness. Mrs. Hamer said, "When the people came to Mississippi in 1964, to us it was the result of all our faith—all we had always hoped for. Our prayers and all we had lived for started to be translated into action. Now we have action, and we're doing something that will not only free the black man in Mississippi but hopefully will free the white one as well."[104] In the generous reach of Mrs. Hamer's love of God, the doors and windows of the church swing wide, open to anyone who shows concern for others. Christ is discovered in living for others; in the performance of being out there where it's happening.

Questioning America

By the middle of July, the upcoming Democratic National Convention in Atlantic City, scheduled to begin on August 24, had become the strategic focal point of the Summer Project. SNCC continued to coordinate voter registration and Freedom School activities throughout the state, but the organizing of a new alternative political party moved to center stage. The Mississippi Freedom Democratic party (MFDP), or the Freedom Democrats, as the party was sometimes called, had been formed in April for the purpose of challenging the legitimacy of the all-white state Democratic delegation. As an "independent movement-led party," the MFDP would also introduce black men and women to the empowering prospects of political ownership—which they had experienced almost solely, if at all, in the black church. Bob Moses's "Emergency Memorandum" of July 19 to all COFO field workers stressed the need to convert the summer's successes into concrete political power. He insisted that "*everyone* who is not working in Freedom Schools or community centers . . . devote all their time to organizing for the convention challenge."[105] The immediate task was to encourage black people to defy the state's traditional Democratic establishment, which had both systematically excluded blacks from all levels of participation and aggressively opposed federal programs assisting minorities and the poor. So committed were the "regular Democrats" to the preservation of the status quo that they had thrown their support behind the candidacy of Republican Senator Barry Goldwater, spurning their own party's president in office, the much-loathed traitorous Texan whose fondness for civil rights legislation had become an outrage in the South.

However, the Freedom Democrats wanted more than recognition as the authentic delegation from Mississippi to the Atlantic City convention, more even than forcing some of the white regulars to work with them. Cleveland Sellers, a SNCC staff member in Holly Springs, explained, "If our venture there was successful, we intended to utilize similar tactics in other Southern states, particularly Georgia and South Carolina. Our ultimate goal was the destruction of the awesome power of the Dixiecrats, who controlled over 75 percent of the committees in Congress. With the Dixiecrats deposed, the way would have been clear for a wide-ranging redistribution of wealth, power and priorities throughout the nation."[106] The Freedom Democrats would test the limits of liberal democracy, taking to the highest level of the political ladder folks who had fallen through the cracks of the system as it had operated until now.

The MFDP believed it could use to its advantage the discriminatory practices and disloyalty of the Mississippi regulars in persuading the Credentials Committee in Atlantic City of its legitimacy. Party members also hoped that the national scrutiny of the state sustained throughout the long, hot summer would give widespread popular support to the party's challenge. In fact, national scrutiny of Mississippi had reached a new level of intensity. Two days before the MFDP assembled in Jackson for its first state convention, FBI agents uncovered the bodies of James Chaney, Andrew Goodman, and Mickey Schwerner from a dam under construction in Neshoba County, having heard of their whereabouts from a paid informant. When the MFDP convention convened in Jackson on August 6, the two thousand people who overflowed the Masonic Temple in Jackson had good reason to believe that public support had shifted in their favor. In the convention hall, participants listened to speeches by movement veteran Ella Baker and the party's legal council, Joseph Rauh; rallied support for the Atlantic City challenge; and broke out time and again into thunderous renditions of Freedom songs. The electrifying atmosphere helped to give many Mississippi blacks and civil rights workers a new perspective on the struggle. One volunteer wrote excitedly:

> Man, this is the stuff democracy is made of. All of us here are pretty emotional about the names of the counties of Mississippi. Amite and Sunflower and Tallahatchie have always meant where this one was shot, where this one was beaten, where civil rights workers feared for their lives the minute they arrived. But on Thursday Amite, and Tallahatchie, and Sunflower, and Neshoba didn't mean another man's gone. They meant people are voting from there, it meant people who work 14 hours a day from sun-up to sun-down picking cotton and live in homes with no plumbing and no paint, were casting bal-

lots to send a delegation to Atlantic City. As [Ella Baker] said, it was not a political convention, it was a demonstration that the people of Mississippi want
to be let into America.

Waving American flags and county signs, balanced with "humility and
pride, fear and courage," the convention crowd displayed patriotism at its
best.[107]

The sixty-eight delegates picked to represent the state included a number of established black leaders—the sort one volunteer maladroitly called
"the comfortable, middle-aged 'We Don't Want Any Trouble' Uncle
Toms"—but it included even more grass-roots organizers. Charles McLaurin, Lawrence Guyot, Annie Devine, E. W. Steptoe, Victoria Gray, and Fannie Lou Hamer were among the latter. Guyot was elected as the party
chairman, Aaron Henry the delegation's chairman, Fannie Lou Hamer the
vice chairwoman, and Annie Devine the secretary. Victoria Gray, a church-
woman in the forefront of the movement in Hattiesburg, along with Ed
King and four other officers, were elected as representatives to the Democratic National Committee.[108]

The MFDP hoped, and increasingly believed, that Atlantic City would   curious
provide the opportunity for black Mississippians to claim their rightful
place in the Democratic party. Personal accounts of black life in Mississippi would be aired not only before the convention delegates but, via television, to a national audience that had heard precious little from poor
blacks themselves. Most of the media's interest in the Summer Project had
been focused on the white volunteers. An Ivy League man decked in khakis
and rumpled-up workshirt conjured just the kind of image that captured
white America's moral imagination. Rarely had Americans the chance to
hear blacks tell their own stories. Importantly, the MFDP would seize the
Democratic National Convention in Atlantic City as the perfect forum for
local people's own testimony to the nation, and at the perfect time. Most
of the delegates maintained a guarded optimism about the challenge; in
fact, during the summer three states (Oregon, New York, and Michigan)
had passed resolutions calling for the seating of the party.

Fannie Lou Hamer may have gone to Atlantic City with some trepida-
tion, but once there she shook the political establishment like Jesus among
the money changers. On Friday, August 21, the caravan of unairconditioned buses and automobiles arrived at the convention city. Mrs. Hamer
and the other MFDP representatives, as well as the handful of summer volunteers who accompanied the delegation, checked into the low-budget
Gem Hotel on a back street. The "pop-art, circus quality of Atlantic City"
seemed a surreal contrast to the summer's landscapes of dense, withering
vegetation, sweltering heat and violence.[109] The large group of black men
and women, which included schoolteachers and domestics, plantation
workers and businessmen, caught the media's attention—and everyone

else's in Atlantic City—from the moment they arrived. The Freedom Democrats, hoping to spark keen media and popular interest in their presence, brought along numerous artifacts of Mississippi life. Along the boardwalk were displayed notarized depositions from victims of violence and discrimination, photographs of living conditions for black people, reports on economic and medical deprivation, and a list of the churches and homes bombed by the Klan (the White Knights would not systematically target synagogues until 1967).[110] The MFDP delegation displayed every available symbol and document that served to bolster support of their seating in place of the regular Mississippi Democrats, including a burned-out Ford stationwagon, transported from Mississippi on the back of a flat-bed truck, which reminded viewers of the one in which Chaney, Goodman, and Schwerner took their fateful ride into Neshoba County; including sketches of the martyred civil rights workers, nailed to pieces of wood and waved in the air to remind the nation of the murders; and including the bell from the Mt. Zion Methodist Church near Philadelphia, which had been burned to the ground after opening its doors to Schwerner's voter-registration initiative. Still, it was Mrs. Hamer—singing her rendition of "Go Tell It on the Mountain to Let My People Go" and addressing the MFDP vigils on the boardwalk—who seemed always to be at the center of the network news shows or a circle of reporters.[111]

The Freedom Democrats' immediate goal was to garner the favor of the Credentials Committee by winning over at least 10 percent of the committee members, which amounted to eleven votes. If successful, a minority report in behalf of the MFDP would come to a discussion on the convention floor. Once on the floor, the support of eight states would be needed to get a roll call, which would then require every state to go on record with its position on the seating. Although earlier in the summer numerous state conventions had voiced support of the MFDP's seating in Atlantic City, the task of getting the 10 percent vote was now an uphill battle. As the official body in charge of reviewing the credentials of all state and territorial delegations, the committee was home to many of the national party's regulars, and their primary interest lay in making sure that the proceedings went off smoothly and without any unexpected problems.[112] Certainly the last thing Lyndon Johnson needed was some last-minute glitch in the machinery of his presidential campaign. This would be the year he finally moved into the spotlight, out of the shadows of other men.

But with the arrival of the Freedom Democrats, the "Johnson Convention" seemed to be straying from his advisers' script. He was irate that Joseph Rauh, a long-time activist in the Democratic party, had agreed to represent the MFDP as its lawyer. He was angry that the Freedom Democrats had even come to town. When Johnson saw Mrs. Hamer on a news broadcast leading a group of people in the chant "eleven and eight, eleven and eight," he called Senator Hubert Humphrey (himself hoping for the vice-presidential spot), and barked, "You tell that bastard goddamn lawyer friend of yours that there ain't gonna be all that eleven and eight shit at the convention."[113] To make matters worse, Johnson had also been informed that five delegations from the South would walk out of the convention if the black Mississippians were seated in place of the regulars. He worried that excessive patronizing of the MFDP would cost him the entire southern vote.

Nonetheless, all the behind-the-scenes political maneuvering seemed momentarily unimportant when the Credentials Committee proceedings commenced on Saturday afternoon, and all the major networks went live to national coverage. Aaron Henry began with a brief speech outlining his efforts as head of COFO's voter registration during the Summer Project. Henry explained that the very presence of the MFDP delegation in Atlantic City might be cause for arrest when they returned home to Mississippi. Already, the state attorney general had obtained an injunction barring their attendance at the convention on the grounds that they were using the word "Democratic" illegally. Yet in spite of these and other threats, Henry resolved before the committee and the nation, "If jail is the price that we must pay for our efforts to be of benefit to America, to the national Democratic Party, and to Mississippi, then nothing could be more redemptive."[114]

Ed King, the vice chairman of the delegation, was the next to testify. On King's face was a bright red arch from his right cheek to his chin, the scar from an automobile accident in Jackson a few weeks after the murder of Medgar Evers, which King believed to have been orchestrated by the Citizens' Council.[115] King described how costly, indeed how dangerous, were the consequences of dissent from the prevailing orthodoxy of the closed society. But it was still important to remember that there were whites sympathetic to civil rights for blacks, even though fear had immobilized almost all disagreement and self-criticism, King said. "I know many Mississippians in the last several years, over one hundred ministers and college teachers, [who] have been forced to leave the state. This nation is being populated with refugees from the closed society in Mississippi."[116] Those white men and women courageous enough to speak against the day could expect relentless intimidation by the Citizens' Council or the Ku Klux Klan; and ultimately they could expect to lose their jobs and become exiles in their own country.

When Reverend King concluded, Mrs. Hamer took the microphone. In a proud, solemn voice, she began, "Mr. Chairman and Credentials Committee, my name is Mrs. Fannie Lou Hamer, and I live at 626 East Lafayette Street, Ruleville, Mississippi, Sunflower County, the home of Senator James O. Eastland and Senator Stennis."[117] Mrs. Hamer told her story to

America. Patient and composed, she recalled the ordeal of registering to vote in 1962 and the violent attacks encountered as a result; she recalled the horrors of the Winona jail and concluded her story with the terse observation, "All of this is on account we want to register, to become first-class citizens, and if the Freedom Democratic Party is not seated now, I question America." On the verge of tears, she left her astonished audience with the question, "Is this America, the land of the free and the home of the brave where we have to sleep with our telephones off the hooks because our lives be threatened daily because we want to live as decent human beings—in America?"[118] When Mrs. Hamer finished, she was not the only one in the room on the verge of tears. As Cleveland Sellers said, "Some of the rest of us were too."[119]

The several million Americans watching the Credentials Committee hearings by television were forced to miss the final minutes of live coverage. "In the White House there was panic," civil rights historian Len Holt said.[120] Or as Joseph Rauh put it, "Johnson saw her and blew his stack." Fearing the damage Mrs. Hamer's account might bring to his long-awaited nomination, the president interrupted live televised coverage for a press conference on an unrelated matter. However, by the end of the afternoon, the major networks, realizing they had been manipulated by the president, responded to his trick by playing one of their own: they broadcast the tape of Mrs. Hamer's testimony from start to finish during the evening convention coverage.[121] Thousands of telephone calls and telegrams poured into the Credentials Committee throughout the afternoon and evening and the next day. Although Johnson's ill-conceived press conference did little to diminish America's sympathy for the black Mississippians, his advisers and convention strategists knew their continued proximity to presidential power depended on keeping "that illiterate woman" (as Johnson called Mrs. Hamer) out of the spotlight and putting a quiet end to the challenge.[122]

Johnson dispatched his "trustworthy troops," Hubert Humphrey, Walter Mondale, J. Edgar Hoover, and Walter Reuther. Humphrey's task was clear and simple: if he wanted his name to appear as vice president on a Johnson ticket, he would need to dismantle the MFDP challenge. (With regard to his selection of a running-mate, Johnson had stated in no uncertain terms, "Whoever he is, I want his pecker to be in my pocket.")[123] In turn, Humphrey assigned the young Walter Mondale to the nitty-gritty work of hammering out a compromise. If Mondale hoped to become the successor of the Minnesota senator, he would have to wield his position as chair of the special subcommittee to convince the MFDP to accept his "two-seat" proposal. Rounding off the team of political insiders was J. Edgar Hoover, who was more than willing to deploy his favorite surveillance techniques in SNCC and MFDP gathering places and in Martin Luther King, Jr.'s, hotel room. For his part, Walter Reuther, president of the

United Auto Workers, interrupted high-level negotiations with General Motors to intervene in the Atlantic City crisis, appealing to his beneficiaries in the Southern Christian Leadership Conference to accept the compromise.[124] The eventual support of Martin Luther King, Jr., and SCLC for the "two-seat" plan had as much to do with Reuther's dimly veiled threat to withdraw financial support from SCLC as with King's wish to placate Johnson. The MFDP's rich depository of principle was no match for the man who held his hands on the purse strings of the United Auto Worker's treasury.

The proposed compromise hammered out by Senator Humphrey and the White House would preclude any full-scale replacement of the Mississippi regulars, and would grant the MFDP general recognition as honored guests of the convention with only two at-large delegates, Aaron Henry and Ed King. In addition to the two-seat plan, the Humphrey and Mondale compromise recommended that only those Mississippi regulars be seated who supported the convention's nominees, not Barry Goldwater, the Republican presidential nominee whose states rights rhetoric had captivated the white South. The proposal also recommended that the Democratic National Committee require all delegations at the 1968 convention "to assure that voters in the state, regardless of race, color, creed or national origin . . . have the opportunity to participate fully in Party affairs."[125]

Humphrey hoped the Mississippi delegation would not only accept the compromise but would also show some appreciation for the efforts made by the national party in taking their challenge seriously. In arguing the merit of compromise, Humphrey appealed to their political sense. He reminded the party of his liberal views on civil rights, of the president's concern for poverty in America. He encouraged realism, savvy. Concessions must be made at this level of the game. His political future and his job were hanging in the balance. Could the MFDP not appreciate his point?

As a black woman from the South, Mrs. Hamer could certainly understand concessions. But in her mind this was not about concession or compromise. She said to Humphrey, "Do you mean to tell me that your position is more important to you than four hundred thousand black people's lives?"[126] For Mrs. Hamer, this was about the ascendancy of truth over politics; divine justice over liberal shrewdness. This was about "the beginning of a New Kingdom right here on earth," about curing "America's sickness"—and not with another remedy from the prevailing ethos of utility and power but with an injection of new vision and energy; not with a view toward political expediency but with a view from below.[127] Mrs. Hamer continued, "Senator Humphrey, I know lots of people in Mississippi who have lost their jobs for trying to register to vote. I had to leave the plantation where I worked in Sunflower County. Now if you lose this job of vice president because you do what is right, because you help the MFDP, everything will be all right. God will take care of you. But if you take [the vice-presidential nomination] this way, why, you will never be able to do any good for civil rights, for poor people, for peace or any of those things you talk about. Senator Humphrey, I'm gonna pray to Jesus for you."[128] This was about faithfulness to the call.

The architects of the White House-supported compromise did the rest of their work largely in secret. Fannie Lou Hamer was deliberately excluded from all further discussion. Mrs. Hamer's passionate witness on behalf of the poor seemed as out of place in the war rooms of partisan maneuvering as among the elegantly appointed plantations of the Mississippi Delta. As Kay Mills explains, "She had not been processed through any part of the system that usually renders someone controllable, at least in the eyes of those in power. She wasn't a product of the educational system or a labor union or the political system. She owed nothing to no one. She was uncompromising."[129] Mrs. Hamer had spoken the truth to power, and power responded with silence and rejection.[130] Listening to Mrs. Hamer finish her remarks, Humphrey's face bore an "empty sadness" (as Ed King recalls), his genuine sympathy for her story checked by his incapacity to invite her into the political process and to take her witness to heart.[131]

By Tuesday, August 25, the eleven votes needed for the Credentials Committee support had evaporated. Lyndon Johnson demonstrated his well-earned reputation as a political heavyweight. In addition to the defection of Martin Luther King, Jr., from the MFDP challenge, one member of the committee reversed her support when told by a Johnson aide that her husband would lose any chance of a federal judgeship. Another member changed sides when threatened with the elimination of all poverty programs in his Congressional district. Yet another learned that a vote for the Freedom Democratic party might guarantee the loss of a government contract his firm was pursuing.[132] Courtland Cox, a SNCC staffer working for MFDP, recalls, "Every member of that credentials committee who was going to vote for the minority, got a call. . . . And you began to see how things worked in the real world. I mean everybody, including a number of the people in the civil rights movement, a number of people in the religious community, a number of people in the liberal community, all came out and tried to blunt the thrust of the MFDP to take its rightful place as the lawful delegation from Mississippi."[133] The MFDP watched as their fragile coalition of backers began to crumble. By the time Johnson and company finished their hard hitting, support on the Credentials Committee for the Mississippi challenge had dropped from 18 to 4.

All the while, in his negotiations with MFDP representatives, Humphrey was brandishing just the sort of political cunning that would soon seal his spot on the presidential ticket. Supported by his new converts, Martin Luther King, Jr., Andrew Young, Bayard Rustin, and Walter Reuther,

Humphrey conferred with MFDP representatives Aaron Henry, Ed King, and Bob Moses at the Pagent Hotel and urged them to accept the compromise—and quickly. Humphrey had to explain that the delegation would not even be allowed to vote on their own two delegates because the president feared the MFDP would elect Hamer. At the same time, Mondale was railroading the compromise through the Credentials Committee hearing. Henry, Ed King, and Moses were under the impression that their conference with Humphrey was pivotal in negotiating the challenge, that the decision of the Freedom Democrats would be taken seriously by the committee, despite the fact that Humphrey clearly wished to settle the issue promptly without further delay. But that illusion was shattered when one of the senator's assistants rushed into the meeting room to announce that an important news report was about to be made on television. The news was that the Credentials Committee had unanimously approved the two-seat plan; that civil rights forces had won a remarkable victory by forcing the president of the United States to compromise. Bob Moses was livid. "You tricked us!" he shouted at Humphrey, as he stormed out of the room, visibly enraged.[134] Feeling "completely manipulated," Moses hurried to the Union Temple Baptist Church, where he explained to the confused delegates that he had not accepted the compromise.

On Tuesday night, as the temporary chair dismissed any dissenting voices from the floor with a bang of his gavel, the recommendation of the Credentials Committee was approved.[135] Johnson's convention could now proceed without further aggravation. Aside from an MFDP sit-in in Convention Hall, the continued vigils outside, and the predictable protestations of betrayal and political trickery, the delegation had run out of steam. The challenge was finished.

The Freedom Democrats had only then to meet and decide whether to accept or reject the compromise. Obviously, the two-seat proposal had many enthusiastic supporters, from Humphrey to Martin Luther King, Jr., to the northern news media. Even MFDP's own Aaron Henry and Ed King agreed in the end with the compromise. But Mrs. Hamer and the rank-and-file delegates, particularly the women and the sharecroppers and the poorer members of the party, remained unyielding in their call for true representation. Mrs. Hamer said, "If something was supposed to be ours 300 years ago, no one has the right to hand us only a *part* of it 300 years later."[136] Having too long accepted the leftovers from the white man's table, Mrs. Hamer refused what she considered a political handout. The compromise was an offense to those thousands of local black men and women, nameless and without voice in the national political scene, who, as Victoria Gray explained, "had not only laid their lives on the line, but had given their lives in order for this particular event to happen."[137] They would no longer accept the crumbs of liberal charity. Mrs. Hamer said baldly, "We didn't come all this way for no two seats."[138] The Freedom Democrats rejected the compromise.

The Mississippi delegation began to cast about for a way to understand the defeat. Some SNCC members seemed ready to wash their hands of the whole political establishment, citing the obvious failures of liberal democracy. "Atlantic City undermined my faith in the democratic process," said one summer volunteer.[139] "My hopes and dreams of being part of the National Democratic party were dead," said SNCC's Curtis Hayes.[140] Cleveland Sellers gave voice to an anger that propelled many SNCC members toward a more militant agenda in the months to follow. Sellers said, "The National Democratic party's rejection of the MFDP at the 1964 convention was to the civil rights movement what the Civil War was to American history: afterward, things could never be the same. Never again were we lulled into believing that our task was exposing injustices so that the 'good' people of America would eliminate them. We left Atlantic City with the knowledge that the movement had turned into something else. After Atlantic City, our struggle was not for civil rights, but for liberation."[141] For his part, veteran SNCC activist Ed Brown left Atlantic City with a intensified awareness of the either/or situation at hand, which he called the new "religious" impulse of the movement. "The world was now defined between us and them," Brown said, "in the way a religious person defines the world between believers and nonbelievers. We were pure and good; all the others were corrupt, even those middle-class blacks who wanted to compromise at the convention."[142]

Most everyone mourned the fact that the Democratic establishment had passed on a rare opportunity to truly be the representative party of the poor and the oppressed.[143] Bob Moses lamented this failure above all. Perhaps there was room for black professionals in the party, but there was no room for "the grassroots people, the sharecroppers, the common workers and the day workers." Of course, there might be room for them "as recipients of largesse, of poverty programs and the like," he said, but not as "participants in power-sharing."[144] Although Bob Moses returned to Mississippi after the National Democratic Convention, his distrust of organizations had intensified to a feverish high in Atlantic City, making it difficult for him to give much more to the movement. "Go where the spirit says go, and do what the spirit says do," he began urging SNCC workers in late 1964. He withdrew from Mississippi the next year.[145]

Mrs. Hamer was also angry and tired. But like most of the local people representing the Mississippi Freedom Democratic party (and unlike most of the younger SNCC staffers), Mrs. Hamer had long possessed a sober realism toward racial politics. She did not need Atlantic City to convince her that "the white man is not going to give up his power to us." Atlantic City only broadened that realism, teaching her that racism "is not Mississippi's problem, but America's—that 'the land of the free and the home of the brave is all on paper.'"[146] The enemy was no longer the familiar cast of bigots and klansmen but "the powers in high places."[147] She questioned America. But she did not despair. In fact, Mrs. Hamer and the Freedom Democrats proved their claim as Mississippi's legitimate Democratic delegation by supporting the Johnson-Humphrey ticket in November, unlike all but a few white regulars, who catapulted Goldwater to an overwhelming victory in the state polls.

In the closing hours of the Atlantic City convention, the MFDP held its final vigil on the boardwalk. Sally Belfrage described the mood that prevailed at the gathering as one of solemn but steadied determination, radiating from the indefatigable presence of Mrs. Hamer. The hard lessons of the summer's end seemed only to strengthen her resolve.

> At the vigil again quite late we stood and sang "We Shall Overcome"—remembering all the impossible times, unlike any others, when we had sung it before. The only song that has no clapping, because the hands are holding all the other hands. A suspension from color, hate, recrimination, guilt, suffering—a kind of lesson in miniature of what it's all about. The song begins slowly and somehow without anticipation of these things: just a song, the last one, before we separate. You see the others, and the instant when it comes to each one to think what the words mean, when each merely breaks, wondering: shall we overcome? The hands hold each other tighter. Mrs. Hamer is smiling, flinging out the words, and crying at once. "Black and white together," she leads the next verse, and a sort of joy begins to grow in every face; "We are not afraid"—and for just that second no one is afraid, because they are free.[148]

When the vigil ended, Mrs. Hamer, along with her fellow Freedom Democrats, returned to Mississippi—"proud and unbowed."[149]

But free? Does not Belfrage's artfulness obscure her historical judgment? On the contrary, her observation is characteristically prescient. In defiance of the compromise, Mrs. Hamer and her Mississippi comrades were freed by the moral clarity that comes from resisting temptation, freed by their refusal to sell out, from the illusion that the solution to their problems would come from the powers of the political establishment.

Their perceptions clouded by fatigue and anger, Mrs. Hamer and the MFDP had no way of realizing that their labors in the Summer Project and at Atlantic City would help usher in the Voting Rights Act. Indeed the victories of the Freedom Democratic party were not moral or spiritual alone. By the summer of 1968, 42 percent of the black people living in Sunflower County had registered to vote. In other Delta counties like Leflore, Coahoma, and Issaquena, the percentage was even higher. Compared to the early 1960s, when only 250 blacks were registered in Leflore County and fewer in Sunflower, the MFDP and SNCC summer initiative had been a strategic success. As political scientist Leslie McLemore summarized in his analysis of the party, "The FDP's Atlantic City performance represented the coming of political age of Black people in Mississippi in a way that had not been seen since Reconstruction."[150]

The Welcome Table

Mrs. Hamer's life after 1964 mirrored her conviction that God's power—God's concrete, worldly presence—was with the poor. After traveling to Africa with Harry Belafonte and a group of SNCC veterans in September 1964, she returned to her home in Ruleville, Mississippi, where she lived in poverty until her death on March 14, 1977. Mrs. Hamer continued to organize Freedom Democratic initiatives to build black power in the state. Although defeated in her own bids for public office and in her 1964 and 1965 congressional challenge, she represented the state as a member of the official (and biracial) delegation of Mississippians in the 1968 National Democratic Convention in Chicago, where she strongly supported anti-Vietnam War actions. She helped organize the Child Development Group of Mississippi, and when that failed became a champion for other grass-roots Head Start programs.[151] She directed the Freedom Farm Cooperative in Sunflower County, obtaining several hundred acres of land for planta-tion workers who had lost their jobs to farm mechanization. She also played a critical role in Martin Luther King, Jr.'s, Poor People's Campaign, which worked to create a multiracial political coalition of the poor and dis-possessed.[152] In the last years of her life, she battled a devastating assault of cancer, heart disease, and diabetes, along with severe mental strain and depression. Her lack of any disability income intensified the stress and re-sulted in inconsistent health care.

Through it all, the Summer Project remained for Mrs. Hamer the most powerful memory of the movement, a reminder amidst much personal suf-fering that God had been present in the struggle. In her final interview, given three months before her death, she recalled: "A living example was Andy Goodman, James Chaney, and Michael Schwerner that come down here. And I remember talking to them the Sunday before they went to Ox-ford, Ohio, for the orientation where we had to drill or talk [to the volun-teers] about what they might be faced with. Even when Christ hung on the cross, he said greater love has no man than the one who is willing to lay down his life for his friends. Even though they was aware they might die, they still came. These are the things we have to think about. These are the things we can't sweep under the rug. And these are the things that still give me hope."[153] In Mrs. Hamer's way of seeing, the thought of the three civil rights workers dying like Christ on the cross was not an exhibition of any sort of Christian imperialism—claiming the two Jewish men as martyrs for Christ. Rather, her perception was shaped by the utterly straightforward conviction that if Jesus is the one for others, then surely he welcomes all who follow after, no matter whether they confess some other name or no name at all.

Fannie Lou Hamer gave voice to a distinctive Christian discourse, evangelical in the most vigorous sense of the term, a robust and disciplined love of Jesus of Nazareth, of the whole scandalous story of his life, death, and resurrection. At the same time, her love was a great big love, open to anyone who cared for the weak and the poor. Was this not the message of the Gospel? She believed it was: "The churches have got to remember how Christ dealt with the people," she testified, "like in the 4th chapter of St. Luke, and the 18th verse, when Jesus said, 'The spirit of the Lord is upon me, because he hath anointed me to preach the gospel to the poor; he hath sent me to heal the brokenhearted, to preach deliverance to the captives, and recovering of sight to the blind, to set at liberty those that are bruised.'" Jesus was God's son, sacrificed on the bloody cross for the sins of the world, raised miraculously from the dead on the third day, coming again in glory to judge the world and gather home his children. But Jesus was also a "radical" and a "militant," and were he living in the Delta in 1964, he would be branded a "red."[154] Christ was a real revolutionary, "out there where it's happening."

In this context Mrs. Hamer spoke of the Summer Project as "the beginning of a New Kingdom right here on earth." She compared the student volunteers to the Good Samaritan, reading Jesus's famous parable as a description of the New Kingdom emerging amidst the scorched summer fields of the Mississippi Delta. Like the self-righteous priest and the Levite in the biblical account, who passed by the wounded man without concern for his welfare, southern white Christians had turned their sights from black suffering—and "never taken the time to see what was going on." But this was not true of the summer volunteers who came to Mississippi. Although strangers like the Samaritan in Jericho, they never hesitated to act with compassion toward people they found hurting and oppressed. "Although they were strangers, they were the best friends we ever met," Mrs. Hamer said. "This was the beginning of the New Kingdom in Mississippi. To me, if I had to choose today between the church and these young people—and I was brought up in the church and I'm not against the church—I'd choose these young people. They did something in Mississippi that gave us the hope that we had prayed for so many years. We had wondered if there was anybody human enough to see us as human beings instead of animals. These young people were so Christlike." The volunteers, often

[handwritten marginal note: Says more about the author than Jesus — also over used]

boasting secular ideals of justice, appeared to Mrs. Hamer as instruments
of divine grace and compassion—their naïveté, bookish agnosticism, and
occasional patronizing notwithstanding. In Mrs. Hamer's view, their commitment was a beautiful and holy thing. She said, "If Christ were here
today, He would be just like these young people who the Southerners
called radicals and beatniks. Christ was called a Beelzebub, called so many
names. But He was Christ."[155] In Mrs. Hamer's keen theological imagination, the radical, beatnik Christ was taking shape in the texture of compassionate service for others. ("Bob Moses was my little Jesus," Curtis
Hayes once confessed.)[156] This far outweighed, in her mind, the contentious matter of whether the students had purged themselves of whatever cultural stereotypes continued to distort their self-perceptions and
perceptions of local people.

Like any good evangelical theologian, Mrs. Hamer's discourse was full of
subversive undercurrents and iconoclastic impulses, spirited with energy
moving into action. Her words disarmed: they were comforting and familiar on a literal level, agitating and sly beneath the surface. She liked to describe salvation as a welcoming table (as in the well-known spiritual)
where everybody was invited to come and eat, even Ross Barnett and
James O. Eastland—but they would have to learn some manners. For
those who had ears to hear, she added, "It's a funny thing since I started
working for Christ; it's kind of like in the 23rd Psalm, when David said,
'Thou preparest a table before me in the presence of my enemies. Thou an-
nointeth my head with oil.'"[157] She would only be working now for Jesus,
but look what had happened; in a comic reversal of roles, Jesus had prepared a feast for her, where the governor and the senator would be the
strangers in need of hospitality.

Thus, two interconnecting images of Christ shaped her piety: the historical, miraculous, resurrected Christ, on the one hand, and the gritty,
revolutionary Christ, on the other. Was there not a contradiction between
these images? Though there might be for the intellectual aristocracy, for
the folks in high places, there was not for Mrs. Hamer. For she rehearsed
a synthetic ingenuity born of experience, as adept as the most sublime
philosopher in weaving contradictions into an integrated whole. Yet Mrs.
Hamer did not rely on philosophical or theological systems to reconcile
opposites. Indeed, it might seem ludicrous to state this, were it not for the
fact that her way of holding together the two thoughts of the miraculous
and the militant Christ exhibited a creative and conceptual power every bit
the equal of our canonized masters of conceptual thought. The animating
center of her piety was her voice, which time and again energized people
into action. She used the singing of spirituals.[158]

Consider the way she combined two slave spirituals, differing in theme
and structure, into a new song with resonances specifically attuned to the

movement.[159] Apart from any formal theological training, Mrs. Hamer grasped with keen insight the connection between Easter and Passover, between personal salvation and the liberation of the people of Israel from bondage. She took the Christmas spiritual, "Go Tell It on the Mountain":

> Go tell it on the mountain
>   over the hills and everywhere;
> Go tell it on the mountain
>   that Jesus Christ is born.

She combined it with the song, "Go Down Moses":

> When Israel was in Egypt's land, let my people go,
>   oppressed so hard they could not stand, let my people go.
> Go down Moses, way down in Egypt's land;
> Tell old Pharaoh, let my people go.

She then sang:

> Paul and Silas was bound in jail, let my people go.
> Had no money for to go their bail, let my people go.
>
> Paul and Silas began to shout, let my people go.
> Jail doors open and they walked out, let my people go.
>
> Who's that yonder dressed in red? Let my people go.
> Must be the children that Moses led, let my people go.
>
> Who's that yonder dressed in black? Let my people go.
> Must be the hypocrites turning back, let my people go.
>
> Who's that yonder dressed in blue? Let my people go.
> Must be the children now passing through, let my people go.
>
> I had a little book he gave to me, let my people go.
> And every page spelled victory, let my people go.
>
> Go, tell it on the mountain, over the hills and everywhere.
> Go, tell it on the mountain, to let my people go!

Here is Mrs. Hamer's retelling of the Gospel story. My sins are forgiven; my life is made new; the angel of death has passed over me; I have been rescued from an eternal perishing. Still, much more is at stake than the fate of my individual soul. For since the good news is proclaimed, I can stand up to Pharaoh, look him in the eyes and say, "Let my people go." There *is* a land beyond Egypt.[160] The song builds momentum until the final verse repeats the phrase, but now no longer as a plea but as a demand of the Gospel—"Let my people go." The Gospel—"go tell it"—becomes the theological framework for the liberation of people from oppression.[161]

Thus, the death for which Christ has atoned—my death, humanity's death—is also the death of bondage to fear and oppression—a resounding "No" to Jim Crow.[162] And importantly, both deaths, the atoning death of Christ and the death to slavery, can—and must—be claimed in the here and now. In Mrs. Hamer's mind, this is what Moses—that is, Bob Moses—had tried to explain when he said, "The thing was not how you're going to die, but how you're going to live."[163] The solitariness of one's own death—of one's own self—is taken up in the historical unfolding of the demand, "Let my people go," a demand that is also a promise, that also gathers up the particularities of our individual stories into the spirit's movement toward freedom. The Good News is this: that the core of who we are as individual selves is no longer enslaved in the cotton fields of the Mississippi Delta or shut up in a Winona prison; it is now free for others, open toward life. The lady who sang understood:

> I've got the light of freedom
> I'm gonna let it shine.
> Jesus gave it to me,
> I'm gonna let it shine.
> Gonna shine all over the Delta,
> I'm gonna let it shine.
> Let it shine, let it shine, let it shine.

TWO

High Priest of the Anti–Civil Rights
Movement: The Calling
of Sam Bowers

The Making of a Christian Militant

WHEN Sam Bowers surveyed America's social landscape from his beloved Mississippi in early 1964, he did not simply lament the changing South—the desecration of "sovereign" southern states, their time-honored practices attacked by liberal politicians, northern media elites, and civil right workers. The world Bowers saw was more menacing and full of dangers greater than even these assaults on caste and custom. Right before his eyes, on the alluvial soil of the very heart of the Confederacy, appeared all the signs of a two-thousand-year war between the idolatrous agents of Baal and the soldiers of the one true God, the "Galilean Jesus Christ."

As Imperial Wizard of the White Knights of Ku Klux Klan, Bowers ruled over a four-year campaign of pervasive white terrorism during which he was suspected of orchestrating at least nine murders, seventy-five bombings of black churches, and three hundred assaults, bombings, and beatings. From 1964 until his conviction in 1967 on federal civil rights violations in the triple murder of Michael Schwerner, James Chaney, and Andrew Goodman, Bowers was the animating force behind white Mississippi's journey into the heart of militant rage, the Kurtz at the heart of darkness of the anti-civil rights movement. Standing before what he considered a world-historical moment, Bowers believed he was called by God to accomplish the urgent task of eliminating the "heretics."[1] He described the moment in a recruiting poster that appeared on telephone poles, church bulletin boards, café windows, and front porches throughout the state:

The administration of our National Government is now under the actual control of atheists who are Bolsheviks by nature. As dedicated agents of Satan,
they are absolutely determined to destroy Christian Civilization and all Christians. . . . [Our] members are Christians who are anxious to preserve not only
their souls for all Eternity, but who are MILITANTLY DETERMINED, God willing,
to save their lives, and the Life of this Nation, in order that their descendants
shall enjoy the same, full, God-given blessings of True Liberty that we have
been permitted to enjoy up to now.

We do not accept Jews, because they reject Christ, and through the machi-
nations of their International Banking Cartel, are at the root-center of what
we call "communism" today.

We do not accept Papists, because they bow to a Roman dictator, in direct
violation of the First Commandment and the True American Spirit of Responsible, Individual Liberty.

We do not accept Turks, Mongols, Tarters, Orientals, Negroes, nor any
other person whose native background of culture is foreign to the Anglo-
Saxon system of Government by responsible, FREE, Individual Citizens.

If you are a Christian, American Anglo-Saxon who can understand the
simple Truth of this Philosophy, you belong in the White Knights of the Ku
Klux Klan of Mississippi. We need your help right away. Get your Bible out
and Pray! You will hear from us.[2]

When Bowers described the deluge of civil rights workers and federal law
enforcement agents in the summer of 1964 as a "crucifixion" of the "innocent people" of God, the stage was set for a holy crusade to purge the land
of those who had betrayed his Lord. Bowers resurrected the Klan's Christian identity with a fanatic's zeal and, as journalist Wyn Craig Wade wrote,
"restored to the hackneyed word *crusade* its thirteenth-century purpose of
murdering the infidels."[3] He was determined to fight the battle until the
bitter end.

Sam Holloway Bowers, Jr., was born in New Orleans on August 6, 1924.
His biography defies stereotypes of klansmen as backwoods, semi-illiterate
rednecks. His father was a salesman from Gulfport. His mother, the former
Evangeline Peyton, was the daughter of a wealthy planter.[4] Bowers was
supremely proud of his family pedigree. His grandfather, Eaton J. Bowers,
was a prominent Mississippi attorney who had been admitted to the bar at
the age of nineteen and served three terms in the United States Congress
from 1903 until 1911; he was the most revered male figure in Bowers's
life.[5] Bowers also claimed to be a direct descendent of "the first president
of the first constituted legislative assembly on this continent, the Virginia
House of Burgesses."[6] For three generations, the Bowers family were practicing Methodists; Dr. Charles Betts Galloway (the father of the well-loved
Methodist bishop of Mississippi from 1886–1909, Charles Betts Galloway, Jr.) and Bowers's great-grandfather, Eaton Jackson Bowers, Sr., married the sisters Adelaide and Sallie Lee Dinkins.[7] The grandfather Eaton J.

Bowers had been a trustee and steward in his Methodist church in Bay St. Louis, Mississippi.[8] In fact, Sam Bowers himself might have gone on to Millsaps College and become "a great Methodist man" had he not early suspected that even the most benign authorities posed grave personal dangers to him.[9] Baptist theology and polity, with its happy distrust of creeds and hierarchy, better fit his anti-clerical bent. In 1966 Bowers joined the Hillcrest Baptist Church in Laurel, Mississippi, where he taught (and continues to teach) an adult men's Sunday school class.

Bowers's parents were divorced when he was fourteen. After a series of short stays with his father in Florida, the Mississippi Gulf Coast, and New Orleans, he moved to Jackson, Mississippi, in the summer of 1939. His mother Evangeline took a secretarial job at the Agricultural and Industrial Board and later at the Department of Motor Vehicles.[10] In Jackson, Bowers and his mother lived in a apartment on North West Street near the state capitol, a few blocks away from Jackson's largest churches, including the Capitol Street Methodist Church and First Baptist Church. In the nearby Belhaven neighborhood, Ross Barnett, the successful attorney who would later become governor as a die-hard segregationist, lived in a house on Fairview Street; as did William Simmons, the man who later ruled over the Citizens' Council of Mississippi. On Pinehurst Street, Eudora Welty had settled into her brilliant writing life, having returned from New York in the early 1930s to live in the neighborhood of her childhood.

Bowers's mother was a woman of strict discipline and deliberate erudition, who insisted he learn from her example. He would mind his manners and his language. Certain forms of civility would be expected of the boy at all times: polite forms of address, eloquence in conversation, refined tastes—nothing less would be suitable to his upbringing and lineage. Should an ungrammatical phrase or sentence pass from his mouth, it would not be tolerated without punishment. Evangeline believed that eloquence and skillful rhetoric made a child virtuous; "purify a young man's speech, and his heart and mind will follow," Bowers recalls his mother saying. Yet he believed that her discipline was tempered with genuine affection. She wanted her son to seek learning not solely out of a sense of duty but for the sake of a higher principle. Although she was adamant that the boy abstain from reading trash books and dime-store novels, it was the "majesty of language" that fueled her demands. "She did not dogmatically state her views, but would say things like, 'you would be so much better off reading the classics.' She had a gentle way about her. She was a master psychologist in this manner." With the same persuasion she attempted to keep her son interested in his school life. "I know you aren't terribly interested in school," she would say, "but please try to do better. These years will pass soon enough." Yet notwithstanding his mother's admonitions and lofty expectations, he found it impossible to treat his school teachers with the respect they demanded.[11]

By the time Bowers entered Jackson's Central High School, he had begun to feel threatened by the "adult world" of his teachers, refusing to conform to their standards of appropriate behavior. In fact, he took "secret pleasure" in performing poorly in school; he enjoyed thwarting his teachers' efforts to instruct. They tried to reassure Evangeline that her son had "so much potential if he'd just apply himself"; nonetheless, it gave him "some sense of power" to confound and aggravate intrusive adult authority. He would skip school and race boxcars on a hilly road near Millsaps College. He defied anyone to take measures of discipline against him. "The adult authorities could not socially stigmatize me because I succeeded in frustrating the adult world," he said. And this was crucial, especially at a time when he was feeling "almost fully powerless and at the mercy of stronger personalities"—feeling intruded upon, as though outsiders were interfering with his "childhood mission." His mission, even in these early years, was to preserve innocence before the crushing blows of nihilistic authority; to defy the authority of those who were "bent on making impositions" on him. "Many great men, like Douglas MacArthur, were really just mama's boys," Bowers once said. "They were children to the end."[12]

Yet, as he soon discovered, a child "cannot take too much overlooking or imposition before he must rage out against those powers which are seeking to tear him away from his equanimity." By age fifteen Bowers was deeply resentful of all authority figures, whose degeneracy he claims to have felt with a visceral intensity. He exhibited his anger and frustration in a kind of hyperactivity that sometimes gave way to temper tantrums and other times to wild and exaggerated humor. "The adult authorities were bent on making impositions on my childhood, and I despised them for it." Bowers abruptly returned to New Orleans in the fall of his senior year—at his father's insistence—and attended Fortier High School. But he was so furious for having been taken away from Jackson that by the middle of the fall semester he dropped out of high school and joined the Navy—even against his mother's wishes—shortly after Pearl Harbor in December of 1941.[13]

Bowers would later understand his childhood abhorrence of adult imposition—or "outside agitation"—as a "predestined formation," which prepared him well for future battles with "the alien prophets of Baal." However, he had to undergo a series of formative religious experiences before his militant vocation became clear to him—before he was able to understand that God had singled him out for a high and holy calling. The first took place just after V-J Day, in August of 1945. Having been stationed with the Navy in the Pacific, Bowers had discovered that the discipline imposed by the military was able to accommodate his visceral rage against outside agitation and put that rage (at least temporarily) to positive, mostly patriotic, use. Discipline or authority did not necessarily signal conformity and self-disintegration, rather it could channel hostility toward the elimination of specific, justifiable targets. Whereas the adult, "academic" authorities seemed to persecute Bowers "for the sake of their own gratuitous pleasure and gratification," the Navy gave him a reason to accept discipline—for "the country's honor and health were at stake." On this day after the news of the Japanese surrender and the end of World War II, Bowers got off duty and climbed to the top of the ship's deck. It was a clear, blue morning, he remembers—the sea had never looked so beautiful. Recalling the immense sacrifice his countrymen had made for the sake of freedom, and his comrades who had died in combat, tears came to his eyes. Full of sadness, yet deeply grateful for his privilege to stand before this moment, Bowers uttered the prayer: "I thank you Lord. There were many better men than I who perished in this war. I don't know why you spared my life, but I appreciate it. And for the rest of my life I'll seek to understand the purpose of your mercy, and to live accordingly."[14] He sensed the great, incomprehensible mystery of God's sovereign plan, and the growing recognition of his unique role in it. He was ready to pursue an immense destiny, marked by the Almighty God himself.

Bowers was honorably discharged as Machinist Mate First Class in December 1945. For the next two years he studied engineering at Tulane University and the University of Southern California (although he did not receive a bachelor's degree until his incarceration in the mid-1970s at McNeil Island federal penitentiary in Washington state, when he completed formal theological studies through Pacific Lutheran University's prison program). In the late 1940s Bowers returned to Laurel from the West Coast, where he tried his hand without much success in various business ventures before setting up a vending machine operation called the Sambo Amusement Company. He began reading Nazi and racist philosophy and the novels of Thomas Dixon, which he later required his fellow klansmen to read. Such Dixon novels as *The Leopard's Spots* and *The Clansmen*—which D. W. Griffith would make into his epochal film, *The Birth of a Nation*—offered depictions of "African barbarism" and black sexual degeneracy in contrast to "God's first law of life," the "white man's instinct of racial purity."[15]

Even friends who shared Bowers's interests and genuinely enjoyed his company found him alternately eccentric and frightening. Stockpiled in his living quarters were original manuscripts on religion and political philosophy, racing car paraphernalia, guns and ammunition, a collection of masks (large rubber caricatures of presidents, movie stars and blacks) and his wardrobe of fashionable suits and ties. One acquaintance described his habit of wearing a swastika armband and of clicking his heels in front of his dog, saluting the canine with a "Heil Hitler!"[16] Bowers's unpredictable capacity for anger always kept other men at a distance, even at times his roommate and best friend, Robert Larson, who accompanied him to Laurel from California and shared his living quarters in the back of the company's clapboard building. When Bowers was angry, a former colleague noted, he would "stalk rapidly back and forth, fists clenched, countenance . . . fierce enough to make any target of his rage quickly back off."[17]

The second formative experience in the development of Bowers's priestly self-consciousness proved more specifically religious, and more commanding than the earlier. In 1955, he was arrested for illegal possession of liquor—a demeaning ordeal for a man who took pride in his aristocratic lineage. He pleaded guilty and was fined one hundred dollars.[18] Bowers's arrest, combined with the collapse of another business venture, brought him to the brink of self-destruction. He felt unraveled and desperate. Family memories haunted him. The brilliant victory at war was now darkened by his own disjointed past and an unpromising future—unfinished degrees at two universities, job failures, career uncertainties, personal fears, and an arrest. "Sam had failed me totally—economically, personally, ethically, and in every real way," he recalled. "I felt totally crushed by life, and wanted to destroy everything, including myself." He looked on God "with absolute antipathy."[19]

But all that changed in an experience of "overwhelming grace." Like Paul's conversion on the Damascus road or Martin Luther's encounter with his St. Ann while walking along an empty road during a thunderstorm, Bowers was also on a journey. On a drive along a two-lane highway on a late summer afternoon in south Mississippi, contemplating suicide and equipped for the task, Bowers felt suddenly transported by a power greater than he had ever before experienced. In a moment of mystical intensity, God spoke to him the words, "Don't be afraid; everything is all right." Bowers explained, "The living God made himself real to me even when I did not deserve it." It was not a vision he beheld; there was no blinding light or appearance of a holy personage. Rather, his was an "ecstatic realization." Although moments earlier he had wanted to destroy everything including himself, he now felt his whole identity melt into divine bliss. His inner anguish vanished; hope was renewed and energy restored in an experience of "unmerited grace." The effect was not to leave him blinded or in any way incapacitated. God "used his blackjack on Paul a lot more vigorously than he did on Sam," he insisted. Yet like Paul with his vision of dazzling light, strange voices, and terrifying blindness, Bowers received the clear and overwhelming conviction on which his life would be forever after based: that he had seen and witnessed the living God, that this God knew his name and had called him for a special purpose. "To be saved one must go to the point of insanity," Bowers said. One must realize there is nothing left to do but throw oneself into the hands of divine mercy, perform any task, fulfill any demand for the saving God.[20]

Behind the wheel of his pickup truck that summer evening, Bowers discovered that God's love was wholly unmerited; that "all the horrible experiences of [his] life could be redeemed by the unbounded goodness of the one
true God." He felt "on air for three days," his thoughts about suicide having
given way to the new perspective his life had been given. "Sam Bowers," he
resolved, "I'm going to live the rest of my life with you, but don't expect me
to take you quite so seriously again. Your life is no longer your own: it is
God's." With the world around him reconfigured and full of sense, he gave
himself to his work, his friends, and the nurturing of his divine call.[21]

Soon thereafter Bowers's religious identity acquired its decisive Christian
character, when a young friend prevailed upon him to take a more active
role in the study of Scripture. Here is Bowers's account: "A boy was working with me in one of my side occupations. We supplied cigarettes to the
cigarette machines around town. We would wake up early Monday mornings and make the rounds refilling the machines. This boy was always
fresh from his Sunday sermon, which he always found inspiring and in-
vigorating. In his presence, I restricted my anti-clerical venom, which I
often spewed out on friends, even though I took my spirituality very seriously. We would sometimes debate certain topics, like the infallibility of
Scripture, or the authorship of the New Testament books. The boy's
knowledge of the Bible, though a naive one I thought, was very much alive
to him. As a result of these discussions, I decided I needed to get more familiar with the Bible, so I purchased a King James Bible at the local Baptist book store. When I read the epistolary dedicatory, I realized that these
guys were speaking the truth—and, of course, I've always been interested
in the majesty of language."[22]

The embracing sense of divine peace that Bowers had experienced on
the deck of the naval vessel and in his pickup truck epiphany he now discovered in the words of Scripture, particularly in the Elizabethan eloquence of the King James Bible. A magnificent new world opened up to .
him; it was as if the *sensus literalis* of Scripture gave Bowers a new way of
seeing the realities of his own distinctive geographical and spiritual place.
An indissoluble link with the prophets and the fiery convert Paul was
forged in his religious self-understanding. These biblical writers seemed to
speak directly to him. As he gave himself to the study of Scripture, Bowers began to realize that his rage (which at times dissipated only to return
with new intensity) could be put in service to the work of the Lord. His
anger found a religious energy and thus a warrant to the career awaiting
him. No one less than Jesus Christ himself was calling him to the priestly
task of preserving the purity of his blood and soil. To his education in the
literature of racial superiority and cultural nationalism, Bowers added a
disciplined study of the Bible. He would never stray from the conviction
that he had been called according to God's high purpose.

Patriots for Jesus

Since the 1954 Supreme Court decision in *Brown vs. Board of Education* that outlawed segregation in public schools, the Citizens' Council in Mississippi had labored long and hard to preserve the "Southern Way of Life." When federal marshals arrived at Oxford in 1962 to enforce James Meredith's enrollment at the university, however, popular sentiment held that once again the state's sovereignty was under attack by outsiders posing as legitimate authorities. "The Battle of Ole Miss" was simply the most recent chapter in the long, tragic story of the South's stolen dignity. The following year, in 1963, white fear intensified as CORE and SNCC began to turn their full attention to Mississippi as the primary target of voter registration in the South. Throughout the state, rumors spread of the upcoming Summer Project, of an outside invasion far greater than that at Ole Miss, an invasion the size of which the South had not experienced since Sherman's cruel march in the final days of "the War for Southern Independence."

Although Bowers had been a member of the Original Knights of the Ku Klux Klan of Louisiana in its Mississippi chapter, he began to organize a new Klan that would be more responsive to his state's unique concerns. On February 15, 1964, at a meeting in Brookhaven, Bowers, along with two hundred other dissenters from the Louisiana order, pledged his loyalties to a new, highly secretive organization, the White Knights of the Ku Klux Klan of Mississippi. These "Christian militants" would dedicate themselves "to oppose in every honorable way possible the forces of Satan on this earth, and in particular his agency which is called by the name of 'Communism' today."[23] Bowers, the Imperial Wizard of the new White Knights, described the Klan's mission in his "Executive Lecture":

> The world and all of the people in it are torn between two exactly opposite forces:
>
> 1. The Spiritual Force of Almighty God Championed by our Savior, Christ Jesus.
>
> 2. The negative, materialistic force of destruction championed by Satan.
>
> It is necessary that each and every member truly understand the above before he can ever become effective in this organization. . . . Until we all realise [sic] that we are up against a SUPERNATURAL Force, against which our FINITE minds and emotions and abilities are, by themselves, POWERLESS to defeat, we shall continue to suffer disappointments and defeats again and again.[24]

Violence would not be spared in this mission of protecting the purity of God's people. Had Elijah spared the prophets of Baal?

Bowers wanted to distinguish the White Knights from other Klan groups not only by their vigorous piety but also by their practices. The White

Knights would not display their members in senseless public rituals. No klansmen from this order would be found in uniform at a Little League fish fry or driving a go-cart in a Memorial Day parade. Rather, these holy warriors would remain hidden from view. Their concealment would obscure their violence, and at the same time heighten the terror of their enemies. Acts of sabotage would erupt often without ostensible logic, creating an environment of fear as inscrutable as divine wrath. Calculated harassment would intensify the sense of unpredictability and confusion. As Bowers explained, "The Acts [of harassment] themselves should always appear to aliens as ridiculous and unimportant. Harassment itself should never aim at accomplishing any goal DIRECTLY. The purpose of harassment is to stir up and fret the enemy, then step back and wait for him to make a mistake, meanwhile preparing calmly and soberly to exploit any mistake that he does make to the maximum advantage to ourselves."[25] To "stir up and fret the enemy," Bowers offered an extensive list of "equipment" that could be used with favorable results in acts of calculated harassment: "roofing nails, sugar and molasses, firecrackers, snakes and lizards, mad dogs, itching powder, stink bombs, tear gas, sling shots, marbles, BB guns, Air Rifles, Bow and arrows . . . and the proper use of the Telephone."[26] Crosses might be burned on the lawns of the state's eighty-two courthouses on the same night, even though the White Knights were largely concentrated in no more than ten counties. On one occasion, in May of 1964, Bowers ordered the bombing of the local newspaper offices, the timid, uninformative *Laurel Leader Call.* Although the paper was owned by a British company, it had shown no signs of advancing a liberal or moderate racial position. Even so, after the bombing, Bowers sent word to the befuddled editor that his paper had been targeted "not for anything you did to us, but because you did not do anything for us."[27]

When harassment was violent, Bowers insisted it be carried out in a way that appeared random, thus fostering an atmosphere of intimidation and fear, a prevailing sense of danger. A sample from the long chronicle of the Department of Justice serves as grim evidence of the strategy:

February 15, 1964—Adams County. A Negro man, Winston, was attacked and beaten by masked and armed men asking if he was a member of the NAACP.

February 16, 1964—Adams County. Two Negro men, Curtis and Jackson, were beaten by five armed men wearing white hoods down to their waists. The men questioned the two Negroes about their membership in the NAACP.

February 18, or 25, 1964—Lincoln County. A 28-year-old Negro man was beaten by a group of four white men who stopped his car while he was returning home from work. He was accused of following a white lady, taken out into the county, and both his eyes were blackened.

March 25, 1964—Hinds County. The plate glass windows in the grocery store belonging to a Negro active in the civil rights work in Jackson, Rev. Smith, were broken. A Klan pamphlet was discovered in the debris.

April—Panola County. West Camp Church was broken into and its windows were smashed and chairs inside the church were damaged. This church has been used for voter registration purposes every other week.

April 4, 1964—Neshoba County. A dozen crosses were burned at various spots throughout the county.

April 5, 1964—Adams County. Richard Joe Butler, Negro, was stopped outside Natchez by a group of white men wearing hoods. He was shot several times and seriously wounded, requiring hospitalization.

April 9, 1964—Jones County. Two crosses allegedly burned at the home of Ollie Cole and the home of Sam Merrill, both Negro employees of the Masonite Corporation in Laurel.

April 24, 1964—Statewide. Crosses were burned across the state. The Highway Patrol received reports of 71 crosses being burned in 61 areas of Mississippi including Jackson, Hattiesburg, Vicksburg, Utica, Crystal Springs, Greenwood, Natchez, Greenville, Meridian, Fayette, and Winona.

June 4, 1964—Hinds County. Ethel Jordon and Alvin Higgins, both Negroes, were beaten on their way home after they stopped to assist a white man in a car that appeared to be disabled. Jordon suffered a fractured rib and a tremendously swollen left side of the head, and a severely contused hand.

June 6, 1964—Amite County. Roland Sleeper, a Negro, was taken from his home near Liberty, Mississippi and whipped by four white men who also threatened to kill him. He was asked if any NAACP people were staying at his home.

June 11, 1964—Pike County. Ivey Gutter, a Negro male who resides near Summit, was beaten by unknown white males who were armed and wore black hoods.[28]

Days of harassment and violence might be followed by days of calm, when known or suspected klansmen, dressed in plain clothes, would appear at civil rights gatherings, just to stand at the periphery of the crowd or to sit in a pickup truck, smoking cigarettes and laughing.

The quality of this dialectic—appearance and disappearance, presence and absence, aggression and passivity—would imbue even their everyday discourse. Thomas Tarrants, a former explosives specialist with the White Knights, described his conversations with Bowers in this manner. When speaking directly about Klan activities, the two men would take separate cars, frequently separate routes, and meet in a wooded area outside Laurel, where they would walk silently into the densest and most remote part of the woods and communicate in whispers. On occasion, if matters were urgent, leaving them no time to quit Klan headquarters, Bowers would insist that the conversation be written in a notebook, which was handed back and forth; after each exchange the page would be torn out, burned with matches, and then flushed down the toilet.[29]

While protecting the secrecy of his organization, Bowers tirelessly spread the news of his clandestine patriots to those men he considered congenial to the militant call. He proselytized a wide spectrum of the white community; not only did he target men working in blue-collar jobs but, as journalist Jack Nelson noted, he also recruited "law enforcement officers, jackleg preachers, ragtag attorneys and other professionals and semiprofessionals who enjoyed a measure of respect in their communities."[30] Bowers was persuasive and charismatic. In conversation with ministers and pious Christians, he could quote freely from the Bible while describing his religious vocation and God's desire to raise up a band of holy patriots against the infidels. With a rowdier crowd, he could talk guns and drag racing and "nigger knocking." With the racist ideologues (and there were those, too), he could hold forth on such influential racist thinkers as the German theologian Paul de Lagarde (1827–1891), or Wagner's half-English son-in-law, Houston Stewart Chamberlain (1855–1927), or the Frenchman Count Arthur de Gobineau (1816–1882), whose famous *Essai sur l'inégalité des races humaines* described the Aryans as the people predestined to live as God's chosen race.[31]

In all his solicitations, Bowers capitalized on the gathering storm of intensified social unrest and ominous forecasts for the future. The Sambo Amusement Company was located directly across the street from Laurel's largest employer, the Masonite plant, where the time was ripe for his message. Increased demands for labor equity by black employees had recently exacerbated the already mounting racial tensions, and would continue to escalate until a violent strike erupted in 1967. Although the thriving town of Laurel was not a primary COFO target, it had not been overlooked by civil rights organizers in their statewide attempt to register black voters and develop freedom schools. In early summer 1964, in a town that had experienced little racial unrest since the highly publicized execution of Willie McGee in 1951, the headlines of the local newspaper warned, "Racial Violence Flares at Home," after a group of blacks was met by hostile whites while trying to integrate a popular hamburger joint.[32]

Bowers could point out to his embittered sycophants that the socialist invasion was not only raging in places like McComb, Jackson, and Greenwood but had reached their very doorsteps. As a recruiting trump card, he could recite in dramatic detail a plot involving the federal government's support of an African military force, presently being trained in Cuba for an invasion of the Mississippi Gulf Coast. The militia would be deployed by Defense Secretary Robert McNamara in cooperation with a nationalized State Guard for the purpose of winning Mississippi for the Negro, after which white residents of the state would be exiled to the chilly regions of the northern plains.[33] Whether Bowers actually believed this conspiracy, as the House Committee on Un-American Activities earnestly documents, is unclear; that Bowers could get great recruiting mileage from the account is beyond doubt. Bowers knew what to say and how to say it. As one state investigator put it, "He could get these people to do damn near anything."[34]

Nonetheless, although Bowers considered the White Knights as part of a noble tradition of aristocratic and intellectual racialists, most of his early recruits were working-class men. And he secretly despised them. Bowers confided to one of his few bookish associates, Delmar Dennis, "The typical Mississippi red-neck doesn't have sense enough to know what he is doing. I have to use him for my own cause and direct his every action to fit my plan." The work of the Lord required "A HARDENED MENTAL ATTITUDE"— Bowers could certainly count that among his spiritual gifts.[35]

The Warrior Priest

Bowers could think of the "invasion"—or "crucifixion"—of Mississippi in terms that resembled, in part, many of the familiar conspiracy theories about an international banking cartel's unlimited will to power. The domestic agents of socialism, according to this theory, poor and beleaguered black folk though they sometimes might be, had yielded their hearts and minds to a vast bureaucratic machinery, driven by the banks' insatiable need to consume and flatten. Most right-wing malcontents were—and continue to be—attracted to some version of the Jewish banking cartel theory.[36] Bowers's account turned with singular intensity on his utter contempt for the "pagan academy." Even more insidious than the banks' control of money or the media's manipulation of information was the activity of the intellectual elite, whose thoroughly godless institutions perform the nitty-gritty work of initiating men and women into the brute anonymity of the "socialist universe." The academy—abhorred by Bowers since childhood—intrudes and corrupts; it tears apart the exquisite fabric of particular differences, of regional taste and etiquette, of rituals and dialect. And it does so by any means possible, through the promise of exhilarating freedom or through coercion and deceit. Nonetheless, Bowers's theory of outside agitation gave way to a deeper theological conflict that was, in his mind, even more serious than political, social, and intellectual decay.

He fastened onto two biblical sources as fitting illustrations of the holy war taking shape and of his divine calling to take a stand in it. The first was the story of Elijah the Tishbite, told in the book of 1 Kings in the Old Testament; Elijah who wandered into Israel from the edge of the desert across the river Jordan, declaring a famine in the name of Yahweh.[37] His message was unequivocal: God's people must place their allegiance in Yahweh alone. They must abandon their worship of the foreign Canaanite Baals. Elijah's question of King Ahab cuts to the heart of God's demand of Israel: "How long halt ye between two opinions? If the Lord be God, follow him." After demonstrating to his people that the God of Abraham, Isaac, and Israel was the one true God—only this God could unleash fire from heaven to consume the burnt sacrifice—Elijah commanded the crowd to apprehend the false prophets and lead them down to the Kishon brook. There the four hundred and fifty were slaughtered in obedience to Jehovah. Pleased with the day's rewards, Elijah said to an impressed King Ahab, "Get thee up, eat and drink; for there is a sound of abundance of rain."[38]

Bowers's deep affinity with Elijah's story speaks volumes not only of his perception of the civil rights movement but of his own self-understanding. Elijah's ultimatum to King Ahab made perfectly clear that the coexistence, or coalescence, of two sorts of allegiance is intolerable.[39] From Bowers's perspective, the American South had come to a similar fork in the road. The day of reckoning had arrived. God's people—those simple, hard-working white folk ordained as guardians of their forefathers' faith—could not countenance divided loyalties, halting between two opinions. They must honor either the God of the covenant, the One who had sheltered their beautiful land, empowering its people with a special capacity for piety and respect, or the Baals, the gods of the Canaanites, the intrusive, foreign powers, tethered to immoral desires, corrupting the young.[40] These alien deities appeared in the early 1960s much as they had in the 600s B.C.E., as "disintegrating forces" eating away at the unity of God and his people.[41] According to Bowers, Baalism taunted the South with its own vanishing ideals: never should the region sacrifice its tradition or sacred identity to the chaos of these outside authorities.

Equally telling is the manner in which Elijah carried out the slaughter of the prophets of Baal. That is, the sentence was not meted out as an act of passion or vengeance or fanaticism. Elijah was only giving rational effect to an ancient law that required the death penalty for any apostasy from Yahweh: "He that sacrifice unto any god, save unto the Lord only, he shall be utterly destroyed."[42] Bowers took this to heart, admonishing his Klan confederates toward a similar impassibility when distributing vengeance: "As Christians we are disposed to kindness, generosity, affection and humility in our dealings with others. As militants we are disposed to use physical force against our enemies. How can we reconcile these two apparently contradictory philosophies? The answer, of course, is to purge malice, bitterness and vengeance from our heart." Divine retribution demands gravity and resoluteness. The Imperial Wizard instructed, "If it is necessary to eliminate someone, it should be done with no malice, in complete silence and in the manner of a Christian act."[43] For if someone becomes an agent of Baal, then that person, however innocent his motives might be, has put himself on the battle line. Rage should take the form of righteous indignation; laws governing civil society must be suspended so that a new social logic can take shape. Those priests called by God into holy service must willingly perform the task required of them in face of heresy: eliminate it![44]

If Elijah inspired Bowers's holy militancy against the foreign gods, it was the apostle Paul who instructed him on the actual doctrinal content of his priestly mission. The theological detail herein illustrates both the complexity and the startling, albeit convoluted, orthodoxy of Bowers's faith. He pointed to Paul's first epistle to the Corinthians as the most powerful rendering of his own vocation:

> But if there be no resurrection of the dead, then is Christ not risen: And if Christ be not risen, then is our preaching vain, and your faith is also vain. . . . But now is Christ risen from the dead, and become the firstfruits of them that slept. . . . For as in Adam all die, even so in Christ shall all be made alive. But every man in his own order: Christ the firstfruits; afterward they that are Christ's at his coming. Then cometh the end, when he shall have delivered up the kingdom of God, even the Father; when he shall have put down all rule and all authority and all power. For he must reign, till he hath put all enemies under his feet.[45]

The foundation of Bowers's militant vocation was the resurrection of Jesus Christ in the fullness of physical flesh; the resurrection was nothing less than the very axis on which world history turns. "There is one simple, and central, Empirical Fact, of manifested human history," Bowers explained. "That Empirical Fact, of course, is the Physical Resurrection of The Galilean."[46] History itself is simply the time between the resurrection and the return, the turning wheels of promise and judgment. That "Fact" must be defended to the bitter end; when denied, either explicitly or implicitly, the disciple has no alternative but to strive toward that great day when all Christ's enemies will be put under his feet. Bowers read the Bible with all the passion of a fundamentalist Baptist. When he turned to Scripture for comfort and guidance, he found his own calling delineated no more clearly than in Paul's story of the triumphant Christ.

Ken Dean, a white Southern Baptist minister from east Tennessee who came to Mississippi at the end of 1964 as director of the Council on Human Relations and later became a friend of Bowers, described the former Imperial Wizard as one who "in the most radical sense possible, is a believer in the sovereignty of God."[47] God may use different means to accomplish his purposes—fire falling directly from heaven, priests slaying the heretics at the Kishon brook, or klansmen pledging militancy beneath a Mississippi winter sky—but his purpose shall come to pass without fail. Bowers's God demands unquestioning loyalty; all time and space, history and eternity, are gathered up in the majesty of the sovereign will. God looks on his children with a severe mercy, ruling over creation with absolute power.

Dean is no doubt correct in his assessment. However, it is Jesus Christ, or the "Galilean," Bowers says, who alone enables people to call upon God and be received as his children—indeed as children spared a just and harsh punishment. Jesus has made peace on the believer's behalf, atoning before the Father for a punishment fully deserving of the sons and daughters of Adam. In this manner, Bowers as theologian is, in a most radical, perplexing, and bizarre sense, a believer in the Christ-centered shape of all reality. All knowledge of truth, both natural and supernatural, is based on "the Fact" that God came to the world in the saving event of his son Jesus Christ. "The genuineness of Faith," Bowers wrote, "is in the Omnipotent Power of God to perform the Miracle: The certainty of rational human knowledge is that the Resurrection did occur: As an Empirically manifested Fact."[48] If Jesus Christ has not risen from the dead in all the splendor of a real, live human being, then truth disassembles, creation slides away into chaos and clutter. Happily, however, the message of the Bible speaks otherwise: Jesus was in fact raised from the dead. If you were there that Sunday morning at the empty tomb, you would have seen him with your own eyes, you could have touched his flesh with your own. If you had been there with the advantage of modern technology, you could have photographed him. He was really alive. And more: having risen from the dead, Christ now reigns supreme over creation, until, as Paul says, that time when he has put "all things in subjection under him," that time when he will hand the kingdom over to his Father, when the last enemy is destroyed.

Yet for all his appreciation of Paul's vocation as the great evangelist of Christ, Bowers's own ministry required even more of him than the proclamation of the Good News. He described his calling by analyzing the difference between a preacher and a priest. A preacher, he says, points people toward the truth; whereas a priest "arranges the means and operations to implement the truth into concrete action." A preacher is an evangelist; he will tell people what to do, but "he will not arrange the means and operations to implement this into concrete action." A priest is interested in "visible, public power operations"—"this is what makes him powerful like a warrior." Priests, like warriors, do not simply administer the forgiveness of sins or the terms of surrender. When heretics arise, the priests respond with a calculated and confident militancy; for heresy cannot be forgiven, it can only be eliminated. The preacher rails long and hard about the wages of sin; but God forgives the repentant sinner. The priest searches out the heretic, who cannot be forgiven but only destroyed. Bowers explains, "Priests and warriors are necessary for the guardianship of America—with their attack upon the power structures and as instruments of divine grace and judgment."[49]

Who were the heretics, the enemies of Christ in the early spring of 1964? When Sam Bowers looked at Mississippi from his monastic dwelling at the Sambo Amusement Company, he saw with a righteous rage especially those volunteers rolling in from the north across the state line—and not four hundred and fifty false prophets this time but over a hundred thousand, it was rumored, fresh from the pagan academies, with "the whores of the media" in tow. Communists, homosexuals, and Jews, fornicators and liberals and angry blacks—infidels all. And singing:

> Michael, row the boat ashore, Alleluia
> Christian brothers don't be slow, Alleluia;
> Mississippi's next to go, Alleluia.

As the high priest of the anti-civil rights movement in Mississippi, Bowers called upon all his "white, Protestant, Christian, Gentile patriots" to take up their cross (and, of course, burn it on occasion), to dedicate themselves to the sober task of protecting the godly heritage of their sovereign state.

Eliminating the Heretics

On the morning of June 7, 1964, the members of the recently established White Knights met in a piney woods near Raleigh, in the center of the state. Armed with rifles, pistols, and shotguns and protected by men riding horseback through the woods and by two Piper Cubs circling the property overhead, the klansmen gathered in the Boykin Methodist Church. The "Grand Chaplain" of the White Knights ascended to the pulpit and read a prayer to the new recruits:

> Oh God, our Heavenly Guide, as finite creatures of time and as dependent creatures of Thine, we acknowledge Thee as our sovereign Lord. Permit freedom and the joys thereof to forever reign throughout our land. May we as klansmen forever have the courage of our convictions and that we may always stand for Thee and our great nation. May the sweet cup of brotherly fraternity ever be ours to enjoy and build within us that kindred spirit which will keep us unified and strong. Engender within us that wisdom kindred to honorable decisions and the Godly work. By the power of Thy infinite spirit and the energizing virtue therein, ever keep before us our oaths of secrecy and pledges of righteousness. Bless us now in this assembly that we may honor Thee in all things, we pray in the name of Christ, our blessed Savior. Amen.[50]

The congregation echoed "Amen."

Then the Imperial Wizard took the pulpit and announced to his fellow klansmen, "You know why we are here. We are here to discuss what we are going to do about COFO's nigger-communist invasion of Mississippi which will begin within a few days."[51] In a sermon to his fellow militants, Bowers defined the moment in all its world-epochal immensity:

This summer, within a very few days, the enemy will launch his final push for victory here in Mississippi. This offensive will consist of two basic salients, which have been designed to envelop and destroy our small forces in a pincer movement of agitation, force by Federal troops, and communist propaganda. The two basic salients are as follows, listed in one-two order as they will be used.

One. Massive street demonstrations and agitation by blacks in many areas at once, designed to provoke white militants into counterdemonstration and open, pitched street battles, resulting in civil chaos and anarchy to provide an "excuse" for:

Two. A decree from the communist authorities in charge of the national government, which will declare the State of Mississippi to be in a state of open revolt, with a complete breakdown of law and order; and declaring martial law, followed by a massive occupation of the state by Federal troops, with all known patriotic whites placed under military arrest. If this martial law is imposed, our homes and our lives and our arms will pass under the complete control of the enemy, and he will have won his victory. We will, of course, resist to the very end, but our chance of victory will undoubtedly end with the imposition of martial law in Mississippi by the communist masters in Washington. . . .

When the first waves of blacks hit our streets this summer, we must avoid open daylight conflict with them, if at all possible, as private citizens, or as members of this organization. We should join with and support local police and duly constituted law enforcement agencies with volunteer, legally deputized men from our own ranks. We must absolutely avoid the appearance of a mob going into the streets to fight the blacks. Our first contact with the troops of the enemy in the streets should be as legally-deputized law enforcement officers. . . .

In all cases, however, there must be a secondary group of our members, standing back away from the main area of conflict, armed and ready to move on very short notice, who are not under the control of anyone but our own Christian officers. This secondary group must not be used except in clear cases where law-enforcement and our own deputized, auxiliary first groups are at the point of being over-whelmed by the blacks. Only if it appears reasonably certain that control of the streets is being lost by the establishment forces of law can the secondary group be committed. Once committed, this secondary group must move swiftly and vigorously to attack the local head-

quarters of the enemy, destroy and disrupt his leadership and communica-
tions (both local and Washington) and any news communication equipment
or agents in the area. The action of this secondary group must be very swift
and very forceful with no holds barred. The attack on the enemy headquarters will relieve the pressure on the first group in the streets and as soon as
this has been done, the second group must prepare to withdraw out of the
area. They will be replaced by another secondary group standing at ready. It
must be understood that the secondary group is an extremely swift and extremely violent hit and run group. They should rarely be in action for over one-
half hour, and under no circumstances for over one hour. Within two hours of
their commitment they should be many miles from the scene of action. . . .

When the black waves hit our communities, we must remain calm and
think in terms of our individual enemies rather than our mass enemy. We
must roll with the mass punch which they will deliver in the streets during
the day, and we must counterattack the individual leaders at night. . . . Any
personal attacks on the enemy should be carefully planned to include *only*
the leaders and prime white collaborators of the enemy forces. These attacks
against these selected individual targets should, of course, be as severe as circumstances and conditions will permit. No severe attacks should be directed
against the general mass of the enemy because of the danger of hurting some
actually innocent person. The leaders, of course, are not innocent, and they
should be our prime targets, but the innocent must be protected. . . .

We must always remember that while law enforcement officials have a job
to do, we, as Christians, have a responsibility and have taken an oath to preserve Christian civilization. May Almighty God grant that their job and our
oath never come into conflict; but should they ever, it must be clearly understood that we can never yield our principles to anyone, regardless of his
position. Respect for Christian ideals can not yield to respect for persons nor
statutes and procedure which have been twisted by man away from its original Divine design.[52]

Bowers's message amounted to a declaration of holy war against the civil
rights movement.

In Meridian, a city sixty miles northeast of Laurel, the Klan's surveillance
of civil rights operations had focused on a white civil rights worker named
Mickey Schwerner. Schwerner had alarmed local militants when in Janu-
ary he and his wife Rita arrived from New York City to direct the Freedom
House established under the auspices of the Congress on Racial Equality
(CORE). Although there had been talk among the Klan since early spring
of a terrorist attack against his life, by the month of June, the White
Knights' interest in Schwerner had reached a point of feverish obsession.
The sight of the young Jewish man, wearing his signature bluejeans and

goatee, working with black children around the community center and co-ordinating voter registration, struck a deep nerve with the White Knights. Schwerner, or "goatee" as Bowers called him, was considered "a thorn in the flesh of everyone living, especially white people."[53] When klansmen re-ported to Bowers the rumor that Schwerner, a confessed atheist, had been seen with black men and women on the steps of local white churches seek-ing to integrate worship services, Bowers announced that the New Yorker "should be taken care of."[54]

All the details of Bowers's plan to kill Schwerner will probably never be known. What we do know makes up, as John Dittmer says, "the most de-pressingly familiar story of the Mississippi movement."[55] On the evening of June 16 (the same day the Democratic party of Mississippi set aside for precinct meetings to select delegates to county conventions), several truck-loads of Klan terrorists drove to the hamlet of Longdale in rural Neshoba County and quietly surrounded the Mt. Zion Methodist Church as the weekly meeting of "the leaders and stewards" was concluding. When the meeting adjourned, the parishioners walked toward the parking lot where they encountered a mob—as many as thirty men in all—holding rifles, shotguns, and billy clubs, surrounding the church people in a semicircle. The Mt. Zion members—ten in all—passed by the white men and headed to their cars and trucks to return home.[56] Some of the people drove north on Longdale Road to get to their homes, while other church members, like Roosevelt Cole and his wife Beatrice (known to friends as "Bud" and "Bid-die"), headed south.

A few hundred yards from the church, the Coles in their car and another black couple in their truck were forced to the side by a pickup truck. A group of white men then approached the vehicles and ordered the drivers to turn the headlights off. The Coles and the other couple were seized and interrogated. "Where are the guns?" they were asked, exposing the Klan's fear that local blacks were storing up ammunition. "Where are the white men who were here?" a klansman continued, indicating some knowledge of Mickey Schwerner's recent visit to solicit the church's involvement in voter registration.[57] "We know they had meetings here. Have they been having them over at the old school?"[58] (No other church in the county had yet joined Mt. Zion in hosting organizational meetings.) Unsatisfied with the Coles's answers that they and the other parishioners harbored neither guns nor Schwerner, the klansmen proceeded to beat Mr. Cole, repeatedly striking blows to his neck and back with an iron tire jack and kicking his head and hip until he lay motionless in the dirt parking lot.

Such savagery still did not satisfy one of the assailants, who warned Mr. Cole that unless he could give the white men some useful information, he would be killed. Mrs. Cole pleaded with the klansmen to stop their torture, hoping against hope that she could reason with the mob. "He can't say nothing, he's unconscious," she said. Her memory of what happened next is worth documenting at length:

> I began to pray. I was praying very hard. I was just praying, "Lord have mercy, Lord have mercy, don't let them kill my husband." And then I heard a voice sound like a woman scream down the road just a little piece below me and then a man walked up with a club and I continued saying, "Lord have mercy," and he drew back to hit me and I asked this man that was standing by him would he allow me to pray. The one on the right side says if you think it will do you any good you had better pray. The one on the left says it is too late to pray. But I said, "Let me pray." I stretched out my hands. Then I started praying to God that he would spare my husband, that God would spare his life. I kept praying and praying, and then I remembered a hymn. It just fell into my heart. I said, "Father I stretch my hand to thee, no other help I know. If thou withdraw thy help from me where shall I go?" That's what I prayed. And when I said that, the man who was beating my husband just stopped. Someone said, "leave him living." And I went there and tried to lift my husband up, once, then again, and I couldn't do it. And I tried a third time and he just fell back to his knees. Finally, he stood up and I drug him to where the car was. And I put him in the car. And about that time the crowd of white men just disappeared. I didn't know nothing else to do but call on God. And God just got in the midst.[59]

The klansmen moved aside as "Biddie" Cole carried her husband to the car and drove home. "Bud" Cole's life was spared as a result, although the beating permanently damaged his hip. However, the Klan did not spare the church, which Mr. Cole and his fellow parishioners had built with their hands. From the front window of her home nearly a mile away, Mrs. Cole could see on the horizon a fiery glow illuminating the night sky. Mt. Zion was burned to the ground. The affidavit filed by Michael F. Starr of the National Lawyers' Guild read: "At the church site itself all that is now to be seen are a few bricks and some twisted metal roofing lying where it fell. There is not one piece of timber left, charred or otherwise. All that remains is that metal and some ashes."[60]

The purpose of the Klan attack on the night of June 16 is not entirely clear. Mickey Schwerner was nowhere near Mt. Zion. He was in Oxford, Ohio, at the orientation for the summer volunteers—a fact the Klan would have known. The Klan probably wanted to set a trap for Schwerner when he returned to Meridian the following week. Schwerner would be likely to investigate the church burning, since he had initiated COFO's relationship with Mt. Zion. And if he could be lured back to rural Neshoba County—with its "duly constituted law enforcement officers"—then the Klan could carry out a "number 4" (a killing) with impunity.

In fact, five days later, on Sunday, June 21, just hours after returning from Ohio, Schwerner, along with James Chaney (a local black CORE activist from Meridian) and Andy Goodman (a white summer volunteer from New York on his first day in Mississippi) drove COFO's white station wagon northwest on highway 19 into Neshoba County. There they visited the Coles and other members of the church, who told the civil rights workers of the terror-filled night of June 16. Shortly after leaving Longdale, the three men were arrested by deputy sheriff Cecil Price on the outskirts of Philadelphia and locked up in the Neshoba County jail. They were released later the same night, around 10:30, on the orders of Sheriff Lawrence Rainey, but then were stopped again by Deputy Price after a high-speed chase. Price then turned the three civil rights workers over to Klan assassins, who drove them to an abandoned dirt road south of town.

Just before firing at point black range into Schwerner's chest, klansman Alton Wayne Roberts asked, "Are you that nigger lover?"

"Sir, I know just how you feel," Schwerner answered directly.

Roberts then fired one fatal bullet into the back of Andrew Goodman. Klansmen Jim Jordan, motivated by Roberts's willingness to act, jumped out his car and shouted, "Save one for me!"[61] After firing repeatedly on James Chaney, he told his friends, "You didn't leave me anything but a nigger, but at least I killed me a nigger."[62] Three "heretics" had been eliminated.

On Tuesday afternoon, a man from the Neshoba County Choctaw tribe discovered the white station wagon, still smoldering, behind a thicket of burned brush at the edge of the Bogue Chitto Swamp. The bodies of the dead were still missing, however, having been buried miles away beneath an earthen dam on klansman Olen Burrage's farm. To assist state police officials with their search (Price and Rainey actually helped coordinate local efforts), four hundred sailors from the U.S. naval base in Pascagoula were dispatched to comb the area for the missing men, while 153 FBI agents spread out from Neshoba County looking for clues. The news media descended on the state in large numbers. In the company of fellow klansmen, Bowers appeared "gleeful," elated that his Christian patriots had successfully "planned and carried out the execution of a Jew."[63] Publicly and in various pseudononymous writings, his apocalyptic rhetoric intensified as the presence of outsiders increased in the wake of the murders. He vehemently denied any involvement in the disappearance and used the new wave of national (and now international) scrutiny as further demonstration to disgruntled whites of the growing anti-Christian invasion. He penned an angry diatribe against those in the media and the academy who had begun to cast blame on the White Knights for the prevailing atmosphere of violence, calling their actions nothing less than a "crucifixion" of the good white people of his sovereign state:

We are now in the midst of the "long, hot summer" of agitation which was promised to the Innocent People of Mississippi by the savage blacks and their Communist masters. . . . We were NOT involved, and there was NO DISAPPEAR- ANCE. . . . We refuse to be concerned or upset about this fraud. What we are concerned about is the welfare of the citizens of the State of Mississippi. . . .

We are going to serve notice that we are not going to recognize the au- thority of any bi-racial group, NOR THE AUTHORITY OF ANY PUBLIC OFFICIAL WHO ENTERS INTO ANY AGREEMENT WITH ANY SUCH SOVIET ORGANIZATION. We Knights are working day and night to preserve Law and Order here in Mis- sissippi, in the only way that it can be preserved: by strict segregation of the races, and the control of the social structure in the hands of the Christian, Anglo-Saxon White men, the only race on earth that can build and maintain just and stable governments. We are deadly serious about this business. . . . Take heed, atheists and mongrels, we will not travel your path to a Leninist Hell, but we will buy YOU a ticket to the Eternal if you insist. Take your choice, SEGREGATION, TRANQUILITY AND JUSTICE, or, BI-RACISM, CHAOS AND DEATH.[64]

Bowers was not alone in denying any responsibility for the disappear- ance. Many white Mississippians regarded the alleged murders as a hoax played out at the state's expense. As one white man shrugged to a news re- porter, "I believe those jokers [who] planned it are sitting off up there in New York laughing at us Mississippi folk." Others put the matter differ- ently, saying "If they're dead, they asked for it"; and more, "Martin Luther King may run the rest of the country, but he ain't gonna run Mississippi. And every Communist-atheist-nigger-loving-bearded-Jew-sonofabitch who comes down here looking for trouble is gonna find it!"[65] Governor Paul Johnson conjectured that James Chaney, Andrew Goodman, and Michael Schwerner had run off to Cuba. Robert Shelton, the Grand Dragon of the United Klans of America, believed the same. Traveling from his home in Tuscalousa, Alabama, to Neshoba County, the klansman told the sailors in the presence of several journalists, "Cuba is 300 miles in the other direction."[66] Shelton's skewed geography notwithstanding, his idea that the disappearance was planned by COFO to bolster its fundraising ef- forts was shared by extremists and moderates alike. Even the state's mod- erate Baptist newspaper, *The Baptist Record*, in a front-page article on June 25 addressing the matter of church members who have "moved but left their church letters behind," chimed in with the mocking headlines:

Search Begins for Three
Million Southern Baptists

But when the bodies of the three civil rights workers were discovered on August 4, the hoax theory vanished in silence and into "muted talk," as one of Philadelphia's few white liberals put it.[67]

Bowers, on the other hand, revved up the propaganda machines. One week later, on the opening day of the hugely popular Neshoba County Fair, an airplane dropped leaflets welcoming people to the event in behalf of the White Knights, announcing in Bowers's inimitable style, "Schwerner, Chaney and Goodman were not civil rights workers [but] Communist Revolutionaries, actively working to undermine and destroy Christian Civilization."[68]

Bowers had little fear of prosecution. By the end of the summer, the White Knights had grown in membership to 6,000. After the summer, Bowers's militancy became even more reckless and arrogant. "A jury would not dare convict a white man for killing a nigger in Mississippi," he would boast openly. In fact, in 1965 and 1966, the Klan struck more than fifty times in the Laurel area alone; there were cross burnings, house bombings, shotgun blasts, harassing phone calls, store burnings, and repeated attacks on the local COFO house (which finally closed its doors in defeat). Just months after he was subpoenaed for hearings before the House Un-American Committee in October 1965, Bowers is alleged to have ordered a "number 3 and a number 4" (a burning and a killing) on Vernon Dahmer, the former president of the Forrest County branch of the NAACP and voter registration organizer in Forrest County, who owned a prosperous farm and business in the Kelly Settlement, about a half-hour drive from the Sambo Amusement Company.

In the early hours before daybreak on January 10, 1966, members of the White Knights entered the Dahmer property, driving two automobiles, and tossed Molotov cocktails into the windows of Dahmer's home. As flames engulfed the house, klansmen opened fire on the windows and the porch, where Dahmer stood with his shotgun aimed at the retreating cars. Dahmer's shots missed their target, although one klansman accidentally blasted a hole in the tire of the other car, forcing it to be abandoned in the hurry to reach Laurel before sunrise. Mrs. Dahmer and the children escaped the burning house; but on the porch, Vernon had inhaled what would prove to be fatal lungfulls of smoke and flame, although he managed to drive his family to a hospital in Hattiesburg before collapsing. A few hours before his death the next morning he told a friend, "People who don't vote are deadbeats on the state. I figure a man needs to do his own thinking. What happened to us can happen to anybody, white or black. At one time I didn't think so, but I have changed my mind."[69]

However, with this new wave of violence, Bowers had gone too far. Most white Mississippians were beginning to find him and his White Knights a disgrace and an embarrassment. As the former district attorney in Laurel explained, "We were becoming aware of ourselves as a lawless society."[70] In Laurel, Mayor Henry Bucklew, a staunch segregationist and popular evangelist, took to the airwaves on October 18, 1966, to denounce the Klan "fanatics [who] talk so much about God."[71] The Jones County Baptist

Association and its forty-six churches passed a resolution in support of the mayor's condemnation.

The Dahmer killing also marked a new stage in the FBI involvement in civil rights. Throughout the early 1960s and during the Mississippi Summer Project of 1964, the FBI had often played softball with the Klan. To local black people and civil rights activists who complained that the harassment and beatings they routinely received from white terrorists seemed immune from prosecution, the FBI repeated that it was not an investigative but a law-enforcing agency. But all this changed in early 1966 when local white leaders and law enforcement officials in Jones and Forrest counties, tired of the Klan's violence and lawlessness, gave the FBI carte blanche to wipe out the White Knights by any means necessary.[72]

Bowers stood four trials for the murder of Vernon Dahmer; all ended in mistrials or hung juries. However, a Forrest County jury handed out convictions to four members of the Klan, including three life sentences. Bowers had also escaped conviction in his previous trials for the Neshoba murders, although his luck would eventually run out. On October 20, 1967, he was convicted for conspiracy to violate the civil rights of Andrew Goodman, James Chaney, and Michael Schwerner and sentenced to ten years in federal prison. Bowers entered the federal penitentiary at McNeil Island, Washington, on April 3, 1970. He was released in March of 1976 and returned to Laurel to resume his work as a self-described "Mississippi native pin ball operator and preacher of Jesus the Galilean." The Sambo Amusement Company, where he still resides, is today a neglected and run-down building, surrounded by a fifteen-foot-high chain link fence, in a neighborhood that is mostly black.

Against the World Rulers of This Present Darkness

Unclear in the foregoing is how, or exactly why, Bowers linked the invading hordes of civil rights activists—and all those local people who were taken up into the spirit of the moment—with the enemies of Christ. It is tempting to write it off to a strange psychology. His identification of outside agitators with the false prophets of a pagan god must harken back to some aspect of Bowers's early abhorrence of intrusive authority. No doubt, psychoanalytic interpreters would have a field day with Bowers's complex childhood. Consider the possibilities of Norman Cohn's observation that in the fantasies of much popular eschatology, history tends to be construed "as a mortal struggle waged by good fathers and good children against bad fathers and bad children."[73] Raging against an adult world that constantly threatens his maternal intimacy, Bowers presents himself as an extraordinary case study. Nonetheless, the task of sorting out the psychological sources of his—or anyone's—religious ideas is a task that too easily lends itself to oversimplified reductions.

Beyond the question of which came first in Bowers's case, the psychology or the religious ideas, it is undoubtedly of great value to pay attention to his own claim that the identification has a rational structure. That is, Bowers believed that his perception of civil rights workers as "agents of Satan" was warranted by the metaphysical nature of reality as such. Although Bowers's perception did not evolve in isolation from other influences, real theological structures both shaped and legitimated his understanding of the situation at hand. What then is the inner logic of his peculiar way of seeing the movement?

Let us return to the basic point: the unfolding of a two-thousand-year war between the idolatrous agents of Baal and the soldiers of the one true God was a palpably real event for Bowers and his fellow klansmen. A question in one of the White Knights' issues of *The Klan Ledger* illustrates the point: what is the "essential reality" of the present situation? The answer, drafted by Bowers, reads: "It is simply what it has always been for centuries: Christ versus Satan."[74] The anatomy of this reality must be our present concern. For only by understanding the "cosmic battle" being waged in Mississippi can we hope to understand the connection in Bowers's mind between the civil rights movement and heresy against God.

Bowers's white militancy was not grounded primarily in his analysis of the centralized bankers or the socialist homogenization of regional and racial difference; these factors, although important, were derived from his basic perception that "Jesus the Galilean is Lord of all." His *Klan Ledger* became a kind of catechism of the prevailing orthodoxy: "We place our ultimate faith in Jesus Christ rather than in the ballot box to save America from Satanism." "We have no cause but Christ." "Christ will triumph, never fear!"[75] But who is Jesus the Galilean? Who is Bowers's Christ?

Unlike many Christian theologians of the past, Bowers made no attempt to characterize biblical Judaism as spiritually bankrupt or to deracinate Christianity from Jewish antiquity.[76] The Hebrew Bible is essential to the story of Jesus and must not be disconnected from the New Testament. This is a perplexing attitude in someone who would eventually claim that Jews were the driving force behind the civil rights movement and its demonic attempt to destroy "white Christian Civilization through mongrelization." Yet Bowers parts company with more familiar anti-Semitic thinkers on the matter of Christianity's Judaic roots.[77] He writes, "The foundation of Christianity lies in the ancient Hebrew Law and the Teachings of its Prophets. That Law and [those] Teachings actually and clearly foretold and acurately [sic] described the coming of the Christ."[78] The complexity lies in the fact that although the Christian faith must not be severed from Judaism, something new and decisive enters salvation history with the story of Jesus

Christ: namely, the binding of all Jews to Jesus in his messianic and eternal reign. Thus, "in the true religious sense," there is no longer any such thing as "a real Jew."

Bowers's logic runs as follows: because Christ is now the Lord of the Jew, as well as of the Gentile, a Jew who accepts Christ is not really a Jew but a Christian, while the Jew who rejects Christ is also not a Jew inasmuch as all genuine Jews now accept Christ. Bowers's reading of the Hebrew Bible as fully anticipatory of the coming of Jesus is part of the makeup of this logic. "In rejecting Christ, [the Jew] thereby rejects his own teachings in over 300 instances."[79] But there is more at stake. When Jesus refused to stand in solidarity with the "Temple Business" during his earthly ministry, he was throwing down the gauntlet to the "hierarchy" and "religion profession."[80] No wonder that his murder came at the hands of those who controlled the "political machine." But Jewish rejection of Christ brought about the rescinding of the divine election of Jews, while demonstrating the anti-Christian character endemic to the ideological, religious, and political establishment. Bowers concludes that there are really no Jews left in the world; for "the word Jew is correctly used only in connection with those who were members of a monotheistic sect which existed in Palestine prior to, and only shortly after the first coming of Jesus Christ two thousand years ago."[81] Those who claim to be Jews—"the modern, world-wide, international cartel"—may presume to cloak themselves "in the garb of this ancient, long dead, theological system," but in fact they are "completely materialistic" and "deny the true, Spiritual principles upon which the worship of God must be based, in accordance with the First Commandment."[82] Thus, the Jews are the Antichrist(s).

Was Jesus a Jew? No, for Bowers, Jesus was "a Galilean," not a Jew. The appellation invokes the ideas of the influential racist historian and theologian Houston Steward Chamberlain, whom Bowers admired. In Chamberlain's landmark book, *The Foundations of the Nineteenth Century* (1899), he argued that Jesus, as a Galilean rather than a Jew, was a descendent of Aryan colonists in ancient Galilee. Although he came of age in a Jewish ethos, his racial distinctiveness compelled him in the fullness of time toward a unique understanding of God. With a twist (and twisted reading) of Hegel's religious philosophy, Chamberlain argued that Judaism or Pharisaism gave birth to Jesus, after which Jesus nullified Judaism in order to give the world Christianity. In stark contrast to Jewish legalism and formalism, Jesus inspired a profound personal and worldly freedom; against Jewish utilitarianism and materialism, Jesus fashioned new values and ideals, encouraging simplicity and quiet nobility. No wonder the Jews plotted to crucify Jesus, Chamberlain reasoned, for he had staked the "flag of idealism" on the soil of their "obstinate materialism," decimating Judaism at its very center.[83] Jesus was then not a Jew but, of course, there are now no more real Jews. The conclusion of Chamberlain's description is apropos of

Bowers's own crusading zeal: if one is not a follower of Christ, then one is a rejector of Christ. You either stand for Christ or for Mammon.[84]

Yet, again, how does this theological commitment shape Bowers's perception of the civil rights movement as the invidious purveyor of idolatry and impiety? It is tempting here to appeal to popular fears about communism and all its godless, anti-republican consequences. Certainly there is much truth to the description of Bowers as a staunch anti-communist. As we have seen, he tirelessly fulminated against the "red menace" in his numerous Klan publications of the period. Undoubtedly, the cry of "communism" would have sufficed to rally most Mississippi klansmen to militant action against outside agitators. And Bowers deftly exploited this fear in his role as master strategist of the White Knights. Nonetheless, Bowers interpreted the civil rights movement in decidedly more complex detail, thanks to his ambitious architectonic design of America's sacred history, named "The Five Tiered Crystallized Logos of Western Civilization," which he conceptualized in rudimentary terms in his crudely published "encyclicals" of the 1960s.[85] Taken as a whole, Bowers's grand narrative offers a way of envisioning an "American national political orthodoxy" that is based on the "Empirical Fact of the Resurrection of Jesus Christ."

At first glance, "The Five Tiered Logos" might seem hopelessly idiosyncratic—even akin to psychotic rambling. Yet his theological interpretation of America, with its steady progression of world historical (or Christological) moments leading up to the present, has an internal coherence that authorizes—in Bowers's mind—his terrible vocation. It gives him strength to issue the clarion call that "the events which will occur in Mississippi this summer may well determine the fate of Christianity for centuries to come."[86] The "Five Tiered Logos" also has affinities with more mainstream fundamentalist and popular millinarian readings of America as the "new Israel."[87]

As the story goes, America is the apotheosis of a sacred history inaugurated by the empirical fact of the resurrection of Jesus Christ. America is a divine miracle. In this manner, there is an ontological connection between the miracle of God's raising Jesus from the dead and the forming of the republic. Bowers's system elucidates this formation and its theological antecedents as "The Five Tiered Crystallized Logos of Western Civilization":

1. The empirical fact of the resurrection of Jesus Christ
2. The Reformation: (four sides)
   a. Lutheran
   b. Calvinistic
   c. Thomistic
   d. Bunyan or outlaw
3. The Declaration of Independence
4. The Constitution
5. The Great Writs of Common Law

"The Five Tiered Crystallized Logos of Western Civilization" is intended to describe the dispensations in which God's sovereign will takes shape in world history. Clearly Bowers's conception has deep roots in nineteenth-century philosophical and theological thought, particularly in the encyclopedic systems of the German speculative thinkers. The extent to which Bowers derived his architectonic design from the views of his intellectual progenitors is unclear; what is certain is that he used the schema to legitimate his own standing before a world historical moment—"Christ versus Satan"—and to emphasize the necessity to seize the moment with great purpose.[88]

The first tier of the crystallization of logos in western civilization is, not surprisingly, the risen Jesus. At the empty tomb Western history finds both its origin and its telos, such that all reality now turns to God's raising Jesus Christ from the dead as its "ultimate reference point." Unfortunately, the miracle was not received by either the church or the surrounding culture as the all-sufficient fact that it is. Worldly powers—the academy, the religious elites, the "cathedral"—co-opted the miracle, turning it inevitably into legality and drudgery.[89] The result was a fifteen-hundred-year development of dogma and law; unnecessary accoutrements of grace, distractions from the simplicity of discipleship, and intrusions by outside authorities. The church's unwavering loyalty to the resurrected Jesus was compromised in its subservience to Rome.

Happily, God would not allow this degeneration to continue unabated. The second crystallization of logos took place during the Protestant Reformation's protest against hierarchy and outside authority. Luther's doctrine of the priesthood of believers, the belief that all people have access to God through the freedom of the Scriptures, shattered Rome's foreign domination.[90] "Freedom in Christ," as Luther advanced the notion, empowers the believer to resist religious authority with vigor. Bowers understood the German reformer to claim that when any outside authority calls the Christian away from Jesus, that person is authorized to take matters into his own hands and fight for the purity of the faith, in whatever way the situation demands.

The historical and spiritual momentum of the resurrection and the Reformation takes consummate form in the miracle of America, when logos is crystallized in the Declaration of Independence, the Constitution, and "the Three Great Writs of Common Law"—the third, fourth and final tiers of Bowers' typology of sacred history. Bowers's typology of definitions governing the meaning of law was as follows:

LAW: the holy sovereign will of God
Law: God's will as most perfectly perceived and implemented by man
law: natural man's best efforts
legality: pharisaism

The resurrection remains the paradigmatic case of these subsequent miracles, the condition of their possibility. The resurrection burst into time, shattering the pretensions of pharisaic legality, and established a new reality, a new kingdom and a new standard of law: the absolute LAW of "the holy sovereign will of God" revealing itself in the ordained Law of God's self-witness in Jesus Christ. Still, the founding of the republic was, if not equally, at least derivatively miraculous. Like the resurrection, the Declaration is "illegal" but "lawful," that is, it violated established legal canons (thus its illegality) and at the same time gave birth to new foundations of individual and communal identity (thus its lawfulness). The Declaration is a "secular rendering" of the notion of the priesthood of all believers. Again, the Declaration is illegal in a historical sense of actually violating the British law at the time of rebellion; lawful because it succeeded. As such, the miracle of the Declaration of Independence lay not only in its "appeal to God for the rectitude of our beliefs" but in the very fact of its imbrication in our national identity. The final two tiers are legal and lawful; which is to say, less miraculous than the resurrection/Reformation/Declaration narrative, but as much spiritually and ontologically linked to the resurrection as the Reformation and Declaration.

Importantly, if Bowers was enforcing a theocracy—or any political vision that would demand of the citizenry a collective profession of Jesus Christ as Lord—it was sufficiently nuanced to avoid a reconstruction of democracy on the basis of biblical homogeneity. He explains: "As national Americans, we have an absolute political right to hold one another to the final three points—to the Declaration, the Constitution, and the three writs. To be sure, under the First Amendment we are prohibited from going back to an earlier document for metaphysical or legal grounding. So we cannot demand the resurrection belief of every American. But we can hold his feet to the fire on his commitment to the Declaration, and indeed on his commitment to the Declaration as orthodoxy."[91] One of the tests in the secular, public sphere of an individual's fidelity to God is his fidelity to the lower three tiers. Yet understanding the origin of these inevitably leads the individual to confront more explicit theological demands. Bowers asks: "Where did the Declaration come from? How did Thomas Jefferson come to say as a citizen I am among equals with George III? Or Luther, I am among equals as a priest with the Bishop of Rome?"[92] Jefferson's claim is in fact "a fundamental predicate of the Reformation," namely, the notion of the priesthood of all believers. It is called into being by Luther's discovery that if one is a believer, then that miracle of belief qualifies the person as fully competent to interpret Scripture and to address God without hierarchical mediation.

Luther's and Jefferson's doctrines ought not be taken as justifications of natural or even civil rights. Rather, they are revealed and as such are miraculous. One cannot appeal to natural law as warrant for human dignity or the common good (let us dare not forget the universal scope of human sinfulness, or "the despicable worm we are," Bowers counsels).[93] Any affirmation of the rights of man is fully contingent on the non-necessary, gracious event of the resurrection of Jesus Christ. If Jesus Christ has not risen from the dead, then reality and truth fall apart, creation recedes into nothingness, and the republic's inscribed ideals appear whimsical and groundless.

The result confirms the suspicion that, yes, the denial of America's sacred doctrines represents an implicit but real denial of the resurrection.[94] Granted, there would seem to be a place for those people who do not believe in the resurrection but hold faithfully to the lower three tiers. Such people would seem appropriate co-belligerents in the war against heresy, and for a time they might be. However, lacking the theological repertoire to discern the deeper holy war and the degree of force required to win it, they will inevitably shift allegiance out of fear, bourgeois wisdom, and a petty sense of legality. Be that as it may, as long as a co-belligerent upholds the republic's ideals, he stands within a narrow (and narrowing) field of grace, and ought to be spared.

But *no mercy should be shown the heretic*. Bowers draws the battle lines: "As Americans, we can and should hold one another to the binding character of the lower three tiers. If an individual will not confirm those lower three, he is a potential heretic. If he denies them in word or deed, he is a heretic."[95] In opposition to the civil rights activists in Mississippi in 1964, God called from among his faithful an "elitist priesthood" whose task it was to eliminate the heretics. God placed in the hands of this priesthood the responsibility of silencing the infidels—a responsibility to which in turn the rank-and-file white believer either forthrightly or tacitly gave consent.

Someone has to get serious. The government will surely not volunteer for the job, insofar as it is "too much tied in with legality to take care of business." The democratic society and its vast bureaucracy cannot call open season on civil rights activists. The canon of laws created by government protects both itself and others from itself. But the elitist priesthood is held to a higher standard; a standard Bowers describes as "transmoral, transnational, and transsocial," nothing less than "the Holy Sovereign Will of God" (the LAW), radiating out into the divine will "as most perfectly perceived and implemented by man" (the Law).[96] The divine will measures justice in absolute terms, never bending to the extenuations of precedent, adjudication, and interpretation: the "thou shall not" of the Decalogue admits little room for quibbling.

To some people the elitist priest will seem indistinguishable from the warrior. For Bowers that it is as it should be. Priestly authority transcends the particular moral traditions of the nation or state. "Did not Paul say, all things are lawful unto me, but not all things are expedient?" Thus Bowers believes that the "war of the 1960s will never be over, because it is not a war of the 60s as such, but a history-long struggle for the soul of a people, a flareup of a larger, ongoing battle."[97]

What finally tagged the civil rights movement in the 1960s as heretical was its massive effort to replace sovereign independent states with the "soviet" or "soviets," defined lugubriously by Bowers as "an extra-territorial or non-territorial organization which presumes to exercise and or replace the sovereignty of a territorial state by racial or economic metaphysics." Like the villainous "black soviets," now popping up in unlikely backwaters all across the deep South, the soviet is aggressive, anti-democratic, and godless; it aims to usurp the autonomy of local jurisdictions and to violate the organic purity of place and practice. Bowers said in a 1994 interview: "There is a potential of grace in nationalism which cannot possibly exist in socialism. What does it mean to say 'one nation under God'? It means there is a sense of shared destiny, a *collegia*. How many soviets can exist under God? This is unanswerable for the fact that soviets militate against any form of unity. A soviet is simply one leg on the temple of Baal."[98] The "soviet" invasion and all the scary side effects its alliterative kin evoke—"sinister," "seditious," "subversive," "satanic"—brought the armies of the civil and anti-civil rights movement to an insurmountable crisis. In early 1964 Bowers described this point of no return: "We are NOW, right now, each and every one of us going to begin NOW to LIVE IN WITH and FOR the Spirit of Christ Jesus in ourselves and our civilized brethren about us, and thus purified, without Malice or Vengeance, begin, systematical [sic] to DESTROY the atheistic, Satanic agents of communism in our midst, OR, we are going to see, before our very eyes, our society degenerate into a savage melee of brutal, humanistic animals, snarling and fighting among themselves for the bare necessities of animal existence."[99] There must be those who will offer their physical lives in opposition to the idols; as Bowers says, "in not only reforming this establishment from the inside out, but in attacking it at the very center of its power and prestige."[100]

But this is not the end of the matter. The soviets are not self-driven in their unrelenting move toward leveling and coerced equality: behind them stand the academy, the media, the central bankers, and ultimately the metaphysical powers that seek to defeat Jesus Christ. Bowers tells the story in a way that seems to blur the political-economic account and the theological. He explains at length:

> What happened in America is that the central bankers in Europe displaced the authority of the Cathedral (London had the paper money and petroleum and Zurich had gold and Central Europe). Marx had been right; production

of labor is no longer the central factor in light of technology and automation. What the bankers discovered is that automation is producing so much that consumption is the problem. The central bankers said: we've got to do something concerning consumption. Where are the population markets? In the third world, they answered, but the third world is backward. We will then bankrupt the national governments that control these countries. So we will take their territory and their resources—all their life forces.

The bankers also saw the southern United States, and said we need to start hollering about civil rights, despite the constitution. It doesn't matter what sort of anarchy happens, because we are the ones who decide what the standard of living is. We are in charge, and we will stay in charge. We know how to utilize fear and greed. And we will drive our interests hard. The bankers may have admitted that some people had a genuine thirst for righteousness. But they said to themselves, let's not ignore that, let's pervert it. So the bankers exploited fear and greed; and wherever there was a leader who had different views, they bribed him or assassinated him.

But there arose an elite priesthood. We knew that something was wrong— we knew that black persecutions were exaggerated; we knew that the powers behind the civil rights movement were only interested in control and economic domination.

As an American priest and a patriot, I take my liberty as common or as nothing. Liberty is not individual but common. I cannot deny other citizens their rights to full citizenship; I cannot violate his citizenship. If a black man stands up and demands his constitutional rights, I must support that man as strongly as I wish him to do for me; but if he permits himself to be deluded by socialism, he's become devoid of grace. *He must be eliminated.* God will permit his common liberty, but he will not permit Baal to come and corrupt his liberty and his citizenship.

As I see it, this is the basic premise of the anti-civil rights movement. The civil rights movement was devoid of grace; it was using many despicable and some unfortunate people as means to a communistic end. The whole motivation of the movement was wrong; in other words, when a local person stood up for his rights, there was sometimes a nobility to it; but when socialism was advanced from outside, fostered by the bank, justified by the academy, promoted by the media, buttressed by the judiciary, then Baal-worship was put in place of honor due the one true Lord, Jesus Christ the Galilean.[101]

To say that there is a perilous conflation of the theological and the political, as though this might help explain the menacing confusion between political and religious perception, fails to appreciate the level of theological realism in Bowers's analysis. The banks, the academy, the media, the state, and the soviet are first and foremost metaphysical realities; only secondarily and "operationally" can they be construed as institutions or social entities. Looming above the desperate, driven zeal of Bowers and his Christian patriots, as they pursued their mission of eliminating the heretics, was the specter of the civil rights workers and the Jews existing primarily as demonic powers—as emissaries of darkness, as the Antichrist(s). As Bowers concludes, everything that is true of the Antichrist is also true of the "soviets" or "outgroups" that serve him.[102]

Therefore, the soviets' attack on the South—on soil long saturated with love of Jesus the Galilean—amounted to an attack on the last refuge of holiness in the darkening republic.[103] The defilement of Mississippi by the alien prophets of Baal had to be countered by swift and decisive action. Bowers turned to the apostle Paul for the most graphic description of Mississippi's social landscape in 1964: "For we wrestle not against flesh and blood, but against principalities, against powers, against the rulers of the darkness of this world, against spiritual wickedness in high places. Wherefore take unto you the whole armour of God, that ye may be able to withstand in the evil day, and having done all, to stand" (Ephesians 6:12). The Christian had to make himself ready for combat; he had to become "strong in the Lord and in the power of his might" (Ephesians 6:10). The stakes could not be higher.[104]

THREE

Douglas Hudgins: Theologian of the Closed Society

The Closed Society

A COLUMNIST in the *Jackson Daily News* once joked of three black men sitting on a stile in a churchyard, staring at the cemetery. One man named L.C. says to his friends, "Boys, I'll tell you what. When us gets unsegregated, I'm gonner dress in my Sunday best and go up town to that big white church, and I'm gonna march down to the first bench and set; and I'm gonna sing louder than all them white brethren." Friend Gabe agrees with L.C.: "Yeah, I'm gonna put on my glad rags and some perfume; and I'm gonna walk right in that swell Country Club out on Ash Cat Avenue. I'm gonna tap the swellest blonde and I'm gonna tell her, 'Miz, Madam, dis here next dance is mine.'" John Lee, patiently hearing his friends out, concludes, "Well, after you all does that, I'm gonna get out my good blue serge suit and buy me a white carnation for my button hole and I'll mosey down to the I Hope to Rise Funeral Parlor and set up with two deceased pals."[1]

There was nothing unusual about the notion that a black man should be lynched for showing affection toward a white lady. A formidable number of the nearly five thousand blacks lynched in the South since the Civil War were accused of some kind of sexual impropriety. But the coupling of sexual prohibition with the integration of the church—the insinuation that worshiping in a white congregation was no less a violation of racial doctrine than slow dancing with "the swellest blonde"—attests to a dimension of white anxiety that easily evades theological analysis. The purity of the white church must be guarded with the same vigilance given the protection of white feminine virtue.[2]

Inherent in the mission of the segregated church was the preservation of racial purity. The risks of opening up the doors were great, inviting menacing images of forbidden sexual desire and contamination. As a Jackson civil rights leader speculated, "Perhaps there is even a darker mystery in this. Could it be that the presence of the Black man inside the Sanctuary of the White Church was the 'abomination of abominations' even as the presence of the seed of the Black man in the womb of the white woman was the most dreadful thing that could be imagined?" Opening up the doors aroused the deepest and most frightening transformations of ecclesial, but also social and sexual identity. "If the Black man was allowed to penetrate the doors of the Church what was the violation that followed?"[3]

No doubt, the white Christian establishment had convinced itself that this and other changes in race relations defiled all that was sacred and pure. It chose to batten down the hatches, to guard itself against further advances with clenched fist and tightened jaw. In the end, it gave John Lee the voice of its own unbending determination: you would surely not want to be the man who broke through.

In the aftermath of the 1954 Supreme Court ruling that segregation in public schools was unconstitutional, white Mississippi became obsessed with the preservation of social orthodoxy.[4] John Dittmer has written that *Brown vs. Board of Education* compelled whites to develop "a siege mentality so pervasive it encompassed virtually every citizen and institution." As the Red Scare of the fifties was declining in the rest of the country, Dittmer explains, "a homegrown McCarthyism took hold in the Magnolia State. Books were banned, speakers censored, and network television programs cut off in midsentence."[5] The white public appeared collectively devoted to the protection of a state autonomy undefiled by federal impositions. A pro-segregationist student newspaper at Ole Miss, *The Rabble Underground*, captured the mood in its 1964 "Ode to Sovereignty":

> O Sons of Mississippi,
>   Remember your mothers;
> Remember your fathers and
>   grandfathers.
> Remember your greatgrandfathers
>   and great aunts.
> Remember and salute.
>
> How, in this wilderness, they sowed
> And we reap what they sowed.
> It is *all* for us, the Sovereign
>   State
> Of flowing rivers and happy
>   Delta land. . . .

O Sovereign State, pure and white.
O Sovereign State, where might . . .
    makes right.
O Mississippi, our words are trite
But Thou art precious in his sight.

O Sovereign State!
    Dear Homeland!
Stand ye firm in these crisis days.
Let not Truth confuse thee;
God is on our side.[6]

The poem is not likely to be anthologized as an example of the state's rich literary heritage, but it does give vivid expression to the belief that God, no less—the God of their grandfathers and great aunts—has empowered the guardians of orthodoxy. With the bold invocation of providence's election of all people "pure and white," powerful forces in the state responded to the Supreme Court decision with a broad range of defensive and counteroffensive measures, strengthened by the belief that God was on their side.

Agencies like the Mississippi State Sovereignty Commission and the Citizens' Council (or "the uptown Klan," in the words of progressive newspaperman Hodding Carter) were created as guardians of racial separation, vigilantly monitoring the goings-on of outsiders and dissidents. The Citizens' Council had been formed just two months after *Brown vs. Board of Education* by a group of thirteen civic leaders in the Delta town of Indianola. Ostensibly, the Council eschewed the violent measures later associated with the White Knights of the Ku Klux Klan, advocating instead the use of economic and social pressure to enforce segregation. But John Dittmer is correct to remind us that its constant attack on human rights "fostered and legitimized violent actions by individuals not overly concerned with questions of legality and image." By 1956, the Citizens' Council boasted a membership of eighty thousand people, scattered throughout most of the state's eighty-two counties, including all six congressional districts. The organization's two main publications, the newspaper *The Citizens' Council*, and then, after 1961, the journal *The Citizen*, offered a wide range of prosegregationist opinion—from Paul Harvey reprints to quasi-scientific accounts of black inferiority to biblical defenses of white supremacy. It also published a number of occasional pamphlets, including the extremely popular *Racial Facts*, which warned of "Negroid blood like the jungle, steadily and completely swallowing up everything."[7]

At the heart of white fear was the terrible certainty that the new social landscape would encourage intimacy between blacks and whites—the dreaded "mongrelization" of the races. The editor of the *Jackson Daily News* lamented the *Brown vs. Board* decision as "the first step, or an opening wedge, toward mixed marriages, miscegenation, and the mongrelization of the human race."[8] Judge Tom P. Brady, the most revered intellectual of Mississippi white resistance, got to the bottom of the matter in his widely read polemic of 1954, *Black Monday*. Brady explained: "Very few negroes have true respect and reverence for their race. They sense their racial limitations. If there is a short cut they want it. They are unwilling to try to evolve and develop through growth and struggle as has the white man. Evolutionary advancement, the only way in which a substantial lasting contribution to their race and to this country can be made, is far too tedious and slow. Oh, no, they desire a much shorter detour, via the political tunnel, to get on the inter-marriage turnpikes. These Northern negroes are determined to mongrelize America!"[9]

The Princeton-educated judge (and later Mississippi Supreme Court justice) then forecast bleak consequences for the future in a telling juxtaposition of images: "When a law transgresses the moral and ethical sanctions and standards of the mores, invariable strife, bloodshed and revolution follow in the wake of its attempted enforcement. The loveliest and purest of God's creatures, the nearest thing to an angelic being that treads this terrestrial ball is a well-bred, cultured Southern white woman or her blue-eyed, golden-haired little girl."[10] Brady's claim to a pure Southern Anglo-Saxon identity was indissolubly linked with the "purest of God's creatures"—that swellest blonde again.[11]

In 1956, a new organization appeared, predisposed to the same political concerns as those articulated by the Citizens' Council, but now underwritten by the state legislature. The Mississippi State Sovereignty Commission was formed to broaden the scope of protecting "the Southern Way of Life."[12] The commission's expressed purpose was "to do and perform any and all acts and things deemed necessary and proper to protect the sovereignty of the State of Mississippi, and her sister states, from encroachment thereon by the Federal Government."[13] Nevertheless, it operated as "something akin to NKVD among the cotton patches," as journalist Wilson Minor put it.[14] With an extensive surveillance network solidly in place, the Sovereignty Commission vigilantly monitored civil rights activists and any Mississippi citizens suspected of heterodoxy—"persons whose utterances or actions indicate they should be watched with suspicion on future racial attitudes."[15] The commission pursued its ordained work by dispatching investigators and spies to gather information on civil rights workers, white liberals, and anyone else suspected of racial indiscretion. By 1967, the commission had amassed an archive of more than ten thousand reports on people who worked for or represented "subversive, militant, or revolutionary groups."[16] By 1974, the files would grow to 87,000 names.

Although the Sovereignty Commission's principal motivation was "to prevent encroachment upon the rights of this and other states by the Federal Government," as the charter stated, its obsession with racial purity could not be entirely explained by states' rights fervor. The commission's agents seemed to spend as much energy tracking down reports of mixed-race babies and children as it did investigating the activities of subversive, militant, and revolutionary groups. Sadly, a reading of the available Sovereignty Commission files regarding rumors of interracial sex show us (in Adam Nossiter's words) "cool accounts of lives damaged, destroyed, or threatened because black men were suspected of consorting with white women."[17]

Then there are reports that are stranger than fiction. In the case of the woman Louvenia K. and her two sons, Edgar and Randy Ed, the director of the commission himself, Erle Johnston, Jr., wrote an eight-page, single-spaced report in December of 1963 exploring the racial composition of the boys and their mother. The complexity of the case—or better, the twisted nature of the investigation—makes the report almost unbearable to read. At stake was the situation of the two boys, eight and nine years old, who had been turned away from the local white school because of questions regarding their racial identity. Even though Louvenia told investigators that her family "had always considered themselves white, that they did not associate with Negroes and [that] she objected to Negro children attending white schools as much as any other white person," and even though her two boys were sandy-haired blondes, a mistaken reference to her as "colored" on her birth certificate sent school officials into a frenzy of racial panic. Suffice it to say that sovereignty commission officials investigated every available past and present reference to Louvenia K.'s family in order to determine whether she was "colored," and if so, how much colored, and then to what percentage her sons were colored. All this was critically important because, according to Mississippi law, if the sons were "1/8 Negro" or more, they would be considered black; if not more than "1/16 Negro," they would be considered white.

To insure that the investigation was conducted as thoroughly as possible, Director Johnston noted that he spent "considerable time studying" a historical novel called *The Echo of the Black Horn*, in which was contained a reference to "an unusual Mulatto with blue-green eyes" named Rachel, alleged to be the great-grandmother of Louvenia, no less—and thus the great-great-grandmother of Edgar and Randy Ed. The woman Rachel, about whom there apparently existed genealogical references in nonfictional sources, had been a slave of Newt Knight, a deserter from the Confederate army who founded the free state of Jones County—a county in Mississippi that seceded from the South after the South seceded from the Union, and that fought against both the Confederate and Union armies. As Erle Johnston reports, Rachel was the "villain" of the case, the one who "infused Negro blood into the white blood of the descendants of Newton Knight"—including Edgar and Randy Ed. Johnston surveys the worst-case scenario in breathtaking detail: "If Rachel was pure Negro, then her son Jeff was a Mulatto, her grandson, Otho, was a Quadroon and her great grand-daughter, Louvenia, is an Octoroon, meaning that she is 1/8 Negro. Following the same line one step further, any children of Louvenia, assuming that the descendants of Rachel all intermarried with [pure] white mates, would be exactly 1/16 Negro, which under Mississippi law would classify them as white. If Rachel was *not* pure Negro, then Louvenia and her brothers and sisters by the same parents would be less than 1/8 Negro and the two sons, Randy and Edgar W. would be nearer 1/32. A family tree outline is attached to and made part of this report."[18]

Although the commission concluded that the boys were legally white, the local school board had reached "a stalemate" in its own deliberations on the matter. As a result, the two boys, who had attended less than one day of school during their entire lives, were left to help their parents raise chickens on the family's small farm in Jones County.

Despite this and other numerous exhibitions of race obsession by the guardians of orthodoxy, we must be cautious with Dittmer's claim that the siege mentality "encompassed virtually every citizen and institution."[19] There is another side of the analysis that must be considered. The historian James Silver, who became a household name in Mississippi in 1964 with the publication of his blistering attack on the state, described to readers a "closed society" in which, by and large, white people nonchalantly accepted the "all-pervading doctrine" of white supremacy, justified by a professed belief in states' rights and religious fundamentalism. "In such a society," Silver wrote, "a never-ceasing propagation of the 'true faith' must go on relentlessly, with a constantly reiterated demand for loyalty to the united front, requiring that non-conformists and dissenters from the code be silenced, or, in a crisis, driven from the community."[20] Silver emphasized that the state leadership in such a crisis would inevitably be the extremists—those hard-jawed incorrigibles whose every move was "determined by their conformity to the orthodoxy." Silver's analysis went directly to the heart of the state's repressive ethos.

Yet what should be added to both accounts is the sensibility of the larger mass of white people shielded from intrusion and dissent—those whose thoughts were more with the prospects of the Ole Miss football team or the upcoming Miss Mississippi pageant than with the subtleties of racial politics. Their outlook on life took a form different from that of extremist zealots. One of Silver's friends, the historian and native white Mississippian David Donald, observed in a letter to Silver, "The Mississippian has always lived in a self-contained world. When he traveled, he went to Memphis (where he met other Mississippians in the lobby of the Gayso Hotel) or to his own Gulf Coast. When he traded, it was with other Mississippians. When he read, it was his own local newspapers, edited by Mississippians. When he got an education, it was at Mississippi colleges, where Mississippians taught. . . . These people had no idea that there was a world beyond themselves."[21] In the tranquil spaces carved out by the guardians of orthodoxy (however diminished they became in time), something like a serene aloofness to the outside and to the other became an attainable luxury—a pleasing detachment from everything and everyone different. Not even *Brown vs. Board of Education*, nonviolent direct action and boycotts, sit-ins, COFO workers, the Summer Project, or the Civil Rights Act of 1964 could fully diminish this composure once it took hold in the white public imagination.

In his 1965 essay, "Mississippi: The Fallen Paradise," the novelist Walker Percy held up the "the wacky logic of white supremacy" to critical analysis (the phrase is not Percy's but William Faulkner's).[22] Percy—who was born in Alabama and raised in Greenville, Mississippi, by his uncle William Alexander Percy—reached the conclusion that in the attempt to reconcile increasingly contradictory claims about social life under Jim Crow, segregationists had forged a discourse wherein all assertions became both equally true and equally false, "depending on one's rhetorical posture." Percy explained, "When Senator Eastland declares, 'There is no discrimination in Mississippi,' and 'All who are qualified to vote, black or white, exercise the right of suffrage,' these utterances are received by friend and foe alike with a certain torpor of spirit. It does not matter that there is very little connection between Senator Eastland's utterances and the voting statistics of his home county: that of a population of 31,020 Negroes, 161 are registered to vote." A disconnection is made between language and reality: arguments advanced in support of the status quo create in turn their own logic and credibility. As a result, the prevailing syllogism goes as follows: "1. There is no ill-feeling in Mississippi between the races; the Negroes like things the way they are; if you don't believe it, I'll call my cook out of the kitchen and you can ask her. 2. The trouble is caused by outside agitators who are Communist-inspired. 3. Therefore, the real issue is between atheistic Communism and patriotic, God-fearing Mississippians." How did it happen, Percy asks, that a fairly decent people has become so completely deluded about itself, "that it is difficult to discuss the issues with them, because the common words of the language no longer carry the same meanings?"[23]

One large piece of the puzzle was indisputably theological. In the sermons and Bible studies delivered zealously from the pulpits and fellowship halls of the white Protestant churches, the disjunction between language and reality gained powerful reenforcement. A certain deracinated piety created a strange, new world (pearly clean and tidy) that resided in but not of the old world (where darkness, difference, and clutter prevailed). No better illustration of the theology that shaped this world can be found than in the career of the state's preeminent Southern Baptist preacher, Douglas Hudgins, who presided over the congregation of First Baptist Church in Jackson from 1946 until his retirement from the ministry in 1969.

First Baptist Church, which occupied an entire city block near the state capital building, was the single most powerful religious institution in Mississippi during the civil rights years. Among its well-known members was Ross Barnett, vociferous supporter of white supremacy as governor of the state from 1960 to 1964 and long-time teacher of the Men's Sunday school class. Barnett had made international headlines in 1962 by arrogantly defying the Justice Department's order that the black student James Meredith be enrolled at Ole Miss. "We will not drink from the cup of genocide," Barnett had proclaimed.[24] Also at First Baptist were Thomas and Robert Hederman. Owners of the two largest newspapers, the militantly segregationist *Clarion Ledger* and *Jackson Daily News*, the Hedermans were the church's leading patrons. Hodding Carter, Jr., the Pulitzer-prize-winning and iconoclastic editor of the *Greenville Delta Democrat-Times*, once described the Hedermans as a homegrown product of Jim Crow racism and Christian fundamentalism. Hodding Carter III, who had written an undergraduate thesis at Princeton on white resistance to civil rights in Mississippi, was even more candid than his father in his assessment. "The Hedermans were to segregation what Joseph Goebbels was to Hitler. They were cheerleaders and chief propagandists, dishonest and racist. They helped shape as well as reflect a philosophy which was, at its core, as undemocratic and immoral as any extant."[25] Not to be overlooked among the church's members was Tom Etheridge, the *Daily News*'s main political columnist and savage interpreter of the civil rights movement to the paper's 100,000 readers.

Doug Hudgins, or "Mister Baptist" as one Jackson columnist called him, took full advantage of his influential pulpit, winning a wide range of civic and political honors: he was chaplain of the Mississippi Highway Safety Patrol, director of the Jackson Chamber of Commerce, member of both the Masonic order and the Chamber of Commerce, and president of the Jackson Rotary Club (in 1961).[26] As the shepherd of First Baptist's highly influential congregation, Hudgins preached a gospel of individual salvation and personal orderliness, construing civil rights activism as not only a defilement of social purity but even more as simply irrelevant to the proclamation of Jesus Christ as God. The cross of Christ, Hudgins explained at the conclusion of a sermon in late 1964, has nothing to do with social movements or realities beyond the church; it's a matter of individual salvation.[27] The congregation at First Baptist knew exactly what Hudgins meant. Had he stated the matter more explicitly, he might have said that the cross has nothing to do with the civil rights of black Mississippians. On the other hand, the cross ought to inspire decent white people toward the preservation of the purity of the social body. And it certainly did.

Douglas Hudgins was the premier theologian of the closed society. He articulated in his sermons, Bible studies, and occasional writings, and embodied in his church leadership, an austere piety that remained impervious to the sufferings of black people, as well as to the repressive tactics of the guardians of orthodoxy, many of whom were lodged in his own congregation. Hudgins's faith contained elements of traditional Southern Baptist theology, anti-modernist fundamentalism, and republican civil religion, but these were put in the service of his distinctive emphasis on personal and spiritual purity.[28] In Hudgins's view, the important matters of faith were discovered in the interior dimensions of the soul's journey to perfection. He proclaimed in a televised sermon in the early years of the civil rights era, "Now is the time to shift the emphasis from the material to the spiritual."[29] The greatest influence on Hudgins, the Baptist theologian E. Y. Mullins, once wrote, "The Bible places nothing between the individual soul and God."[30] Sadly, the fair-minded Mullins had no way of knowing the various misuses awaiting his peculiar Southern mysticism when he declared a generation earlier: "Soul competency means to me that I find truth when I am furthest removed from the distractions and contingencies of people and things and authorities—again, when truth takes forms which are unique to me and my understanding of the Bible."[31]

An Uncluttered Life

Doug Hudgins was born on May 4, 1905, in Estill Springs, Tennessee, which he once described as "a little wide place in the road, but primevally beautiful."[32] He counted among his forbears the colonial settlers of King and Queen County in Virginia, where his paternal grandfather Henry S. Hudgins was born.[33] Henry Hudgins eventually became one of the pioneer settlers of Tennessee and a planter in the Rock Creek settlement near Tullahoma. Hudgins's father, William Douglas, worked as a merchant, a farmer, and a cattleman until the Baptists established an encampment in Estill Springs in 1908.[34] That was the year he sold his business interests and "surrendered" to full-time religious work with the Sunday School Board and the Baptist Young Person's Union in the Tennessee Baptist convention. His "six-step program" toward establishing a successful Sunday school was frequently cited throughout the state as an effective, brass-bolts strategy for a certain increase in numbers. The elder Hudgins instructed: "1. Find 'em. 2. Fetch 'em. 3. Fix 'em. 4. Fasten 'em. 5. Follow 'em. 6. Finish 'em."[35] Hudgins's mother, Lelia Barrow Hudgins, was the daughter of a Baptist minister in Kentucky, a faithful member of the Women's Missionary Union, and a woman fully committed to raising her two sons in the faith.

The traditional Southern Baptist culture in which Hudgins was raised nurtured a distinctive moral and religious sensibility. In historian Ted Ownby's words, this culture offered a life "without chance or risk . . . where permanent values and moral development held worldly excitements in check."[36] Just as faith's purity required protection from all forms of foreign corruption—including, as the Alabama Baptist newspaper maintained, the "vainglorious scholarship" of "German born vagaries" who were corrupting Holy Scriptures through historical-critical research—so should the body and mind be protected against moral impurity. Even Scripture itself existed as a kind of pure body, thus needing to be guarded with unceasing vigilance. A fierce sectarian self-consciousness shaped domestic and moral etiquette and equally influenced patterns of religious feeling and understanding. In defiance of outside threats to Southern culture, evangelicals placed an almost exclusive emphasis on individual regeneration and the competency of the soul before God.[37] One Southern Baptist pastor of the 1920s noted that "having considered the matter, [he was] convinced that the religion existing among the whites of the South was of a purer form than that existing in the North."[38] The individual soul and body were the proving ground of salvation's efficacy.

Agitation could very likely assume the form of libidinous forces plaguing the self. In the world of Hudgins's Southern Baptist childhood, many preachers blamed contemporary fashions in women's dress for unsettling men's fragile concentration on things spiritual. Reverend John W. Porter, editor of the *American Baptist* and pastor in Kentucky, mourned that "scant dress is usually accompanied by scant morals. . . . If some of the dresses continue the same ratio for the next twenty-five years that they have maintained for the past ten years, they will be exactly fifteen feet above the head."[39] Not surprisingly, motion pictures took an equally hard shot from the Southern Baptist moralists. In 1926, the convention announced its "uncompromising disfavor for the salacious and character-destroying [motion] pictures produced and shown the public." Cinemas invited men and women to enjoy the cool comforts of a darkened room and then bombarded them with "vulgar styles of dress (or undress)" and "the shameless exposure of female nakedness," and with images "utterly putrid, indecent, vulgar, saturated with sex," all the while leaving "an indelible blot upon the minds" of the viewers.[40]

If moving pictures stirred up impure desires, imagine the possibilities of the dancing female body. Southern preachers did, and what they saw was not pretty: "waltz, turkey trot, grizzly bear, bunny hug, buzzard lope and the shimmy, ad nauseam ad infinitum," intoned the Reverend Porter.[41]

Not only was dancing simply too much fun, as Ownby surmised, displaying a wild disregard for evangelical values of serenity and introspection, but it exhibited a veritable feast of sexual debauchery. The worries of one Georgia minister were shared by many: "the close relations into which the sexes are thrown are such as to inflame the animal passions to a very high degree."[42] The Southern Baptist Social Service Commission offered the appropriate conclusion to the issue of secular entertainment by declaring that dancing, "accompanied, as it is, by immodest dress, by close physical contact of the sexes, and by its lack of restraint, is undoubtedly doing much to undermine the morals of the young people."[43]

With all this worry about personal purity, it was no wonder that little attention was given to the concrete application of Christian teachings to racial and economic issues. An attempt at a meaningful social analysis published in the Georgia Baptist newspaper illustrates the degree of the difficulty: "The majority of the poor, 'the submerged tenth,' the begrimed masses who swarm in the slums and wretched tenement houses of our large cities, some of whom are also found in the smaller towns and even in the country, are dissipated, vicious, wicked, and immoral. Many reformers of the day teach that, if you improve their surroundings and educate them, you can lift them up. . . . But what these people need is to be made over again. There is but only one power in the world that can do this, and that is the gospel of the Son of God."[44] The Southern Baptist Convention of 1921 resolved that "nothing but the power of the gospel in regeneration of individual men in large numbers can ever make the world safe for the highest happiness and most real peace."[45] As one Baptist minister declared, "The best thing men can do is spread the Bible and to get it read and obeyed. This would be the end of hard times, of poverty, of unemployment, of injustice, or wrong, or war [sic].'"[46] As Hudgins himself preached two decades later, "America's Imperative Need is a soul-stirring, life-changing, God-sent, spirit-filled prayed-down revival of religion."[47] A steady concentration on the soul's regeneration and an attentiveness to the body's concomitant tidiness were enough to concern the righteous man. Everything else was clutter.

Of course, simmering fears of racial contamination heightened white anxieties. The dangers of impurity connected with each other in all sorts of intricate ways. Not only was racial homogeneity necessary in maintaining the clean blue lines of Anglo-Saxon gene pools, it was also ordained by God as part of his design for the created order. The protection of the soul's purity depended, in large part, on the preservation of racial homogeneity. The story of the "curse of Ham" added much-needed theological reinforcement to the more general speculations about God's creation of separate races.

As the story goes, Noah lay in a stupor after a long night of drinking. Ham—Noah's son—saw his father's nakedness. He told his two brothers what he had seen, but Shem and Japheth, unlike Ham, did not look upon his body but instead placed a garment over him. When Noah awoke, he was filled with anger toward Ham and declared of Canaan, the son of Ham, "Cursed be Canaan, a servant of servants shall he be unto his brother." That is the end of the story, an unlikely source indeed for the fantastic racial readings that followed. What actually angered Noah is unclear from the narrative, thin as it is on detail. The most plausible conjecture is that the son committed an act which, in his father's eyes, was regarded as a sexual abomination, a violation of sanctioned sexual etiquette.[48]

Yet by the early 1900s many Southern Baptists had come to read the story as a convincing account of the origin of the black race, condemned to a legacy of perpetual servitude. (Noah's intemperate response to a humiliation of his own doing was never questioned.) In its most bizarre configuration, an additional racist component to the Genesis account was developed to show that blacks and other dark-skinned people were created before Adam and Eve, on the day God created animals. The account claimed that when Eve was tempted in the Garden, Satan did not assume the form of a serpent but that of a "negro gardener." As if this were not enough, theologians further pondered the existence of "pre-Adamite negroes" who inhabited the Land of Nod (where Cain went and fathered children), making the cursed son of Ham the first amalgamationist.[49] Accordingly, the mother of all sins, the sin that brought on the calamitous flood and all things invidious and corrupt, was miscegenation. Mongrelization was the root of all evil after all.

Even aside from the popular influence of the Ham theory, racial separation most commonly meant white superiority. In 1912 the Home Mission Board of the Southern Baptist Convention—the agency in charge of religious instruction for minorities and the poor—called on white Christians to help blacks reach their full potential as a separate race, for in so doing, the report stated, "we shall save Anglo-Saxon supremacy." Far less charitable was the writer of an article in Mississippi's *Baptist Record*, who argued that God intended for the white race to rule supreme over blacks, because "a race whose mentality averages on borderline idiocy" is quite obviously bereft of any divine blessing.[50] (The writer's stab at biblical exegesis was no compliment to the capabilities of white "mentality": "Christ would not that the inferior mind should rule, for he said to the disciples who wished a superior place that if they were able to drink the cup with him, they would be granted the petition. The black race is not able to drink the cup of authority with success.")[51] White supremacy was the "divine law," intoned the *Laurel Leader Call*, "enacted for the defense of society and civilization."[52]

When white Christians feared that blacks wanted more than their natural lot warranted—and were seeking to drink "the cup of authority"—any
means to preserve Anglo-Saxon supremacy was justified on broad religious
and moral grounds, including lynching. Writing in a Mississippi Baptist
publication, the minister P. I. Lipsey defended the barbarous practice as
"the wholesome desire to maintain the inviolability of the home." "Nothing stirs the blood of white men like a wrong committed upon a white
woman by a negro," wrote Livingston Johnson in the *Biblical Recorder*.[53]
The ideal of personal purity had to be defended at all costs, mandated as
it was by God for maintaining creation's harmony and coherence.

Douglas Hudgins grew in favor with the cultural and religious sensibility of his region. His spiritual development followed traditional Baptist
form. At the age of ten, he made a "public profession of his faith in Jesus
Christ" and was baptized in the saving waters of muddy Taylor's Creek.
His conversion, "void of the dramatic," was, in his words, "a simple, quiet
thing." Hudgins's account of the experience is notable for its straightforward, unemotional earnestness: "In the spring or early summer, during a
revival meeting held under a tent on the school ground in the little Middle Tennessee community, I came to feel a desperate need for a Savior. On
a Sunday morning at the close of the evangelist's sermon, I responded to
his invitation, saying that I felt the need of Christ, and really wanted to become a Christian. The following morning, while seated on the front porch
of my father's home, the family's pastor appeared and began to talk with me
about the desire I had expressed the day before. Quietly he told me about
how to be saved. He asked that we pray, and while he did he asked the Lord
to save me. When the prayer was completed the pastor said to me, 'Son,
will you accept Jesus as your Savior?' To that question, I remember I
replied, 'Brother Byrom, I trusted the Lord while you were praying.'"[54]

Ten years later, he "surrendered to special service in the Christian
cause," sensing that he felt God's call to the ministry. At the time, Hudgins
was a junior pre-med student at a small Baptist college named Carson-
Newman, "the Baylor of Tennessee," he liked to say. He had been
"wrestling with the impression" that he should give his life to the ministry,
but dreams of medicine continued to steer his decisions about the future.
It was during a revival service at the college, led by well-known evangelist
Finley F. Gibson, that Hudgins felt compelled to take his father's vocation
one step further and become a preacher in the Southern Baptist Convention. "During the service that morning I had the incontestable impression
that the Lord wanted me in the ministry. Almost before I realized it, I
found myself making my way out of the choir and into a small group who
had responded to the invitation. I realized that we had been singing, 'I'll
Go Where You Want Me to Go,' and I almost said aloud, 'I wonder where

the Lord will send me.' Several others that morning made similar decisions and as I called my parents that evening, I fully committed myself to being a preacher."[55]

On his twentieth birthday, Hudgins was ordained to the ministry in the First Baptist Church of Jefferson City. He recalls the afternoon: "Ordination was a real experience. It certainly was no child's play. . . . On the way from the men's dormitory to the church that afternoon to meet with the examining council, I was caught in a sudden driving rain—sans raincoat or umbrella. My only recourse was to run—and run I did. When I arrived at the church five minutes ahead of time I was out of breath and soaking wet—exhibiting more the appearance of a wet airedale than a human being. But there was no time for a clothing change. Four o'clock came and I was launched into the inquisition. For more than an hour I was questioned by first one and then the other of the nearly fifteen brethren present—with not the least of the questions being asked by my own deacon-father."[56]

Hudgins began pastoring churches during his undergraduate years, preaching in towns like Bull's Gap and Lenoir City—towns scattered throughout the hollows of Loundon County. After marrying Blanche Jones in 1927, a trained musician and vocalist who "bears out the Tennessee tradition of beautiful women," Hudgins worked on the staff of Knoxville's Fifth Avenue Baptist Church and soon became senior minister at First Baptist, La Follette, Tennessee.[57] But in 1931 he left the pastorate to begin studies at the Southern Baptist Theological Seminary in Louisville, Kentucky, the largest Protestant seminary in the world and the most academically demanding in the Southern Baptist Convention.

Southern Seminary had taken a moderate view on the race issue. Though the founding fathers of the school had uncritically accepted the practices of racial separation in antebellum South Carolina (where the seminary was established in 1859), a racist ideology had never prevailed in the life of the school. The aristocratic James P. Boyce, a founder and first president of the seminary, described himself as "an ultra-proslavery man," but later confessed, "I feel that our sins as to this institution have cursed us . . . and I fear that God is going to sweep [it] away."[58] By the time Douglas Hudgins arrived in Louisville in 1931, courses on race relations had been part of the curriculum since 1918, taught first by the remarkable Charles Spurgeon Gardner, and then by the racial progressive Jesse B. Weatherspoon. In his classes, Gardner had taught the brotherhood of humanity in Jesus Christ as the basis of any adequate Christian moral thought. He once responded to a student's question of whether blacks would go to heaven by saying, "In my judgment the Negroes have a much better chance than a preacher who would raise such a question."[59] Jesse

Weatherspoon, whose course on "Christianity and Race Relations" provoked intense debate among the seminarians, would soon become a leader in race reform both at Southern Seminary and in the Southern Baptist Convention. Not only did he espouse a biblical ethic of racial equality in the tradition of his predecessor Gardner, but he also encouraged his students to think about concrete political solutions to social issues, and called for full voting rights for blacks, equally distributed educational funding, fair economic policies, and the elimination of all discriminatory laws.[60] In 1950, Weatherspoon fought successfully for the integration of the seminary and later, in 1954, he provoked the wrath of Baptist segregationists throughout the nation by lobbying (also successfully) for the support of *Brown vs. Board of Education* at the annual Southern Baptist Convention, just weeks after the Supreme Court decision.

The president of Southern during Hudgins's student years was an Alabamian named John R. Sampey. Trained as a Hebrew scholar, Sampey had high academic standards and demanded that his seminarians perform accordingly. He emphasized above all the faculty's responsibility to prepare men well for the "art" of preaching.[61] Hudgins steered toward homiletics and would soon come to take pride in his oratorical skills, even though he could never shake the nasal twang of his hill-country upbringing. A better preacher was what Hudgins hoped to become—one more theologically and biblically sophisticated. Besides, racial progressivism was certainly no way to work oneself up the ladder of pulpit prestige. His dedication to homiletics at Southern Seminary paid strong dividends. In little time, Hudgins's eloquent pulpit style came to revered throughout the Southern Baptist Convention—the ideal of many an aspiring young preacher, the envy of many less polished others. "An orator of no mean ability" and "golden-voiced, silver-tongued" were some of the accolades he received. One leader in Texas Baptist circles emoted, "Dr. Hudgins can stand on any platform or grace any pulpit. He combines the qualities of Demosthenes the Athenian, Cicero the Roman, and Jonathan Edwards the American—Demosthenes, whose voice could be heard above the roaring sea; Cicero, whose tirades against the traitor Catiline, cowed the latter like a whipped dog in a corner; Jonathan Edwards, whose descriptions of Hell were so real that sinners held on to the pillars of the church to keep from sliding into Hell."[62]

By all accounts Hudgins was a man of impeccable taste. More than one admirer called attention to his refined and meticulous manner in both personal and professional affairs. "A very thorough man, who paid attention to the smallest detail," wrote the historian of the church in Houston that Hudgins pastored in the early 1940s.[63] Jackson parishioner Lewis Wilson, owner of an upscale habidashery near the state capitol, once told a fellow church member that it was easy to admire a pastor who "was always so smartly dressed and conscientious about style."[64] Dark elegant suits with pin stripes, crisp white shirts, silk ties, and black leather shoes, shined and buffed with abandon: "He dressed like a Philadelphia lawyer," former parishioner and philosophy professor Clayton Sullivan noted in his memoir, "he was a man of manners and suaveness."[65]

One early newspaper profile described the young Hudgins as "a Godly man, who frowns on levity, looseness and lack of correlation in the church" ("correlation" meant decorum and propriety). The article praised Hudgins's belief that "a church service in its uniformity is not unlike a beautiful piece of jewelry." All the elements that go into making the service a work of art must be finely wrought, and then preserved against defect and blemish. The article further commended his distinctive "method" of conducting the "ordinance" of baptism ("ordinance," not "sacrament," for reasons I will explain later). "In a baptism which takes approximately two minutes, a candidate under his guidance enters the baptismal pool and assumes what appears to be a submerged horizontal position. Only the nose and a part of the face of the candidate remain out of water. Then the doctor places his left hand, in which he holds a handkerchief, on the candidate's face, gently and briefly allows the face to be submerged."[66] To be sure, it was not unusual for the Baptist minister to employ a white handkerchief in the baptism "ordinance"—grown men might otherwise come rocketing out of the water, coughing and gasping for air if their mouths were not properly covered during immersion. But Hudgins's method, and the exquisite detail of the two-minute procedure, is more indicative of his own spick-and-span take on religious life than of an ordinance that, at least in Baptist tradition, has no ritualized form. Hudgins showed that every aspect of church life must conform to a high standard of exactness and orderliness. (A Jackson journalist noted that on the day the new educational building was occupied, the pastor, "mindful of the fresh carpets, followed the movers up and down the corridors with a vacuum cleaner.")[67]

Consider his opinions on "furnishing the pulpit." In an article written for *The Baptist Program*, Hudgins exhibited a breathtaking fastidiousness: the "pulpit and the platform on which it is set" should be maintained with considerable care; its size should be "compatible with its surroundings" and its style in keeping with the architectural theme of the sanctuary with a pleasing finish and decorative scheme. Above all, it must appear pure and simple: "even the most streamlined reading lamp detracts." Hudgins felt this strongly: "The pulpit should not be a catchall for a couple of hymnbooks; notes left over from a departmental or general superintendent; bulletins three or four weeks old; small articles lost by members of the congregation; or other miscellaneous material. If a microphone is used, let it be as inconspicuous as possible. (Ours is 'hidden' by an ingenious inner installation.)" There should be no incongruity of upholstery in the chairs behind the pulpit; no mixing of varnish tones or furniture styles. "Neither put a pair of incongruous upholstered lounge chairs behind a correctly styled pulpit. Let the furniture 'flow' together so that it becomes a 'whole.'" The meticulous detail of Hudgins's pulpit was intended to command the congregation's complete attention; as he said, "all furnishings and decorations should let the eye focus itself on the pulpit area—*not away from it*."[68] Hudgins's extraordinary conclusion is a fitting metaphor of the closed society over which he faithfully presided: "Keep the platform and the pulpit free from all clutter. Let them be an attraction to the spirit of worship."

Civil Rights Distractions

Ten years before the Summer Project tried to force Mississippi's hand on desegregation, the state's most renowned Baptist minister—and a budding leader in the Southern Baptist Convention—found himself forced to speak publicly on racial politics. Hudgins would have preferred avoiding the matter of *Brown vs. Board of Education* altogether, but a sequence of events made it impossible for him to remain silent.

The Supreme Court decision came to public debate at the 1954 Southern Baptist Convention in St. Louis, less than a month after the May 17 ruling. By a surprisingly overwhelming majority, the messengers to the Convention voted in favor of a report advanced by the progressive Christian Life Commission supporting the Supreme Court decision. The report stated that *Brown vs. Board* was "in harmony with the constitutional guarantee of equal freedom to all citizens, and with the Christian principles of equal justice and love of all men." The Christian Life Commission also pledged Southern Baptist support to the public school system as a whole, calling it "one of the greatest factors in American history for the maintenance of democracy and our common culture" and urging continued support of public schools as "one of the foundations of our democracy."[69] Messengers at the convention—not only pastors but lay people with differing educational backgrounds and professions—not only accepted the Supreme Court decision, but encouraged fellow Baptists to apply a "Christian spirit" to the hard task of working out the implications of the new law. Although the report praised the high court's delay of the decision's effective date, the Southern Baptist Convention had decisively put its support of *Brown vs. Board of Education* into the public record.

And it put Douglas Hudgins into the national spotlight, testing his hitherto unmitigated loyalty to Baptist life and denominational service. How would he explain his congregation's (and his own) disapproval of the Supreme Court decision—thus pleasing his constituents and saving his job—and also maintain good standing with his denominational peers? Hudgins quit the convention before the vote was cast. He left behind a vote in opposition to the report, hoping to spare himself conspicuous attention on the convention floor. However, his vote was read to the messengers by Jay Storer, the president of the Southern Baptist Convention. And it was read after two men—both denominational unknowns—acrimoniously voiced their opposition to the report. One W. M. Nevins, a pastor of a small, firebrand church in Lexington, Kentucky, took to the microphone to warn the convention that "soon . . . some of you who sit in this audience today will have grandchildren with mixed blood." Next came Arthur Hay, a dentist from Albuquerque, New Mexico, who held forth on the perils of amalgamation, quoting a variety of Bible verses and offering anecdotes about "white girls dating Negro men, and Negro girls dating white men" at a local university. He finished his comments by declaring that he was "a friend of the Negro" but that "Negroes are descendants of Ham," and "we whites must keep our blood pure."[70] It was an embarrassing moment, even to most of the messengers in the audience who held similar views.

GIANT

Without even so much as acknowledging these two opinions, Professor J. B. Weatherspoon rose to the occasion, and the racial progressive from Southern Seminary explained to the convention, in his melodic baritone, the reasons Southern Baptists should affirm the report. Directing the convention's attention to the large banner above the speakers' platform, where the words "Forward in Christ Jesus" were emblazoned in red, Weatherspoon told the messengers, "We're not going to shut our eyes to the fact that ours is a critical period, our nation needs men of faith, men who believe in Jesus Christ . . . to understand what is the most Christian thing to do in a most difficult time."[71] He urged the convention to support the Christian Life Commission report and register its support of *Brown vs. Board of Education*. A vote was then taken, and fewer than one hundred of the ten thousand messengers voiced opposition to the report.

Hudgins's hopes for a graceful exit were dashed when his name appeared alongside those of Nevins and Hay in numerous media accounts of the convention, prompting him to break with routine and speak directly to the issue on his first Sunday back at First Baptist Church in Jackson. (At the conclusion of Weatherspoon's remarks, Jay Storer abruptly announced that his "very good friend Doug Hudgins" had left behind a vote against the report.) In his comments to the church, Hudgins appealed first to the issue of congregational autonomy so basic to the faith and practice of Baptist churches. He reminded his people that the Christian Life Commission report, even though it had passed overwhelmingly at the St. Louis convention, had no binding authority on the local church. "If, perhaps, you are not familiar with Baptist church polity," he said, "let me remind you

that every Baptist congregation in the world—if it be truly Baptist in its position—is a democratic entity, and is responsible to no other body or individual, but is under the leadership of the Lord." The decisions of convention reports and resolutions are "actions of subjective co-operation.
They are not authoritarian nor disciplinary." He added that the report had
a "very large disagreeing vote," referring to what he considered a large
number of nonvoting messengers. But the heart of Hudgins's remarks was
his claim that the Supreme Court decision was "a purely civic matter" and
thus "not appropriate nor necessary before a religious body."

His concluding statement cast in theological language the sentiment of
his instructions for furnishing the pulpit: "Brethren, a church, in our interpretation of the New Testament, is a group of baptized believers, equal
in rank and privilege; but a study of the New Testament further reveals
that a church is a fellowship. If the fellowship of the church be broken, the
idealism of the first is very definitely retarded." Intercourse with other,
outside realities cheapens the church's serene repose, threatening her purity, her unbroken fellowship.[72]

As the 1964 Summer Project took shape and rumors of "outside agitators" invading Mississippi increased, Jacksonians were treated to daily ha-
rangues in the local media against the civil rights leaders and volunteers.
First Baptist parishioner, Tom Etheridge, in his column "Mississippi Notebook" in the Clarion Ledger, never disappointed his readers. "It is logical to
assume," he wrote, "that Communists may have some sort of active role in
the so-called Mississippi Summer Project, which reportedly will bring
hundreds of leftist students and many potential troublemakers to our state
before long."[73] The Jackson Daily News warned: "We are presently under attack as no state has ever been."[74] The Hederman paper further observed:
"It appears to be more than coincidence that racial disorders always seem
to develop somewhere in the South at the very time Communism takes another step forward in the Caribbean area at this country's doorstep."[75] Not
to be outdone, the Citizens' Council circulated numerous cautionary
leaflets and flyers. One of its open letters encouraged white Mississippians
to show special support for the local police, for "the coming violence in the
name of 'civil rights' appears to be the climax of the Communist takeover
of the United States. Washington has been taken over by Communist influences and for all practical purposes the communists are in working control of the federal government."[76]

In the summer and fall of the previous year, the civil rights movement,
which had hitherto existed well outside the immaculate lawn of First Baptist Church, appeared on the front steps of Hudgins's cavernous sanctuary
in the form of students from Tougaloo College, a private black school in
Jackson. Under the leadership of Jackson civil rights leader Medgar Evers
and the college chaplain, Reverend Ed King, the Tougaloo group sought

permission to worship with the regular members of First Baptist Church, just as they had sought to do in their numerous visits to other white churches in the city. From Hudgins's perspective, these visits (like the *Brown* decision) "imposed some difficult problems on the First Baptist Church," but it still remained a political concern and warranted no pastoral consideration.[77] Hudgins would not meet with Evers or the students, nor would he meet Ed King, whose custom it was to discuss the intent of the visits with the white ministers. The church visitors posed only a strategic nuisance, and the matter was promptly turned over to the deacons for resolution.

On June 9, 1963, one week after the first confrontation with the students from Tougaloo and two days before the murder of Medgar Evers (and the night of Mrs. Hamer's torture in Winona), the lay leadership of the church proposed a resolution to the congregation that was later adopted by a unanimous standing vote. The resolution lamented "the present social unrest brought about by agitators who would drive a wedge of hate and distrust between white and colored friends." However, it would be necessary for the First Baptist Church to "confine its assemblies and fellowships to those other than the Negro race, until such time as cordial relationships could be reestablished."[78] The disingenuous notion that cordial relationships would be reestablished once the agitators were gone bears some explanation. The last black members of the church—former slaves—had been expelled in 1868 as white Southerners responded to Reconstruction fears of black enfranchisement. The church's in-house historian justified the expulsion by reference to the fundamental difference in black and white styles of worship—and the need to preserve the solemn eloquence of white religion. "There was a great deal of rejoicing," he wrote, "creating a loud noise and otherwise conducting themselves in a manner that did not meet the approval of the members of the church."[79] Suffice it to say that the singing and praying of the church visitors on the front steps nearly a century later met with equal disapproval. The church visitors were turned away with the threat that arrests and jail sentences would result from further attempts to sully Hudgins's sanctuary.

In the deacons' meeting on June 11, 1963 (hours before Medgar Evers was murdered less than a mile from First Baptist), the shared sense was that the worst had passed. As the minutes indicate: "The Pastor spoke briefly of our church's problems and asked for the Board's continuing prayers. He also announced that he and Mrs. Hudgins were planning on having the Deacons and their wives over to their new home on June 25." Hudgins called for "loyalty to the Church's worship and other services, in spite of and even because of the tensions which might be in our city." The meeting was then turned over to the Property and Maintenance Committee, which discussed its progress report on the construction of an elevator and the cleaning of the sanctuary.[80] No mention was made of the decision to withdraw the church's annual $1,500 contribution to a local colored seminary.[81]

After the start of the summer project, Hudgins was visited by an old acquaintance and classmate, H. Hansel Stembridge, Jr. The two had enjoyed theological discussions and social outings together during their student years at the Southern Baptist Theological Seminary, though they had not maintained strong ties since graduation in 1934. Hudgins and Stembridge would exchange courtesies if they saw each other at the annual Southern Baptist Convention, but the dramatically different directions their ministries had taken made it difficult for the two to find common ground.

Stembridge had become increasingly drawn to a faith that fostered racial justice; his tenure at churches in Georgia, Tennessee, Kentucky, North Carolina, and Virginia was always fragile, and sometimes shortened by his unwillingness to keep quiet on controversial issues. In 1961, while pastor at the First Baptist Church of Lynchburg, Virginia, Stembridge welcomed into the Sunday morning service a group of black students from the local Lynchburg Seminary. At the end of the service, church leaders complained to Stembridge about his decision. They emphasized to him the congregation's complete support of the church's closed-door policy: blacks would not be allowed to enter the church. After a week of soul searching, Stembridge explained in a sermon the following Sunday that if a segregated church was what parishioners wanted, then he could not continue as their pastor. Aside from the support of a local rabbi and Catholic priest—which heightened evangelical resentment—Stembridge stood alone with his theological convictions. The church leaders encouraged a speedy resignation.

The Lynchburg experience solidified Stembridge's growing awareness that ministry in a mainline Southern Baptist church was incompatible with his understanding of faith. To be sure, the denomination counted among its members courageous clergymen like Clarence Jordon, T. B. Maston, Will D. Campbell, and Stembridge's close friend, Carlyle Marney, but the difficulties of sustaining a pastorate in a traditional setting seemed to be insurmountable. Although the Southern Baptist Convention had voiced support of *Brown vs. Board of Education* in 1954, segregation continued to be widely accepted as God's good design for humanity. And in Lynchburg, segregation was preached with cavalier assurance by the town's Protestant clergy, including the young Jerry Falwell, whose newly founded Thomas Road Baptist Church adhered to strict closed-door policies. (In these years, Falwell stated in no uncertain terms his opposition to any meddling of Christians in political matters: "Nowhere are we commissioned to reform the externals. We are not told to wage war against bootleggers, liquor stores, gamblers, murderers, prostitutes, racketeers, prejudiced persons, or institutions, or any other existing evil as such.")[82]

Stembridge and his wife took up residence in San Francisco. There he attended classes at the Baptist Seminary in the Graduate Theological Union in Berkeley and began changing affiliation from the Southern Baptist Convention to the more liberal American Baptist Convention. He continued to support civil rights causes, largely through his daughter, Jane Stembridge, who had recently left her organizational post with SNCC in Atlanta to help develop a field office in Greenwood, Mississippi. (In 1960, Jane had interrupted her own theological studies at Union Seminary in New York and come south.). Stembridge admired his daughter's commitments; he and his wife had always encouraged her to think about the social dimensions of faith. But the parents' fears for their daughter's safety were difficult to bear. With the Klan killings of Schwerner, Chaney, and Goodman and the national media coverage of intensified anti-civil rights violence, Stembridge decided to travel to Mississippi. There he would spend time with his daughter and see first hand the situation reported almost daily on television and in newspapers in the bay area. He also would visit his old seminary classmate and encourage Hudgins to use his influence by preaching against violence and racism.

In July of 1964, with the financial support of a parishioner in his new congregation in Daly City, California, Stembridge flew to Mississippi on what he called a "tour of reconciliation." On the first day of his visit, Stembridge and his daughter drove northwest of Jackson toward Yazoo City to observe the ruins of a bombed black church—where still-smoldering foundations were all that was left of the building. The church was located in a settlement several miles off the main highway, reached only by a narrow dirt road that ended just beyond the church. While Stembridge surveyed the tragedy—this was his first close-hand look at Klan terrorism—Jane talked to her father about the movement and about her hopes for the Summer Project. She talked about the three missing civil rights workers. "No one else should die down here. Nobody should die anymore," she wanted her father to know.[83] But the sudden roaring of engines put a quick end to her reflections. As several cars and pickup trucks pulled into the church parking lot, a group of young white men, with their wives and children, proceeded to get out of their vehicles and walk toward the church. Stembridge and his daughter headed directly to their rental car, locked the doors, and began driving cautiously toward the road, their eyes straight ahead, purposefully avoiding eye contact with any of the men. The crowd stood their ground for one terrifying moment, but then moved slowly aside, allowing the minister and his daughter to drive back to the main highway and then on to Jackson.[84]

That night Stembridge and his daughter visited Douglas Hudgins and his wife. They were served coffee in the Hudgins's living room, and talked politely about seminary and denominational affairs. Then in his gentle, al-

most naive way, Stembridge asked Hudgins the question (in the same kind
of pained, brotherly manner he had asked a Birmingham minister after the
Klan bombing of a church had killed four black girls in their Sunday
school class): "How can it be, Doug, that you are here in this town preaching the Gospel and there's all this hatred and violence?" Hudgins was momentarily silent. Then he said, "You simply don't understand. You know
Baptists have no business tinkering in political matters".[85] Hudgins invoked the familiar claim that civil rights for blacks has nothing to do with
the Gospel.[86]

Stembridge came away from his meeting in despair, with the sad feeling that Hudgins was a man who "wanted to be blind."[87] But even more,
it appeared to Stembridge that Hudgins had developed a "Messianic complex"; he had deceived himself with the arrogant belief that white Mississippians were the last to save the Southern Way of Life—"even to save
America itself." Hudgins was unmoved by the visit. He simply refused to
see how Stembridge's worries had anything to do with his responsibility as
a preacher of the Gospel. Stembridge concluded, "At least I ascertained
who the Freedom Workers could depend upon and whom they couldn't."[88]
His old seminary friend could not be counted among the former.

Anti-civil rights violence did not subside at the end of Freedom Summer.[89] Klan terrorism became more random and unpredictable in the three
years following. Moderate whites and blacks became targets of violent attacks and harassment. Increasingly, the Klan directed terrorist campaigns
against Jewish Mississippians—not just Jewish civil rights workers—who
emerged in the Klan's paranoid imagination as the driving force behind the
civil rights movement.

Shortly before Thanksgiving of 1967, a bomb ripped through the home
of Rabbi Perry Nussbaum, just weeks after his Temple Beth Israel's newly
constructed building had been greatly damaged by a Klan bombing. The
explosion destroyed the kitchen, dining room, living room, and parts of a
bedroom. Miraculously, neither Rabbi Nussbaum, who publicly supported
desegregation, nor his wife was harmed; both had been asleep in their back
bedroom. When firemen, reporters, police officers, and neighbors arrived
at the scene, Arene Nussbaum, the rabbi's wife, was found standing beside
the rubble of the explosion, crying hysterically, picking splinters of glass
from her hair, face, and clothing. As journalist Jack Nelson tells the story,
Nussbaum stood beside his wife in his bathrobe, saying over and over that
while this was the work of Ku Klux Klan, the "atmosphere of violence" was
the work of Christian leaders who did nothing to change it.[90] His first
thought turned to Douglas Hudgins. Go call Hudgins, Nussbaum said to
Reverend Ken Dean, a neighbor who had been awakened by the explosion.
Tell Hudgins that he needs to make a public statement against all this
violence.[91]

When Dean called the First Baptist pastor early the next morning, Hudgins told him he resented his call and was capable of taking care of his own business. He should never call him again.[92] Dean explained that Rabbi Nussbaum simply wanted Hudgins to use his influence to condemn the Klan violence, but Hudgins hung the phone up without replying.

Less than an hour later Dean returned to the Nussbaum's house, and was surprised to find Hudgins and Nussbaum standing on a pile of scorched two by fours that had once been the back porch. Alongside Nussbaum and Hudgins stood Governor Paul Johnson and Lucian Harvey, Jr., a friend of Hudgins and current president of the Jackson Rotary Club who often described his friend and pastor as a man "well-liked by Jew and Gentile."[93] While Charles Quinn from NBC filmed the scene, Nussbaum waved his finger in Hudgins' face and shouted: "If you had spoken out from your pulpit after the synagogue was bombed and told your people it was wrong to have done that, this wouldn't have happened!" Hudgins tried to tell Nussbaum he was deeply sorry about what had happened, but Nussbaum was not interested in pastoral platitudes. He continued, "Don't tell me now how sorry you are. Those sons-of-a-gun attacked me and my family! They've attacked my house! I don't want to hear how sorry you are!" Hudgins was shocked, as were the governor and Mr. Harvey, that Rabbi Nussbaum would dare "deliver such an attack on Mississippi's most prominent religious figure." But Nussbaum was not finished. "Doug, if you're really sorry about this," he said, "get on the pulpit Sunday and tell your people this is wrong. Talk to those segregationists that fill up your church."[94]

With that he turned to Ken Dean, who as the director of the Mississippi Council on Human Relations had always considered himself allies with Nussbaum in a common struggle against racial prejudice. Nussbaum exclaimed, "You're a white Christian—a Baptist, the worst kind for Jews. You've got a responsibility for what happened too. It's the Sunday-school lessons from the New Testament in Baptist churches that lead people to commit such terrible acts."

On the Sunday morning after the bombing, Nussbaum listened by radio to Hudgins's weekly broadcast of the worship service at the First Baptist Church. The sermon was a typical example of Hudgins's otherworldly piety. He made a general reference to the terrorist attack, saying it was regrettable that houses were bombed and wrong to bomb another man's house. He did not mention Nussbaum by name, nor did he mention that the house bombed most recently had been the rabbi's. "The Lord works in mysterious ways," the minister concluded on the subject, before turning to an exposition of a scriptural text.[95] Nussbaum found Hudgins's words outrageous.

In his cryptic remark, Hudgins was not exactly saying that Klan violence had a divine though inscrutable purpose. More than anything else, Hudgins was retreating to a piety that disconnected language from reality, which fashioned a serene, self-enclosed world, undisturbed by the sufferings of blacks and Jews.

A Piety of the Pure Soul

The writer Lillian Smith once described the religion of her southern childhood as one "triangulated on sin, sex and segregation." There was a God in heaven who loved the world and gave his son as a sacrifice for its sins; but this same God would consume in eternal flames anyone who displeased him. Then there were parts of the body that must be separated from touch and curiosity, honored but feared. The lesson on segregation seemed only "a logical extension" of the lessons on the erotic body and the inscrutable God. Smith wrote, "The banning of people and books and ideas did not appear more shocking than the banning of our wishes which we learned so early to send to the Darktown of our unconscious."[96] Purity held everything together. If the encumbrances of the flesh were allowed to agitate the soul's equanimity, then the delicate balance of communion with God would be disturbed—and the individual soul would collapse into chaos and despair.

Douglas Hudgins's piety of the pure soul betrayed this kind of anxious need to save the individual from incoherence and disintegration. The Christian life is about personal union with the saving God, secured in one decisive but continually repeated encounter with the risen Jesus. Nothing else matters. If the Christian admits other concerns into the event of salvation—like good works, doctrinal or creedal confession, or mediations like church tradition and hierarchy—then the purity of the soul's intimacy with God becomes threatened. The impure soul, like the defiled body of the white women (and like the integrated church) signals more than the tragic consequence of sin—it represents the fraying of the self's unbroken union with God, nothing less than the disintegration of the self.

The imprimatur of the Baptist theologian E. Y. Mullins is clearly present in Hudgins's understanding of personal regeneration. Like many of his generation, Hudgins came of age theologically under the influence of Mullins's austere theology. Mullins had been president of the Southern Baptist Theological Seminary until his death in 1928, and was widely regarded as one of the denomination's seminal minds.

Here is Mullins's description of the competency of the soul in communion with God, from his landmark book, *The Axioms of Religion*:

> Observe then that the idea of the competency of the soul in religion excludes at once all human interference, such as episcopacy, and infant baptism, and every form of religion by proxy. Religion is a personal matter between the soul

and God. The principle is at the same time inclusive of all particulars. . . . It must include the doctrine of separation of Church and State because State churches stand on the assumption that civil government is necessary as a factor in man's life in order to [sic] a fulfillment of his religious destiny; that man without the aid of the State is incompetent in religion. Justification by faith is also included because this doctrine is simply one detail in the soul's general religious heritage, from Christ.

Justification asserts man's competency to deal directly with God in the initial act of the Christian life. Regeneration is also implied in the principle of the soul's competency because it is the blessing which follows close upon the heels of justification or occurs at the same time with it, as a result of the soul's direct dealing with God.[97]

On the basis of his definition of the Christian life, Mullins developed his famous "Six Axioms of Religion":

1. The theological axiom: The holy and loving God has a right to be sovereign.
2. The religious axiom: All souls have an equal right to direct access to God.
3. The ecclesiastical axiom: All believers have a right to equal privileges in the church.
4. The moral axiom: To be responsible man must be free.
5. The religio-civic axiom: A free Church in a free State.
6. The social axiom: Love your neighbor as yourself.

For his part, Hudgins revised the list to a neater threefold definition: "The New Testament is Our Only Rule of Faith and Practice," "Individuality in Matters of Religion," and "The Autonomy of the Local Church."[98] These three "principles" stem from the fact that faith's chief concern is "the soul's competency before God."[99]

What does it mean for the New Testament to be "our only rule of faith and practice"? Hudgins emphasized that Baptists have no creed or "ecclesiastical mold or tradition"—no authority or edicts—that might impose "regulatory and compulsory power over the individual church."[100] Just as the individual is alone competent in matters of faith, so "the relationship of pastor and people is one between him and the local church." No outside group has any right to intrude upon this intimate union of shepherd and flock. No ecumenical agency or worldwide religious association dare suggest to the individual congregation how it should structure its beliefs and practices. Everything hangs on the person's regeneration in the experience of inviting Jesus to come into his heart. The only standard against which soul competency can be judged is the witness of the New Testament—understood not as a book of doctrine but as the life and breath of the spirit, kindling the soul's passion for perfect union with the Lord.

If everything hangs on personal regeneration, any trace of what Hudgins calls "sacramentarianism" vanishes. When salvation is interiorized to the soul's competency before God, every reality outside this encounter, which is to say all worldly reality, is stripped clean of sacramental consequence. There are then no sacraments in the church, but only what Hudgins grimly called the two "ordinances" of baptism and "the memorial supper." But these ordinances bring no grace: to those who go down into the saving waters or eat the bread and drink the wine (or the Welch's grape juice), no real presence of God is touched and received. Hudgins calls the ordinances "symbolic" (without regard for how the term was used by many theological modernists to divest Christian doctrine of its literal sense). If one were to consider baptism and the "memorial supper" sacraments, then one would not only steer perilously close to the Roman Catholic mistake, but also cheapen the purity of the ordinances. For the ordinances, Hudgins warns, should be observed with "reverence, dignity and beauty"; they dare not be "practiced loosely, carelessly, shoddily or hurriedly." The pastor must approach their practice with "unhurried gentleness," "simplicity," "quiet dignity," and "precision."[101] A solemn vigilance must guard these tranquil silences from looseness and contamination. Yet even aside from the ordinances, it is equally important to emphasize that there is nothing in the texture of worldly experience—in love or charity, desire or sorrow—that radiates a sacramental light. You will not find, feel, or experience God in compassionate acts or in life with others; you will not find, feel, or experience God anywhere but in the solitude of your own walk with Jesus in your private spiritual garden.

Hudgins's second principle is "Individuality in Matters of Religion." This principle is really first in order of theological importance, though it is certainly understandable why Hudgins would want to begin with the New Testament as the basic rule of faith. Hudgins does not intend to model Christian faith on individual experience as such. This would entail a concession to relativism or pragmatism that Hudgins dare not make (the inevitable concession to a gnostic detachment is far more encompassing and unavoidable), even though every single aspect of his religious thought threatens to end in relativistic or pragmatic reductions. His intentions notwithstanding, to him the individual context of religious experience governs all church teachings and polity, and the authority of scripture as well. Quoting the theologian Mullins, Hudgins explains, "The individual, not man en masse, is the primary object of God's love. 'God loves the whole world, but the whole is reached by contacting individuals one by one.' Individuals do not respond to God as a part of a group; each acts on his own responsibility. Each must act in his own sovereign power of choice. 'The individual not only must act for himself; he is the only one who can. God has made him competent.'" What matters spiritually and above all is that

individuals or sovereign entities act for themselves alone. "A man's relationship to God is his own responsibility," Hudgins asserts.[102]

The autonomous, local church thus becomes an extension of individual
souls and their interior walks with Christ. By analogy, no one can tell my
particular congregation how it ought to conduct its business. This is the
third principle, the lesson of "The Autonomy of the Local Church." "No
conference, presbyter, diocese, council, association, or convention has any
right of dictation to the individual church or its membership," Hudgins
says. The local church is free to do its own thing—as long as the spirit
leads. But since there is "a direct relationship between the Spirit and the
individual," and since congregational polity best accommodates this relationship, there is no external body or authority to judge decisions made by
particular congregations.[103] Thus the Holy Spirit, in the form of the Board
of Deacons, inevitably shapes the congregation in its own image. Importantly, this kind of autonomy put extraordinary pressure on Baptist ministers throughout the South to maintain the status quo; if a minister rubbed
the congregation the wrong way on the race issue, or any other matter, he
would be promptly dismissed. The polity structure that promised maximum individual freedom ironically proved to suffocate individual freedom
by group consensus.

The question Hudgins could not answer, and did not ask, is what exactly the individual does in the experience of personal regeneration. Does
he confess a creed? No, Baptists have no creed. Does he make a covenant
with God for the salvation of his family? No, there is "no such thing as family or proxy faith." Does he do good works? Of course not; this is papist
nonsense. What then does one do to be saved? In the end, no one can tell
the believer what he or she should do; the salvation experience is pieced
together from whatever fragments of desires, prejudices, and dreams one
brings to the event. Hudgins writes, "If the individual is responsible to God
for himself, then there must be an experience of personal commitment to
the saving grace of God before he can be received into the fellowship of
other equally transformed individuals."[104] Other equally transformed individuals will bring from their solitary encounters a common conviction and
a common identity.

But what creates commonality here? In good Baptist form, Hudgins admits that infants and small children cannot be part of the church; they are
simply not yet equipped with the spiritual tools necessary for personal regeneration. Is there anything then left of the church, of the spiritual community's interrelatedness or worldly presence, not to speak of the Pauline
doctrine of the church as the mystical body of Christ? It seems unlikely.
What could link together these spiritual atoms in a common identity and
shared conviction? Hudgins is left with the accidents of race, class, and
custom. Add to this a final problem. In his insightful book on American

religion, Harold Bloom shows that such spiritual architectures as the one bequeathed by Mullins ironically and inevitably lead to the conclusion that the interiority of the soul's communion with God precedes all religious authority, including not only Roman Catholic hierarchy but even quite possibly the infallible Bible itself. Bloom writes, "If one's undying spirit accepts the love of Jesus, walks with the resurrected Jesus, knows what it is to love Jesus in return, alone with Jesus in the only permanent and perfect communion that ever will be, then there can be no churchly authority over me. As for the authority of Scripture, even it must yield to the direct encounter with the resurrected Jesus."[105] The Spirit blows most vigorously when the shackles of hierarchy and ecumenism are removed; conviction comes down to a fellowship of one.

The will to pure freedom betrays an all-too-typical Baptist quandary. The soul that breaks free from the authorities of scriptural interpretation, hierarchy, and state, not to mention from the demands of justice and mercy, cannot tolerate the limitlessness of its possibilities. (Klansman Sam Bowers and his insatiable drive for world historical greatness prove an exception here.) So the church is created as a depository of shared feeling—local and autonomous—determined by whatever traditions and customs prevail. To be sure, Hudgins would not concede this point for a minute. As he writes, "The only church the New Testament projects is a local, autonomous, independent body, functioning under the leadership of the Holy Spirit."[106] Yet although Hudgins (for obvious theological reasons) must locate final authority in the individual congregation as governed by the Holy Spirit, and not in the individual person, the cards are stacked against the move. Final authority on matters of Christian faith and practice resides in the individual's soul competency before God, configured in community by the historical and social contingencies of the self. The theological content of personal regeneration vaporizes under close scrutiny. All that is left of the experience is the individual's inchoate longing for holiness, a holiness which, in Hudgins's case, approximates the Southern Way of Life.

It bears repeating that the forces threatening piety and holiness are forces that absorb individuality into anonymous collectives. Of the federal government, Hudgins would say, "No one but a moron could fail to see the insidious trend in the last thirty years toward a continuous centralization of government."[107] Hudgins would address political concerns to the extent to which these appear to infringe upon individual competency. In fact, it is surprising how often Hudgins did address political matters, his clearly drawn lines of demarcation between church and state notwithstanding. The cross of Jesus may have nothing to do with social movements like civil rights, but it seems altogether pertinent to states' rights, not to mention moral issues like promiscuity and alcohol and the playing of cards.[108] As the uncensurable Mississippi newspaper editor, Hodding Carter, once said, "It is reasonably certain that if a reincarnated General Sherman were to run for governor of Mississippi as a prohibitionist and Marse Robert E. Lee opposed him as an advocate of repeal, General Sherman would be elected, because more than seventy-five per cent of our population are Baptists, who are committed ideologically to an eleventh commandment: 'Thou shalt not drink'—an admonition which has not prevented dry Mississippi from consuming illegally more whisky per capita than do the adjoining wet states of Arkansas, Louisiana, and Alabama."[109] The point clarifies Hudgins's concerns. When the "wild and socialistic fanaticism" of "the group" intrudes upon the integrity of the individual, Christianity does indeed have social relevance, if only to point out that God is on the side of sobriety, wholesomeness, and individual initiative.[110]

Take the case of "minority groups." Hudgins declares, "Minority groups—and there are many of them—with shrewd planning and political pressure, thrust their wills upon the great majority and those of us who do not wish so to be manipulated are maligned, caricatured and despised."[111] That these groups were often represented by religious persons only emphasizes the insidiousness of the problem. Hudgins bemoaned the pronouncement of "philosophical sophistries" by ministers who seemed more concerned with "Thus saith the people" than "Thus saith the Lord."[112] The fact is: you either rally around the "brotherhood of man" and "ecumenical acceptance" or you rally around "new life in Christ" and the true faith. Those who want to change the social order inevitably put their trust in Washington rather than in God's "regeneration of the individual." Thus reliance on the federal government to solve problems amounts to a betrayal of faith in God (that is, in individual soul competency). Unless the social order mirrors the spiritual order—arranged in autonomous, individual, self-determining units—the potential for danger reaches the whole way down to the individual's spiritual freedom.

Here is exposed the two competing themes of Hudgins's theology: the interiorized experience of the saving Jesus and the articulation of that experience in social existence. Hudgins cavalierly presumes in his sermons and public discourse that these two themes fit together, or rather that the latter follows from the former, or in any case, that there is a quality of evidence in biblical faith that not only legitimates but demands the values of the closed society—that is, states' rights, decentralized government, and the like. But as we have seen, the core experience of salvation—the soul's direct encounter with God—is individual in essence. It cannot graduate into larger corporate or covenantal forms. As Hudgins says, without any recognition of the consequences for church life, "the 'competency of the individual soul' sets the policy and the polity of Baptists."[113] Still, since personal regeneration remains essentially spiritual and asocial, what accounts for Hudgins's ideas about the church views on race and civil rights? Are they taken simply from available cultural and social traditions? Obviously, this is true in part. But not in full.

The experience of personal regeneration does give a certain shape to social existence. The experience is unbroken, unmediated, seamless: it is virginal in texture, guarded against intrusion from external powers. Not to be overlooked is that unmediated harmony with God—the soul's marriage to its heavenly bride—commands powerful racial meanings. The notion of lives triangulated on God, the body, and social purity turns racial homogeneity into a theological—if not a metaphysical—necessity. This is the sad legacy of the Baptist doctrine of "soul competency" as it played itself out in the career of Douglas Hudgins.

The Interior Battle

Like Sam Bowers, terrorist and high priest of the White Knights of the Ku Klux Klan, Hudgins saw the present historical moment as the field of a cosmic battle between spiritual and material forces. "As was the case with the disciples—OUR FUTURE IS NOW! The world in which we will live tomorrow depends on what we do today," Hudgins urged. Resting on the promises of God to save from eternal damnation, Christians "must face the compelling responsibilities of the immediate present." Whatever these responsibilities may involve in exact detail, they are in any case "staggering," requiring nothing less than "the reshaping of the concepts of a pagan world." Hudgins preached, "Worship must change into work; adoration must turn into action; fear must give way to faith; security must be supplanted by self-abandonment. The FUTURE must give way to the PRESENT!"[114]

Hudgins agreed with Bowers that Christians must prepare themselves for combat, but the battlefield, as Hudgins saw it, remained largely interiorized and incorporeal. "Our greatest enemy is not flesh and blood," he said, "it is the intangibles," the "rulers of the darkness of this world," the "spiritual wickedness in high places."[115] The "things" that matter most cannot be won through material struggle or through mortal combat. For the spiritual world reigns supreme over the quotidian matters of our earthy toil. "We deal with [worldly] things," lamented Hudgins, "but place too little value on things of the soul. We have unlocked many secrets of the material world about us . . . but in spiritual conquest we have little experienced the wonder-working constructive power of God made effective by the reality of personal prayer." Herein lies the real landscape of spiritual warfare. When the preacher must speak against the impurities of the day, he does so almost regretfully, certainly hesitantly, because what matters most, and what ultimately matters solely, is that "you, dear friend, individually become a Christian, a follower of the Son of God, a new and transformed person through the spiritual alchemy of regeneration by means of faith in Jesus Christ as your Savior."[116]

Hudgins offered America the chance to repent. (We know by now that Sam Bowers would never extend the possibility of forgiveness to the heretics.) Those sins America ought confess, when they reached some sort of social expression, were nonetheless highly individualized or carnal in nature. "Barbarism, butchery and the concentration camp are not our greatest tragedies." "Paganized materialism" needs to go, as do the more pervasive sins of "promiscuous sex indulgence," "the rise in perversion," "the mania for gambling," and "the wild abandon in revolt against authority."[117] In this manner, sin could take shape in massive powers and institutions but only in ways that threatened the individual's quest for purity: powers like communism and ecumenism, and institutions like the federal government or even, at times, the agencies of the Southern Baptist Convention, especially the Christian Life Commission.[118]

In his widely circulated speech on the "Decade of Destiny," Hudgins forecast the "soaring sixties" as America's pivotal moment. "What is achieved, or not achieved, by the people of God in this ten-year period immediately ahead of us will determine, in my judgment, the continuation of our Christian witness to a needy world, or the deterioration and decay of our citizenship as a nation."[119] Recall Sam Bowers's prediction in early 1964 that "the events which will occur in Mississippi this summer may well determine the fate of Christianity for centuries to come," and the two men both seem eerily posed to seize the world historical moment for all its immense promise. But again, while the forecasts for the future looked very much alike, the theological responses differed dramatically. Hudgins's retreat to a spirituality unspoiled by intercourse with the civil rights movement shies away from the kinds of assaults against authority encouraged by Bowers. If God wishes to bring judgment and retribution against the heretics, he will have to do it himself. And, of course, God will if America continues unrepentently down the path of sinfulness and impiety. But even more importantly, Hudgins urged his listeners to prepare themselves for the "decade of destiny"—for combat with "idolatry and evil"—by nurturing "a Christian concept of moral integrity" that places "the individual soul in harmonious fellowship with a redeeming God."[120] The best way to counter the rulers and powers of the present darkness is to cultivate the inner disciplines of the spiritual life. Only in this way can Christians hope to provide the solutions to problems facing America in the "soaring sixties."

Hudgins's proposal for social change surely would not win him the respect of the White Knights of Ku Klux Klan, who in 1964 began waging
violent war against blacks and civil rights workers. For Hudgins never
failed to remind his listeners and readers that the best way to be about the
business of the soul's competency with God was through faithful attendance of worship services and various other church activities. "The neglect
of public worship, family prayer, and Bible study are greater enemies than
any armed force," he said.[121] Wholesomeness was of the essence. Although
Hudgins did not want to turn faith into morality, as he imagined the social
gospel theologians doing (those modernist liberals in Boston and New
York who threatened the faith's miraculous inner sense), he did not avoid
reducing the visceral intensity of the faith—with the bleeding body of the
Lord at the center—to the cultivation of character and social refinement.
In other words, faith in the cross of Jesus must inspire wholesome living,
civic responsibility, and all around niceness. "Our standard of morals must
be lifted; our social conduct must be elevated," he says.[122] This is an important point. Hudgins would never suggest that the piety of the pure soul
underwrites any sort of asceticism. God forbid the insinuation of a monk-
ish renunciation of the world. Rather, Hudgins was convinced that the individualized nature of the person's relationship with God emphasized in
turn the social value of individual initiative and purity as well as the goods
associated with these values. The church was responsible for the preaching of the Gospel and the nurturing of the soul's perfection, but the
preaching of the Gospel ought to make people industrious, thrifty, and
wholesome.

As pastor of a congregation ever eager to grow in membership and budget, there was also, of course, an undeniable savvy in his contention. By
the year 1964 the membership of First Baptist significantly declined to the
middle 4,000s from a high of 5,556 in 1952. Hudgins needed to get people back into the pews of his sanctuary, and back to his downtown church
from the suburbs. Certainly, he would not for a moment have suggested
that regular church participation was tantamount to genuine religion.
Church membership represented the proper and indeed the only context
for nurturing the individual soul's fellowship with God and the attainment
of "new and higher standard of morality and personal character."[123] But by
calling the faithful away from civil rights and social existence, Hudgins was
able to preserve the purity of the closed church and the closed society for
the sake of the closed Gospel. It is no exaggeration to say that one can simply not understand white indifference to black suffering and liberation
during the civil rights movement without understanding the religion of
William Douglas Hudgins.[124]

There are meaningful differences between the revered and genteel minister to Jackson's political and social elites and the seething Imperial Wiz-

ard of the White Knights of the Ku Klux Klan. Nonetheless, the success of Bowers's violent mission depended largely on the kind of Gospel Hudgins eloquently preached to white Christians in the spacious sanctuary of the First Baptist Church and over the airwaves of the state and throughout the South. If you were a Klan militant searching the night for the civil rights heretics, you would count it fortunate that the pure souls had turned their sights inward.

FOUR

Inside Agitator: Ed King's Church Visits

Breaking Free

WHEN Ed King surveyed the white Christian establishment in Mississippi on the eve of Freedom Summer, he saw a people afraid to let go, paralyzed by an intricate knottiness, binding the heart and the soul; he saw people whose imaginations had closed tight against the hurt of others. Here was segregation: the image of a man in the mental hospital at Whitfield, walking four steps out, and four steps in, unable to walk further because he has sketched out an invisible line around his little world and is afraid to step outside it.[1] Perhaps the man has once or twice moved beyond his boundaries, but having caught sight of a great unrest, retreated with heightened fears and panicky condemnations. What he fears is the letting go, the openness to the new, the unshackling of his self-imposed tutelage to tradition. He fears energies unchecked and uncommon; fierce passions of the spirit and of the senses, energies offending the pure of heart.

Ed King knew well this bondage, this captivity to fear and custom. As a child in Vicksburg, he had lived the same kind of segregated life as any other white Southerner. He learned "the racial facts of life early."[2] He learned that the patterns of segregation were absolute, so deeply ingrained in social existence that they did not need to be explicitly defended, articulated, or otherwise thought much about. He was taught that he was superior "not to people but to hate and resentment," and that no member of the King family should look on others with condescension. He was told to use good manners, courtesy, and the Golden Rule, and to revere "traditional American beliefs about democracy, justice, and equality."[3] At the same time, white superiority was a fact taken for granted. King found no better description of his own Mississippi upbringing than Lillian Smith's reflection on her Southern childhood: "I do not remember how or when, but by the time I had learned that God is love, that Jesus is His Son and came to give us more abundant life, that all men are brothers with a common Father, I also knew that I was better than a Negro, that all black folks have their place and must be kept in it, that a terrifying disaster would befall the South if ever I treated a Negro as my social equal."[4] This knowledge was absorbed by King as part of his coming of age in the closed society.

Yet none of the teachings that shaped this ethos seemed overtly racist: most white children of educated parents were discouraged from using "nigger" as an epithet or exhibiting crude forms of racism in polite company. Middle-class whites liked to imagine such behavior as more characteristic of lower-class whites and white-trash types whose pedigrees were often more suspect than those of many black people. King rehearsed a different social convention. You were to stick yourself into the world with the confidence of an aristocrat, with the conviction that the racial universe you inhabited represented God's and nature's careful selection and civilization's finest work. Because the future belonged to you, you were to think— if you must think at all—that Jim Crow is fine, that this is the way things are in the South and the way they will always be. The ordering of things, you were taught, ought never engender unkindness or cruelty, but the noblest of affections. Black folk and their humble lot could even be romanticized. The patrician sentiments of William Alexander Percy's widely read *Lanterns on the Levee* continued to rule the hearts of many white Christians. "The black man is our brother," wrote Percy, "a younger brother, not adult, not disciplined, but tragic, pitiable, and lovable; act as his brother and be patient."[5]

In Vicksburg, where King was raised, black yard men worked silently under hot suns and driving rains, always taking their meals on the backs steps of the house or under a shading tree. Their names were mysterious and exotic, like the Kings' hired hand, Mose. Black "mammies" patiently cared for children, and let them fall asleep in their arms. In the early mornings and late afternoons black women walked to and from white homes to do the washing for their employers. Colorful bundles of laundry wrapped in bedspreads were balanced on their heads as they made their way through the streets, sometimes humming or singing a spiritual.[6] Black people came into white neighborhoods almost every day on their mule-drawn wagons to sell fresh vegetables. King enjoyed the sight of these wagons slowly moving down boulevards beneath canopies of oak trees; sometimes he got to ride along, or even hear a story from an old bearded man who kept the reins.

Shanties and shot-gun shacks were considered quaint features of the Southern landscape, even though few whites ever set foot inside the dwellings of their domestics and hired hands. In Vicksburg, whites lived in spacious homes along the lush hills near the Mississippi river; blacks lived mostly in the hollows below, untouched by roads, sidewalks, plumbing, and electricity, with only dirt trails to connect their commons with the town. Rusted mailboxes leaned in crooked rows at the start of the paths; not even the U.S. mail traversed farther to the homes of blacks. In winter the smoke from the wood fires rose to the whites on the hilltops. When a shanty caught fire, as often happened with the poorly built chimneys and fireplaces, whites would send old clothing and canned goods through delegates from their churches and civic organizations. Helping the poor blacks in wintertime was "the proper role of a white Christian," as King described the conventional wisdom, even though a vocal minority of white church goers always insisted that the "nigras" should take care of themselves, even when homeless and destitute.[7]

During the Christmas vacation of King's senior year in high school in 1953, one of the many tornados that sweep through Mississippi in the winter hit Vicksburg. The result was massive destruction of homes, churches, and public buildings. More than forty residents of the town were trapped under collapsing structures and killed, including several of King's school acquaintances. King had lost a close friend in an automobile accident only weeks earlier; now in the aftermath of the tornado's trail of destruction and death, he was brought face to face with human suffering and mortality unlike any he had encountered before. As he began volunteer relief work with the Red Cross, he was brought into contact with black victims of the storm, seeing for the first time, in the prevailing atmosphere of tragedy, the poverty and squalor of his black neighbors. "I stood in the hilltop yard of a friend and looked down on what had once been a black neighborhood in the valley below Fort Hill. The streets were not paved and firetrucks and ambulances had been unable to drive in the mud after the storm. Injured people had to be carried to the hilltop. Several blocks of houses had been completely burned out. I was not the only student to realize this was partially the result of segregation, that there was no such thing as separate but equal. Before this I had been blind."[8] The appearance of the black houses, yards, and gardens, still burning days after the fires in white neighborhoods had been controlled, opened his eyes to black suffering. These families did not lose their homes as a result of the tornado's aftermath, he concluded; they were victims of a social system that was not willing either to protect them or provide them with equal treatment. His moral imagination was stretched in new and unfamiliar ways—so much so that when he stood at the crest of the hill in Vicksburg in the wake of the devastating tornado and looked down upon the waste of houses and buildings in the black quarters below, he was ready to rethink those patterns of segregation that he had once considered part and parcel of God's natural design.

King's broadening social vision had profound religious sources. Ironic though it may seem, the white segregated Methodist church in Mississippi prepared him for a new perception of race and social order. The discovery that the national church held views radically different from those of his fellow white Mississippi Methodists raised unsettling questions in King's mind about the faith of his fathers and the theological presuppositions of the closed society. He recalls, "I soon became aware of strong liberal statements of the national church favoring integration (and the contradictions of the actual practice of segregation in the church)."[9] The church introduced him to a theological and moral debate on racial segregation, pointing to it at annual youth conferences and in national publications like *Concern* and *Motive* as a practice incompatible with the Gospel. In fact, as early as 1944, the General Conference of the United Methodist Church had stated that "no race is superior or self-sufficient" and had proudly affirmed the equal protection of all races "through the agencies of law and order."[10] The 1954 Supreme Court decision in *Brown vs. Board of Education*—coming a year after the Vicksburg tornado—would be supported widely throughout the denomination's leadership, garnering the formal endorsement of the Woman's Division of Christian Service (May 1954), the Council of Bishops (November 1954), and the Board of Social and Economic Relations (January 1955). A decade of progressive social teaching on race pointed conclusively toward integration as the social policy most consistent with Christian faith and practice. The 1955 statement by the Board of Social and Economic Relations was a natural extension of the denomination's tradition, encouraging as it did all Methodist congregations to "move resolutely forward toward the goal of full participation of the people of all races in the life of the church and the community."[11] Through its progressive agencies and publications, the church carved out a social space where "gradual change in our own thought patterns was possible," initiating King and other young men and women into a community of students and ministers who encouraged each other to question "the system."[12]

Doubts about his family began to plague him. He wondered why his parents cautioned moral restraint, even as the savage inequalities of Jim Crow became open to rare public scrutiny in the aftermath of the storm. Charity alone did not satisfy. The Gospel he heard preached in church and nurtured at home required more than getting things back to normal. He had assumed his parents understood that. But he began to have doubts. His father and mother, whom he had greatly admired, seemed reluctant to follow through on their own admonitions of toleration and decency.[13] There was something wrong with a people—and not only his parents but the adult leaders of the church and the community—who preached love for all humanity but who, at the same time, forced him, with direct and indirect threats of shunning and shame, to renounce love and to distance himself from blacks. King began to see that his parents had betrayed a principle they had held dear. He came to believe that in sequestering black people in their dismal quarters and bottoms, whites had also sequestered themselves in spiritual and physical isolation. He began to understand "that the warped, distorted frame we have put around every Negro child from birth is around every white child also." He felt shamed by his parents' failure, and frightened, and yet at the same time strangely liberated, for he understood "that they were no longer as powerful as I had thought."[14] He would not seek their approval of his vocation in civil rights.

King entered Millsaps College in the fall of 1954. Although his decision was based largely on the prestige of the school in Methodist circles, many of the school's faculty members and students had begun participating in an interracial alliance called the Intercollegiate Fellowship, which included Ole Miss, Jackson College (later named Jackson State University), Mississippi State University, and Tougaloo College. (An informal relationship between faculty and students at Millsaps and Tougaloo had existed since the 1940s.) The president of the Intercollegiate Fellowship was Tougaloo professor C. B. Lawyer, and King himself served as secretary. But the driving force of the interracial alliance was Tougaloo professor Ernst Borinski, a Jewish humanist who fled Nazi Germany in 1938. After serving with the U.S. forces in the war and later earning his doctorate in sociology, Borinski had picked Tougaloo College as a fitting home for his radical scholarship and activism. From his "Social Studies Lab" in the dingy basement of a class building, he introduced students to innovative theories on racial justice and social order; lively debates gave birth in time to the bimonthly meetings of the Intercollegiate Fellowship. That is, until the Citizens' Council learned of the meetings and of Millsaps's support, and of the even more unsettling fact that Borinski had been tutoring an interracial group in the Russian language in the Millsaps-Wilson Library. Pressure was immediately put on administrators at the participating schools to disband the fellowship. Reports in local newspapers of Borinski's insidious influence on Mississippi's impressionable young people further intensified the concern.[15]

Still, nothing much came of outside pressures until King's senior year. In the spring of 1958, the Millsaps Christian Council, under the leadership of King and philosophy professor Robert Bergmark, organized a forum on "The Christian and Race Relations." The Millsaps group invited to campus a young Methodist layman named Glenn Smiley, who was also a leader in the Fellowship of Reconciliation, a Quaker peace initiative. When the Citizens' Council learned of Smiley's affiliation with the New York-based organization, it quickly made the college public enemy number one. Professor Borinski's scandalous comment during a related event that "racial segregation violates Christian principles" solidified white opposition to the forum.[16] The Citizens' Council moved into action, with Ellis Wright, the president of the Jackson chapter, telling college administrators via newspaper reporters, "It is intolerable for Millsaps College, right here in the heart of Mississippi, to be in the apparent position of undermining everything we are fighting for. I tell you frankly and without rancor that the time has come for a showdown."[17] It was not enough that Millsaps administrators cancel the race relations forum. The Board of Trustees wanted to know how Millsaps stood on the central issue of the day: did it support integration or segregation? After deliberations, the Board issued the statement that "segregation always has been, and is now, the policy of Millsaps College. There is no thought, purpose, or intention . . . to change this policy."[18]

By the time King graduated with a degree in English literature in May of 1958, his commitments to racial justice were solidly in place. His decision to study theology at Boston University seemed to him a natural next step, even though it created inevitable conflicts with his parents and the Mississippi church. Boston University was the alma mater of Martin Luther King, Jr., and was widely known as a hotbed of social gospel teaching and radical political activism. His teachers in the School of Theology would include Paul Deats, Walter Muelder, Harold Beck, and Allan Knight Chalmers.

Deats, a native Southerner and later chairman of the Fellowship of Reconciliation, had moved to Boston University from a school in Texas, where his support of racial equality had made his academic post unrenewable. In the School of Theology he taught courses on pacifism and race relations. Muelder, along with Peter Bertocci and Richard Millard, continued to work in the spirit of the influential school of thought known as Boston personalism, in vogue in American philosophy circles since the 1920s. The Boston personalists sought to rescue human sociality as the "ontological ultimate" from positivistic and materialistic views of the self. Many theologians found the personalist philosophy helpful in developing ontologies of social compassion and radical community—foundations for the more explicit social gospel theologies and biblical hermeneutics aired throughout the School of Theology.[19] Muelder, who served as dean of the School of Theology from 1945–1968, had written extensively on social ethics and Christian responsibility and had also taught courses on "History of Theories of Social Reform" and "Christianity and Race Relations."[20] For his part, Harold Beck was considered the "patriarch of the Old Testament Department," whose courses on the prophets and biblical exegesis illumined for King the rich Judaic sources of Christian social justice.

The most tireless champion of race relations among the Boston faculty, however, was Allan Chalmers. In 1948, Chalmers arrived at the School of Theology from his pastorate at Broadway Tabernacle in New York City to help establish the Department of Practical Theology. Chalmers had once been the chairman of the NAACP Legal Defense Fund, a member of the

Board of the American Civil Liberties Union, and a key player in the 1931 acquittal of the Scottsboro boys (which he described in 1951 book, *They Shall Be Free*).[21] His courses on homiletics and social ethics were deeply informed by his political commitments; but even more, students learned about racial matters from anecdotal reports of—and sometimes participation in—his weekend trips to New York, to Washington, and to the deep South in the cause of social justice.[22]

King also studied with the black theologian and dean of Marsh Chapel, Howard Thurman, whose reflections on prayer and mysticism profoundly shaped his own deliberate piety. Thurman's far-ranging intellect and interest in mysticism were not without a keen political dimension. His contemplative essays and books were balanced by meditations on "Jesus and the Disinherited" as well as by socially concerned articles in religious magazines. "Jesus rejected hatred," Thurman wrote in a prose poem published in the Methodist student magazine *Motive*. "It was not because he lacked the vitality or the strength. It was not because he lacked incentive. Jesus rejected hatred because he saw that hatred meant death to the mind, death to the spirit, death to communion with his Father." [23]

Through the consortium of theological schools called the Boston Theological Institute, King attended lectures by Paul Tillich and Reinhold Niebuhr, who both taught at Harvard at the time (the latter as a visiting professor). Niebuhr introduced King to the theologies of Karl Barth and Dietrich Bonhoeffer (the latter had been Niebuhr's personal friend until his execution in a German concentration camp in 1945). The writings of these theologians helped the young Mississippian nurture a confessional radicalism that balanced theological integrity with political involvement.

In Boston, King also discovered a wide range of work groups exploring the intersections of faith and social justice. His commitments to many of these groups became more important to him than academic life. In particular, through the American Friends Service Committee and the Fellowship of Reconciliation, he came into contact with Quaker pacifists and religious radicals who were turning their sights toward civil rights causes in the South. Although King had always assumed he would finish seminary and serve as a pastor in a local Methodist church back in Mississippi, his increasing interests in progressive social movements led him in a different direction.

In March of 1960, a month after the first of the sit-ins in Woolworth stores in Greensboro, North Carolina, he took a leave from seminary to volunteer in Montgomery, Alabama. In a role similar to his later activism in Mississippi, King worked in the Alabama capital city as a pastoral liaison between student activists—incarcerated and often beaten—and white ministers and church women. His purpose was to set up interracial meetings and associations in hopes that whites and blacks together might be able to talk and pray through the long night of desegregation.

King had not intended to get himself arrested. Plainly, the nature of his role as a mediator between whites and blacks was at cross-purposes with such an outcome—as was his unfinished bachelor of divinity in Boston. Nonetheless, a police raid of the black-owned Regal Cafe at lunch on March 31 found King in company with a student group from MacMurray College in Jacksonville, Illinois, and local and black activists, some of whom were affiliated with Martin Luther King Jr.'s, Southern Christian Leadership Conference.[24] Twenty persons in all were arrested and found guilty of disorderly conduct—behavior "calculated to create a breach of the peace," as Judge D. Eugene Loe stated. Local press coverage of the story described a racial situation taking shape inside the café, led by the white Illinoisans and Ed King ("a minister from Boston" stated the *Montgomery Advertiser*), with police officers arriving on the scenes just in time to spoil the plans.[25] King's innocence was lost, and with it his naive thoughts of returning to Mississippi the courageous and esteemed preacher of the social gospel. For, as he now understood, "to be a prisoner accused of being a traitor made it virtually impossible to come back home and assume a regular ministry."[26] Howard Thurman had been right when he told King one day after class that he should not expect anything like an ordinary vocation in the church.

Yet if King had been concerned about appearances before his arrest, the actual experience of incarceration only intensified his zeal for the movement. He reemerged unbowed, telling reporters in Alabama that the arrest of the integrated diners came about because "police state conditions" prevailed under Governor John Patterson's rule.[27]

On the afternoon of June 7, two hours after receiving a $100 fine for participating in the March 31 luncheon, King and a fellow Methodist minister, Elroy Embry, were arrested for attempting to eat together in the restaurant of a downtown hotel. The second arrest played to King's inimitable brand of dark comedy. King had been boarding for several days at the Jefferson Davis Hotel, and had previously dined with white clergymen in the hotel restaurant. So when he asked the hotel manager on the morning of the trial if he could bring a minister to lunch that day, the manager seemed surprised he had even asked. Sure he could, he was a guest of the hotel. At noon King arrived with a black colleague to the Plantation Room of the Jefferson Davis Hotel and took a table. Thus the second arrest. King was convicted of trespassing in his own hotel and sentenced to hard labor for a week. In local and national papers, King explained to reporters that the long of days chopping wood and cutting grass, supervised by guards riding horseback on the roadside, caused him no despair; on the contrary,

he had been "morally strengthened" by his attack on the "idol of segregation." He told an Alabama reporter, "I consider myself in approximately
the same situation as early Christian martyrs who were put to death for refusing to put incense on the statue of the emperor. We refused to put a
pinch of incense on the idol of segregation." For those white Christians of
Montgomery who could not understand the significance of the analogy, he
offered the following observation: "I'm getting along all right with the
other prisoners and, call it irony if you will, Embry and I cut grass together
Wednesday and we probably will again today."[28]

Still, he refused to give up all hope of parish ministry in Mississippi. He
would just need more time and patience. He believed he could stall, stay
away from Mississippi a few more years, finish his coursework from the
spring semester and his degree in divinity, perhaps work in Northern and
Western parishes for a while, and eventually the dust would settle, making it possible for him to return home without fears of a hostile reception.[29]
Eventually King did return to Mississippi, but not because the dust had
settled. Rather he found himself compelled to rethink his idea of the Christian ministry. Elroy Embry's pastoral advice hit home. "[You] have made
many friends here," Embry wrote to King, "not with the upper class but
with the middle and lower class people." Embry charged his white friend
to have courage, to lay aside his fears, "because as long as I live I will stand
by you in whatever takes place." The black pastor spoke with prescience
of King's coming vocation when he concluded: "Don't forget, 'We are fools
for Christ.'"[30]

Embry's words took root in King's imagination. Shortly after receiving
the letter, King wrote to a ministerial colleague in Mississippi, "There is
still one other possibility. If I want to be minister of a Christian church and
if I really believe the Christian Church offers the only possibilities of any
real solutions to any problems, then I must broaden my conception of the
Christian Church—and even of the Methodist Church."[31]

In 1960 King's parents, Ralph and Julia, were forced to move from the
state. Although King's father had worked in Vicksburg as an engineer for
the Mississippi River Commission (an agency operated by the federal government and thus not directly affected by the Citizens' Council boycotts of
traitorous businesses), the Council had other ways of informing mothers
and fathers that they had failed in their duties as guardians of the closed
society. With help from the Sovereignty Commission, the Citizens' Council put direct pressure on the King family (rather than on the employer)
through carefully placed innuendos and hints. Look at the parents of Ed
King, the rumors spreading around Vicksburg cautioned: imagine the kind
of people whose son becomes a communist sympathizer and champion of
black revolutionary activity. These parents must not be the patriots and
good Americans we thought. Friends soon stopped speaking to the Kings;

social engagements came to a standstill. Ralph and Julia were embarrassed and ashamed, and they were also frightened for their son. But they were also frightened of him, of what he'd become, of the company he kept, of what good white townspeople continued to say about him.[32]

In 1960, shortly before they left Mississippi, the parents were visited by J. W. Legett, the district superintendent of the Methodist Church for the region covering Vicksburg. His purpose was to console the parents, to reassure them of his prayerful support during these difficult times when friends and neighbors, even fellow members of their church, scorned them. In their home that evening, the superintendent told the Kings: "I want to tell you something very important, and I hope this makes you feel better. I do not for a minute believe you are communists. I have listened to some of the people who say you are, and I don't accept their arguments. However, I'm afraid your son is."[33] The truth of the matter—that Ed King was no more communist than Medgar Evers or Fanny Lou Hamer, that the closed society needed convenient categories in which to impound its dissidents and critics—was of no consequence. The image of the King family had been irreparably soiled. The parents' disgrace could only be suffered in exile.

In June of 1961, Ed King moved to Montana with his wife Jeannette, where he spent the summer circuit preaching in a number of small rural churches. Ed and Jeannette (also a Mississippi native) had met in college at Millsaps. Jeanette had earned a master's degree in social work at Boston University while Ed completed his theological education. In the fall of 1961, the two moved back across country to Massachusetts, where he took a Methodist parish in Worcester and Jeannette worked with children in a community center and an orphanage. King's spotted police record occasionally made him consider putting down roots in Massachusetts, but as the weeks rolled passed—and as he watched the drama of James Meredith's integration of Ole Miss unfold from his parsonage in New England—he began to think that the closed society might be cracking at last, "that the process of change was really starting to happen." He wanted to be a part of that change. To be sure, King had received no encouragement from Mississippi Methodist leaders to return to the state. In fact, in the spring of 1961, Bishop Marvin Franklin of Mississippi, fearing reprisals from Citizens' Council bullies and mobilized parishioners, had ordained King to the ministry of the Christian church without any denominational affiliation to a conference of the United Methodist Church.[34] But the unusual ordination only underscored the peculiar nature of his calling, and pushed him to rethink further his understanding of the Christian church and his own identity and vocation as a Christian minister. "I had agonized for years about how I could go back and be a priest in the church. But I had never really understood that I had defined the church as the white church. Now it was time I simply say of myself: I am called to be a priest in the Church. I will see now what's possible and what's not." He realized he had defined the church in "racist terms," as the *white* church no less, but now he opened himself up to "the Lord's call whatever it might be, wherever it might lead him."[35]

In November of 1962, King returned from Boston to Alabama on one of his many trips to stand trial for violating private property rights. After the familiar routine was concluded, with a guilty sentence handed out and an appeal filed, he traveled to Mississippi for Thanksgiving and met with several white friends from Millsaps and a few sympathetic representatives of the Methodist church. The message he got from them was "never come back—leave, leave, leave. Never come further east in the South than Austin, never further south than Chapel Hill."[36] But King also visited with two old acquaintances from the Intercollegiate Fellowship, Ernst Borinski and Medgar Evers. Borinski emphasized the strategic advantages involved in King's ministry in Mississippi as well as the possibility that progressive whites might help check the "complete demoralization" of the state."[37] For his part, Medgar Evers, who had become the NAACP field secretary for Mississippi, told King point blank he should return; in fact, he must return to fill the vacancy of the chaplaincy at Tougaloo College. King recalls Evers's words: "You have to come back because we need you, because this, my friend, is your calling."[38]

The Kings returned to Mississippi in January of 1963. Ed came as "a white Christian minister in the black Church" and Jeannette as a part-time instructor in psychology and sociology at the college.[39] The Methodist hierarchy looked on him with suspicion as the native son who had already made a name for himself through his civil rights activities and his arrests. He had not only embarrassed the white church, which certainly had no idea what else was in store for it, but also brought humiliation on his mother and father, living now in Memphis. But King's thoughts were not with the opinions of the state's church leaders or even with his parents. For the twenty-six-year-old white Methodist minister who had heard the Lord's perplexing call in 1953 (and Medgar Evers's in 1962) and followed after, the composition of family and social relations had been entirely reshaped. His family was now his brothers and sisters in the movement. His Tougaloo congregation and colleagues, his fellow clergy committed to justice, his friends in SNCC—these were all like blood kin. Along with Evers and John Salter (a white sociology professor at Tougaloo), King became one of the key organizers of the civil rights movement in Jackson.[40] In John Dittmer's view, King was "the most visible white activist in the Mississippi movement, and he paid a heavy price for honoring his convictions."[41]

Once back in Mississippi, King entered the whirlwind. On May 28, he appeared with Salter, Ann Moody, and Joan Trumpauer in a Woolworth sit-in; the photograph of white hoodlums pelting Salter, Moody, and Trumpauer with ashtrays, catsup, and cigarettes illustrated to an international audience the gratuitous violence of Mississippi's closed society. On June 12, his friend Medgar Evers was murdered as he returned home after a speaking engagement. Several weeks later, after King helped organize massive demonstrations in the wake of Evers's murder, he and Salter barely survived an automobile accident when their Rambler was hit by a car driven by a black woman, who had swerved to avoid colliding with a car driven by an Ole Miss student. King suffered a deep gashing scar that disfigured the right side of his face. Although the accident strengthened his resolve to keep going; it also gave him pause (and ample material) to consider the dark magnitude of his struggle. King claimed that accident had been orchestrated by the Citizens' Council, basing his judgment on the fact that the student's father was a leader at the time in the Jackson Citizens' Council. (John Salter's own report disavows any conspiracy.)

In October of 1963 he was selected by Bob Moses as the Freedom Vote candidate for lieutenant governor of Mississippi, as the running mate of the black Delta pharmacist Aaron Henry.[42] The following year King and his wife Jeannette served as local organizers of the Summer Project and the Mississippi Freedom Democratic party. Though neither joined SNCC—the line between members and nonmembers at the time seemed to them porous and appropriately undefined—King and Jeannette were fully involved with the voter registration initiative, the formation of freedom schools, and the MFDP challenge. Still, his most remarkable civil rights activity, certainly from the perspective of his vocation as pastor to a movement congregation, was his leadership of the extraordinary church visits campaign—an attempt to desegregate and agitate white conservative and moderate churches, which (as he saw it) set the stage for the necessity of Freedom Summer.

Inside Agitator

On Easter Sunday 1964, about twenty minutes before the eleven o'clock worship hour—sadly depicted by Martin Luther King, Jr., as the most segregated hour of the week—a black and a white man stood together outside the doors of Jackson's prestigious Galloway Memorial Methodist Church. The two men introduced themselves to the church guards whose business it was to protect the church sanctuary from black or interracial groups of worshipers: Bishop Charles F. Golden of Los Angeles, the leader of the black Central Jurisdiction for the Methodist Church in Mississippi, and Bishop James K. Matthews of Boston.[43] The two men hoped to worship at Galloway on Easter morning. But one of the church guards had said that would not be possible. The bishops should attend a black Methodist church or even better return to their home state and go to church some place there. Bishop Golden replied that Mississippi was his home state, and he wanted to worship with his Christian brothers and sisters at Galloway.

A man named Nat Rogers, chairman of the board at Galloway and a prominent banker and civic leader in Jackson, soon arrived on the scene. His tone was less confrontational than the ushers, almost apologetic. Still it would not be possible for the bishops to attend the service. The church's policy, enacted a year earlier on January 14, 1963, was clear on the matter: "It is not un-Christian that we prefer to remain an all-white congregation. The practice of the separation of the races in Galloway Memorial Methodist Church is a time-honored tradition. We earnestly hope that the perpetuation of that tradition will never be impaired."[44] While Rogers informed Golden and Matthews of the policy, several policemen gathered in the periphery, awaiting the go-ahead from the ushers to arrest the intruders and take them to city jail. More than a dozen people had been arrested at Galloway during the previous weeks; nine more would be arrested on Easter Sunday outside other churches in Jackson. The Methodist bishops, however, would be spared. Nat Rogers and his church guards escorted the two men around the church to a side walkway, where, out of the eye of curious church members, they told Golden and Matthews to leave well enough alone and take off. The bishops obliged, but not before leaving with the guards copies of an open letter to the congregation.

The bishops' letter is a gentle, prodding entreaty to fellow Christians who have (it was hoped only momentarily) forgotten the central message of the Gospel, namely, that all humanity is reconciled to God and each other through Jesus. "There cannot . . . be any true Christian worship at all which is not intercession in behalf of all mankind," the bishops said, "for Jesus Christ died and rose again for *all*." How tragic that a church could so misshape the Gospel that the Easter celebration becomes removed from the lived experience of social relations. The letter continued: "For *this is* Easter Sunday, which offers not only victory over death, but infinite possibility for renewal of individuals and of churches and of society. Easter is an occasion for entirely new attitudes and fresh beginnings. We believe that the Feast of the Resurrection affirms life for *all* men. All Christians together believe that Jesus, the Christ, is the Living Lord of *all*. Furthermore, for Christians every Sunday is a commemoration of Easter and its meaning."[45] That afternoon, the Reverend W. J. Cunningham, Galloway's pastor of six months and successor of Dr. W. B. Selah (who had resigned in protest of the church's closed-door policy), painfully reflected on the letter and the events of the morning with a senior member of the church. Cunnginham had told Rogers before the worship service that the two bishops should be admitted to the sanctuary "on my responsibility."[46] But his recommendation had been ignored, not only by Rogers but also apparently by his young assistant minister, Clay Lee. As Cunningham began to unburden his heart and express his great distress with their decision, he broke down and wept. He told his parishioner that "the mental and emotional stress of [his] ministry at Galloway had become almost unbearable." Even though Cunningham had nowhere else to go and only recently had assumed the pastorate of the church, he would have to step down.

The Easter visitation at Galloway was part of an ongoing effort to crack the iceberg of the closed society at its most sensitive point, its extraordinary devotion to the church. Led by Ed King, along with a student volunteers, ministers, and professors, the church visits were exercises in civil disobedience informed by a radical theological vision that sought "creative revolutionary interpretations of Christian responsibility embedded in practical experience," as one northern minister explained.[47] As the campaign played out during the following months, it had all the makings of a theater of the absurd, wherein the myriad religious and racial contradictions of the closed society became evidenced and pantomimed. King was relentless in his role of the Lord's prophet, rendering judgments and demands with a righteous anger bordering on arrogance. Reverend Cunningham breaking down under the weight of emotional stress was a small price to pay for such dramatic symbolism as the church guards forcing away vicars of Christ himself.

The initiative in Mississippi was inspired, in large part, by civil rights events that had taken place in Birmingham in the spring of 1963. Martin Luther King, Jr., had organized a massive protest against the city's Jim Crow ordinances, especially its segregated public accommodations. Much of the nation had watched in horror as Police Commissioner Bull Connor—a practicing Methodist layman—commanded his police force to repel nonviolent demonstrators in Kelly Ingram Park with police dogs and firehoses. During Holy Week, small, sometimes integrated, groups of churchpeople were blocked from attending Protestant services at numerous white churches in Birmingham. Watching the story unfold from Jackson, Ed King believed that the hypocrisy on display in Birmingham's churches was not lost even on white Mississippi Christians. Look at Birmingham! Here are people who profess faith in the reconciling God actively turning away from the church their black brothers and sisters in the faith. King found the subversive and symbolic possibilities of the so-called "church testings" irresistible. He intended to make them an integral part of the Jackson movement.

King knew well the enthusiasm his fellow Mississippians exhibited toward matters ecclesiastical. If not "Christ-haunted," as Flannery O'Connor described her low-church Georgian compatriots, they were certainly Jesus's very good friends. He walked with them and talked with them throughout the Magnolia State. Evangelistic crusades in every hamlet summoned thousands of the unsaved and the backsliding to surrender their lives to Jesus; to trust in the one whose blood ransom paid the debt of their sins. People's minds were stirred by images of the dying Christ, bleeding and suffering for the sins of humanity, hanging on the cross, ridiculed by the sinister mobs. If they believed in Jesus, they would some day, in the twinkling of an eye, in a moment no man knows, be taken up in to the sky, there to meet their savior with millions of living and millions more sleeping, now-awakening souls. In Mississippi, thousands sang, in tiny wood-framed churches and in modern, plush sanctuaries:

> All to Jesus I surrender, all to him I freely give;
> I will ever love and trust him, in his presence daily live.
> I surrender all, I surrender all;
> All to Thee, my blessed Savior, I surrender all.

Ed King knew this language and loved its evocative energy and visual concreteness—its remarkable power to transform lives. But the time had come, he believed, for the white church to live out the Gospel much more concretely than in the past. The white church needed a visceral reminder that it was steering perilously close to idolatry in its devotion to the Southern Way of Life.[48]

King also understood the deep interconnection between the church and other dimensions of social and political life. "As well as being friends, comrades, and neighbors," he explained, "white Mississippians were often blood relatives, cousins of fairly complicated computations, and truly an inclusive family. To be an unquestioning [and] accepted member of this family could be a beautiful thing."[49]

His strategy in the months leading up to the summer of 1964 was to crack the church's closed doors in hopes that a breakthrough would shake the foundations of the state's public institutions, social practices, and political establishment. He hoped that the opening up of the closed doors would inspire, in turn, the opening up of the closed society. He said, "If white moderates, stirred by a Christian conscience that had been pricked at one of their few vulnerable points, began to support any kind of change in racial patterns in Jackson, even (or, perhaps, especially) at the Church—then the door was open, not just the church door, but the door to the possibilities of moderate, gradual change in all Mississippi."[50] Thus was born the campaign of the "church visits" in Jackson.

What did the campaign accomplish? By objective measures of success, it seems ill-fated and fruitless; not much changed as a result. Yet of all the acts of nonviolent direct protest leveled against the closed society, none registered as a more painful reminder of the South's own failed ideals than the pervasive inhospitality displayed toward black and interracial groups of Christians seeking a space on a pew. Ed King was the driving conviction and animating humor of the church visits—the principal organizer of the campaign against the segregated church in Jackson.

The thinking he brought to the task was simple at its heart, and yet severe in its demands. If a person calls himself a Christian, he must give up everything and follow Christ. In Mississippi in 1963 and 1964, "everything" meant, first and foremost, giving up the practices of white supremacy; but it also meant giving up class privilege, educational pretension, anything that kept one from opening up and going the whole way. The Christian life must be lived for others. There is something miraculous and mysterious, and possibly even hilarious, about the idea of people being recreated for solidarity with the outsider and the oppressed, tangled up with the struggles and delights of others. For King, this was the message of the Gospel, the joyful news of salvation.

Ed King's mission as church reformer, and at times theological prankster, of the civil rights movement was to enact the subversive implications of the Christian's new creation—to demonstrate that obedience to Jesus's call leads one out of oneself into a strange, new world of agape love and compassion. The church visits campaign embodied this mission in an unforgettable way, enacting time and again spectacular scenarios that teased out of the various antagonists darkly comic, ironic, and self-contradictory assertions about God, Jesus Christ, and the church. The moral and, even more, the theological bankruptcy of the white church was dramatically expressed. Once they took root in the Jackson movement, the church visits would come to illustrate (from King's perspective) the theological context in which Freedom Summer became a strategic necessity and a prophetic demand. King's relentless and creative confrontations earned him the description by *Christian Century* magazine of "Mississippi's Pastor Niemöller," the Christian minister who worked in the German resistance against Hitler. At the same time, his feverish activism also inclined local religious leaders like J. W. Legett to brand him an "unfrocked minister" and "an irresponsible troublemaker with mental problems."[51] Or as one critic in Ohio penned, "a lazy no good bum and a hypocrite."[52]

The Church Visits

In late May of 1963, a year before the two Methodist bishops' visit to Jackson, King conducted a biracial pray-in on the steps of the downtown post office. Wearing a clerical collar and purple yoke, he refused to leave when confronted by law officials; as two black inmates carried his outstretched body to a police wagon, he was heard singing "God is on our side."[53] But the first organized visits to churches were not made until June, when groups from Tougaloo College appeared on the front steps of the First Baptist Church and the Galloway Memorial Methodist Church. First Baptist's refusal of the group was immediate and unmitigated, surprising no one. More unexpected was the reaction at Galloway Memorial.

Dr. W. B. Selah, Galloway's much admired pastor of nineteen years, noticed on his way to the morning worship service that a group of blacks was standing together in the street near the church entrance. Dispatching his assistant, Jerry Furr, to investigate the situation, Selah learned minutes later that five blacks had been refused entry by the ushers. Dr. Selah cut short his sermon and made a brief statement: he loved his parishioners at Galloway but he could not serve in a congregation where any one was turned away on account of the color of their skin. Either he would be forced to deny the Gospel he was called to preach or he must tender his resignation. Selah had already stirred controversy when in January he signed the "Born of Conviction" statement with twenty-eight other Mississippi Methodist clergymen, declaring—in a style reminiscent of Martin Luther's "Here I stand. I can do no other!"—his support of the law of the land, of public schools, and of the national church's affirmation that "all men are brothers in Christ."[54] Now the time had come to make an even bolder stand. He explained to his parishioners, "I know in conscience there can be no color bar in a Christian church, so I will ask the bishop for another appointment."[55]

Galloway's new minister was appointed in late summer, the scholarly and amiable Reverend W. J. Cunningham, who preferred a more gradual pace for desegregation in church and society. As Cunningham would later explain, "I could not concur in the racial policy in effect in our congregation, [but] I would try to look at it understandingly and work with our people lovingly and patiently toward the Methodist ideal of the church in the stress of these days of social change."[56] The Saturday evening before he was slated to preach his first sermon—always a time of heightened apprehension for any new preacher—Cunningham received a telephone call from Ed King. King identified himself as a Methodist minister and chaplain at Tougaloo. Without any preliminary chit-chat, King informed Cunningham in his high-pitched voice that he could chose one of two options: either he could expect a group of black people at church the next morning and risk an unpleasant disturbance on his first Sunday in the pulpit, or he could expect the group the following Sunday, allowing himself a week to get better acquainted with his congregation. Which would it be? Cunningham replied that he "could not propose when any one should or should not attend church," and he "sincerely hoped that no one would be arrested" (such would surely be without his consent); in any case, the final decision would have to King's own. Cunningham notes, "Our brief conversation ended with his sardonic laugh."[57]

It became part of Cunningham's weekly routine to accept many of these church visitors in his office for conversation on Saturday afternoons, the day before their appearance on the church steps. Most other white ministers, such as Douglas Hudgins, would never in their wildest dreams grant King and his "trouble makers" a visit. Guilt by even the remotest association could prove fatal. But Cunningham was open to a dialogue with the Tougaloo group. Often he would invite an associate minister or lay leaders to speak to the matter of the church's closed-door policies. He hoped the visitors would learn, as had he, to put Galloway's recalcitrance into broader perspective: there was work being done on the inside that might some day graduate into new, more inclusive policies on church attendance. King should just learn a little patience. Cunningham not only tolerated these Saturday meetings, but also listened attentively to his black and white callers. He would not, however, make promises on desegregating the church—even though in 1965 he would courageously lead a successful campaign to reverse the church's closed-door policies, and lose his job as a result.[58]

Nonetheless, Cunningham's moderation in 1963, however reasonable and well-intentioned, earned him the wrath of Ed King. In his memoir, Cunningham remembers one unpleasant exchange. "During several of the Saturday afternoon interviews with Negro and white delegations from afar, the Rev. Edwin King, white chaplain at Tougaloo, entered my office half way through the interviews and seated himself. So, these were his visitors! They were being sponsored at Tougaloo, officially or not, while they were in town and he was acting as host. At least his entering in this strange way gave credence to that idea. Why did he not enter with them at the beginning? Why had he hovered behind the scenes at all? He said nothing during the interviews, and when they were finished he was the first to leave. He never introduced himself to me personally."[59] This was King's style, elusive, unpredictable, and agitating, presenting himself as a kind of aggravating parable, an unmistakable reminder that all was not well in the house of the Lord.

One Sunday morning during the autumn of the church visits crusade, King drove a group of Tougaloo students (in the car named known by friend and foe as "King's Rambler") to Galloway for an early morning communion service. The ushers, who had not been prepared for the visitors' arrival, rushed to the front of the chapel—where smaller informal services were held—and formed a human barricade at the double doors. The church regulars were forced to find their way to the chapel by entering the main building on the opposite side of the grounds. As the church ushers held their ground, refusing to engage in yet another theological tête-à-tête with civil rights activists, King and the students leaned over the outstretched arms of the Methodist men and began knocking on the heavy wooden closed doors of the chapel. People were kneeling inside at the altar, waiting to receive communion, but the loud knocking at the back doors echoed furiously through the recesses of the interior. There was great apprehension inside about what to do. In the end, many people remained in the pews instead of walking to the altar to take communion, so annoying was the sound of fists striking against the closed doors of the Galloway chapel. The theological prankster had struck again. His vexing reply was aimed to agitate. "If we can't worship the same God together inside the same church buildings, then we will still knock on your door and so irritate you that you cannot worship your white God in peace, that you cannot escape thinking about the problems of segregation even on Sunday morning, that we are just letting you know that every single aspect of your Southern Way of Life is under attack."[60]

The Jackson police began making routine arrests of the church visitors in October of 1963. The first to be jailed were three women from Tougaloo College—Bettye Poole and Ida Hannah, two black Southerners, and Julie Zaugg, a white northerner from Oberlin College studying at Tougaloo for the year—during their visit to the Capitol Street Methodist Church, a massive edifice near the state capitol. According to Hannah's written description of the arrest—a testimony solicited by Ed King—the three women had asked one of the usher-guards at the front steps of Capitol Street if they could attend the eleven o'clock service. The church official, standing ranks alongside a policeman, told Bettye Poole that the women were not welcome. When Poole asked for an explanation, the policeman told her to shut up and move on. "If you want to worship," he said, "there are nigger churches you can go to." Poole agreed that there were Negro churches that would welcome them, but today she and her friends wanted to attend Capitol Street. The policeman replied, "You have two minutes to leave or I'll have him call the paddy wagon." He then grabbed Poole's arm and pushed her to the sidewalk. (Poole was probably singled out for harsher treatment by the police because of her prior arrests earlier in the year as a student leader in Medgar Evers's demonstrations in Jackson.) When Poole responded by telling the policeman not to push her, he barked in response, "I'll not only push you, I'll slap your goddamned face." King's hastily written notes speak of the policemen as "so furious he could not finish sentence, only grits teeth and scowls."[61]

Poole smoothed over her dress and looked up at the usher-guard. She asked him what he thought about the way his church was treating fellow Christians: didn't he realize that they were all brothers and sisters in Christ? The usher told her point blank she was no Christian. None of her types were Christians. They were communists and trouble makers and didn't care about the church—they were just trying to make white people look bad. Poole disagreed. She was indeed a Christian and cared deeply for the church.[62]

Ida Hannah reminded the usher of the bitter irony that this particular Sunday was World Wide Communion Sunday, when Methodists from around the globe celebrated the unity of all Christians in Christ. The usher acknowledged the fact with a nod, but restated his belief that the Tougaloo students should go to their own church. The policeman, even more uninterested in ecumenical matters, told the group the police wagon was on its way. If the women wanted to avoid arrest, they should leave immediately.

Julie Zaugg ignored the warning and asked the usher if she and her friends could kneel on the front steps and pray for the unity of the church. She invited the usher to join her, but he shook his head. Hannah told him that she really could understand his reluctance to open the doors, but it was still sad he could not understand their view. She asked him if he would accept a copy of Martin Luther King, Jr.'s, "Letter from Birmingham City Jail"—this might help him appreciate their concerns. The usher said no and looked away. However, the policeman, ready to take matters into his own hands, again fastened onto Bettye Poole and pushed her in the chest.

Poole and her two friends took stock of the situation. Deciding there was little more to do or say, the women turned and walked away. But they had pushed the issue too far. As the three were leaving the church grounds, they were apprehended by the policeman, handcuffed, and arrested on charges of "disturbing worship services" and "refusal to leave private property."[63]

During their interrogation at the city jail, a police officer told Zaugg that if she really wanted to attend Capitol Street, she should send her money there. He then grabbed a church offering envelope out of his pocket and tossed it in her direction. On the cover of the envelope was a picture of a communion table, displaying the elements of the eucharist, surrounded by five hands reaching for the wine. "The hands were of different colors: black, pink, and white," Hannah's affidavit states. The officer had not noticed the picture, so Zaugg brought it to his attention. "Sir, do you see these hands reaching for the wine, the different skin colors coming together in communion—this is what we are trying to do." The officer laughed and replied, "If God had intended for the nigger and the white man to be together he never . . . " but then he stopped abruptly, mumbled something under his breath, and continued with a look of perplexity, "he never would have made the nigger and the white man."[64]

Late that Sunday night, Ed King called the minister of the Capitol Street Methodist Church, Reverend Seth Granberry, to talk about the arrests. Granberry told King that as a well-known moderate on racial issues, he was embaressed by the whole ordeal. He insisted his church had not asked for the arrests. Sure, the police had said earlier in the week that arrests of church visitors would be the next stage in subduing the campaign. But he had assumed that that meant arrests would take place only at the request of any church that barred blacks and interracial groups. "As far as I know," he said, "the churches have not authorized the police to arrest anyone." He, the Reverend Seth Granberry, certainly had not. In any case, there was nothing he could do now.[65]

Granberry also doubted, as had the church guard earlier in the day, that the women were sincere in wanting to worship at Capitol Street. He suspected their true motives had little to do with God and Jesus Christ. King argued in response that Granberry and the church leadership had a moral responsibility "for what the police had done and what they might do." But Granberry washed his hands of the matter. He had done nothing to cause the problem. There was nothing he could imagine doing in the future that would help. Again, there was nothing he intended to do now.[66]

King wrote disingenuously in his notebooks that Granberry's defensive aloofness both surprised and hurt him. The fact of the matter was that King had Granberry just where he wanted him. He could now state publicly that the widely esteemed denominational leader had relinquished his right to speak the word of God with credibility. Granberry's church had, at the very least, given tacit approval to the rejection, abuse, and arrest of three women seeking to worship on World Wide Communion Sunday. In a certain sense, King could count Granberry's abdication of responsibility as both a theological and a personal victory. Personal because Granberry had been King's pastor in Vicksburg. Granberry and his wife had been instrumental in encouraging the young King to ask questions about segregation—questions "that came as a result of my developing loyalty to the church"—and to hold up the racial practices of the closed society to the light of biblical principles of justice. It was Granberry who encouraged King as a young man to consider devoting his life to full-time Christian ministry. But Granberry was a moderate; to be sure, as King wrote, "an excellent preacher and a sensitive, wonderful minister to the needs of his people, that is, the traditional needs of all people, visiting the sick, comforting the bereaved, spreading healing, love and good will." But a moderate nonetheless. Granberry could speak with great conviction about the evils of communist police states in eastern Europe, but "there was no point in talking to him about police-states in Christian Mississippi, in God-fearing America. He could not understand."[67] In fact, no one was spared King's opinions about the Mississippi police state.

From King's perspective, Granberry was a quietist, a man who would rather turn his back on oppression and brutality than risk soiling his career and reputation. "[He] just wanted things to move along slowly and the church to be left alone."[68] King found in Granberry and Cunningham and in the other white ministers of Jackson's segregated Protestant churches a vivid demonstration of the theological bankruptcy of white moderate Christianity. As the summer of 1964 drew near, King was able to say with heightened prophetic certainty that one was either for the movement or against it: if a person abdicated the right to speak of racial justice for the sake of the Kingdom of God, then he was giving support to the brutal ethic of white supremacy. However unwitting that capitulation might be, it was equally damnable before God. There was no middle ground.

When the case of Bettye Poole, Ida Hannah, and Julie Zaugg came to trial the next week, they were handed stiff sentences of one year in prison and a thousand dollar fine. But the sentence only fueled their determination. After an appeals bond was posted by the Women's Division of the Board of Missions and the Board of Christian Social Concern (both agencies of the National Methodist Church), the women were back at it again the following Sunday—"same church, same police, same charges, same jail."[69] Unlike their first visit, this time the women were accompanied by nine companions, including a Tougaloo professor, fellow students, and several Methodist ministers from Chicago, all of whom were arrested. King, while continuing to organize other church visits around the city and work behind the scenes, visited the twelve in the segregated Jackson jail. His description of an afternoon with the Chicago ministers is a remarkable portrayal of the theological conviction slowly taking shape: that the movement, wherever it appeared, in whatever form or figuration, was now the true body of Christ, the worldly presence of God:

> In the cellblock with the ministers we talked of the state of the church and the world, of God and man, and laughed at the absurdity of so much that was happening to us all. And we had a celebration of Holy Communion. I was asked to lead the service. The cell was our chapel. On the low ceiling above us we could read the names of those who had been imprisoned—for freedom, for faith, before us. Recent names from the demonstrations of the 1963 summer, before the death of Medgar Evers. Earlier battles and names of soldiers—students, other minsters on the 1961 Freedom Rides. Sometimes a name was familiar to one of the Chicago men; many of the names were familiar to me. Scrawled among the names of these men—and of all the regular lonely prisoners and more traditional criminals—were simple messages, slogans of freedom, "Ten more days to go," of the petty thief and alcoholic who slept here last month; verses or lines from Freedom songs barely legible under the more recent pornography. . . . We commented on these names and hopes and fears written around us; I told some stories about some of the names I recognized. It was easy to move into a spirit of worship; the recent

past and the ancient past both seemed close. Our altar-Communion table was the long, simple metal-covered all-purpose table the prisoners used for their meals and their card games. One of the men brought out a hard biscuit, left over from the meager breakfast. This became our Communion loaf. The Communion wine (smuggled in from the outside world) was poured into our chalice—a prisoner's battered tin drinking cup. I read the words we all knew; we joined in the prayers; we sang together; we had silence together; we broke bread together, we shared the cup of wine, the Body and the Blood. We felt unity, and strength, and humility, and love. There was a kind of awe, as though our little band of five prisoners (and I always thought of myself as a prisoner) were the only people present in some immense cathedral, kneeling before some small crucifix in a tiny chapel on the side aisle, waiting, in no hurry, to walk back out into the great building around us. We knew strength, and we knew peace.[70]

King had asked J. W. Legett to celebrate the eucharist with the incarcerated ministers, but the district superintendent had refused. "To bring the sacrament in such surroundings would be a sacrilege," Legett announced.[71]

Even after the twelve were released on a $1,000 bail—thanks to the tenacity of lawyers Arthur Kinoy and William Kunstler—the church visits continued throughout the fall of the year and into the winter and early spring of 1964. More than forty people were arrested during the campaign. The ushers' prepared statements were more or less the same familiar retreats to church policy and God's design for separate races; the police charges always "disturbing a worship service" or "trespassing." But the theological meaning varied in intensity: sometimes it was mixed with pathos and sadness, sometimes with incredulity and the absurd.

Perhaps the strangest visit of the fall campaign involved John Garner, a white physics teacher at Tougaloo College and parishioner at Galloway, who was arrested for attending his own church.[72] John and his wife Margrit had been among a few members of Galloway actively to encourage the clergy and laity to reconsider the church's closed-door policies. With King's encouragement, the Garners had joined the church for the very purpose of encouraging white moderates and conservatives in the congregation, most of whom were afraid to speak out. Now that the church visits had hit home, John decided to pursue direct action himself. On October 13, he invited one of his students, Joyce Ladner, and two white out-of-state Methodist ministers, Joseph Buckles and Elmer Dickson, to be his guests at Sunday school.[73] On a warm and balmy Sunday morning, the integrated group entered the educational building without resistance, though not, as it turned out, unnoticed. Once they were in Garner's Sunday school class, several policemen paraded into the room and made arrests. Joyce Ladner, who had warmed to the kind remarks of two white women, began quietly sobbing as she saw the police, the "looks of hate on some white faces, and the even more terrible look of fear and shame on the faces that were turning away" (although for the moment preceding the raid, "it was beautiful," Ladner said).[74] The two ministers tried to explain to the policemen that they could not arrest Methodist clergy inside a Methodist church, but denominational polity was lost on Jackson's finest. The ministers asked the mortified church members to find Reverend Cunningham and bring him to the scene at once, but Cunningham never appeared. John Garner then began calling on his fellow churchmen in the room by name, asking each one to inform the police of the absurdity of the arrest: he was a member of this church! But his classmates remained silent, except for one woman who looked on the scene and began crying—whether with shame or sadness, Garner never knew—and then covered her face with her hands and ran down the hall out of sight. The police led the integrated group out of the church into the police wagons and into city jail. Along with his guests, Garner was arrested for trespassing and disturbing public worship. Although many people had certainly been arrested for praying or worshiping God in prohibited places, no one in the civil rights movement (or perhaps in the history of the Christian church) had ever been arrested for the crime of attending his own church.

Ed King's church visit campaign elicited, time and again, symbolic gestures and comic self-contradictions that caricatured the closed society's celebrated piety. In King's mind, these moments during which white Christians betrayed all manner of theological incoherence were often just as important as gaining a place in the pews. When a black woman tried to engage an usher-guard in a dialogue about the church's racial policy, only to hear the response, "Please don't try to appeal to my conscience" or "Just leave Jesus out of this" or "This is a Christian church and we intend to keep it that way," the result was a dramatic default of theological credibility.[75] King could then ascend to speak the prophetic word to the historical moment. In full view of divine and public scrutiny, authority was relinquished to the "outsiders"—and in a way that became deeply empowering, even reassuring. *God must be on our side. He's surely not with the white church!*

The confrontations between integrated groups of church visitors and the white religious establishment created a space where previously unspoken ideas on religion and race came quickly to the surface. The most common of these was the shaky, troubled inclination to value the Southern Way of Life over the integrity of the Gospel. When that inclination reached public articulation, as it did in the varied responses to the church visits, the default of theological credibility bore severe consequences—none more striking than the white church presenting itself as hostile to the Gospel, indeed to Christ himself. Even an occasional open door, in the final analysis, only confirmed to King the white church's failure to reckon with the cost of true discipleship—the all or nothing, the willingness to give up the security of culture and custom and even the ecclesiastical institution itself for the sake of bearing witness to the power of the resurrection. As the two bishops had said on Easter Sunday 1964, the "Feast of the Resurrection affirms life for *all* men." And the feast was not reserved for the members of one's own tribe or clan, but for all humanity, and especially the brother or sister on the other side, for the ones who suffered under the brutalities of the Jim Crow milieu, whose lives buckled beneath the iron-hard blows of white supremacy.

Ed King pushed the matter hard: if the white church really believed what it preached, it would not simply open its doors (and this in a pretense of welcome that was really condescension). If the white church really believed what it preached, it would change its ways, it would give itself away and live for others. That most of the churches targeted by King and his cohorts were moderate only underscored the symbolic power of the campaign. Even the moderates capitulated to comfortable standards of compassion. In a society of increased anti-black violence, there was no longer any gentlemanly compromise, no polite middle ground. "The 'Christian' moderates were no longer free to do good, even to be decent."[76] What was made plain through the confrontations of the church visits was the secret of the moderates' hitherto unspeakable solidarity with racial extremists. As King maintained, "There is a line from the lynch mob, through the jury exoneration of every white man accused of murdering a black man, to the denial of the right to vote to the black man and the closed doors of the church."[77] The closed doors of the church authorized and sustained the brutalities of the closed society, so that, in the end, the closed society "gradually became the police state," governed, King said, by "Nazi laws."[78]

By the middle of June in 1964, the church visits had reached an impasse. A few white churches had made some concessions to the Tougaloo visitors, but, by and large, the institution stood unmoved. At the same time, the frequent cross burnings turned into church burnings. Black churches, especially those that had opened their doors to whites, burned at a rate of one every week and would continue to do so for the next year.[79]

One of the first to burn was the Mt. Zion Methodist Church in Neshoba County, which had opened its doors to CORE staff member Mickey Schwerner for use as a Freedom school and voter registration training center. From King's point of view, the burning of Mt. Zion and the murders of Schwerner, Goodman, and Chaney were theologically interconnected with the closed doors of the white church. Confirming the belief for King was the fact that after visiting Mt. Zion on the afternoon of their fateful trip into Neshoba County, the three civil rights workers had come to a stop in the parking lot of the First Methodist Church of Philadelphia.[80] While standing around the car fixing a flat tire, Chaney, Goodman, and Schwerner were approached by the town deputy and his assistant, and then taken to city jail. Journalist William Bradford Huie reports that from their cells, Chaney, Goodman, and Schwerner could hear the singing of "Blessed Assurance Jesus is Mine," "My Faith Look up to Thee," and "What a Friend We Have in Jesus," from the congregation of the First Baptist Church a block away from the city jail.[81]

The sad truth of the parking lot scene was hard for King to take, that "the last possible chance they had for escape was that very church," the First Methodist Church of Philadelphia, even though none of the men would have considered the church a refuge from danger.[82] The tragedy of the situation was compounded by the fact that the new minister of the First Methodist Church was Clay Lee, the same man who had one year earlier advised W. J. Cunningham, as his assistant pastor, against support of the church visitors at Galloway Memorial Methodist Church in Jackson.

When King heard of the disappearance of his fellow workers on the morning of June 22, he sought out numerous religious leaders in Jackson, hoping to convince someone of the gravity of the moment and his certainty that the three men were dead. The church had to condemn the killings, he argued. But no one wanted to hear from King—not the Methodist bishop, not even the liberal editor of the Roman Catholic newspaper in Mississippi, Father Bernard Law. King said, "My picture of a Mississippi where crosses burned nightly, where Black churches were being bombed, where people were being killed by police working with klansmen was just something they could not tolerate."[83] As a result, King turned his anger into a readiness for the new work at hand. For the morning of June 22 also marked the beginning of the 1964 Summer Project.

In the end, the white church's failure to open its doors signaled the need for dramatically more radical action. "We needed something new or we needed to quit," King observed.[84] The harsh truth had now to be made evident: salvation would come only from the outside, as a violent, intruding event, crashing into history, exploding the old order, establishing the new. Freedom Summer was the graphic articulation of this stark conclusion. It would come like a prophetic warning: unless the white Christian establishment repented and changed its ways, a time of punishment—of confrontation and violence—could not, and would not, be avoided.

Burying the Dead

By the end of the summer there had been a "slight shift" in the position of the white church toward both the struggle for civil rights and the increased anti-civil rights terrorism of the Klan.[85] According to King, the initial response had been one of disinterest and denial. The church simply denied reports that violence was on the rise. As astonishing as such a perception may seem, it must not be forgotten that the state media had systematically ignored incidents of Klan terrorism in its coverage of "Negro life." Recall also that local reporting of the murders of the three civil rights workers had presupposed that the whole situation was a hoax created by SNCC to attract critical national and international attention. If the case could be made that there was no crisis, "then nothing was demanded of the church or the moderate."[86]

Yet eventually denial wore thin and the grim facts of violence could no longer be whitewashed. As black churches and homes exploded with alarming frequency, and terrorism and white militancy were everywhere present, the moderate response became that of blaming the outsider. King explained, "No one could say, could prove, that white Mississippians were guilty of this violence. It might be the Communists. It might be the civil rights workers."[87] Tom Etheridge for one, the Jackson newspaper columnist, worked hard to convince Mississippians that church bombings were "inside jobs" that were "financially or psychologically profitable to leaders and adherents of the Negro revolution."[88]

Nonetheless, by the time the bodies of Chaney, Goodman, and Schwerner were unearthed on August 4 on Olen Burrage's farm in Neshoba County, the admission became inescapable that some white Mississippians were guilty of "some small degree of violence." Popular sentiment then shifted toward condemnation of these violent acts because they might very well threaten the "the traditional good race relations (i.e., white supremacy and docile happy Blacks) in Mississippi." Condemnation, however, took the peculiar form of "disindentification" (as King said). For whites uncomfortable with the Klan, disindentification served the useful purpose of pushing white militancy "so far outside the circle (and class) of the religious moderates that there was still no need to accept any responsibility for their (the Klan, the red necks, the poor whites, the hill billies, the white trash, etc.) violent acts." The mainline white church could continue telling itself that Mississippi—all those good, decent Christian people—had been wrongly accused by the liberal media and was innocent of "all the terrible things said about the State."[89]

In the end, the "slight shift" did little to trouble business as usual. Even the few initiatives to rebuild black churches and parsonages destroyed by Klan firebombs failed to address the sources of anti-black violence—and often even failed to acknowledge that the churches had been bombed, rather than accidentally burned.[90] Not only had the church visits campaign failed to crack the doors of the closed society but the dramatic infusion of summer volunteers seemed only to harden the hearts of white Christians. Freedom Summer may have come like the prophetic warning that unless white Christians repent and change their ways, a time of reckoning would follow; but it was a prophetic warning unheard and unheeded. What should one do and say now, King wondered.

On the night of August 7, 1964, a memorial service was held in Meridian for slain black civil rights worker James Chaney.[91] Local black people assembled in various churches in the early afternoon, and after a period of prayer, singing, and mourning with fellow members of their home churches, proceeded to walk silently to the First Union Baptist Church, where they gathered together with movement activists from around the state. By the time the service began, more than seven hundred people packed the pews and aisles of the church sanctuary. For nearly an hour, ministers from Meridian delivered a series of composed, almost placid eulogies, which were, as John Dittmer says, "careful not to inflame the emotions of the congregation."[92] Then David Dennis rose to the pulpit.

Dennis, a young black freedom rider from New Orleans who had taken over as CORE's Mississippi field secretary in the summer of 1962 and had remained active in the movement ever since, had become disillusioned of the whole Christian witness of nonviolence. The murders of James Chaney, Andrew Goodman, and Michael Schwerner had confirmed his growing suspicion that pacifist strategies resulted in "a waste of good lives."[93] He could no longer countenance the platitudes of the cautious clergy, etherealized eulogies of the young dead activist that preceded his remarks. Dennis's first words before the congregation made clear that something different was on the way. "Sorry," he began, "but I'm not here to do the traditional thing most of us do at such a gathering, and that is to tell of what a great person the individual was and some of the great works the person was involved in. I think we all know that." I am not here to mourn James Chaney, he added, for "he's got his freedom and he's still fighting for it."[94]

Rather, Dennis intended to mourn those people who don't care, who "don't have the guts to stand up." That included the president of the United States, the government of the state of Mississippi, and, anybody sitting before him at First Union Baptist Church who was not prepared to stand up and fight back. Dennis called to mind the black people murdered in the south—Emmett Till, Mack Parker, the four girls in the Birmingham church, Medgar Evers, and so many others whose memories had faded into obscurity. He pledged to the church, "I'm sick and tired of going to memorials; I'm sick and tired of going to funerals. I've got a bitter vengeance in my heart tonight . . . and I'm not going to stand here and ask anybody here not to be angry."[95]

Dennis acknowledged that he and his black brothers and sisters had long fought the struggle with love in their hearts. But look where that had led them, he shouted. To yet another memorial service, to more irrelevant eulogies. Dennis declared that the time comes when it is necessary "to put some injury on your enemy to get respect."[96] He deplored the fact that many people will say tonight "what a shame" but then go back to their homes and pray to the Lord as they've done for years. Or worse, "[They'll] go back to work in some white folks' kitchen tomorrow and forget about the whole God-blasted thing." But if you're really angry, Dennis said, don't "get your frustration out by clapping your hands." Rather, "resolve among yourselves not to take it any longer, not to let the white man run you down." "Holding our hands up high," he continued, "[tell] them that if they're not ready for us, too bad, baby, 'cause we're coming anyway." Dennis's searing conclusion hit hard: "I'm going to tell you deep down in my heart what I feel like right now. If you do go back home and sit down and take it, God damn your souls!"[97]

He then collapsed as he turned to walk back to his chair. Ed King, who had been standing near the podium, caught him in his arms, and embraced him until other friends received his body and carried him outside for water and fresh air.[98]

The congregation seemed visibly shaken by Dennis's final remarks and his fainting. As King prepared to deliver the final eulogy of the service, he paused and asked the people to sing the slow, hopeful anthem, "Oh Freedom."

> O freedom, O freedom, O freedom over me, over me
> And before I'll be afraid I'll be buried in my grave
> And go home to my Lord and be free, and be free
> No more killing, no more shooting, over me, over me.

When the singing was over, King told the congregation he was happy David Dennis had gotten angry. He said, "Any of you who are not angry in your heart will not find the strength to go on. You have to hate this thing that has been done." But King broke away from the drift of Dennis's rage, saying, "And then you have to somehow be able to forgive the people who have done it." Forgiveness cannot be cheap or "automatic," King hurried to add. Much needs to be said and felt before forgiveness can be real. "If we cannot admit when we feel pain, when we feel anger, when we feel hate, then we are not using the feelings that God gave us." He confessed to being unable to understand fully how Dennis felt on a night like this. Still, King felt called to say what God has laid on his heart. "My white brothers have killed my black brothers. Somehow you have the greater burden to be able to forgive the people who do this and through your forgiveness bring salvation to them for they are in a living hell and will not admit it. Their souls are being destroyed by the hate and fear they bear towards all of us."

But what also needed to be said was a word of judgment on all those who had given their consent to the murder of James Chaney. And who were they? Not just the vicious klansmen who carried out the assassination. James Chaney's blood lies on the hands of the FBI and the United States government, on complacent Americans from all parts of the country, but especially on the silent white Christians of the state. These people are just as guilty as the "sick white Mississippians" who carried out the brutal murder, "and more damned in their souls because they know it's wrong." King said, "The greatest tragedy that has occurred here is not just these deaths but the failure in the white community that has brought this about, that has tolerated it."

Then King's thoughts shifted toward the extraordinary conclusion. The death at the center of his eulogy was no longer James Chaney: it was white Mississippi, the white church. "Many white people talk of being Christians. They are afraid of Christianity as much as they are afraid of you. They are afraid of a guilty conscience. Afraid that you would treat us as we have treated you. I don't believe that it will be that way, but that is what they fear. So their fear allows a few men to commit murder. But it doesn't matter if a few men do the murders and burn the churches, the rest of the people are responsible." Can the true people of God forgive these tormented souls—souls "being destroyed by hate and fear," confined "in a living hell"? King asked the congregation to pray for them; but then in a startling, though perhaps unavoidable move, he proclaimed that their prayer should be one for the damned and the dying. "The white Christians of the city of Meridian, tonight, need your prayers because God almighty sees them and knows in his eyes that *every white Christian that did not come to this church is no Christian.*"[99] Every white Christian who did not come to this church is guilty, not only of violence and cruelty, but of forsaking and betraying the call of Christ.

Look! The symbol of white Mississippi has become a burning cross. What more graphic expression of its own death could be imagined? King lamented before the congregation that the white church has tragically but quite willingly destroyed the image most precious to its proclamation: the miracle of God's sacrifice in Jesus Christ, the miracle of God's laying down his life for humanity, the miracle that God is a God for others.

Yet King refused to give the white segregated church the final word on the matter. In the closing moments of his eulogy, he offered a bold reclaiming of the cross as the symbol that most eloquently expressed James Chaney's and the movement's hard sacrifices. He exclaimed, "[Our] cross is not a burned cross, it is the one cross of Calvary that is stained with the blood of Jesus, God's son. God gave his son for all of us and this is the cross that we follow—the cross that means victory, not emptiness and decay; the cross that means victory over death, the victory in this life; the cross that means we can forgive, that God will help us to love; the cross that means we will have a new beginning, a new resurrection, a new birth."[100] The members of the Meridian COFO staff then walked to the front of church and joined hands, and with all the people gathered in the crowded sanctuary, began to sing, "We Shall Overcome." When the singing came to an end, the congregation scattered into the warm, August night.

The Countercultural Christ

A northern minister writing in the Methodist magazine *Behold* concluded after returning from a Sunday with Ed King's church visitors, "What has happened in Jackson, Mississippi not only dramatizes the segregated nature of the church and its false unity, but also reveals that the church has capitulated to the culture in which it dwells. . . . The church, like a chameleon, blends in with its background so that it loses its identity."[101] The white church that sanctified and blessed the Southern Way of Life preached a gospel of comfort. A pleasing correlation adhered between proclamation and culture; and in any case, those untamed or sinful elements in culture which threatened piety's innocence were reproached by a faith almost completely purified of compassion's harder demands. In King's view, the white church had forgotten that it had a right to exist—more, was called into being—only when it continually gave itself away. The church had only deceived itself by thinking otherwise, though such deception often became irresistible by its wealth of associations, councils, bureaucracies, ecclesiastical agencies, and (as the theologian Karl Barth said in a different context) its "interesting nooks for the soul, of dogma, cultus and morality." The white church did not, and would not, tolerate the possibility of its own relativity; of the fact that its confidence and traditions hovered above an abyss of increasing self-doubt. Not even the spectacle of the church visits could bring home this sobering fact. In the end, the white church lacked that character of pilgrim, stranger, and peculiar people which alone could distinguish its presence as "the body of Christ." People spoke, without blushing, of "Christian" morals, values, families, clubs, and society—even of "Christian fun and wholesomeness." The closed society had taken the divine into its own possession; it had brought God under its nervous management.[102]

As King understood the Gospel message, becoming a new creation required leaving the old behind, turning away from the familiar and crossing over to the "everything new." If that means rejection, ridicule, and persecuting, then that's what it takes. If that means anarchy and madness, then that's what it takes. If that means breaking the hearts of the mother and father who raised you, then that's what it takes.

Following the countercultural Christ was a terrifying prospect to a white Christian born and reared in the segregated south. For this Christ stood outside the closed society, outside the doors of the segregated white churches, beyond the Southern Way of Life. This Christ signaled the power of the new breaking into the old. No wonder that those who follow after in obedience cannot help but appear peculiar and alien, always the outsider, their commitments propelled by a "grammar of dissent."[103]

King came to recognize faith as an unconstraining will to freedom, a freedom that wages war against the idols of the old regime, enlivened by the promise that the Lord's reign is at hand. Ed King's theology was like a tapestry of differing layers and textures, like a dense foliage of contrasting shades, full of movement and energy, resisting fixed structure, permanence, and rigid orderliness. In a striking sense, the shape of his theology paralleled the manner of his activism, appearing in fresh and often unexpected forms, always turning against the grain, calling into question the established system, subverting any effort to consume the diversity of experience into one overreaching totality. Fixed structure and permanence too closely resembled the closed society of the Jim Crow South—a totalizing system wherein all particularity and difference were accounted for and controlled.

Yet King's vocation involved more than sheer iconoclasm: more than the negation of all idols, more than the perpetual overturning of system and establishment. There was a ground, an energizing core, that gave life to a field of living faith. This core—this animating center—was God's jubilant invitation to open up and let go. Following after the countercultural Christ meant living one's life "in the spirit"—in the spirit who frees, reshapes, transforms. Those doors swinging inward, the spirit causes to swing outward. The self that had become twisted in an intricate, insidious knottiness loosens and opens up. The spirit recreates the person, entangling it with others, not only with one's friend and comrade but with the enemy as well. The spirit frees women and men for a new order—for a new individual, social, and political identity—for the spirit means newness, life, togetherness, and power.

Toward this end, Ed King understood his ministry in the movement as both priestly and pastoral. In his priestly role, King believed himself anointed to bless and to ordain those people, white and black, men and women, Christians, Jews, and atheists, who had yielded their hearts to the calling of the spirit—who had said "yes" to the summons to cross on over to the land of promise. At the training session for Freedom Summer volunteers in Oxford, Ohio, in June 1964, King had presided over an ordination service that included prayer, supplication, and the laying on of hands. In his pastoral role, King listened to his movement brothers and sisters in their distress, prayed with them in celebration and anguish, visited them in prison, and kept fellowship with his coworkers as they faced death together. (Many shared the sentiment of one volunteer who said, "We all thought we would die that summer.")[104] The movement community became King's congregation, his church, even though many in SNCC never fully trusted him nor could make any sense of his theological vision. Still, for King, all who had answered the call were gathered in as part of this new community—indeed as part of the Kingdom of God.

Like Mrs. Hamer, King believed in all the miraculous detail of the Christian story; and like Mrs. Hamer, he believed that the doors of the Kingdom of God were wide open for all who heard the call and pursued justice. "What of those people who were not Christians as such?" he asked. "These people had still yielded their hearts to the call. And what call was that? The call to leave their individuality and let go of things."[105]

In this manner, it became clear to King that the movement was not a struggle between liberal and conservative ideologies. Long before the Atlantic City's rejection of the MFDP's platform, King knew that the issue at stake in Mississippi was not a stronger federalism, or any shift, subtle or revolutionary, within the existing political framework.[106] It was the advent of an altogether new framework; not simply a reversal of power, wherein poor would replace rich, black replace white, and the structures of economic distribution flip flop accordingly. "It would not be correct to say that we thought we were building the Kingdom of God," King says, "we were working *for it* and making the kinds of sacrifices we hoped would foster the Kingdom's realization. This hope sustained and inspired us, and opened us up to a new frame of reference beyond the existing framework of Mississippi."[107] The new framework represented a step beyond the reversal of social oppositions, a step beyond all that was familiar, a transformation to a reconciled, a beloved community. To be sure, King did not know exactly what this meant, what the new framework would look like, what it would require of his own life. What he did know was that blacks and whites gathered together in prayer on the steps of white churches, in late-night assignments in COFO offices, in mass meetings in black churches, in smoky debates in the back room of his house at Tougaloo College (which, as Julie Zaugg wrote in her notebooks, "Mrs. King has graciously . . . opened to students to be used as a meeting, study and coffee room"), and throughout the fellowship of the movement, signified the place—the literal, geographical location—where the new framework was taking visible, albeit temporary, form.[108] King mused, "There were no answers. All we had was each other—and whatever brothers and sisters belonged in the beloved community. Our band was wide, our circle full—but we needed to feel the presence and the faith in that fellowship of all the people who held that dream who had ever lived—or ever would. The world was so much bigger than SNCC—or Mississippi—or the Movement."[109]

The meaningful though ultimately frustrating experience of the church visits convinced King that the reconciled movement congregation must itself form the primary religious witness against the sin of segregation; all subsequent political activism would have to radiate out from this center to the larger public spaces. Yet the strategies of nonviolent direct action carried out in Jackson from 1962 through the spring of 1964 in protest of segregated institutions (of course, there were other desegregation campaigns

Fannie Lou Hamer at the 1964 National Democratic Convention in Atlantic City. (UPI/Corbis-Bettmann)

Workers picking cotton on a Delta plantation. (Mississippi Department of Archives and History)

A circuit clerk in Mississippi administers the "literacy test" for voter registration. (Mississippi Department of Archives and History)

Mrs. Annie Devine, Mrs. Hamer, and Reverend Edwin King (seated) in the convention hall in Atlantic City. (UPI/Corbis-Bettmann)

The welcoming woman. (Bruce Davidson, Magnum)

Sam Bowers after he was found guilty on conspiracy charges in the slaying of Michael Schwerner, James Chaney, and Andrew Goodman. (AP/Wide World Photos)

Klan rally in south Mississippi. (Mississippi Department of Archives and History)

A cast iron bell lies among the ashes of the burned Mt. Zion Methodist Church near Philadelphia, Mississippi. (UPI/Corbis-Bettmann)

The bodies of the three civil rights workers are uncovered on August 4, 1964, from an earthen dam on a farm near Philadelphia, Mississippi. (UPI/Corbis-Bettmann)

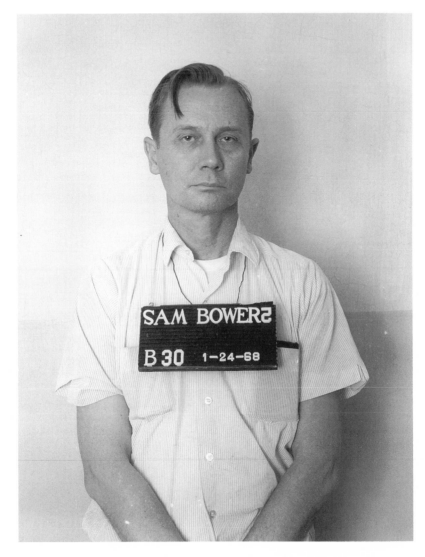

The high priest of the anti-civil rights movement. (Mississippi Department of Archives and History)

Reverend Douglas Hudgins. (Historical Commission of the Southern Baptist Convention, Nashville)

The 1954 Southern Baptist Convention in St. Louis, where messengers voted to support *Brown vs. Board of Education*. (Historical Commission of the Southern Baptist Convention, Nashville)

Church ladies
hosting a
shower.
(Johnson Family
Papers, McCain
Library and
Archives,
University of
Southern
Mississippi)

The "white
waiting room" at
the Trailways
Bus Terminal in
Jackson,
Mississippi.
(UPI/Corbis-
Bettmann)

First Baptist Church, Jackson. (Historical Commission of the Southern Baptist Convention, Nashville)

Reverend Edwin King. (State Historical Society of Wisconsin)

Volunteers remove debris from a building destroyed in the 1953 Vicksburg tornado. (Mississippi Department of Archives and History)

Black inmates are forced to carry Ed King to a police wagon after a 1963 demonstration in Jackson. (Mississippi Department of Archives and History)

The theological prankster. (UPI/Corbis-Bettmann)

Cleveland Sellers (in white T shirt), Stokely Carmichael (directly behind Sellers), and Martin Luther King, Jr. (directly to Seller's right), at the 1966 Meredith March Against Fear. (Archive Photos)

National Guardsmen armed with pepper gas, rifles, and bayonets stand rank in Cambridge, Maryland. (UPI/Corbis-Bettmann)

National Guardsmen in Cambridge, Maryland, attack SNCC photographer Cliff Vaughn during a demonstration in May of 1964. (Danny Lyon, Magnum)

A house in Mississippi where student volunteers lived during the summer of 1964. (Johnson Family Papers, McCain Library and Archives, University of Southern Mississippi)

The message of the 1966 Meredith March: "Move on over or we'll move on over you." (Johnson Family Papers, McCain Library and Archives, University of Southern Mississippi)

Cleveland Sellers leaving the Release Center of the South Carolina Department of Corrections on August 31, 1973, after serving a sentence for conviction of riot charges in Orangeburg. (UPI/Corbis-Bettmann)

in progress as well) came to very little. From King's perspective, it now became as important simply *to be* the beloved community as *to act* in specific revolutionary ways. King began to see that the movement congregation did not need to make a great show politically, or to execute revolutionary action in calculated or strategic ways. "I believed we were asked not only to let go of our individual selves and open up to the new, but also to let go of the fellowship of SNCC and the revolution itself if all that became for us an idol." He believed it was necessary for his brothers and sisters in the movement to live in the present time that kind of reality which the revolution was going to bring about later. Being and acting were ultimately part of the same dialectic of justice. "The cause of the Movement was to live the kind of life we wanted for the world in the midst of the struggle to change the world—for civil rights or anything else."[110]

The unsettling but unavoidable thought took shape in King's mind: perhaps the movement church, as it stood outside the institutions of the closed society, united together in opposition to the existing framework, *was* the beloved community. Perhaps it was the beloved community only as long as it stood outside the closed doors of Jim Crow, knocking, stirring, and agitating. As SNCC staffer and poet Jane Stembridge had written:

> This, is . . .
> as much of community
> as we will ever know.[111]

Perhaps the beloved community could not be translated into a broader, more embracing social reality. Whatever the case, King understood that even as the movement continued to remind the white church that its worship was idolatrous, at the same time it had constantly to fortify itself against the expectation that its knocking, stirring, and agitating—however prophetic these actions might be—would make the beloved community permanent and enduring. In time, the movement's witness would disappear like a prophetic lightning flash across a dark sky.

What would become of a movement community so configured? What of its strategic initiatives in voter rights, education, and desegregation? Would these goals become secondary to the prophetic witness of the reconciled society? The answers disturbed. Obviously, the institutions of the white Christian religion had proven illegitimate. Though there might come a day when the white segregated church would open up its doors to all races, that day would only be reached through concession and resignation, with the regretful nod that "well, if you have to sit next to Colored people in the movies, the cafes, and the school room, we might as well let them into the churches too."[112] White resistance seemed to be settled in for the long haul. And on the side of the movement community, emotions were at a breaking point. By summer's end, King recalls, we "were worn out; we had given everything we had. None of us realized how strong the evil was that we fought, and how much a part of American power it was."[113] Some movement activists, as David Dennis had made clear, had begun questioning pacifist strategies, exploring violence as a means of pursuing the urgent objectives of black liberation. King himself sometimes felt tempted by the exciting possibilities of militancy: "How long could anyone in SNCC, black or white, keep going without breaking, without advocating first self defense then some kind of traditional armed deterrent? How long before we ourselves would break? What were our own motives? Had we joined the Movement to promote pacifism, love, and integration as more important than freedom?"[114]

However, as he further reasoned, the turn to "some kind of traditional armed deterrent" would too easily lead to a reversal of power wherein the movement community would end up embracing the same dehumanizing practices characteristic of white supremacy. He could not accept violence as an inevitable or legitimate option. When love is negotiated in a way that preserves a place for hatred, hatred proves all-consuming: "the brothers and sisters would turn the hate reserved for the enemy on the other brothers and sisters, the band would be broken, the 'beloved community' would become just like the world we fought and sought to change. We would have nothing to offer any man or woman and nothing would change, whether we were defeated or we were victorious. To abandon nonviolence was to open the way for fear and hate and to lose love; it was to lose the Movement."[115]

Theological integrity necessitated this resolve. The divine call to follow after demanded everything; its costliness could not be negotiated with armaments. The God who called men and women out of themselves demanded a peaceable witness at all costs. And to reinforce King's resolve was the stark, distorting image of segregation: four steps out, and four steps in, a prisoner to a self-inscribed world of paranoid and paralyzing fears.[116] He could not endorse the same sensibility in his movement comrades that he had vigorously condemned in the militant guardians of the closed society. Rage enslaved; it dissipated the spirit's liberating energies, convoluting them, turning them in and against themselves. King saw everywhere he looked a people imprisoned by these fears—and King himself, in ways he both could and could never understand, was threatened by them as well.

As King considered his responsibility to the Gospel, it became clear that the strange, new world he inhabited imposed a demand on the civil rights struggle different from the achievement of political power. The theme of Christ as the suffering servant loomed large in his mind, not only as a theological expression of the movement's hard journey but as a basic requirement of following after. His meditations drifted to various biblical reflections on suffering. "For it has been granted to you that for the sake of Christ you should not only believe in him but also suffer for his sake" (Phil. 1:29); "For his sake I have suffered the loss of all things, and count them as refuse, in order that I may gain Christ and be found in him . . . that I may know him and the power of his resurrection, and may share his sufferings, becoming like him in his death" (Phil. 3:8, 10). If the movement was the beloved community only as long as it stood outside the closed doors of Jim Crow society—knocking, stirring, agitating—perhaps it was also true that the movement could remain the beloved community only as long as it suffered for the sake of the peaceable Kingdom. The movement's suffering sharpened and preserved its prophetic edge: to the extent to which it graduated into institutional power, or gave way to violence, it risked forfeiting the very element that sustained its witness—the willingness to open up and let go.

FIVE

Cleveland Sellers and the
River of No Return

Into the River

CLEVELAND SELLERS had a happy childhood in Denmark, South Carolina. His mother, Pauline Sellers, came from a middle-class family, which made possible a bachelor's degree in home economics and a master's degree in education. Although she worked full time as a dietician at Denmark's vocational school, she always managed to set a generous table for dinner and to keep her children well clothed and entertained. It was his mother who first took Sellers to the Edisto river, one of the longest black-water rivers in the country, where she taught him to fish for bass, muds, and carpie in the river's dark waters—using a rod and reel, not the cane pole used by most poor people.[1] His mother inspired confidence in Sellers and his sister, always encouraging in them a sense of freedom and adventure.

For Sellers's father, Booker T. Washington's glorification of common labor and self-reliance could not be improved upon. If you were poor and black and wanted a better life, you had better get off your ass and work like hell.[2] As Sellers recalls, "If the people next door got up and began working at five o'clock in the morning, my father would get up at four o'clock." As a man who had grown up in a working-class family, Cleveland Sellers, Sr., was proud of his accomplishments. He had resisted a life wasted by "white lightnin'" and "store-bought alcohol," not because white people on the other side of the tracks had made life any easier for him, but because he had damn well decided to.[3] First, he bought a few acres of land to farm. Then when he had saved enough money, he bought a restaurant and a taxicab. Working three jobs, he began buying houses to lease or sell. By the time Cleve was a teenager, his father owned more than twenty homes and had become a leader in Denmark's black community.[4] He also had four jobs and worked hard at all of them. Sellers's father was living proof that Washington's hard-work ethic remained gospel truth; neither he nor any of his brothers had ever worked for white people. To make his point perfectly clear, he would not shy away from airing his opinions on poverty for anyone who cared to listen. Sellers says, "I had heard him say on many occasions that anybody who really wanted to work did not have to be poor."[5] Still, he bent over backward to help the destitute people who often gathered outside his restaurant; and he tried to be a lenient and responsible landlord, usually allowing his tenants an extension on their rent if they were short of cash.

As a way of certifying their good fortune and growing social prestige, the Sellers family joined the St. Philip's Episcopal Church, located on the campus of Denmark's Voorhees College, a historically black school founded by the Protestant Episcopal Church. It did not matter that his father had been raised Baptist and his mother Methodist; the Episcopal church was "the place to worship for Denmark's up and coming black middle class."[6] Church membership had as much to do with civic responsibility as with spiritual matters: it was an essential part of good citizenship and all around conviviality—and, of course, it cemented business relations and social contacts. Yet the young Sellers wanted more out of religion than good manners and a pat on the back. He exhibited a sharp and restless intellect that would not tolerate simplistic answers to important questions about God and human existence. Salvation would not be a matter of good breeding alone.

At St. Philip's, Sellers found more. The church's young rector, Father Henry Grant, was energetic and provocative. Although Grant was no social radical, he kept an eye on the burgeoning civil rights movement in the South, often referring to it in his sermons as an example of a living faith. Grant had supplemented his theological education at Johnson C. Smith University with a master's degree in political science from the University of Iowa.[7] He quickly recognized in Sellers a soul mate and encouraged him to become an acolyte. Grant gave Sellers opportunities for leadership in the church, and also introduced him to the discipline and rich complexities of the Episcopal tradition. Sometimes he would even drive his young friend to other parishes in the diocese, where the two would observe and discuss different styles of worship. So taken was Sellers by Grant's ministry at St. Philip's that he soon became deeply involved with the church and increasingly more comfortable with its rituals; he even began thinking that he would also become a priest one day.

Above all else, Sellers was taken by the orderliness of the liturgy and the beauty of the eucharistic fellowship—the way men and women were drawn into the mysterious world of the sacraments. He also appreciated the aesthetic richness of the tradition, and a certain apprehension of nature and the sacred that came alive when he entered the darkened foyer of the chapel. "The earth is the Lord's for he made it," read one of Sellers's favorite prayers in the Psalter. There was a quality in the Episcopalian psyche that lent itself to a worldy openness and refreshment. Perhaps this was a result of the centrality of the eucharist, the sacrament animating all other parts of the Anglican communion, in which the wine and bread—objects of the natural world—were transformed by the divine mystery. Sellers came to believe in the goodness of the world and in a good God—and he trusted his desires, never feeling inhibited by his religious convictions. A sense of God's presence combined with an earthy confidence in his awakening faith. (To wit, he showed a great flair for the scatological, though always outside of his mother's earshot.)

The segregated society of Sellers's childhood was peaceful and predictable. The town lay at the outermost edge of South Carolina's low country, and like most southern hamlets was composed of two worlds, divided neatly by racial lines. Black Denmark was a strong, vital community centered around its college and schools. Sellers was nearly twelve years old before he first became aware of southern racism. Until then every reference point in his life was black—his neighborhood, school, church, friendships, shopping places. Yet far from oppressive, this self-contained world had manifold virtues. "Because I saw black people competently performing all manner of tasks all the time," Sellers explains, "I never had any reason to question their abilities. . . . From a very early age, I was always convinced that I could succeed whenever I really applied myself. As far as I was concerned, white people did not constitute a threat or deterrent to anything I wanted to be or accomplish."[8] Sellers thought nothing of the ascent to the balcony of the movie theater, where blacks were required to sit. He even turned the seating arrangement to his advantage; from his lofty perch, he would fire spit balls and smashed cups onto the heads of unsuspecting whites below, and dash to the back rows to avoid getting caught by the attendant who patrolled the aisles with a watchdog eye.

Although black residents were barred from access to institutional power, white leadership did not flaunt its authority. In fact, as Sellers recalls, no one ever discussed the issue of power. Whites had so effectively marginalized political issues that most elections went totally unnoticed by black people.[9] Whites enforced the Jim Crow restrictions that governed Denmark's public spaces and institutions with a kind of genteel paternalism—certainly not with the violence characteristic of towns in the deeper South. Black people may have accepted these conventions with instincts "almost Pavlovian," but there seemed no reason to call them into question.

At the end of August of 1955, the report of Emmett Till's brutal murder in Money, Mississippi, made national headlines. The ghastly details of Till's lynching, including a photograph of his disfigured corpse, were widely published in the nation's black magazines and newspapers, and discussed with disbelief and anger in Denmark's tightly knit black community. Not only were black Southerners dismayed by the report of another lynching (the Tuskegee Institute had recorded no such murders in the United States since 1951), but the latest victim in Mississippi had been a fourteen-year-old boy.[10]

Emmett Till of Chicago was visiting his great-uncle Moses "Preacher" Wright in Tallahatchie County, Mississippi. Unfamiliar with the complex grammar of southern race relations, and openly boastful of his white girl-friends back home (one of whose photographs was displayed in his wallet), Till defied his taunting cousins and their friends by walking into a white-owned store on the evening of August 24 and asking the woman at the counter for a date. Even when threatened with a gun, Till remained calm, saying "Bye, baby" and "wolf whistling" the woman before going back outside to the parking lot, where a group of astonished people was quickly disbanding and heading for home. The white woman's husband, Roy Bryant, had been away from his store the night of the incident. But two nights later, Bryant along with his half-brother, J. W. Milam, came for Till at Moses Wright's home. Over the next six or seven hours, Till was interrogated, cursed and beaten, and finally thrown into the waters of the Tallahatchie River with a hundred-pound fan tied with barbed wire to his neck—just seconds after taking a bullet to the right side of his head.

Although initially most local whites registered disgust with the murder, they soon closed ranks as the town of Money became populated with members of the national and international press, including reporters from the *New York Times*, *Le Monde*, and the *Daily Worker*. The all-white jury needed an hour and seven minutes to reach a verdict of not guilty. One juror later confessed, "If we hadn't stopped to drink pop, it wouldn't have taken so long."[11]

In Denmark, South Carolina, Sellers—just three years younger than Till—was hit hard by the brutal murder. For the first time in his life, he began thinking about racism, which he had been conditioned to accept without notice. Not only did Sellers see himself in the boy Till—his confident outlook, precocious mind, and playful wit drowned by the half-brothers in the Tallahatchie River. He realized that what had happened in Mississippi was no isolated event but part of the pervasive environment of white Southern racism—a fact tranquil Denmark could no longer conceal.[12] By 1960, other dark images had stirred Sellers's moral imagination: the lynching of Mack Charles Parker in Poplarville, Mississippi, the school integration crisis in Little Rock, the Montgomery bus boycott. At the same time, there also emerged a succession of exciting, empowering images: the faces of Daisy Bates, Rosa Parks, and Martin Luther King, Jr. "I was extremely proud of them," Sellers says, "They were my people. They were standing and fighting a common enemy."[13] He began to take stock.

When Henry Grant organized a "Summer School for Religious Education" at Voorhees College, Sellers had the opportunity to hear progressive church leaders discuss race relations and also meet black high school students from across the South—including a group from a black Episcopal church and school in Okolona, Mississippi, in the northeast region of the state.[14] Civil rights seemed as natural a topic of discussion at the youth conference as prayer and missions. "We'd talk about justice and peace; and basic catechisms that crossed over into civil rights concerns," Sellers recalls.[15] Although Denmark's white Episcopalians worshiped in the segregated Christ Church, located on Main Street a few blocks away from St. Philip's, the General Convention of the Episcopal Church had resolved in 1958 that "discrimination by reason of color or race between men has as its root human sin" and "that the Church must confess its own sin in this area." All men and women, of whatever race or color, the church declared, possess natural dignity by virtue of their having been created in the image of God.[16]

At the summer school Sellers participated in discussion groups with such black Episcopal leaders as Reverend Tollie L. Caution (executive director for racial minorities with the National Council) and Reverend William F. O'Neal (the rector of St. Luke's, Columbia, South Carolina).[17] The week's events inspired Sellers to begin thinking about racial injustice both in and outside the church, about the inequities between white and black communities in Denmark, and about the crushing impoverishment of most southern blacks. He resolved to put his faith into action. "I've gotta help do something about this shit!" he said.[18]

The movement came to Denmark in the middle of February 1960, just two weeks after a Woolworth department store was targeted for sit-ins on February 1 by student activists in Greensboro, North Carolina.[19] Although Sellers was only fifteen years old, he had no difficulty convincing the members of the Voorhees Student Governing Association—the principal organizers of the local sit-ins—that he was ready to move. Nor did he have trouble getting his mother's approval. When he explained his decision to her, "she smiled tenderly" and told him to be very careful but not to worry about the pressures that might be put on the parents as a result. The sit-in itself was completely bereft of drama: the small group of students marched into the drugstore, took seats and asked to be served. The whites sitting at the counter stared straight ahead in dismay, but said nothing to the students and soon left the store. The waitress then explained that the counter was for whites only, but the students remained seated. Police then arrived and began making arrests. The same day Sellers and his fellow students were released into the custody of Father Grant, who drove them back to the campus, where they were met with a mixture of fear and respect.

The sit-in would inspire further demonstrations, both on campus (where reforms in curriculum and student life were demanded) and in the town's business district. Movement fever began to spread slowly among the student body, peaking just around the time Bishop Thomas N. Carruthers of South Carolina visited Denmark in early April.[20]

By the fall, the fifteen-year-old Sellers—honor student, youth leader at St. Philip's, basketball star, and budding provocateur—had emerged as the leader of the Voorhees Student Association. Rebuffed by the local NAACP for his call to escalate demonstrations and marches—"'You young people are trying to go too fast,' they told us."—Sellers visited Rock Hill, South Carolina, where local activists were several months into demonstrations of businesses and public facilities.[21] Having endured numerous hardships and jailings, members of the Rock Hill movement, led by the indomitable Reverend C. A. Ivory from his wheelchair, showed no signs of slowing down. Sellers listened intently to Ruby Doris Robinson, who represented a new organization called the Student Nonviolent Coordinating Committee, as she described the strategy and goals of the Rock Hill initiative. He returned to Denmark determined to launch a challenge to the existing white power structure, and to do so by bypassing the town's diffident black leaders. Sellers was not bothered by the fact that few people in the community shared his zeal for change. Since the recently established SNCC was unable to offer organizational support, Sellers and Grant wrote an application to the NAACP's national headquarters in New York requesting a charter for a youth chapter, and the request was granted.

But Sellers's nascent activism in Denmark would soon come to a screeching halt. Henry Grant, under pressure from the parish chapter at St. Philip's, left Denmark to take a parish in Charleston, South Carolina.[22] Then on the morning of an afternoon rally at one of Denmark's other black churches, Sellers's father confronted his son point blank, "I want you to stop everything you've been doing. Right now. I think you've gone as far as you should go."[23] Sellers well knew his father's misgivings about his activism, but he never expected him to stand in his way. Sellers was incredulous and angry, not simply over the fact that he had organized the event and personally invited several well-known civil rights leaders to speak but even more because he had resolved to enter the movement and had no intention of turning back. He was not the least mollified by father's claim that somebody else would be able to do the work for him. He wanted to scream, "Goddammit, nigger, you're scared! You're scared of what those candy-assed white crackers will do to you!"[24] Nevertheless, on this morning he deferred to his father's authority and asked, "What do you suggest I do?" His father answered, "I suggest that you stay home and not attend that meeting this afternoon. I want you to stop everything right now." Sellers obeyed his father, but in his mind he was packing his trunk, numbering the days until he could go where the spirit said to go. He would not seek his father's advice on civil rights again.

Sellers thought he heard the spirit say go to Howard University. But his first impressions at that college were discouraging. His tattered blue jeans, sweat shirts, and army jackets, not to mention his "swashbuckling boots with d'Artagnanlike flaps" (as Mary King wrote), did not fit the Howard image.[25] A friend reprimanded him. "But Cleve, you'll never get a girlfriend. No girl's gonna be caught dead with you if you keep dressing like a refugee from World War I." But what surprised Sellers even more than criticisms of his sartorial presence was the indifference and boredom that always seemed to greet his effusive talk about the movement. After enduring more than he could stand one night, his roommate shouted, "Don't confront me with that Martin Luther King shit. Everybody's gotta go for himself and I'm going for me. If niggas down South don't like the way they're being treated, they oughta leave. I'm not going to join no picket lines and get the shit beat oughtta me by them crazy-ass Ku Klux-ers!" There were many things his roommate wanted from his Howard education—"a degree, a good job, a good woman, and a good living"—but civil rights for blacks was not one of them. "You and Martin Luther King can take care of the demonstrating and protesting. I have *no* use for them!"[26]

Indifference to civil rights was decidedly not the case for the "tall, lanky junior with sparkling eyes and an infectious smile" whom Sellers met toward the end of his freshman year. Stokely Carmichael, like Sellers, was flamboyant and independent; and having spent the previous summer working for SNCC in Mississippi, Carmichael assumed near-heroic proportions in Sellers's eyes. At Carmichael's invitation, Sellers attended a meeting of the campus organization called NAG (Nonviolent Action Group), an organization that already had experienced success in desegregating more than twenty facilities in Washington, D.C. Since NAG was considered one of the "Friends of SNCC" (an informal affiliate of the Student Nonviolent Coordinating Committee), Sellers became better versed in the emerging strategies for increased student involvement in the movement. Carmichael's apartment a few blocks from campus functioned as NAG's unofficial headquarters, and it soon became Sellers's new home. Almost every night a group of students, including Carmichael, Sellers, Courtland Cox, Stanley Wise, Bill Mahoney, and Ed Brown, gathered in the tiny, crowded studio and argued politics and movement strategy, sometimes until morning.

But even on campus, Sellers's life became consumed by movement fever. His conversations at Howard University with Muriel Tillinghast and Doris Robinson led to a time of serious introspection. Was he willing to take the risks his faith required, he asked himself? "That was the defining moment for me. What I did was try to set up the consequences and the reality of what I was committing my life to, because here I was about to take the step of sacrificing my life and making a long-term commitment. I had to have a deeper knowledge of what I was doing and how I could convey this to my parents. I had to find the courage and strength to become responsible for myself."[27]

In April 1964, during Sellers's sophomore year at Howard, Gloria Richardson, the leader of the civil rights movement in Cambridge, Maryland, and its main organization, the Cambridge Nonviolent Action Committee (CNAC), sent an urgent letter to the Howard group requesting the students' participation in an upcoming demonstration. SNCC had made Cambridge its northernmost target, and as a result the town had been under a modified marital law for nearly a year. Ever mindful of its pervasive slave culture in the early nineteenth century (which Frederick Douglass chillingly depicted in his *Narrative*) and its strong allegiance to the Confederacy, Cambridge and the surrounding region of Maryland's Eastern Shore remained as segregated as any area in the deep South. As historian Dan T. Carter described, "the state's anthem ('Maryland, My Maryland') still rang with protests over Abraham Lincoln's forcible overthrow of the pro-Confederate state legislature: 'The despot's heel is on thy shore / Maryland. His torch is at thy temple door / Maryland.'"[28] Now George Wallace, the governor of Alabama who had recently launched a presidential campaign, was bringing his states' rights/segregationist bandwagon to a large rally at the Cambridge Rescue and Fire Company's arena, sponsored by the Dorchester County Businessmen's and Citizen's Association, the organization opposed to the local movement's proposal for a public accommodations law.[29] NAG enthusiastically agreed to help Cambridge activists organize in protest, as did Sellers, even though his decision to get involved in a situation far more dangerous than anything he had previously experienced would come at a cost: he would flunk out of Howard by the end of the spring semester. Still, he counted that as nothing compared to the higher calling of the struggle for civil rights. The "small war in Cambridge" would be his baptism by fire into a movement life.

The Cambridge crisis was unlike anything Sellers had seen before. In face of hostile and often violent resistance to their demands for economic and social reforms, the town's black residents had ceased "extolling the virtues of passive resistance." Guns were carried as a matter of course by members of the local movement. On the night of Wallace's speech on May 11, an overflow crowd gathered at an Elks Lodge in Cambridge's black community. When the mass meeting adjourned, more than six hundred blacks reassembled outside, forming a demonstration line behind Gloria Richardson and eight priests from Catholic University. Sellers recalled that

while some of the people tried to start up freedom songs, "most of us remained grimly silent." And for good reason. Only a few blocks away from
the Elks Lodge, the marchers were stopped short by a phalanx of national
guardsmen, all armed with rifles and bayonets and wearing gas masks,
standing ranks across the width of the road. As the marchers approached
the barricade, a crowd of several hundred whites slowly became visible on
the sidewalks and surrounding spaces behind the guardsmen. Standing
near the front of the march, Sellers whispered to Carmichael, "Those
mothers mean business."[30] All eyes were on the soft-spoken woman with
the permanent scowl, who was warned by the guardsmen not to proceed
any further. "I'm going through," she said.[31]

Immediately, Richardson and two other blacks were seized, arrested,
and carried away by the military. But Sellers kept walking forward. "The
shit's on now," he thought, as he ducked the swing of a rifle butt aimed at
his head.[32] When Sellers grabbed the gun to avoid further attack, guardsmen fell on him from all sides to make an arrest. He followed his instinct
and went limp, collapsing back into the mass of the approaching demonstrators—fifty or sixty strong. But the guardsmen were prepared for resistance. A man dressed like an astronaut, in an iridescent uniform that gave
off "a soft, eerie glow" (described by SNCC photographer Danny Lyon as
"a vacuum-cleaner salesman from outerspace"), sprayed the crowd from
the two tanks of pepper gas strapped to his shoulder.[33] The demonstrators
took off running in great panic through the streets, realizing that their wet
handkerchiefs were no match for the searing effect of the gas. Sellers wrote
in his memoir, "The gas made our wet handkerchiefs burn like fire. It also
burned our nostrils. When we attempted to breathe out of our mouths in
order to save our nostrils, the gas attacked the insides of our mouths and
throats. My throat and stomach felt as if I had gulped a mouthful of burning acid." Sellers heard the sounds of the advancing guardsmen, "Ah-
HUMP-CLUMP-Ah-HUMP-CLUMP!" and saw "their bayoneted rifles extended
like spears," and then all went blank. He came to consciousness moments
later in the middle of street, on his back "like a dying cockroach." When
someone shouted, "Get up, Cleve! Here they come!" Sellers managed to
rise to his feet and stagger away. Everywhere people were vomiting and
sick as a result of the poisonous gas. Gunfire from the guardsmen exploded into the air. Sellers climbed a fence, two fences, and began running
again. But still behind him was the sound: "AH-HUMP-CLUMP-CLUMP!" "AH-
HUMP-CLUMP-CHOW!" Soon he was surrounded by other people, all running
in collective hysteria. Small groups of black men occasionally broke from
their retreat to fire on the guardsmen, hoping to slow them down.[34]

When Sellers reached CNAC headquarters, he found Carmichael in a
state of delirium, choking on his vomit and nearly unconscious. With the
help of a few men standing nearby, Sellers dragged Carmichael to a car and

set out in search of medical help. Not knowing where to go, and fearing hostile reprisals by whites, Sellers drove to the police station, hoping against hope to get an escort to the hospital. A police officer, after looking at a shivering Carmichael laying in a fetal position in the front seat of the car with his head in Sellers's lap, told Sellers to drive on to the fire station—someone could help them there. But at the fire station, they were greeted by a parking lot filled with state troopers and ordered into the back of a large truck. Several other demonstrators had been transported there by guardsmen for holding and were also being forced onto the truck. When SNCC staff member Cliff Vaughn resisted arrest, saying, "I haven't broken any law and I'm not going to get into that truck," one of the guardsmen shoved a bayonet through his calf, and blood gushed everywhere. Carmichael was dragged away from the group "as if he were a bag of rotten potatoes" and put into an ambulance.[35] Once in the truck, Sellers—and to his surprise Gloria Richardson, NAG member Khaleel Syyed, and SNCC activist John Batiste—were transported to the National Guard Armory in the Baltimore suburb of Pikesville, where they remained locked up for two days before being returned to the Cambridge city jail. The Cambridge Nonviolent Action Committee posted bail shortly after their return.

Sellers returned to Washington exhausted, much in need of a few days' rest. Instead, Stokely Carmichael, recuperated and again ready for action, gave Sellers their new assignment: organize and get prepared for Mississippi. SNCC had asked them to recruit black students for the Summer Project, scheduled to kick off in just over a month. And Sellers and Carmichael were expected to be there themselves.

The Long, Hot Summer

Six weeks later, on June 21, Sellers sat in attendance at the Summer Project training session at the Western College for Women in Oxford, Ohio. While Bob Moses was addressing the packed auditorium of student volunteers, a SNCC staff member walked to the edge of the stage and whispered the grim report in his ear that two CORE workers and a summer volunteer had disappeared near Philadelphia. Moses had not known that Mickey Schwerner had left Ohio, nor that he had taken two of his fellow workers to the scene of the church bombing.[36] When he received the news, he walked back to center stage, but did not speak; he bowed his head and gazed at the floor. After what seemed an eternity to Sellers, Moses, still staring at the floor, informed the audience of the missing civil rights workers. Sellers and most of his black coworkers knew immediately that the three men were dead. "There was no illusion on our part that they were still alive," he said.[37] Bob Moses, with characteristic restraint, explained to the group that John Doar of the Justice Department had been notified and had sent assurances that the FBI and other federal agencies would soon move into action.

Sellers, along with Stokely Carmichael and a handful of others, volunteered to accompany one of the many search parties dispatched to Neshoba County within hours of the announcement. COFO offices in Jackson and Meridian had already sent a number of teams. For the next three days, Sellers and Carmichael stayed with a black family who lived on a small farm near the church. They remained indoors during the daylight hours, helping themselves to a table full of turnip greens, ham hocks, buttermilk, and cornbread, and then met with local black sharecroppers under the cover of night to scour the countryside in search of the disappeared. "Piling from the truck at 1:30 or 2 A.M., we would fan out. Walking slowly, and almost never talking—we searched swamps, creeks, old houses, abandoned barns, orchards, tangled underbrush and unused wells. Most of us used long sticks to probe the many ditches and holes we encountered. When the sticks proved inadequate, as they frequently did, we had to feel about in the dark with our hands and feet."[38] The search party worked methodically, although, as Sellers admits, "we really didn't know what we were doing. We figured we could go into sundry areas and find where they were. We figured they were dead. But we were still caught between reality and an optimism. In our most optimistic moments, we hoped to find our fallen comrades staying in someone's house."[39] The bodies were never found during these nocturnal forays into frightening terrain.

So began Cleveland Sellers's "longest nightmare." He was assigned to the SNCC office in Holly Springs, a town fifty miles south of Memphis in Marshall County, assistant to the project's no-nonsense director, Ivanhoe Donaldson, who on their first day in Mississippi told his recruits point blank that if anyone failed to obey his rules, he could pack his bags "and get his ass out of town." "We're here to work," Donaldson said. "The time for bullshitting is past."[40] Sellers's interpersonal skills, developed as a youth leader in Denmark, served him well for a time. In his first days in Holly Springs, he would greet the sheriff and other city officials by extending his hand for a shake before the white men were able to process the racial indiscretion. "I'm here to work with the people on civil rights," he told them. "And I don't plan on causing any trouble. We want to help these people vote, because that is their constitutional right."[41] The empowering word would soon get out to the black community that one of the civil rights workers had stood up to the sheriff, or to the circuit clerk, and had not appeared intimidated.

Sellers's responsibility was to coordinate voter registration and freedom schools, and to help organize for the Mississippi Freedom Democratic party, particularly in the heavily black "crescent shaped area" west of Holly

Springs in the northern part of Marshall County. He was also asked to help organize SNCC's Freedom Days—communitywide voting celebrations meant to mobilize voters and broaden interest in registration.[42] Freedom Days always lifted Sellers's spirits, especially after the tiresome, often tedious business of SNCC field work. "Sometimes we were on farms and the white folks knew we were there. Credit from the stores would then be cut off, and we'd have to go pick in the fields for them. Nobody had any money. Midway into the summer, most of the money had run out and our diet was beans and peas and cheese, and then beans and beans and cheese, and then finally peanut butter and jelly."[43] But Freedom Days could be "awe-inspiring," as sharecroppers and domestics and black people from other professions made their way up to the courthouse, in their Sunday best and determined to register.

Organizing for the Mississippi Freedom Democratic party was a different matter, for among the local people, the MFDP called to mind the association with Chaney, Goodman, and Schwerner. Sellers soon discovered that to speak to people's fears required more than speaking to their political needs; it required speaking to their souls. By his third week in Mississippi, Sellers had rekindled his skills as a church leader, often visiting black (mostly Baptist) congregations, and in the spirit of Father Grant, preaching "a pretty good sermon" on faith and justice.[44]

Even though the racial climate in Holly Springs was milder than at such SNCC project locations as McComb and Hattiesburg, Sellers had never before encountered anything like Mississippi racism. It was visceral and raw. "Racist militance was more aggressive because Mississippi had gone to war footage," he said. "They were ready for war; everyone in the state had been alerted, the agencies, the institutions, they were all prepared for battle." Fear and anger fused with the steady threat of violence (and the consolation of violence) to create an almost unrelenting anxiety. "If you had an altercation with a white person who was trailing you or giving you the finger, you could be pretty sure that he was not gonna do anything right then. He was gonna go home and organize and come get you. Now, our Alabama comrades would tell us that in that state the white person was gonna get you right then and there. But in Mississippi, things were different. We always had to be ready for attack, at any time or place. If you saw a car coming around your house frequently, you knew something was up: the Klan was casing the joint, or a drive-by shooting was about to happen."[45]

Sellers's experience of Mississippi was equally visceral and intense; at times the summer charged toward an emotional overload. While Bob Moses seemed the calm at the eye of the storm—astonishing his fellow workers by an ability to fall peacefully asleep in the corner of a COFO office just minutes after surviving a terrorist attack or a life-threatening confrontation with white racists—Sellers was constant motion. At every moment he lived in a state of tension, "always stretched like a tight steel wire

between the pit of the stomach and the center of the brain."[46] The steady
threat of violence tested his spiritual and psychological resiliency. The
well-defined world of St. Philip's—and of black Denmark—seemed an increasingly distant memory. When his mother wrote to him that Denmark's
movie theaters had been integrated without incident, he was reminded
again that Mississippi was truly another world.[47] Sellers struggled for a way
to fathom the evil at hand.

On the last Friday night of July, after an MFDP meeting in Layfayette
County, Sellers was leading a three-car caravan through the university
town of Oxford when he observed in his rearview mirror police officers
signaling the two cars behind him to the side of the road.[48] He made a U-
turn and came to a stop. In minutes, several other police cars arrived. The
sheriff walked back and forth beside the three cars, with a smile on his
face, twirling a blackjack. He peered in Sellers's car and asked, "What yo'
name, boy?" Sellers told him his name and where he was from. What business does "a South Carolina nigra" have in Mississippi, the sheriff asked.
Sellers remained silent, although he sorely longed to jettison his commitment to nonviolence and spit in the man's face. The sheriff persisted,
"What's the matter, nigra? Cain't chew talk? Ever' time I turn on the television I sees one of you SNCC nigras talkin' 'bout how bad us white Mississippians is. What chew got ta say now?" With deliberate control, Sellers
told the sheriff he had nothing to say. The officer bellowed in response,
"Git yo' slack ass back in the cah!" If he caught Sellers and his comrades in
his jurisdiction again, he warned, he would make sure they left in a pine
box.

But Sellers was unable to drive away. The SNCC cars were now encir-
cled by a crowd of several hundred people, mostly men, howling "like
spectators at a bullfight." The sheriff had spotted a white woman in the
back of the Sellers's Volvo. "Out of the car!" he barked at Kathy Kunstler,
a summer volunteer and daughter of civil rights lawyer William Kunstler.
"Which one them coons is you fuckin?" he asked in a loud voice. A roar of
approving laughter swelled from the crowd. The sheriff continued, "Slut, I
know you fuckin' them niggers. Why else would you be down heah?
Which one is it? If you tell me the truth, I'll let you go. Which one is it?"
But Kunstler could not be broken, despite the sheriff's continued interrogation and verbal abuse. When he finished, the sheriff allowed her to return to the car, although not before telling the SNCC drivers, "Take your
white whores and get the hell out of Oxford! If I ketch any one of you heah
again, um gonna see to it that you git a quick trip to hell!"

Sellers and the other SNCC workers had barely made it to the city limits when a group of twenty cars began trailing along behind them. Pushing their speed up to 105 miles an hour and swerving perilously close to a
ravine to avoid the roadblock ahead, they were determined not to stop

their cars again—at least not voluntarily. "We drove the thirty miles from Oxford to Holly Springs as if we were Grand Prix racers. Our pursuers slowed down for bridges, sharp curves and small towns. We didn't. Hitting 105, we roared through the small towns along the way with our horns blaring and our gas pedals on the floor."[49] Miraculously, Sellers and his fellow travelers made it back to Holly Springs.

His friends and coworkers Charlie Scales and Wayne Yancey would not be so lucky. The day after the Oxford incident, a call came into the SNCC office in Holly Springs that the two staff members had been seriously injured in an automobile accident. When Sellers and Ivanhoe Donaldson arrived at the hospital, they discovered Yancey's battered body laying unattended in the back of a hearse, his blood spilling out on the concrete parking lot. Beside the hearse, a group of white police officers stood guard, acting "as if all [this] was a circus" (as the SNCC affidavit read).[50] An angered Donaldson demanded to know what was going on. "You cain't move the body," the officer replied, on account of "mayor's orders."[51] One of the white onlookers explained in menacing detail the effect of Yancey's head going through the windshield. The young civil rights worker's mangled face, his shattered leg and the deep cuts in his body immediately conjured in Sellers's mind the photographs of Emmett Till—though there was little time to ponder the haunting sense of déjà vu.

Charlie Scales was struggling for his life inside the hospital, on a table in the emergency room, much in need of the medical assistance that had been refused him by the white doctors and nurses.[52] Sellers and Donaldson tried to rescue Scales and drive him to a hospital in Memphis, but they were stopped by police officers at the front door. Incredibly, one of the officers wanted to arrest Scales for manslaughter since he had been the driver of the car in which Yancey had been killed. Through a combination of "begging, threatening and pleading," Donaldson was eventually able to get the mayor's permission to move Scales to Memphis's Meherry Hospital, where he received successful treatment. Although no concrete evidence was ever found to indicate that the accident was a result of foul play, Scales recalled that when he came to consciousness on the side of the road a white man was standing over him, telling him to be quiet or "you'll get the same thing as your buddy!" Scales claimed that his car was forced into the massive collision with the oncoming automobile when the car he was passing—driven by a white man—would not allow him to yield ahead.[53]

At the time, Sellers was certain that Yancey's death had been somehow orchestrated by whites. It was yet another part of the living nightmare of Mississippi. With the preceding anxious weeks, his friend's death and then, on August 4, the day after Wayne Yancey's wake, the discovery of the mutilated bodies of Chaney, Goodman, and Schwerner, the summer came to a crisis. The pain would not subside: "it was impossible for me to rest or forget what had been done to those three innocent men." "Hate and viciousness seemed to be everywhere," he thought. After staying drunk for several days, Sellers tried to pull himself together, to "keep on keepin' on," but it was impossible. He knew without a doubt that death could come at any moment in any form—"a bullet between the shoulder blades, a fire bomb in the night, a pistol whipping, a lynching." He said, "I had never experienced such tension and near-paralyzing fear."[54]

By the time the Democratic National Convention ended in Atlantic City in late August, Sellers was convinced that the kind of challenge to Jim Crow waged by COFO, CORE, and SNCC in Mississippi throughout the summer—a patient and studied petitioning for civil rights—amounted to precious energy poorly spent. The MFDP's defeat at the convention confirmed that the movement needed to change course; that, as two of its founding members concluded, "we cannot look to the Office of the Presidency, the Democratic or Republican Parties as presently constituted, the redemptive force of love, public moral outrage, the northern political establishment, nor even to the Congress with its 'Great Society' legislation."[55] Sellers was disillusioned and angry. "We had such idealism and hope for the people, most of whom had never been out of the state before. We wanted them to make a difference; to be able to jump for joy and say, 'I did it; we did it.' I, for one, had a lot of hope built around this." Sellers began to turn his attention away from the ideal of the beloved community and toward what he considered more realistic political solutions. Never again, Sellers insisted, should the civil rights forces be "lulled into believing that our task was exposing injustices so that the 'good' people of America could eliminate them."[56] The movement must demand liberation and power.

Beyond the Beloved Community

Sellers returned to Holly Springs after Atlantic City, though not before visiting his parents in Denmark, to unwind after a summer that had been physically and psychologically punishing. His parents tried hard to conceal their distress, but their anxiety was everywhere apparent. It was apparent in the awkward silences that fell between Sellers and his sister; in his father's momentary "look of tenderness and pain" as his son was saying goodbye. It was apparent in his mother's question—restated numerous times throughout the weekend and in subsequent letters—why he had to return to Mississippi. She wrote him shortly after his visit: "I have just finished reading an article in the paper. . . . After Goldwater lost, the Mississippians are planning to go back to their guns. They also said that no one will be convicted for killing the three C.R. workers, in fact, 'a white man will never be convicted for killing a nigger in Mississippi.'" Knowing little about the confrontation outside of Oxford with the sheriff and his mob, Pauline Sellers offered motherly caution: "Whatever you do, don't trust your luck. It makes no difference to an ignorant drunkard about the law unless you have bodyguards—and you don't have them—so be cautious at all times, because I can imagine everyone knows by now the kind of car you drive and has it spotted. I really wouldn't drive at night."[57] In another letter she also made no secret of her wish that her son finish his college degree. "Everybody seems to think that the summer project was OK, but they think it was very unwise to stay out of school. I think so for this reason: you are impairing your health and mind. If you change your mind and decide to go back in school the second semester, I'll expect you home for Christmas. If you still plan to go to school next fall, I'll expect you home in the early summer."[58] On a card with the picture of St. Philip's Episcopal Church on the front, she included news about the family and the high school football team's victory over Fayettesville with the fearful report, "I heard on the T.V. that two churches were burned in Philadelphia, Mississippi, today."[59] But Sellers found himself unable to give his mother a clear answer. "It's something I must do," he could only say of his decision to return.[60]

Although the rolling hills and barren fields around Holly Springs were familiar to Sellers, the landscape of the movement in Mississippi had changed. "The summer volunteers, the newspaper and television reporters and the local hangers-on were gone. For those of us who remained, there was only fear, work and exhaustion."[61] Ivanhoe Donaldson had been transferred to SNCC's National Office in Atlanta, leaving Sellers as project director in charge of Holly Springs. Along with the other directors and staff members in Mississippi, Sellers began the hard work of critically reviewing SNCC's strategies to date, reconsidering the principles and presuppositions that had governed the Summer Project. SNCC's energetic, spontaneous activism, its sense of idealism, and its willingness to embrace diverse ideas and people had served the organization well in the past, but staff members began to wonder whether these attitudes and values were still appropriate to the changing landscape.[62] Moreover, the summer's many successes—the encouragement of local initiatives, the creation of solid financial support, the increased federal commitment to civil rights, and the interracial witness of the summer workers—seemed overshadowed by the defeat in Atlantic City.

Indeed, the defeat of the MFDP challenge to the all-white regular Democrats was much harder for the SNCC staff to take than for the local people, who by and large possessed a stubborn, time-worn realism toward politics. Sellers and many other staffers began to take stock. Should SNCC become a more formally defined organization, better equipped to foster al-

ternative political structures now that the Democratic party and liberal social policy had shown their true colors? Was SNCC's dependence on a
leadership lacking specialized skills adequate to carry the movement beyond the achievements of the first half of the 1960s? Was SNCC's distinc-
tively anti-authoritarian character still appropriate?

These questions came into vigorous debate in November 1964 at a
SNCC staff retreat at the Gulfside Methodist Assembly in Waveland, Mississippi. By drafting and discussing a series of position papers on a wide
range of important issues, SNCC staffers attempted to come to terms with
the organization's new priorities and responsibilities. In the course of these
discussions, it became clear that SNCC was undergoing dramatic change.
One paper, attributed to Bob Moses, illustrated the situation as that "of a
boat in the middle of the ocean," proposing that "[it] has to be rebuilt in
order to stay afloat. It also has to stay afloat in order to be rebuilt. Our problem is like that. Since we are out on the ocean we have to do it ourselves."[63]

Bob Zellner's question went to the heart of many staffers' concerns.
"Where does SNCC fit in politically, ideologically, and religiously in America?" he asked. "This summer we worked for LBJ. We were a tool of the
Democratic Party. What does it mean to be a revolutionary?"[64] Zellner im-
plored his fellow SNCC staffers "to talk about these things rather than talking about talking and procedures." Donna Richards Moses's response that
"it's revolutionary to use the word 'revolutionary' in this country" only illustrated the sort of abstraction against which Zellner cautioned. Although Zellner insisted in the opening session of the conference that "we
have got to be a band of brothers and stay together from now on," the
Waveland meeting made clear that SNCC's survival as an interracial,
loosely knit organization depended on the recognition of disagreement—
the achievement of a unity that included difference. What it meant to be
a revolutionary was complex and multi-layered, even if the context of revolutionary activity was specific to a single county in the state of Mississippi. To be sure, all the staffers were generally committed to "participatory democracy," the notion that local people should work together in the
democratic process to develop the power "to control the significant events
that affected their lives."[65] But participatory democracy, like the idea of a
revolutionary, never came down to the same notion—or the same case.

The Waveland retreat offered a glimpse into the fragile, often cacophonous self-understandings of SNCC on the verge of enormous internal
change. Conflicts came to the surface that had hitherto remained unspoken: between college-educated staffers and those with little formal education, between outside activists and local people; and disputes erupted
concerning administration, strategy, gender inequality within the organization, and white involvement.[66] In the end, the position papers raised
more questions than SNCC could answer. The effect of the Waveland re-

treat, despite whatever urgency the position papers proposed, was to diffuse the organization's attention to specific tasks, while at the same time, to emphasize the particular differences of the individual members and the various ideological clusters. With their faith in the federal government shaken, if not shattered, by the experience in Atlantic City, SNCC staff members began to work more deliberately in directions that mirrored class, gender, and racial identities.[67] No longer did it seem enough to focus on voter registration or the various concrete initiatives of the previous summer: it was important to be a revolutionary. Or if not quite that, at least to talk about being a revolutionary.

Nonetheless, in the months following the Waveland retreat, Sellers began to conclude that the revolutionary ideal—at least as embodied in many SNCC members—had little to do with concrete action toward specific ends and too much to do with an increasingly abstract concept of freedom. A volunteer in Laurel, Mississippi, exhibited an extreme version of Sellers's concern when she stated her belief that the United States and the world could be changed "by nonviolence and real honesty, and letting everybody say things, and not even have to do such things as vote or have leaders or officers."[68] Extreme to be sure, but Sellers detected a similar disposition among many of his SNCC comrades, especially those gathered around the enigmatic Bob Moses. The "philosophers, existentialists, anarchists, floaters, and freedom-high niggers," he called them, "the little Bobs," always high on freedom, positioned against the grain, unified only in their resolute opposition to all forms of organization and structure.[69] Moses had even taken to suggesting that SNCC should abolish all its committees.[70] But Sellers believed it was counterproductive for SNCC to move in this direction. As he explained, "If a confrontation developed in Jackson, Mississippi, and a group of Freedom-High Floaters was working in southwest Georgia, they would pile into cars and head for Jackson. They might return to Georgia when the Jackson confrontation was over—and they might not. No one ever knew for certain what they were going to do or where they might turn up next. They were great talkers, who generally ended up dominating those meetings and conferences they saw fit to attend. Holding forth with long, involved existential arguments, they would take as long as three days of nonstop talking to win a single inconsequential point; but they didn't mind. They loved to bring meetings to a screeching halt with open-ended, theoretical questions. In the midst of a crucial strategy session on the problems of community leaders in rural areas, one of them might get the floor and begin to hold forth on the true meaning of the word *leader*. "What is a leader?" the speaker would ask. The term would be defined and examined and analyzed before proceeding to other matters: "Should SNCC continue encouraging grass-roots leadership— leadership from the ground up—or might it actually be that leaders are born not made?" "Perhaps we are not helping local people become free. Perhaps we are in fact contributing to the oppression of local people by giving them false hopes and unrealistic expectations." "What is freedom, anyway?" Sellers grew frustrated. "SNCC was not a debating society," he said. "It was an action organization."[71]

Sellers was elected program director of SNCC in February of 1965. After his move to SNCC headquarters in Atlanta, he immediately sought aggressive measures to refocus SNCC toward specific, realizable goals. Some of his measures were rhetorical, others were programmatic and procedural. None went over very well with most of his SNCC comrades. Against the "freedom high floaters," Sellers laid down his own hard-line position: pursuing justice for blacks required limits and constraints to individual freedom.[72] The spirit did not just blow where it willed; in good Episcopal fashion, Sellers presumed that it was particular to certain forms and orders. Combining in a sense the virtues of his two fathers, that is, the financial efficiency that had well served the elder Sellers's business ventures and the spiritual orderliness Henry Grant brought to liturgical life, Sellers demanded that all SNCC members begin "to accept at least a minimal amount of discipline." As he said in a letter to staffers after he took office, "Any one who doesn't like things can go home."[73]

Sellers's hard-line reform of SNCC was driven by a spiritual intensity that should not go unappreciated. When he became a member in 1964, he took a vow of poverty on behalf of the struggle for civil rights, resolving to forsake family, education, and the narcissistic pleasures of student life. The sort of "interior spiritual discipline" to which he committed himself meant much more than wearing tattered blue jeans, sweat shirts or overalls—like the "summer soldiers in their artificially faded denim," in the words of one SNCC staffer.[74] The changes taking shape inside the organization—and, of course, outside in the national landscape—demanded sober minds and realistic assessments of the situation. As Sellers saw it, the passage of the civil rights laws of 1964 and 1965 had created the paradoxical effect of fulfilling many of SNCC's persistent demands while at the same time obscuring the more elusive issue of class and caste oppression.[75] Sellers came to see that the structures of white racism oppressed black people quite apart from insulting traditions or the abuse of bigots and know-nothings; these structures needed to be challenged with a renewed energy and a sharper focus.[76] He reached the conclusion that the time of words was over, the time of freedom songs and mass meetings, the time when movement people could sit down together and hold forth on the beloved community.[77] Now—in the language of Ecclesiastes—was the time to cast away stones and to rend.

Inside the organization, the floaters, gathered around Bob Moses, continued to claim that every individual had the right above all else to follow his or her own conscience. They dug in their heels, calling Sellers and the other hard-liners fascist, self-centered, and (worst of all) bureaucratic. Yet Sellers believed his hard-line position was the only adequate response to a heightened atmosphere of "tension, frustration, paranoia and internal hostility." The clash of ideas assumed high dramatic form when Sellers and fellow hard-liners Stanley Wise, Rap Brown, and Stokely Carmichael crashed a late-night rump session of floaters during the 1965 annual fall meeting at the Gammon Seminary in Atlanta. Bob Moses and his "existentialists" were found deep in their musings on the nature of oppression. Sellers listened quietly as one floater ruminated on the question, "Do you remember when you were a child? Do you remember how people oppressed you, not with chains or anything, but because they were always trying to get you to do things you didn't really want to do?" Sellers could not contain his frustration. "What has that got to do with SNCC and the work before us?" he shot back.[78]

A vigorous, increasingly hostile debate ensued, with the hard-liners refusing to shift the ground to philosophical concerns and the floaters maintaining that the hard-liners had grown arrogant and calloused. The floaters questioned even the morality of the Summer Project, going to great lengths—in Sellers's view—to distance themselves from concrete concerns. "We took all those people up to Atlantic City," one floater insisted, "and we accomplished nothing but getting them disappointed." "We gave them unrealistic expectations; we shouldn't have done that. Maybe the whole project was a mistake." The floaters lamented their use of force and coercion (inadvertent though it may have been) in moving local people towards SNCC's own goals. "What we have to do with the people is not coerce them, but wait for them to get to the point where they understand what they are doing, and then move with them." Had SNCC manipulated rural men and women in the MFDP for its own advantage, betraying their sincerity and trust? But Sellers had come to despise what he considered romantic notions of the poor—of "localpeopleitis"—in part, because they seemed condescending but also because he thought such notions mystified the concrete demands of political action.[79] He told his antagonists, "Stick to reality. We are trying to move people from one place to another. Sometimes we have to coerce them. Sometimes we have to shame them. They're frequently afraid and reluctant to do the things we want, but that's the way it is. We are not oppressors. We aren't doing anything we should be ashamed of. We *have* to establish priorities. Getting people to deal with their fears and insecurities is a SNCC priority. There's nothing wrong with that! We don't need to get hung up on a lot of philosophy. What we ought to be discussing is strategy and programs. Where are your programs?"[80] The revolution will require pain and suffering and, yes, even some coercion; but we must move on to the next stage.[81]

What was left of the old SNCC was vividly illustrated in the strange eucharist that followed the Gammon meeting. Moses produced a bottle of wine and a large slice of cheese, and lifted up the elements with raised hands. "I want you to eat and drink," he said. He passed the bottle and cheese to the women and men in the room, even though, as Sellers recalled, the bottle was empty. Moses and his wife then left the room without speaking. Everyone present seemed to recognize that *this* SNCC had taken its last supper together. Not only would Moses soon depart Mississippi for Canada and thereafter for Tanzania (where he would live until 1976) but SNCC as a reconciled brotherhood and sisterhood, sharing a common cause, celebrating shared and sacred hopes, had come to an end.

Sellers was far from lamenting this situation. His surging anger forged the severe point that sometimes reconciliation has "to be put on the back burner." Now was that time, a time for liberation, a time delineated by the recently slain Malcolm X (whom Sellers had begun reading in earnest) in his bold exhortation to his black brothers and sisters, "Don't love your enemy, love yourself." Sellers said to himself, "I'm stepping out here."[82]

Black Power

He began setting the house in order. One way to solve the problems of SNCC, he insisted, was to tighten up the organization's improvisational way of operating, to introduce greater structure, even at the risk of alienating movement veterans. An organization that had once had a staff of 17 people now had 250, a million-dollar budget and a huge fleet of late-model automobiles. Although SNCC had historically resisted any kind of bureaucratic rigor in its organization, Sellers recognized that SNCC had—despite itself—become a bureaucracy through rapid growth and expansion. As such, it had best be an efficient one. "I didn't create the bureaucracy," Sellers said, "but that's what we had. And if we didn't hurry up and deal with that, we were going to trip over ourselves. We had cars running around and we didn't even know where the hell they were. We didn't know where our people were. We were paying folks and we had no idea what they're doing. They might be in Alabama and they'd call and say send me a check to Alabama. And I'd say, weren't they in Mississippi two weeks ago, so why are they in Alabama? 'Well,' someone would say, 'they're just being with people. The spirit called them.' Well hell no. I'm sorry. I'm not gonna do it like that. There was a time when if the spirit moved you, you had to go—and that was fine. But now we have a huge organization and, no, people can't be all over the place doing all kinds of things. There must be some kind of structure in place."[83] Hard-liner John Lewis agreed, asserting that those people who "want to do what they want and go where they want"—those who "want to experiment with personal freedom"—better be "shaping up or shipping out."[84]

Sellers conducted a thorough evaluation of SNCC's operations. When he judged a project unproductive, he promptly terminated it. His judgments were swift and decisive. Sellers's audacity in interrogating and assessing his SNCC colleagues generated immediate resentment. Consider the following evaluation, which reads like a manifesto of hard-liner thought:

Category	Names involved	General Comments
B. Atlanta	Ruth Howard	leaves office on whim and work (Student Voice) gets behind
	Emma Bell	office hours too irregular and has been straightened out to some degree
C.	John Buffington	requested vacation
	Randy Battle	" " " " "
D. Re-assignment	Battiste	left Cambridge to work in Alabama/ haven't heard from him since
	Jimmy Travis	left Atlanta to work in Arkansas, stayed in Jackson one month—leave of absence granted for 1 year
F. Work-study Program	(Ruby can speak to this)	poor programs because no one really works on it and nor do most of the kids. The *executive committee* should resolve this problem.
G. Problems—specific	Fred Meely	to be decided by Silas at this point. took staff car to NY for almost 2 months/new program very hasty . . .
	Cordell Reagon	Muriel suggest dismissal from staff. Misappropriation of monies and general misbehavior . . . wife to be notified when such is passed and given a month to adjust to the decision financially
	G'wood	people sent $5000 food/clothing down from Minnesota Task Force and truck was re-routed to 708 . . . folks up north were upset
	Susie Morgan	Mississippi woman SNCC supported for last 1 and 1/2 years/requested to find other means of support . . .
J. Volunteers	Northern volunteers (procedure and form letters made . . .)	If request from the field, ok., if *not* then we'd tell 'em "no."[85]

In addition, letters were sent to every staff member who did not have a specific and well-defined task; these individuals were required to inform Sellers and the other Executive Committee members, in writing, of their work. A second letter was then sent to those who failed to reply, or to those whose reply was unsatisfactory, informing them they had been dropped from the payroll and could henceforth consider themselves disaffiliated from the Student Nonviolent Coordinating Committee.

Sellers's hard-liners and the fledgling floaters came to blows (almost literally) in the fall retreat of 1965—again at Waveland. Sellers's arrangements for the retreat represented a kind of in-your-face assertion of his new austere leadership. He set up a registration desk, preassigned bedrooms, and printed out programs, session schedules, and meal tickets. The floaters were not amused. On the first night of the meeting, they threw a party on the lawn of the campgrounds and burned their meal tickets in a large bonfire. The next morning, they slept late and missed breakfast. When they arrived for lunch, Sellers and a band of hard-liners stood in a blockade in front of the cafeteria door. "No one eats without a meal ticket," Sellers announced. Furious, hungry—and a little hung over—the floaters retreated momentarily, only to return armed with pool sticks, baseball bats, knives, and a couple of pistols. Jim Forman, SNCC's executive secretary, stepped between the groups before fighting began, telling Sellers to ease up. Undaunted, Sellers thundered back, "No! These guys came here to do just what they're doing. They've got it so nobody in the organization can do a goddamn thing. Every time we try to plan something, they fuck it up with a lot of irrelevant bullshit. Time's up for this shit." But no one really listened, because the confrontation quickly degenerated into a carnival of misdirected tempers. According to Sellers, a cook (unaffiliated with SNCC) swung a meat cleaver at hard-liner Cynthia Washington; John Lewis slapped a screaming floater in the face, making her cry; floater Courtland Cox shouted incomprehensibly from the top of a table. Remarkably, no one was seriously injured, and eventually the floaters backed down and left the cafeteria.[86]

The chaos in Waveland mirrored SNCC's direction under the new hard-line leadership. Sellers commented drolly, "Everyone who ate in the cafeteria for the remainder of the staff meeting used a meal ticket."[87] Although the hard-liners now could boast organizational control, SNCC's presence in Mississippi toward the end of 1965 began to seem desultory and uninspired. Support of the Mississippi Freedom Democratic party and the freedom schools continued, but SNCC, suffering from battle fatigue, internal dissension, and outside distractions, failed to recreate a unifying vision of its work. The ideal of the beloved community, however abstract and ethereal the hard-liners deemed it, had at least given SNCC's initiatives a powerful moral and spiritual warrant. Ironically, without a clear vision, many of the hard-liners began to do precisely what they most despised: they floated. They floated from issue to issue: they "aligned" with northern radical organizations, supported "independent programs" in Chicago, Detroit, and Washington D.C., developed a South America campaign and an anti-apartheid program, and made a series of ad hoc pronouncements on foreign policy. Even SNCC's statement in opposition to the war in Vietnam floated: "We believe the United States government has been deceptive in its claims of concern for the Vietnamese people, just as the government has been deceptive in claiming concern for the freedom of colored people in such other countries as the Dominican Republic, the Congo, South Africa, Rhodesia and the United States."[88] Ivanhoe Donaldson moved to Columbus, Ohio, to organize in an urban community; others also moved out of the South to northern cities, often with the intention of setting up urban outposts for SNCC and expanding the organization into new, more challenging environments.

SNCC's radical alignments, revolutionary promulgations, and urban reform proved inconsequential.[89] For, in the end, floating was not the hardliners' real concern after all. What was really at stake soon became unmistakably clear in Lowndes County, Alabama, where Stokely Carmichael had relocated in the summer of 1965, deep in the heart of the west Alabama "black belt," with his sleeping bag, a few dollars in his wallet, and the name of a local contact person. With a handful of other SNCC staffers, Carmichael worked among local community leaders to form the all-black Lowndes County Freedom Organization (LCFO), whose logo of a snarling black panther unveiled SNCC's new self-understanding—and made for a dramatic contrast to the white rooster of the regular Democrats.[90] Carmichael's contact person was local activist John Hulett, a man of deliberate authority and the first black person to register to vote in the district. Alongside SCLC's Andrew Young and James Bevel, Hulett had helped create the Lowndes County Christian Movement for Human Rights. But when SCLC failed to send a full-time staff person to Lowndes County, Hulett began making contact with SNCC people, many of whom he had met months before at a march in Montgomery.[91] Initially, Carmichael spent his time mobilizing voters among the county's 65 percent black majority, but this changed when SNCC's staff researcher, Jack Minnis, discovered an obscure Alabama law permitting the formation of an independent political party at the county level. The Lowndes County Freedom Organization was soon thereafter established, with Hulett as its first chairman. With an ever-growing sense of political ownership, the LCFO registered nearly 4,000 black people by election day—an achievement made even more remarkable by the fact that not a single black person had been registered to vote in March of the previous year.

Although the LCFO lost in all seven races—two of the three candidates for Department of Education by fewer than three hundred votes (1,669 to 1,937; 1,668 to 1,966)—the party and its tireless organizers successfully demonstrated the hitherto untapped political power of local black people. Of course, the Mississippi Freedom Democratic party had demonstrated as much in 1964, but the Lowndes County initiative was witness to the exciting possibilities of political power created and controlled by blacks alone. As John Hulett said, "We aren't asking any longer for protection—we won't need it—or for anyone to come from the outside to speak for us, because we're going to speak for ourselves now and from now on." Lowndes County's black population had shown that they were "tired of the bones" from the white folks' table. "We are going to have some of the meat too," Hulett promised. As for the bold sketch of the black panther, displayed on the sides of general stores and community centers around the black belt, the message should be clear. "The black panther is a vicious animal," Hulett declared. "He never bothers anything, but when you start pushing him, he moves backwards, backwards, and backwards into his corner, and then he comes out to destroy everything that's before him."[92] Carmichael's comments seemed conciliatory by comparison: "We want power, that's all we want. After we get power we can talk about whether we want all black or not."[93] (In California, Huey Newton came upon a pamphlet distributed by the Bay Area Friends of SNCC describing the Lowndes County campaign and lifted the symbol for his Black Panther party.)[94]

Importantly, whites had not been excluded from the Lowndes County Freedom Organization as a matter of policy; in fact, it was the Klan murder of white Detroit homemaker Viola Liuzzo, a voter registration volunteer in Lowndes County, that originally attracted SNCC interest in the area. But after the success of the Lowndes County project, Sellers and the new SNCC leadership increasingly emphasized the idea of power for black people, commencing to use the word "black" in reference to Americans of sub-Saharan African descent.[95] The success of the initiative confirmed Sellers's hard-line convictions and his belief that action shaped by discipline must yield greater power for blacks. By the summer of 1966, Sellers was convinced that the organization must completely reinvent itself in terms of the new ideology. As the embodiment of a nationalistic black consciousness, SNCC must become the animating center of a new racial spirituality. No longer was reconciliation with whites a part of the movement. "The real issue is power," Sellers said. "Black babies are not dying of malnutrition because their parents do not own homes in white communities. Black men and women are not being forced to pick cotton for three dollars a day because of segregation. Integration has little or no effect on such problems." Sellers never minced his words: "If we have power, we can keep people from fucking us over."[96]

Still, it was not until the summer of 1966 that the message of black power hit white America like a slap in the face. James Meredith, the Air Force veteran who in the fall of 1962 had integrated the University of Mississippi under the hostile scrutiny of Governor Ross Barnett and the protection of a federalized national guard, had assumed a low profile as a student in the intervening years. But on June 5, 1966, the ever-inscrutable Meredith launched a one-man demonstration to show the nation that conditions for blacks had changed in Mississippi. "The old order was passing," he said, black people can now "stand up as men with nothing to fear."[97] Meredith would walk two hundred miles from Memphis to Jackson and demonstrate the point. Sadly, he did not walk ten miles before he was shot in the head and neck by a white terrorist and rushed to a hospital back in Memphis. Within hours, news reports had refocused attention on civil rights issues in Mississippi, a feat that SNCC had been incapable of doing since the media blitz during the 1964 Summer Project.

At the time of the shooting, Sellers, Carmichael, and Stanley Wise had been in Little Rock, Arkansas, seeking to energize floundering projects, but when they heard the news the three men drove to Memphis to see Meredith. Although Meredith had no use for the SNCC radicals, he agreed with SCLC officials that the march should be continued in his absence. The March Against Fear, as it was called, soon became a media showcase for black power, a story made all the more striking by the presence of Martin Luther King, Jr., alongside Sellers and Carmichael. Dr. King wanted the march to focus national attention on President Johnson's new civil rights bill, which included a range of anti-discrimination protections as well as open-housing provisions. But Sellers, Carmichael, and the other SNCC participants wanted the march to highlight black liberation from white racism, and the urgent necessity of eliminating black fear.[98] Beneath a hot summer sun and back again in Mississippi, Carmichael and Sellers charted out a new course for the civil rights movement. Black dignity should be preserved by any means necessary, they told onlookers and reporters. "Does that include violence?" Sellers was asked frequently. "Any means necessary is self-explanatory," was his response.[99] To add muscle to the point, the Louisiana-based black paramilitary group, the Deacons for Defense and Justice, escorted the marchers on their pilgrimage to Jackson. (Perhaps the sight of these armed black men kept Sam Bowers's newest sycophant, Byron de la Beckwith, from engaging in business any more serious than occasional interruptions in his pickup truck.)[100]

On Thursday, June 16, when the marchers—now six hundred strong—stopped for a mass rally with local blacks in Greenwood, Carmichael was arrested on the charge of trespassing on public property. Making bail a few hours later, he ascended the speaker's platform and electrified the audience by howling out that "every courthouse in Mississippi should be burnt down tomorrow so we can get rid of the dirt." "This is the 27th time I have been arrested," he continued, "I ain't going to jail no more. I ain't going to jail no more." Over the thunderous applause, Stokely told the crowd, "From now on when they ask you what you want, you know what to tell 'em." "We want Black Power!" he shouted. "Black Power!" the people shouted back. "Black Power!" "Black Power!" "Black Power!" the chant continued.[101] The next day, as reporters across the country screamed the frightening news of the new racial militancy, white America began to understand what Martin Luther King had tried to explain when he wrote in his letter from the Birmingham city jail that "if our white brothers dismiss us as 'rabble-rousers' and 'outside agitators' those of us who are working through the channels of nonviolent direct action and refuse to support our nonviolent efforts, millions of Negroes, out of frustration and despair, will seek solace and security in black nationalist ideologies, a development that will lead inevitably to a frightening racial nightmare."[102]

Although King had not been in Greenwood to hear Carmichael's speech, on the days he rejoined the march he tried to walk a fine line with reporters by maintaining his commitment to nonviolence without fully denouncing the message of black power. He said, "I'm not interested in power for power's sake, but I'm interested in power that is moral, that is right and that is good."[103] The possession of power is important, King acknowledged, but the seizing of power must proceed in dialectical kinship with the responsibilities of love.[104] He was less reticent in speaking harshly of SNCC. He made no secret of his disappointment with the separatist rhetoric and policies. He had tolerated the presence of the Deacons for Defense and Justice; he had tolerated Carmichael's vitriolic speeches; he had listened patiently as certain SNCC members argued that whites should be kept out of the march, but he was losing patience. "I'm sick and tired of violence," he told an audience in Yazoo City, "I'm sick of the war in Vietnam. I'm tired of war and conflict in the world. I'm tired of shooting. I'm tired of hatred. I'm tired of selfishness. I'm tired of evil. I'm not going to use violence, no matter who says it." He reasserted several times his own unyielding commitment to an interracial movement. "We must never forget that there are some white people in the United States just as determined to see us free as we are to be free ourselves." Above all, he reaffirmed his commitment to the goal of "a truly brotherly society, the creation of the beloved community."[105] Although King's polemics against white racism were second to no one's, his commitment to Christianity "offered him no outlet in the rhetoric of violence" (as the theologian Richard Lischer observed).[106]

Whereas the March Against Fear gave Stokely Carmichael the perfect forum for promoting both Black Power and himself, Sellers seemed awestruck by his first encounter with King. In his memoir, he accounts for part of his admiration by positioning King in close proximity to SNCC's new orientation: King the "staunch ally" and "true brother."[107] Perhaps more important was that Sellers encountered once again—in King's sermons and in the nightly church meetings of the twenty-day march—the theological vision of a just and holy God that had drawn him into the movement more than four years earlier. He recognized that King, often caricatured by SNCC people for his deliberate eloquence, his refined taste and aristocratic airs, was held in great respect by local people, probably with greater respect than SNCC's black radicals. The men and women who flocked to see King during the march looked to him as the "symbol of all their hopes for a better life," indeed as a prophet leading a captive people to freedom.[108] Perhaps "de Lawd," SNCC's sardonic nickname for King, was not so far from the mark.

Be that as it may, Sellers's life was beginning to feel "more and more like a yo-yo, spinning crazily on the end of a taut string."[109] He could only envy King's spiritual equanimity (as he imagined it) and lament that the movement had come to this divide. For Sellers, there was no changing course now.

In the Rapids and Losing Control

Sellers's commitment to black power—which increasingly came to be described as Black Power—brought with it a new standard of purity and virtue, but at the same time it pulled him away from the Gospel preached at St. Philip's by Father Grant. Henry Grant, often invoking the voice of Martin Luther King, Jr., had preached a Gospel of agapeic love. "We love men not because we like them, nor because their ways appeal to us, nor even because they possess some type of divine spark," King had explained. "We love every man because God loves him."[110] Grant clung to that proclamation as the essence of Christian faith and practice. Inasmuch as God's love toward humanity is unconditional—overabounding in grace and mercy—men and women must try their best to mirror God's compassion in their own lives and in their own time. But Sellers had chosen to put the Gospel on the back burner. To be sure, he found it deeply offensive when one of his Black Power comrades claimed that Fannie Lou Hamer was "no longer relevant," no longer at their "level of development," so quaint and embarrassing was her exuberant piety.[111] Nonetheless, the will to purity and the construction of a racial orthodoxy led to narrowing standards of toleration. He would soon argue, even more vigorously than Stokely Carmichael, that whites must be excluded from SNCC as a matter of policy. But even before the decisive showdown on the role of whites in the organization, Sellers shocked many long-time supporters of SNCC by helping to orchestrate the ouster of John Lewis as chairman. This was a decisive moment in Sellers's hard-line pilgrimage.

John Lewis represented the SNCC of the freedom rides, the sit-ins, and the radical witness of nonviolent direct action. Lewis had joined the movement while studying at the American Baptist Theological Seminary in

Nashville, and had since been jailed more than forty times. Lewis was of a generation of black Southerners who had come to civil rights activism seeking not only social justice but their own—and their church's—spiritual renewal. He once said of his calling: "So many black ministers talked about the way over yonder and the afterlife. But when I heard Dr. King preaching on the radio one Sunday afternoon, I was amazed that he did not talk about the pearly gates and the streets paved with gold. He was concerned about the streets of Montgomery, the highways and byways of America." Although Lewis embraced many of the liberationist themes in Black Power—as had Fannie Lou Hamer, who once said that black power was what she had been doing all her life—he continued to preach a truly interracial democracy, the heart of which was his belief that "the movement was based on the simple truth of the Great Teacher: love thy neighbor as thyself."[112]

Yet Lewis's sympathies with Black Power stopped short of racial separatism, which he had begun to criticize openly. The new SNCC vanguard needed little time to judge him expendable. Lewis and his Christian convictions were simply not "what the times required," said Jack Minnis (ironically, the days were also numbered for him and the other remaining white SNCC members). There would be no more singing of the "circle of trust, the band of brothers."[113]

Toward the end of 1966, Sellers was working hard both to solidify SNCC's commitment to Black Power and to translate the new consciousness into concrete policies in black communities. He also spent considerable time deflecting the criticisms and denunciations that had begun to inundate SNCC from white liberal supporters and the national media. Sellers wrote to the Central Committee in late August, "We must pull ourselves together now and understand that we are very rapidly becoming the 'outlaws.' This country will go to any length and extent to maintain racism. We must work hard with the present organizational administration to help build the Black Power base in this country."[114] James Peck, a white man who had been both a SNCC member and freedom rider, gave voice to the criticism that would be aired most widely, writing that Black Power was, in short, a racist ideology. "Black power is no more insurance against social injustice than white power," Peck said.[115] The NAACP's Roy Wilkins— never a fan of SNCC—called Black Power "anti-white power," "a reverse Hitler," and "a reverse Ku Klux Klan," which "can only mean black death."[116] The *Atlanta Constitution*'s Ralph McGill told readers that the civil rights organization had been "taken over by what amounts to a secret klan-type group which openly states its racial hatreds and its objective to foment disaster and chaos in order to destroy Western civilization."[117] Bishop Fraser of North Carolina, writing in the Episcopal denominational magazine, *The Living Church*, agreed with McGill's analogy and then proclaimed that "adherents of either philosophy [black or white nationalism] are not entitled to receive the sacraments."[118] Perhaps the most damaging report came in the form of a *Los Angeles Times* interview with John Lewis himself. Lewis told journalist Jack Nelson that Black Power's symbol and slogan were chosen by SNCC "to scare the hell out of white people." He agreed with Dr. King that "racism is implied in the slogan," and asked, "What is scaring [the] hell out of the people going to do for Negroes in the long run?" Most black people "will never identify with black nationalists and other black reactionaries who talk loud and use cutting words like 'Black Power,' but also never engaged in confrontation to bring about change."[119]

Sellers himself understood the frenzied opposition to SNCC's new identity—the intensity of which he had not anticipated—to be directly related to the fact that "we have lived with Jim Crow for so long that when we talk about being Africanized, it's taken that we're anti-somebody." In any case, there was not much Sellers could do to convince SNCC's critics and estranged friends that all was not as it seemed. "A lot of issues came to the surface," Sellers recalls. "We'd had the riots in Watts and the Harlem rebellion and the murder of Malcolm X; we were in a rebellion stage. We were getting hit from a lot of different sides, so we didn't have much time to make the story. We had people who were just tired of being in the movement, who needed to rotate out for a while. There was a lot of frustration stemming from how the political and economic system was operating. Of course, if justice permeated the world, then we might have had something else to work with. But that was not the case and I was angry. It was very difficult to control. I was really kind of out there."[120]

As field operations continued to deteriorate, Carmichael took to the speaking circuit, and in most un-Snicklike fashion, insisted on traveling first class on airplanes and receiving a thousand-dollar honorarium for a lecture.[121] His popularity in leftist circles and his appearance as a gadfly in public debates about civil rights soon earned him the nickname by both friends and foes of Stokely "Starmichael." At the same time, Sellers was living in a small, run-down apartment in southwest Atlanta, with a woman he had met during the Meredith march, determined to embody a pure hard-line spirituality. He met daily with his brothers to contemplate and discuss ways of connecting black nationalist thought with socially transformative action; but Black Power did not lend itself readily to concrete social existence.[122] The "people" to whom power was summoned seemed less and less connected with real black persons in impoverished southern communities. In turn, Black Power took flight into abstractions about "the restoration of nationhood to the people" and setting afoot "a new man."[123] While Carmichael, Jim Forman, and other SNCC leaders appeared in university lecture halls, on television talk shows, and at cocktail parties, giving speeches on Black Power, the organization's membership withered. In a *New York Times* profile, Gene Roberts described the situation of SNCC in

1966: "In contrast to the past, an average day now will find only a third to a half of the 75 or 80 field secretaries out organizing (the remaining Snick members hold staff or clerical jobs), while the rest of the field workers are on the rally circuit or in Atlanta spinning off ideas and spreading the new Snick gospel."[124]

One way Sellers resolved this quandary was to assume that concrete results depended, first of all, on Black Power's dissemination into the consciousness of black people. The full force of Black Power would be lessened were it defined only in strategic terms; it must be preached and taught as the new black spirituality. With the transformation of the people's collective consciousness, local communities would gain a capacity for autonomy and self-determination long diminished through white oppression and cooptation. Black Power would further inspire "a connectedness between American blacks and Africans, between American blacks and Africans outside the diaspora in Cuba, South America, and elsewhere."[125] As such, the rhetoric of black liberation would replace the language of the Christian faith—a rhetoric ultimately in service to the "feeling of oneness among the people of the African world."[126] Above all, the reclamation of black pride through a spiritual union with "Africa" would mean more than "just being self-assured." As Sellers said, "it also gave us an edge."[127]

By the end of 1966, Sellers could count fewer than a dozen white people in SNCC. There were no whites in positions of leadership except Jack Minnis; but even Minnis had recently been demoted from his position as head of the research department and member of the finance committee. When SNCC hard-liners complained that the organization had fostered a debilitating paternalism in permitting a white man to supervise blacks and to monitor their budgets, Minnis's role in SNCC was scaled down to a largely titular post.[128] The issue of white involvement had been raised in past meetings, and of course it was clearly known that the organization's future lay in black people working in black communities without whites. But a formal policy on the matter was not established until a dramatic staff meeting in May of 1967.[129]

SNCC's best known white members, Bob and Dorothy Zellner, had decided to relocate to New Orleans to work with poor whites. The Zellners had already raised their own financial support for the project, but as loyal movement people, they wanted to work with SNCC's full support, without restrictions on their membership. If Bob and Dorothy had been black, their request would have been accepted without a hitch. Since they were white, the Zellners felt it would be best in the current climate to draft a proposal outlining their project goals and to offer a rationale for SNCC's involvement in their work.

The heart of their proposal was the idea that although it might be possible for black people to work in black communities without whites and avoid racist implications, it was not possible for whites to organize in white southern communities without blacks and avoid racist implications. This was what the Ku Klux Klan does: remember "white power"?[130] The Zellners argued that SNCC's interracial witness needed to be exhibited among poor whites "so that we can have strength in the white community as SNCC does in the black community."[131]

Presenting the proposal in his wife's absence, Bob Zellner appealed to his colleagues' growing cynicism. "In order that we get rid of that racism and get people's minds straightened out," he said, "you are going to have to have some amount of inter-racial cooperation although it may be repugnant to us." He insisted that white organizers needed black organizers: whites needed some visible relationship with blacks in order to attest to new interracial possibilities, otherwise their work would not avoid the appearance of segregation in a new form. Zellner's plea showed how far many in SNCC had come in redressing white racism and white paternalism: he was not telling blacks they needed whites, he was telling blacks that whites needed them.

The bottom line in the Zellners' proposal was their wish that whites who had made important contributions to SNCC—and wished to continue making them—be considered full-fledged staff members. Such people should belong to SNCC without restrictions of race and "with all the rights and responsibilities that any staff member has." The Zellners were forcing the Central Committee to bring the issue of white involvement to final clarity. Were whites in or out? Zellner reminded the committee of the consequential fact that "Dottie and I have been with SNCC for [a] long time. . . . I feel, and have always felt," he said, "that SNCC was as much a part of me as anybody else and that I was SNCC and I will always be SNCC."[132] The son of a Methodist minister and former klansman in south Alabama, Zellner had been a movement activist since his student years at Huntington College in Montgomery. An an undergraduate, Zellner had worked in Martin Luther King, Jr.'s, Montgomery Improvement Association after researching a sociology paper on race relations in his home state (and was subsequently expelled from school).[133] "Bob was one of the few whites who commanded the unqualified respect of everyone in the organization," Sellers made clear. "He was a damned good man. No one questioned his courage or commitment. On occasions too numerous to recall, he had put it all on the line. The brutal beatings he had endured at the hands of irate whites while participating in early SNCC marches in Mississippi and Alabama were legend."[134] Bob Zellner was "a special SNCC person."

Nevertheless, the central committee had no intention of backtracking on the matter of racial separatism. After a lengthy, convoluted discussion, the decision to fire the Zellners was made. Even those few committee members who clearly regretted the decision felt compelled to support the decision. Most staffers agreed that the vote signified "a part of our maturity that people have to develop where we can make decisions and not regard personal relationships." As Bill Ware put it, "We have to rise above the personal friendship level and as a group must strive to be objective as much as possible."[135] What did it mean to be revolutionary, Bob Zellner had asked his SNCC comrades in 1964 at Waveland. This was what it meant.

But there was more. After the unanimous decision, Ware pressed the committee to think how it could still "use" white people for its advantage. In a bizarre analogy, he resolved, "I'm willing to accept [Zellner] as a part of the staff as much as I'm willing to accept the mayor who would operate in France as a stooge for the gestapo."[136] Ware added that Zellner could perhaps be used like those "many women who gave up their bodies during the second World War" and slept with German soldiers in order to get information. Zellner was informed of the decision (which was soon expanded to include five other remaining whites in the organization) and promised to say nothing to the press. He and Dottie kept their anguish to themselves as they began their work in New Orleans in a house on Napoleon Street.[137]

Although Sellers fully endorsed the principle that blacks needed now to work among themselves without white involvement, the firing of the Zellners meant little to him by the time the decision was made. He says, "We were angry because we didn't achieve what we'd hoped to; and I had not achieved what I'd hoped to achieve as program director; we were angry because we were frustrated; angry because we had bought into so much of the hope and we thought it had come to nothing; we were angry at ourselves because of our frailties; we were angry at everything and at everybody." It was time to be angry, "time to shake things up," Sellers said.[138] Since it had become clear to Sellers that the United States would "go to any length and extent to maintain racism," SNCC's black leadership had every reason to pull itself together—to "close ranks," as Carmichael advised— and speak the hard truth to whites.[139] What truth was that? A truth that lay in the bold assertion of difference: we are black and you are not. Whites must deal with a difference they can neither comprehend nor embrace. The fact that Black Power yielded only vague strategies for organizing was now quite beside the point. The symbol of an angry panther had always illumined the deeper sense of hard-line passions.

However, unlike Carmichael, who would offer a definition of Black Power at the drop of a dime (or a thousand-dollar honorarium), Sellers never concerned himself with the task of formulating dogma. Rather, Sellers became Black Power's literal embodiment. He says, "I hit the rapids and lost control."[140] Under the exhilarating spell of the Algerian revolutionary Franz Fanon, Ghana's Kwame Nkrumah, and Malcolm X, Sellers directed

SNCC toward a "Third World Coalition of revolutionaries who were anti-capitalist, antiimperialist, and antiracist." (Ironically, before his death, Malcolm X had softened his earlier commitments to racial separatism.) At the same time, projects collapsed throughout the South. What little philanthropic foundation support remained in SNCC's coffers soon dried up after the organization released a public denunciation of Israel's "Zionist imperialists," who (SNCC claimed) mistreated the Palestinians and exploited Africa for profit and political advantage.[141] Sellers became physically abusive with his wife Sandy when he discovered she had been sleeping with SNCC's new director Rap Brown. Their brief, turbulent marriage ended shortly thereafter.

Then in the late spring of 1967, Sellers learned that he would soon receive draft notices. He was charged with violating the Secret Service law after he informed the draft board that he would "not serve in this Army or any others that seek by force to use the resources of my black brothers here at the expense of my brothers in Asia, Africa and Latin America."[142] Sellers decided the time was long overdue to "rotate out" (as SNCC referred to furlough from action).

In October of 1967, Sellers returned to South Carolina to finish his bachelor's degree at South Carolina State College, located in the town of Orangeburg, just a half hour from his parents' home in Denmark. South Carolina State College, along with neighboring Claflin College, a private black school with Methodist affiliations, brought more than two thousand black students to Orangeburg. The fact that his FBI file arrived ahead of him was enough to provoke constant scrutiny by the Orangeburg police.[143] Yet even apart from his record of arrests, Sellers, sporting a goatee, a mustache, and an "Afro" hair style, presented himself as a threatening presence in a town that boasted the state headquarters of the John Birch Society and the South Carolina Association of Independent Schools, a coalition of private, segregationist academies. Sellers also continued to work informally for SNCC on the campus of the historically black college, hoping to rebuild organizational support on Southern black campuses. Sellers's plan was to pursue his studies and informally discuss various aspects of Black Power with students and faculty. More than anything else, however, he wanted to slow down the pace for a while and live near his family. The work of desegregating public facilities—now under way in Orangeburg—seemed secondary to the steady dissemination of the emerging revolutionary consciousness. Still, he did not refuse to give his seasoned advice when approached by a group of student activists who were organizing a protest outside a nearby segregated bowling alley in February of 1968. Ironically, the man no more interested in integrating a bowling alley than "flying in a spaceship," would forever be associated with the coming massacre in Orangeburg.[144]

After city officials proved unwilling to bring sanctions against the bowling alley's owner and endorse a twelve-point list of requests for improvements in the black community, the South Carolina governor summoned National Guardsmen to Orangeburg for fear that student activists were planning an assault on the town's public utilities. One local white official cautioned that the intention of the "Black Power people" was "to do away with your waterworks, lights, telephone service, so forth, gas and such things as that." Rumors also spread that Rap Brown and Stokely Carmichael were en route to South Carolina, accompanied by the Panthers and other black paramilitary groups associated with the widely feared urban riots. White men could be seen working at gas stations or tending stores with pistols in holsters on their hips. At the same time, several black students were displaying posters around campus that read, "Let the Bricks Swing."[145] Everywhere Sellers went on campus, he heard people saying, "Something's gonna happen."[146]

Toward evening on February 8, a large group of students—more than 150—built a bonfire at the edge of campus. An even larger group of police officials, preparing for combat, assembled at the bottom of the embankment beneath the bonfire: 66 state patrolmen (armed with shotguns and deadly "Number 1" buckshot instead of the birdshot that was routinely used to disperse crowds), 45 National Guardsmen armed with M–1 rifles and fixed bayonets, 25 officers from the State Law Enforcement Division (SLED), 28 local policemen and several sheriffs. Tension continued to mount as some students shouted, "You're mama's a whore, you're mama's a whore"—a chant that prompted some of the officers to lower their rifles as though taking aim at the students.[147] Toward midnight, a student threw two white bannister posts down the embankment at the officers, striking one policeman on the head, crushing his mouth and nose. A rifle fired in response, followed by several shots of warning in rapid succession, sending most of the students running back toward the campus buildings. Some held up their hands, while others dropped to the ground and lay in a fetal position when a volley of shotgun blasts roared into the night, sounds of the small army of officers opening fire on the students.

Sellers had been trying to take a nap in a friend's dorm room at the time. When he heard the noise, he went outside and walked toward the bonfire, into the gunfire, against a growing wave of students. He was hit by buckshot in his left shoulder, like "a power-driven sledge-hammer." The air was knocked out of his lungs.[148] What Sellers remembered next was the nightmare of crawling away from the gunfire, trying to avoid another hit, as a chilling silence descended on the campus, interrupted only by moans of the wounded.

By the end of the night, 33 students had been seriously harmed and three were killed—Delano Middleton, Samuel Hammond, Jr., and Henry Smith. Middleton, a 200-pound high school football and basketball star, told his mother as he was dying, "You've been a good Mama, but I'm gonna leave you now. Tell me the Twenty-third Psalm, Mama." Third-year student Henry Smith died alone, although he had written to his mother the week before his death, "Dear Mother, I am living a relatively normal Christian life. I am going to church more than I did last year. I am trying to do unto others as I would have them do unto me. I think that is about all God asks of a Person." Samuel Hammond simply moaned, "Oh, Lord," as he died from gunshots to his back.[149]

In the chaos of the segregated emergency room at a local hospital, Sellers was arrested, driven to Columbia, South Carolina, arraigned, given seventy-eight years' worth of charges and a $50,000 bond, and locked up in the state prison on death row, when he began to have nightmarish thoughts about Mickey Schwerner, James Chaney, and Andrew Goodman.[150] Although he had been unarmed and defenseless and had not participated in the bonfire demonstration, his reputation as a civil rights activist, his well-known friendship with Stokely Carmichael (who had recently visited Fidel Castro and heaped praise on Cuban socialism), and his reported Black Panther affiliations made him a prime suspect as the instigator of the "student riot." Sellers emerged as the "trained agitator" at the center of the violence.[151] Henry Lake, the spokesman for the State Law Enforcement Division, expressed the popular sentiment toward Sellers: "He's the main man. He's the biggest nigger in the crowd."[152]

It did not matter that Sellers was out on bail three weeks later, or that police panic—not student agitation—provoked the violence; seven weeks after the Orangeburg shooting, and a week before the murder of Martin Luther King, Jr., Sellers was found guilty of resisting the draft by a jury of nine whites and three blacks. The court convicted Sellers even though it knew that the FBI had admitted reviewing Sellers's file at his draft board hearing and monitoring his phone calls.[153] Two weeks later he was given the maximum five-year sentence for draft evasion. He appeared before the court unbowed, asserting that the "only solution to my problem is to fight till my death or to fight until I'm liberated."[154] But that would not happen. Sellers now began the dark journey of incarceration (and was still years away from a conviction for inciting to riot in Orangeburg). He recalls, "I started off in Atlanta City Jail, then two days after that I was transferred to the Fulton County Jail; then two days after that to Newnan, Georgia; then two days after that to a jail in Rome, Georgia; then two weeks later I was transported to the federal prison in Tallahassee, Florida. Then there was a race riot in Tallahassee, which I actually watched from my cell window, but I was identified as a ringleader and brought to the Atlanta Federal Institution, where they kept me for two days. The warden in Atlanta said he did not want me in there, so I was taken to Knoxville, then Nashville, then Louisville, and then to Terre Haute, Indiana, where I spent a month."[155]

When Sellers finally got a hearing date in Atlanta and a new appeal bond, he was released from prison only to be arrested by two deputy sheriffs from Louisiana, handcuffed and transported to Baton Rouge to stand trial on a 1967 concealed-weapons charge—which he had forgotten about. He was found guilty, given a suspended sentence, and released. But for good reason, freedom seemed fragile, if not illusory. "I didn't know if I was going or coming. My life was in total disarray."[156] And SNCC was dead. Most of his fellow travelers in the movement were "scattered like seed in the wind."[157]

In the fall of 1970, the state of South Carolina brought Sellers to trial for his participation in the Orangeburg massacre. Despite the conclusion of state circuit Judge John Grimball after hearing the prosecution's ten witnesses that "nobody has ever put the defendant [Sellers] into the area of rioting on [the night of the shooting]," Sellers was convicted for "refusing to disperse immediately when ordered" on January 6, 1968—two nights before the massacre![158] He was sentenced to another year in jail. Sellers's attorney, Howard Moore, protested, "I'm not surprised in the least bit. Black people believe they can't get a fair trial in racist America and this was proven today in Orangeburg."[159] Tom Wicker, who covered the trial for the *New York Times*, put similar sentiments to his readers, lamenting "how casual is this country's sense of justice for black people, how careless it is of its own humanity."[160]

Pauline Sellers's confidence in her son remained strong. "I've seen [this] happen too many times before," she said. "He wasn't even with the students who went to the bowling lanes earlier in the week," she added.[161] While many friends struggled to say the right thing to the Sellers family, the church offered constant support. Reverend Tollie L. Caution, in whose discussion groups her son had participated in 1960 at the Summer School for Religious Education at Voorhees, wrote:

> I am distressed over the news of your son's difficulties in connection with the trouble at Orangeburg.
>
> Your anxiety and pain must be almost unbearable. I am remembering you in my prayers. We are living in strenuous and unfair times, particularly with regard to our youth who realize the serious problems they face. One cannot but admire their courage in the face of danger as they strive for a better life, recognition and understanding. . . .
>
> It could have been my son or any other Negro's son caught in this web of circumstance. May God bless and keep you and yours. And may we find a happier solution to the ills which now assail us.[162]

Pauline received numerous other letters offering prayers and comfort from religious leaders around the nation.

Still, these gestures of sympathy were lost on Sellers himself. He reflected on his life shortly before entering prison:

I am very tired. With the exception of time spent in jails and prisons, I haven't had a vacation in twelve years. I am always on the job, day and night, summer and winter. I almost never get paid, but I survive. I am sometimes hungry, but never for very long. When I need shoes or clothing, I get them— "by any means necessary." . . .

I am committed to doing whatever I can to build bridges between blacks in this country and revolutionary groups in Africa. Africa has the people, the resources and the power potential to become one of the most dominant powers in the world. American blacks are Africans in exile. When Africa is free, her sons and daughters, wherever they are in the world, will have a solid base for their struggles.

I don't have a personal life anymore. I don't know where Sandy is or what she is doing. I sometimes want to drop everything and search her out, attempt to take up where we left off. It wouldn't work. I know that. Everything I have, all my strength, is still wrapped up in the movement. Things would turn out exactly as they did before.

I am caught up in the strong current of a river of no return. My being is inseparable from the struggle. I have thought about all this a great deal, who I am, where I've come from and where I'm going. I don't expect to live a normal life span. Nor do I expect to die a normal death. I am not unique. It's the same for almost everyone who *lived* the SNCC experience. Stokely, Rap, Jim Forman, Bob Moses, wherever he is, we have become one with the struggle. It doesn't matter that we share disagreements and petty animosities from time to time. We all want the same thing. We are all driven by the same inexorable force.[163]

One staff member remarked in 1966 that "Black power is a search for a sense of home, for something we can call our own." Whether Sellers was searching for the vigor and soul and self-possession of his childhood in Denmark is an interesting question, but unlikely. In the end, he was numbed, and then engulfed, by his grim realization that there was no home for black people in the United States. Maryland, Mississippi, Georgia, South Carolina, and all the other stops along Sellers's journey—each represented America writ small.[164]

SNCC the Closed Society

Black Power eventually found its theologians. In his landmark book of 1969, *Black Theology and Black Power*, James Cone would write, "[If] Christ is present today actively risking all for the freedom of man, he must be acting through the most radical elements of Black Power." In a dazzling theological exercise, Cone systematically redescribed the catalog of Christian

dogma (that is, Christology, salvation, resurrection) in light of black revolutionary activity. In much the same methodological way that classical
German theologians of the nineteenth century had taken such experiences
as intellectual reflection, feelings of the sublime, and moral action as the
stuff of Christian faith, Cone reshaped the basic articles of belief by means
of the ideology of Black Power. The result was an original and revolutionary theological treatise.[165]

But Cleve Sellers never concerned himself with a Black Power retelling
of the Gospel. The new racial consciousness should be neither defined nor
codified; it should only be enacted in lived experience. The inescapable
fact is that Black Power propelled him away from the moral world of the
Christian witness. Turning your back on Fannie Lou Hamer meant turning your back on the Gospel. Sellers's exuberant entry into the movement
had been driven by a keen sense of God's providence—of the God who
was moving time and history toward greater freedom. God was doing a
new thing in this movement of black people from bondage to liberation.
Sellers said, "We really believed God was on our side. We were not making an ideology of salvation, as white Christians had done. Rather, without
demanding anything, without being narrow sighted, we were in touch
with God. We were really doing what we believed to be the right thing, at
the right time, and a deep spirituality went along with that."[166] Reconciliation, or even the attempt to reconcile with others different from oneself,
served as an unmistakable sign of the divine miracle at hand.

Although SNCC is often described as the secularizing wave of the movement, a deep religious impulse had been affirmed as early as the SNCC
staff meeting of April 29, 1962. In one of the organization's founding documents, staffers had resolved their firm commitment to the creation of "a
social order permeated by love and to the spirituality of nonviolence as it
grows from the Judeo-Christian tradition." Love was the "central motif of
nonviolence," the "force by which God binds man to himself and man to
man" which "remains loving and forgiving even in the midst of hostility."[167] More than two decades after his release from prison, Sellers reaffirmed, albeit somewhat cautiously and with chastened expectations, the
commitment that had brought him into the movement. "You never give up
on reconciliation," he said. "We live in a broken world and we must keep
a certain amount of trust in each other in order for us to survive."[168] Yet
after the defeat of the Mississippi Freedom Democratic party in 1964,
SNCC "turned so fully from its former dreams," as Vincent Harding
wrote.[169] Disillusioned and justifiably angry, Sellers did give up on reconciliation. Liberation alone mattered.

Rhetorically, Black Power served as a wake-up call to white America, especially to liberal supporters of the civil rights movement. Psychologically,
it was no doubt freeing to give expression to a long-suppressed rage. As

the former Czech dissident, Václav Havel, said in a different revolutionary context, "No wonder, then, that when the crust cracks and the lava of life rolls out, there appear not only well-considered attempts to rectify old wrongs, not only searchings for truth and for reforms matching life's needs, but also symptoms of bilious hatred, vengeful wrath, and a kind of feverish desire for immediate compensation for all the endured degradation."[170] Ideologically, black nationalism gained authorization in view of a society still governed largely by whites and an economic system favoring the rich. But liberation without reconciliation drifted toward segregationist conclusions, misdirecting precious energy from particular social reforms focused on concrete goals to a deracinated globalism focused on rhetorical militancy. Despite its celebration of the ethnic, cultural, religious, and biological particularities of Americans of sub-Saharan African descent, Black Power—as it played out in the story of the civil rights movement in the South—did more tearing down than building up.

Struggling to create new moral and spiritual sources of black personhood and solidarity, the architects of Black Power seemed more equipped to say what they were not than what they were.[171] Of course, they did say what they were, if the SNCC meetings that began in 1966 are any indication. The consequence was that as the beloved community came to be delimited to those ones who shared the same racial, cultural, and spiritual sub-Saharan lineage, the white person (or anyone different) ceased to register as a real human presence.[172] Mrs. Hamer understood this cruel irony when she said, "If I knew today, [that] Mississippi would be taken over by all the black folk, nothing but Negroes, I'd fight that just as hard as I'm fighting this white power."[173] But with Mrs. Hamer no longer relevant, whites became resources to be manipulated.[174] Recall George Ware's comment on Bob Zellner, that he might be used like those "many women who gave up their bodies during the second World War" to get information from the enemy. Narcissism and cruelty thrive on the utility of persons. By constricting the "beloved" and "the other" to the familiar and the same— to the "ontologically black," in theologian Victor Anderson's words—Black Power turned brother against brother and self against itself.[175] In turn, SNCC became the closed society writ small.[176]

CONCLUSION

Clearburning: Fragments of a Reconciling Faith

WHAT THEN is left at the end? Has the ground been burned clear, prepared for a new planting and harvest?

"A jury would not dare convict a white man for killing a nigger in Mississippi," Sam Bowers is boasting after his indictment for the 1966 murder of NAACP worker Vernon Dahmer. "We do not accept Jews. . . . We do not accept Papists. . . . We do not accept Turks, Mongols, Tartars, Orientals, Negroes," he warns, and with an even greater resolve than in 1964.[1] The Klan's systematic terrorist attacks against Mississippi Jews in 1967 and 1968—while Bowers's own trials for the murders of James Chaney, Andy Goodman, Mickey Schwerner, and Vernon Dahmer proceed in court—indicates finally, and all too familiarly, the true identity of the "heretics." Bowers's grandiosity, his world-historical arrogance, eventually collapses into self-imprisonment. Having been released from Fort McNeil Federal Penetentiary in 1976, Bowers lives today alone in the dilapidated Sambo Amusement Company, surrounded by his half-finished tomes on social and religious philosophy, in a lower-income African American neighborhood.

All the while, Doug Hudgins is proclaiming, "If God is holy, if God be righteous, He must be just."[2] The business of his church is managed with optimum efficiency: sermons are preached; Bible studies are taught; evangelistic crusades reach hundreds of lost souls; the Southern Baptist Convention is faithfully served. But Hudgins cannot see—or dare not preach— that the just God grieves for black suffering. Hudgins's etherealized piety, disconnected so expediently from the concern for African American life, finally denies faith's own life-affirming energies, its resounding "Yes!" to the beseeching other, its exuberant this-worldliness.

In their midst, Mrs. Hamer stands with her feet solidly grounded, the welcoming woman in love with the welcoming God. She shows us that the person of faith dare not retreat into racial narcissism or private virtuousness, but must "drink the earthly cup to the dregs"—and only in so doing know the fullness of God's goodness and the resplendent openness to life and to others that follow.[3] Mrs. Hamer embodied the conviction that the God of biblical faith is a liberating God; and those who would please him do so not for the sake of duty alone, but out of deep love and gratitude.[4] Undoubtedly, she would look upon the deracinated Hudgins and the villainous Bowers with indignation and outrage. Yet her table would not be closed to them. These are men gone astray; but like all people, however hopelessly entrenched in their evils, Bowers and Hudgins remain God's children. "Ain't no such thing as I can hate anybody and hope to see God's face," she reminds us.[5] Her invitation to join the "new Kingdom of God in Mississippi" reaches wide, bursting open the closed doors of the closed society.

What shapes such faith? Mrs. Hamer had "walked through the valley of the shadow of death" and still—and perhaps precisely because she walked through death's valley—she knew that the heart of God is love, *movement* in the most basic sense.[6] Such love arises out of surrender, and equally out of strength, and yet still ultimately out of a place beyond surrender and strength. As Sally Belfrage says, "Mrs. Hamer was free. She represented a challenge that few could understand: how it was possible to arrive at a place past suffering, to a concern for her torturers as deep as that for her friends. Such people were rare. All of them began by refusing to hate or despise themselves."[7] Nonetheless, for Mrs. Hamer, the way beyond surrender and strength was not through resoluteness, habituation, or sheer will power, but through God. Love like this, love like Mrs. Hamer's, cannot ground itself. "Take my hand, precious Lord, lead me on," she testifies.[8]

In the end, Mrs. Hamer shows us that in loving we become the people we are supposed to be (and more than simply people who have or demand), people who cannot cease becoming, moving, freeing; for in opening up to others in love, the goodness that originates in God's own being moves toward lived experience.[9] Or even more strongly put: in creation and preservation, in acts of compassion and mercy, and in the exquisite range of beauty and sadness, God not only declares himself, but also arouses and empowers the world and history, and specific human persons and movements of persons "to a spontaneous work of ordering and fashioning" that corresponds to the specific way *God is*.[10] Importantly, the correspondence is not inherent in nature itself (or in material necessity), but is emphatically specific to who God is.[11] A deep river of spiritual power animates the created order, breaking into expression as love, opening up people, institutions, or societies once blocked by fear and tyranny. As one of Mrs. Hamer's sister travelers, Victoria Gray, explained, "I see the Civil Rights Movement as the journey toward the establishment of the kingdom of God. That's how I understand it now and that's how I understood it then. We were spirit people, seed people; no matter how bleak the terrain looked out there, we were planted for a rich harvest. And it was the church

houses themselves out of which we had to move; these were the center of
our lives. We didn't have much of anything really except the church, and
when we put too much emphasis on these, they were burned down. But
that's what it was—the church as the representation of the spirit of love, of
God."[12] Thus, in loving, the evidence of hope becomes real; divine compassion takes human form. God, no less, remains the goal and genesis of
humanity's coming to itself—and to God.

Bob Moses may have spoken a hard truth when he said that the civil
rights movement only brought Mississippi up to the level of the rest of the
country. Whether the white church was (or will be) judged and punished
is a question that can finally be answered by God alone. Nonetheless, it is
better still to say that Mrs. Hamer's life was a parable of divine love embodied in human history, and that the movement she gave her life to happened as a convergence of wills—of the God whose righteousness flows as
a mighty stream with a people readied by time and cruelty. "The movement was a process," recalls SNCC's John Lewis, "an unstoppable over-
flowing event. Some folks might want to call this the spirit of history or
some other force but I believe the movement happened because we were
in step with the Creator."[13] More than assent was required, and more than
the assertion of righteousness; but the spirit moving, calling men and
women and children from cities, farms, and hamlets, from the south and
the north, to join the great march to freedom.

Listen again to the testimonies. "We were in touch with God because we
weren't demanding anything from Him. We were just doing what we
thought and what we understood to be the right thing," says Cleveland
Sellers.[14] "I felt like I had come home," Victoria Gray Adams affirms.[15] And
Curtis Hayes: "I was in heaven for a minute."[16]

AFTERWORD

ED KING remained in Mississippi long after the summer volunteers had moved on to new causes and new places; long after 60 percent of eligible blacks in Mississippi had registered to vote in 1967; long after the Freedom Democratic party effectively disbanded in 1968; after public schools were desegregated in 1970; after a Mississippi governor vetoed the appropriations bill for the State Sovereignty Commission in 1973; after Fannie Lou Hamer died in 1977; and after an African American was elected to Congress in 1986. Through it all, he stuck with civil rights.

In 1966, King ran as a "peace candidate" on the Mississippi Freedom Democratic ticket for U.S. Congress against incumbent John Bell Williams—"the most conservative and racist of the Mississippi congressmen of his day"—and received 5 percent of the white vote in an election he lost by a landslide.[1] In September of 1967 he resigned from his chaplaincy at Tougaloo College to join the staff of the Delta Ministry, an ecumenical project of the National Council of Churches and the World Council of Churches that launched anti-poverty initiatives and community development programs throughout the state. After 1965, along with most of his civil rights comrades, King broadened the scope of his activism to include the anti-war movement, working in the "Dump Johnson" campaign that his friend Al Lowenstein had organized within the Democratic party.[2] With Fannie Lou Hamer and numerous other members of the MFDP, he served as a delegate to the Democratic national conventions in Chicago in 1968 and Miami in 1972—a clear sign that the MFDP challenge in Atlantic City had changed Mississippi politics forever.[3] Then in 1974 he joined the faculty of the Medical Center of the University of Mississippi in Jackson, teaching in the school of health-related professions.

As happened to many activists after the movement, things fell apart for King. His marriage with Jeannette ended in 1983. Their bitter divorce featured King trying to commit his wife to a psychiatric hospital and his wife's lawyers charging him with spousal abuse. The collapse of the Kings' marriage even became the subject of a novel written by a former civil rights activist in Mississippi. In *Civil Wars* (1984), Rosellen Brown (herself a former student volunteer) tells the story of Jessie and Teddy Carl, veterans of the civil rights movement in Mississippi whose lives are drifting apart in the doldrums of the middle 1970s. Teddy Carl—King was called Eddie by friends—with his scarred cheek and chin, refuses to let go of the movement. His activism, now wearing thin in the post-civil rights years, only masks a callous will to power. He is cynical and insincere in faith, his pursuit of justice a mere pretense for self-gain and cruel arrogance. His attempts to rekindle the spark of activist fervor are pathetic: rushing to an ill-fated demonstration in some forlorn hamlet of the state, and from there to excite racial tensions elsewhere, all the while ignoring his wife and children. Teddy Carl is also paranoid, convinced, as his wife Jessie tell him, that "all the big events, the assassinations and riots, are manipulated."[4] He is obsessed with discerning the sinister forces at work against his desperate crusades. He has become a "master of self-justification," fitting all his disappointments into a grand theory of the movement's undoing.

Rosellen Brown was not the only movement veteran to make King the subject of unflattering analysis. Many others were dismayed when he openly endorsed the anti-abortion group, Jackson Right to Life. Seizing on Fannie Lou Hamer's conviction that "abortion is legal murder" and for black people genocide, and that "the use of pills and rings to prevent God's will is a great sin," King began to describe the pro-life movement of the 1970s as the spiritual successor of the civil rights movement.[5] In interviews and in public lectures, he began speaking of the similarities between the racist medical practices of Jim Crow Mississippi and the "abortuaries" of liberal democracies. The witness of the beloved community, of people committed to redemptive suffering, seemed to him now borne out in groups like Jackson Right to Life or Randall Terry's Operation Rescue—groups that seemed in every way as countercultural as the "beatnik missionaries" of the civil rights movement.[6] In King's defense, his convictions did not signal a turn to the religious right. On hearing of the Supreme Court decision in *Roe vs. Wade* in 1973, King had taken for granted that the decision stemmed from "the anti-poor policies of the Republican president, Richard Nixon." Here was an insidious, and now legal, way of achieving massive cuts in welfare spending by "cutting down on black welfare babies."[7]

In 1994, King denounced the much-celebrated retrial of klansman Byron de la Beckwith for the murder of Medgar Evers. While many Mississippians such as Ole Miss historian David Sansing were proclaiming Mississippi "free at last," King was calling the conviction of Beckwith on February 5 "a miscarriage of justice," so hard-driven by political motives as to have been predetermined at the outset. The prosecution had maintained that Beckwith appeared at numerous civil rights meetings for the purpose of gathering information on Evers. Yet when subpoenaed as a chief witness for the defense, King actually claimed that the "mysterious white stranger" cited throughout the prosecution's arguments was himself. A sad need to connect "all the big events" *with himself*, critics said. But King did not doubt that a white racist had murdered his friend and mentor, or that Beckwith was fully capable of such a crime. Rather, he maintained that the evidence for conviction was lacking. "Even evil Beckwith deserved a fair trial," he said.[8]

Still, King's curmudgeonly activism has extended far beyond his pro-life sympathies and his dissent on Beckwith. A labyrinthine legal case involving the files of the Mississippi State Sovereignty Commission has absorbed more of his time, energy, and money than the abortion—or any other— issue. Recall that the Sovereignty Commission had been the organization funded by the state legislature to investigate alleged violations of the Southern Way of Life. The commission's work involved dispatching investigators and spies to gather information on civil rights workers, white liberals, and anyone suspected of racial indiscretion. When the Sovereignty Commission was finally terminated in 1977, the Mississippi State House of Representatives passed a bill, by an overwhelming majority, that required the files to be destroyed "in their entirety."[9] But a court injunction averted the bill's taking effect, and instead the legislature voted to seal the files for fifty years.

Legal action in response to the legislature's decision eventually took the form of two dissenting views, which came to dramatic conflict when Federal District Court Judge William H. Barbour ruled in 1989 that the files be opened. Public disclosure, Judge Barbour had stated, "would further the general principle of informed discussion of the actions of government, while to leave the files closed would perpetuate the attempt of the State to escape accountability."[10] On the one side, Ed King and fellow Jackson movement activist, John Salter, argued that unlimited access to the Sovereignty Commission files was unfair, potentially damaging to people who had three decades earlier been victims of the commission's tendentious reports. King offered an explanation to anyone willing to consider his position: "The documents would say things like: Reverend X, black pastor, opened his church for a civil rights meeting. This is the same Reverend X who sleeps with Mrs. John Smith, the organist who teaches third grade. Her husband who doesn't know about this is a high school principal, but then he's never known that his wife sleeps all over town."[11] The files might describe movement activists—many of whom had become successful political leaders, teachers, or psychiatrists—as drug addicts and psychopaths. Were the reports true? Who could know for sure? Certainly if motives are considered, the investigations would be widely discredited. Yet, in King's opinion, the media frenzy surrounding the file's disclosure would distort their sleazy history; and, even aside from that, many of the reports were undoubtedly true. Consequently, King and Salter argued that individuals investigated by the Sovereignty Commission should be given the right to keep their files closed.[12]

On the other side, the American Civil Liberties Union (ACLU)—and virtually everyone else associated with the civil rights movement in Mississippi—argued for full disclosure, invoking the Freedom of Information Act, and inspired by the thought of the state coming clean with its dirty secrets. However, the Fifth Circuit Court in New Orleans overturned Judge Barbour's decision and sided with the plaintiffs King and Salter. Privacy must be maintained, the Circuit Court stated. So in 1993, Judge Barbour amended his 1989 decision with a ninety-day grace period, allowing individuals on whom files existed to add information or to block out names. Once done, the files would be placed in the Mississippi Department of Archives and History and made accessible to the public in perpetuity.

Unsatisfied with Barbour's revision, King contended that the ninety-day period was wholly inadequate to protect privacy, since many of the 87,000 individuals named in the Sovereignty Commission investigations did not know enough about the content of the files to assert their privacy rights. The presumption should not be on these individuals to block out their names or to attach explanatory information.[13] King then became the sole plaintiff as John Salter withdrew from the case in 1994, conceding the matter "essentially over in the litigatory sense."[14] Despite a depleted bank account and eviction from his home, King resolved to fight the legal battle to the bitter end; he remained unfazed by frequent criticism of his position. When the Fifth Circuit Court ruled on June 11, 1996, in favor of Judge Barbour's terms, he immediately arranged meetings with the ACLU, hoping, at the least, to convince attorneys of the need to block out the reports' prolific references to sexual affairs. Again he was unsuccessful.

King insists that there is a common thread in all of these diverse commitments. He rejects the notion that the right to abortion presupposes the same privacy rights he invokes in the Sovereignty Commission case, or which indirectly influence his interest in the aging klansmen. Rather, at stake is the idea of what "it means for life to have dignity in mass society."[15] The theologian Dietrich Bonhoeffer once lamented the loss of *hilaritas* in the modern world, of persons embodying "a steadfast certainty that in their own work they are showing the world something good (even if the world doesn't like it)." King's indefatigable, often aggravating confidence in his own iconoclastic fervor, his defiance of popular opinion, displays more than just a hint of such "high-spirited self-confidence."[16] He cites St. John's first epistle, "For whatsoever is born of God overcometh the world: and this is the victory that overcometh the world, even our faith" (1 John 5:4). The world must be seen from a perspective different from the way it sees itself, King insists. "We have to look beyond ourselves and understand that

victory over the dark powers in high places does not depend on us alone."
King is not sure what this means in every lived situation, but he is certain
that whoever is born of God will inevitably appear peculiar. What else
could be expected of people whose speech is born of ultimate honesty?[17]

On a Wednesday evening in early summer, King was invited to celebrate
the eucharist at Galloway Memorial Methodist Church. The church has
long abandoned its closed-door policies, even though the decision has cost
the church dearly in membership and budget. Since 1966, Galloway has
learned to survive its urban setting (while many other white churches relocated to the suburbs) by reinventing itself as a socially progressive congregation, supporting soup kitchens and other social ministries in the
church's surrounding neighborhood (which has become largely African
American). Although King has attended Galloway over the years, and
though he was eventually ordained to the ministry in the United Methodist
Church, he continues to live on the margins of the institutional church. He
was pleased when Galloway's young associate minister asked him to assist
with the eucharist.

As King stood at the front of the sanctuary this summer evening, offering the cup and bread to those people who had made their way to the
front, he recognized a tall, middle-aged man near the front of the line as
the Republican governor of the state, Kirk Fordice. Extending the symbolic
blood and body of Jesus to Fordice, King was momentarily overcome by
the urge to laugh, not with smugness but with a glad heart and a sense of
rejoicing. More than thirty years earlier, King had stood on the outside of
the same chapel, his arms reaching over a phalanx of unyielding church
guards, knocking and banging on the heavy wooden door in protest of the
segregated communion service. Now here he was, presiding over the sacrament, with the governor of the state bowed before him in prayer. There is
in our salvation, at the bottom of it all, a great comedy, he thought. Sometimes, when the long loneliness breaks, scattering the fears of the dark
powers, he can smile with a deep sense of gratitude and delight.

When King reflects on his years in the civil rights movement, he feels
"awed" at how God used him. "I was able to say the right thing at the right
time," he says. And on such occasions as the eucharist at Galloway, King
is hopeful that God is not through with him yet.

When Cleveland Sellers was released from prison in late 1974, he returned to Greensboro, North Carolina, where his new wife and baby
daughter were living. Sellers's decision to remain in the South was based
in part on his wish to live near his parents, though not so close as to make
their life difficult. After living a year in Cambridge, Massachusetts, in
1970, he also realized that he preferred the South. "I like being close to
nature and living off the earth; I like fresh air, open spaces, and honesty,"

he explained. He wanted to live in the region where "the rich heritage of African-American history and traditions and the sense of community remain strong." Returning from prison to the soil that gave birth to the sit-ins enabled Sellers to "extract little things, little memories, in trying to make sense of where I was."[18] He felt an abiding sense of place in the South, and it was there he resolved to live the rest of his life.

Still, healing proved slow and painful. In prison, Sellers had kept himself sane by willfully forgetting as much as he could of the tumultuous years preceding his incarceration. "In prison, you can think only about wherever it is that you are," he recalled. "You don't think about where're you're going, because, of course, you're not going anywhere. You deal with what you have to deal with that day. And the way you do that is to forget about everything you've left behind. You forget about it totally." While forgetfulness may have helped Sellers cope with the monotony of incarceration, his release brought with it an acute sense of loneliness and a flood of distressing memories. He could not shake the sad conclusion that "the bond with those people who had at one time been my brother or sister had, somewhere along the way, been irreparably severed." Reentry to "normal life" was difficult; it was as though he had finally come up for air, but now the year was 1974 and everything was different. "The whole movement—life itself—seemed to have dissolved. The parts and elements were missing that I had come alive with—the people in Mississippi and Alabama." Gerald Ford occupied the White House; the Vietnam war was over; television shows like "Sanford and Sons" and "What's Happening?" had soared to the top of weekly ratings, captivating a younger generation of black boys and girls. Life often seemed surreal. "I'd try to talk to people and it was like I was speaking a different language."[19]

Learning a new language was no easy task. After returning to Greensboro from prison, Sellers was not able to find steady work. He had earned a master's degree in education at Harvard in 1970, and later a B.A. at Shaw University in Raleigh (which he thought he needed as a qualification for a teaching position). Nonetheless, the "disinformation machine had been reloaded" and potential employers were frightened of his criminal record.[20] White colleges might invite the former black militant to teach a course in Afro-American studies or to give a talk on his movement years, but no one gave serious consideration to full-time employment. Black colleges seemed even more inaccessible, citing fears of recriminations from private foundations and boards of trustees. Although Sellers was able to land a one-term appointment at North Carolina A & T, his position was not renewed when the funds were exhausted.

Then, in 1976, a white woman named Kathleen Soles from a prominent family in Greensboro, refusing to be influenced by public opinion, hired Sellers as an interviewer for the city's employment office. He worked in city government for the next decade and a half, receiving a promotion every two years, and becoming involved in numerous community activities—the PTA, anti-drug initiatives in the public school system and tutorial programs. He also worked toward a doctorate in education administration, receiving his degree from North Carolina A & T in 1987.

During these years and in his many responsibilities, Sellers worked hard to find new sources of meaning. He began making new commitments. He participated in a group therapy program organized in Greensboro by an African American psychologist. He and his wife Gwendolyn, the daughter of a Baptist minister in Tennessee and a skilled journalist, had two more children. He tried his hand in politics and ran for a seat on the city council—although he lost the race after encountering strong opposition from the NAACP. He also returned to the church. "I realized something strange and incredible that had never really occurred to me," he said. "I realized that the denomination with one of the largest representations in the civil rights movement was the Episcopal Church."[21] He realized that central to the church's theological identity was (as the House of Bishops once stated) "the reconciling comprehensiveness of the Body of Christ," a conviction reinforced through the Constitution and Canons, Pastoral Letters, the General Convention, the National Council, and the *Book of Common Prayer*. But even more importantly, he met a priest who reminded him of Henry Grant.

Father Carlton Morales, the much-loved rector of Greensboro's Church of the Redeemer, encouraged his parishioners to become champions of social justice—but not without nurturing a deep love of God. Blending soulful preaching with a high regard for the church's liturgical tradition, Father Morales welcomed Sellers "back into the fold."[22] Morales was just the right person to help the healing process. After leaving his native Jamaica in the middle 1950s and before beginning pastoral duties in Greensboro in 1966, Morales had worked with inmates in a Panama prison and with patients in a mental hospital and in a leper colony.[23]

Under Morales's pastoral leadership, Sellers came to see that the "internal moral discipline" he had once known as a young foot soldier in the movement was long spent. Sellers decided to reorganize his life with the church once again at its center. He realized further that the spiritual and moral vigor he had once known had been animated by his engagement in a community "united in purpose and centered on agape love."[24] Sellers felt a warmth and comradery in the church's fellowship during a time when many black people "kept their distance from him."[25] Eventually he reached a conclusion that changed his whole perception of life. "I realized I had not been good to myself as a person, and that I had to deal with an anger which was more intense than ever. But what could I do? I was angry at something I could not change. I couldn't live my life with constant migraines and peptic ulcers. I said to myself, yes it's true, we as black people have had everything done to us that could possibly be done. But I've got to get on with it. It's important that I have a personality and a life. I can't live like some mutant. I've got to move on. We've all got to move on."²⁶

Sellers's father died in 1990. Years earlier their contentious relationship and estrangement during the civil rights years had been dealt with and resolved. In fact, when Sellers's father had received word the terrible night in January of 1968 that his son had been shot in Orangeburg, he rounded up a group of his friends to protect his son. Taking pistols and shotguns, a posse of rural black men drove in caravan to the prison in the capital city of Columbia and there demanded from prison officials that the young Sellers be removed from death row. Although unsuccessful, Sellers's father and his friends stood vigil outside the prison throughout the long night until they were convinced that Cleve's life was no longer in danger. The experience marked a turning point in their relationship. After Orangeburg, his father seemed more sympathetic to his son's concerns; and Sellers began to see a more vulnerable side of his father. "We came so close to losing it all," Sellers said. "I think we both started to see how fragile our lives really were."²⁷

When his mother died in 1992, Sellers, along with his wife Gwendolyn and their three children, without any job prospects, moved back to his home town of Denmark and settled in the same red brick house in which he had lived as a child. And again he applied for teaching positions at nearby black colleges, only to encounter the same fears he had run up against in Greensboro.

Sellers also began seeking a pardon from the South Carolina Probation, Pardon and Parole Board for his conviction in the Orangeburg Massacre. With help from journalist Jack Bass as well as from several movement friends who had achieved national political prestige in subsequent years, his petition was successful. Bass, who with Jack Nelson had written a book-length account of the Orangeburg Massacre, noted in his newspaper coverage that after receiving word of the pardon, Sellers's thoughts had turned to Martin Luther King, Jr.'s, words spoken at the end of the Selma march, "Even though the arc of the moral universe is long, it bends towards justice." Sellers received the pardon graciously, observing that "the state [has] said it's sorry, not to me, but through me to a larger class of African Americans."²⁸ He also told an interviewer, "The pardon is going to give me a little more leverage so I can get the door open and walk in."²⁹ In fact, it was only a matter of months before he was invited by the History Department of the University of South Carolina to replace an instructor on sick leave. Sellers seized the opportunity and demonstrated his seasoned organizational and intellectual skills, though now in an academic context, collaborating with other movement veterans and historians to create a successful civil rights curriculum for college instruction. The following year, the university offered Sellers a full-time position as an assistant professor of history.

Sellers's return to Denmark also brought him back into the small congregation of St. Philip's Episcopal Church. He served as the church's senior warden until 1995, assisting the parish with administrative responsibilities, attending to certain pastoral concerns and, on occasion, playing the role of the rector's spiritual confidant. The Reverend Emmanuel Johnson, the church's new minister, had been president of Liberia's Cuttington College until he was forced to flee the embattled country's tribal wars.

On a summer afternoon Cleveland Sellers can be found working in a small community center in Denmark. In a cramped, unairconditioned gymnasium, he talks with elementary school boys and girls on a wide range of issues: African American history, personal hygiene, good behavior and attitudes, and sometimes his years as a civil rights activist. When he talks to children these days about the movement, he is more inclined to speak of Martin Luther King, Jr., than of Stokely Carmichael or Bobby Seale, even though his love for Stokely is enduring. A photograph of Sellers with Dr. King taken during the Meredith march rests on the coffee table in his spacious new home outside of town. With his son as his partner, Sellers takes the children from the community center on picnics and coordinates a basketball clinic for the boys.

There is a small grassy field next to the cinder-block building where volleyball games are sometimes played, but the children's favorite pastime—much to Seller's bemusement—is the challenge of jumping a small, muddy ditch in the wooded area behind the center. When a child is able to jump the four-foot divide between the two banks of the small creek, she or he is welcomed into a special circle of veteran jumpers. Sellers tells the children they must continue to take leaps of courage, testing their strength in ways that may prove exhilarating or, of course, leave them disappointed and muddy. "I try to still maintain a simple touch," he says. "I think that was the most important part of the movement. So I work very hard to try to have something for these kids to do. I'm an advocate for them; that's the direction I have taken."[30]

Sellers often visits the chapel of St. Philip's in the late afternoon. He goes there now for the same reason he went as a child, to feel embraced by the serenity and mystery of the place, to give himself over to a "certain feel and spirit."[31] Although he recognizes that the most segregated hour of the week is still eleven o'clock Sunday morning, Sellers has helped organize a series of common worship services and fellowships with the all-white Episcopal Christ Church just a few blocks away on Main Street. Even apart from these occasions, however, the congregation at St. Philip's opens its doors to all who want to worship, and among its visitors are Asians, Hispanic Americans, and whites.

Sometimes Sellers thinks about the dream of the beloved community and its disintegration in the cataclysmic years of the late sixties. If the beloved community is still worth pursuing—and he thinks it is—it should be sought in focused and highly particular places, like the community center or the congregation of St. Philip's. Hopes for an all-encompassing movement toward national redemption and social transformation are better left behind.

From the church, it is a short drive down a winding dirt road to a wide expanse of cotton and tobacco fields. There the vegetation becomes dense and wild; the roadside is overgrown with blackberry briars and kudzu vine. Small farms, many of which are owned and operated by African Americans, are visible in the distance through the cleared fields of late summer. Sellers rolls his window down and lets in a warm rush of air and the roar of crickets in the hour before sunset. He says, "There is nothing else anybody can do to shame me or make me feel like I'm not cut out for the life I'm living." He has found a home.[32]

NOTES

Introduction

Faiths in Conflict

1. Karl Barth, *The Word of God and the Word of Man*, p. 37.

2. This is a rephrasing of Richard Lischer's provocative comment on the religious vocation of Martin Luther King, Jr.: "In King's vision of the world, ordinary southern towns became theaters of divine revelation, and the gospel became a possibility for the renewal of public life." *The Preacher King*, p. 10. The novelist Richard Ford describes his state's polyvalent moods, textures, and dissonances as elements perfectly suited for literary reconstruction. "I think when you have built into your society a completely irreconcilable human conflict, slavery and segregation for instance, there are schisms and torques and breakage all around you, both about race and not about race, drama in other words." Cited in Jerry Mitchell, "State's Contrasts Reach to Its Soul," *Jackson Clarion-Ledger*, February 14, 1994.

3. See also C. Eric Lincoln and Lawrence H. Mamiya, *The Black Church in the African American Experience* (Durham: Duke University Press, 1990).

4. Doug McAdam, *Freedom Summer*, p. 5.

5. Flannery O'Connor, *Mystery and Manners*, p. 44; Neil R. McMillen, *Dark Journey*.

6. See Ralph E. Luker's excellent study of the social gospel's diverse views of race and social order, *The Social Gospel in Black and White*.

7. As such, this work falls loosely within what Steven F. Lawson calls the third generation of civil rights scholars—those scholars who "are beginning to reexamine the ideological roots of the freedom struggle," including the legal, theological, and political sources. Steven F. Lawson, "Freedom Then, Freedom Now: The Historiography of the Civil Rights Movement," p. 457.

8. Cornel West describes prophetic Christian thought as an utterly honest confrontation with the tragic character of human history "without permitting the immensity of what is and what must be lost to call into question the significance of what may be gained." At the same time, prophetic religion elevates "the notion of struggle"—not just individual, but collective and thus redemptive—to the highest priority. West explains, "To be a prophetic Afro-American Christian is to negate what is and transform prevailing realities against the backdrop of the present historical limits. In short, prophetic Afro-American Christian thought imbues Afro-

American thinking with the sobriety of tragedy, the struggle for freedom, and the spirit of hope." *Prophesy Deliverance! An Afro-American Revolutionary Christianity*, p. 19.

9. This is true in Kay Mills's otherwise fine biography, *This Little Light of Mine: The Life of Fannie Lou Hamer*.

10. James M. Washington, "Editor's Introduction," *A Testament of Hope*, p. xxiii.

11. The term is John Dittmer's. See his monumental study, *Local People: The Struggle for Civil Rights in Mississippi*, for an absorbing account of the grass-roots origins of black activism. Fannie Lou Hamer's witness is noted in most African American theological literature. For examples, see James H. Cone, *Martin and Malcolm: A Dream or a Nightmare* (Maryknoll, N.Y.: Orbis Books, 1991); Diana L. Hayes, *And Still We Rise: An Introduction to Black Liberation Theology* (New York: Paulist Press, 1991); Dwight N. Hopkins, *Shoes That Fit Our Feet: Sources for a Constructive Black Theology* (Maryknoll, N.Y.: Orbis Books, 1993); and Delores S. Williams, *Sisters in the Wilderness: The Challenge of Womanist God-Talk* (Maryknoll, N.Y.: Orbis Books, 1993).

12. According to Hegel—who is often condemned for his chilling characterizations of the world historical individual—such grandiose self-awareness is one sure way of ruling out a person's epochal significance. Hegel said, "These heroic individuals, in fulfilling these aims of theirs, had no consciousness of the Idea at all. On the contrary, they were practical and political men." Nevertheless, one finds in Hegel ample passages of sufficient vagueness for underwriting all the Sam Bowerses who promise the new millennium. Hegel says, "A world-historical individual is not so circumspect as to want this, that, and the other, and to take account of everything; rather, he commits himself unreservedly to one purpose alone. So it happens that such individuals treat other interests, even sacred ones, in a casual way—a mode of conduct certainly open to moral censure. But so great a figure must necessarily trample on many an innocent flower, crushing much that gets in his way." G. W. F. Hegel, *Introduction to the Philosophy of History*, pp. 33, 35.

13. Sam Bowers, interview with author.

14. Will D. Campbell, interview with author.

15. Douglas Hudgins cited in *The Jackson Daily News*, "A Great Television Sermon by Dr. W. Douglas Hudgins" (Jackson, Miss., n.d.).

16. Cleveland Sellers, interview with author.

17. Cleveland Sellers with Robert Terrell, *The River of No Return*, p. 156.

18. James Forman, *The Making of Black Revolutionaries*, p. 476.

19. Sam Bowers cited in Wyn Craig Wade, *The Fiery Cross: The Ku Klux Klan in America* (London: Simon and Schuster, 1987), p. 340.

20. See Ephraim Radner, "New World Order, Old World Anti-Semitism: The Case of Pat Robertson," *The Christian Century*, 112:26 (September 13–20, 1995), pp. 844–49. Paul Boyer, *When Time Shall Be No More*.

21. James Baldwin, *The Fire Next Time*, p. 81.

Chapter One

Mrs. Hamer's Fight

1. Mississippi represented "the whole vicious system of segregation," said SNCC's John Lewis. "If we can crack Mississippi, we will be able to crack the system in the rest of the country." Cited in James Atwater, "If We Can Crack Mississippi," *Saturday Evening Post*, July 25, 1964, p. 19.

2. Fannie Lou Hamer, in J. H. O'Dell, "Life in Mississippi, An Interview with Fannie Lou Hamer," *Freedomways* (2nd quarter 1965), 231. See also the profile by Phyl Garland, "Builders of a New South," *Ebony*, 21:10 (August 1966), 27–29. Charles M. Payne is correct to remind us that, within the movement, local black people were accorded the respect of "courtesy titles" that the Jim Crow South forbade. Women like Ella Baker, Fannie Lou Hamer, and Annie Devine were called Miss Baker, Mrs. Hamer, and Mrs. Devine. Although inconsistencies in using these "titles" will inevitably arise, I will follow the now standard practice of referring to Fannie Lou Hamer as Mrs. Hamer. See Charles M. Payne, *I've Got the Light of Freedom*, pp. 5–6.

3. Hamer, "Life in Mississippi," pp. 231–32.

4. Hamer cited in "Fannie Lou Hamer: Civil Rights Activist," in *Mississippi Black History Makers*, edited by George Alexander Sewell and Margaret L. Dwight (Jackson: University Press of Mississippi, 1984), p. 125.

5. Fannie Lou Hamer, "To Praise Our Bridges," *Mississippi Writers: Reflections of Childhood and Youth*, Volume 2, edited by Dorothy Abbot (Jackson: University Press of Mississippi, 1986), p. 324.

6. Kay Mills, *This Little Light of Mine*, p. 13.

7. Hamer, "To Praise Our Bridges," p. 321. See also *The Independent Eye* (Cincinnati, Ohio) December 23, 1968–January 20, 1969, Amistad.

8. Fannie Lou Hamer, interview with Neil McMillen, Mississippi Oral History Program, April 14, 1972.

9. Hamer, "To Praise Our Bridges," p. 324.

10. Hamer cited in Mills, *This Little Light of Mine*, p. 24.

11. E. Franklin Frazier cited in Pater J. Paris, *The Social Teaching of the Black Churches* (Philadelphia: Fortress Press, 1985), p. 7.

12. James Cone, *My Soul Looks Back*, p. 23.

13. In *Race, Religion and the Continuing American Dilemma*, C. Eric Lincoln amplifies this point: "Worship, which is the grateful recognition of human contingency, implies a sense of perspective: man needs to know not only that God is, but what God is like. Conversely, he needs to have some authentic notions about himself as an individual, his proper relationship to other men, and his worthiness to be included in the peculiar concern God reserves for those in his own image. In a society where significant truths and values are racially determined, such issues are painfully clouded and frequently compromised. But in the Black Church the nor-

mative presuppositions which gave the American society its racist cast are disregarded, and the equal worth of all races is affirmed as a necessary inference of the common fatherhood of God. The imputation of pariahism, the assumption of privilege, and the demands of prerogative based on racial identity are all rejected. The Black Church perceives itself as an expression of the divine intent that, however nefarious the strategies of men, the faith will not be rendered destitute and the righteousness of God will not be left without a witness. If the established oracles are silent or unreliable, then lo, a voice cries forth from the wilderness." *Race, Religion and the Continuing American Dilemma* (New York: Hill and Wang, 1984), p. xx.

14. The network of black churches, civil organizations and business institutions was mutually empowering, demonstrating, as Steven F. Lawson has written, that "blacks were not simply victims of separate and unequal policies; rather, they retained a measure of social, economic, and political autonomy that under the proper conditions could fuel demands for equality and power." "Freedom Then, Freedom Now," p. 466.

15. Cone, *My Soul Looks Back*, p. 14.

16. Fannie Lou Hamer, "Sick and Tired of Being Sick and Tired," *Katallagate*, Fall 1968, p. 27 (published in Nashville, Tenn., by the Committee of Southern Churchmen).

17. Charles McLaurin, "Voice of Calm," *Sojourners* 11:11 (December 1982), 12.

18. As Neil McMillen explains, to be qualified to take the test, the applicant could not have committed "crimes presumed peculiar to his race" such as bigamy, adultery, theft, perjury, child abandonment, nonsupport, or fornication. Neil R. McMillen, "Black Enfranchisement in Mississippi: Federal Enforcement and Black Protest in the 1960s," *The Journal of Southern History* 43:3 (August 1977), 353.

19. Hamer, "Sick and Tired of Being Sick and Tired," p. 21.

20. Doug McAdam is correct to add, however, "[As] more and more people donned their Sunday best for the trip to the courthouse, a curious thing happened: the daily newspaper lists of those registering to vote were transformed from an effective means of social control into a vehicle for gaining prestige in the black community." As one summer volunteer wrote in a letter, "in Panola County now the Negro citizens look with pride at their names in the *Panolian*; they point out the names of friends and neighbors and hurry to courthouse to be enlisted on the honor roll." *Freedom Summer*, p. 81.

21. Phyl Garland, "Builders of a New South," 34. Mrs. Hamer told historian Neil McMillen that she did not know until 1962 that black people could register to vote. McMillen, "Black Enfranchisement in Mississippi," p. 353.

22. Hamer, "Sick and Tired of Being Sick and Tired," p. 22.

23. Hamer cited in Mills, *This Little Light of Mine*, p. 37.

24. Neil McMillen describes the difficulty: "Many registrars refused outright to permit blacks to make application for the ballot; but even when Negroes were permitted to complete the registration form, their circumstances were not greatly improved. Some were rebuffed when they could not recite the state constitution from memory; others were refused for their inability to identify by name every

officeholder and committeeman in their counties; still others were disqualified for minor omissions and errors. But the white registrar's most common complaint was the Negro's uncertain grasp of the state constitution—a document, according to Theodore G. Bilbo, 'that damn few white men and no niggers at all can explain. . . .' Whether field hand or college professor, domestic servant or physician, a black Mississippian could rarely meet the exacting standards of the county courthouse." McMillen, "Black Enfranchisement in Mississippi," pp. 353–54.

25. McLaurin, "Voice of Calm," p. 13.

26. Hamer, interview with Neil McMillen.

27. Fannie Lou Hamer, "Interview" in Howell Raines, *My Soul Is Rested*, p. 250.

28. Charles McLaurin cited in Tracy Sugarman, *Stranger at the Gates*, p. 66.

29. Mills, *This Little Light of Mine*, p. 16.

30. Hamer in Raines, *My Soul is Rested*, p. 251.

31. Cited in John Egerton, *A Mind to Stay Here*, p. 98.

32. Cited in Mills, *This Little Light of Mine*, p. 39.

33. McLaurin, "Voice of Calm," p. 13. Mills, *This Little Light of Mine*, p. 42.

34. Tracy Sugarman interview cited in Mills, *This Little Light of Mine*, p. 39.

35. Hamer in Raines, *My Soul Is Rested*, p. 252.

36. Hamer, "To Praise Our Bridges," p. 325.

37. Donald W. Shriver, Jr., *An Ethic for Enemies: Forgiveness or Politics* (New York: Oxford University Press, 1995), p. 201.

38. Hamer in Raines, *My Soul Is Rested*, pp. 252–53, and in Edgerton, *A Mind to Stay Here*, p. 100.

39. Hamer in Raines, *My Soul Is Rested*, p. 253.

40. Mills, *This Little Light of Mine*, p. 60; Raines, *My Soul Is Rested*, pp. 253–54; *Local People*, p. 172; Hamer, "To Praise Our Bridges," p. 326; Fannie Lou Hamer, "Affidavit," State of Mississippi, County of Hinds, SNCC Papers.

41. There is much in Elaine Scarry's remarkable study that helps to clarify the complex meaning of Mrs. Hamer's beating in Winona. As Scarry shows, there is no experience in which the obliteration of one's total world occurs in a more immediate, visceral form than in calculated physical violence. "Intense pain is world-destroying," she writes. The torturer's will to unlimited control—governed by the equation "the larger the prisoner's pain, the larger the torturer's power"—depends on a reciprocal demonstration of the victim's diminution and the final disappearance of her world. Elaine Scarry, *The Body in Pain: The Making and Unmaking of the World* (New York: Oxford University Press, 1985), p. 29.

Scarry refers to a description in Solzhenitzyn's *The First Circle* in which prisoners, while sleeping in precise uniform rows of beds, were forced to keep their hands outside the covers. "It was a diabolical rule," he wrote; "It is a natural, deep-rooted, unnoticed human habit to hide one's hands while asleep, to hold them against one's body" (Alexander Solzhenitzyn cited ibid., p. 48. The denial of such simple nurturing gestures, quite apart from the violent physical abuse of the kind displayed in the Winona jail, had the effect of turning the prisoner's body—in its needs and wants, "in its small and moving gestures of friendship toward itself"—

into a weapon of self-torture. In the end, the prisoner's body becomes the enemy itself, so that the world-destroying capacity of torture continues long after the physical violence has ceased: the world lingers as the enduring presence of the torturer. Scarry explains, "The world unmaking, this uncreating of the created world, which is an external objectification of the psychic experience of the person in pain, becomes itself the cause of the pain" (ibid.). When in the Winona jail the sheriff offered to let Mrs. Hamer and her friends go free and return home the night after the beatings, their refusal betrayed the certainty that their lives were in greater danger outside the jail—at home—than inside. Mrs. Hamer said, "I told 'em they'd have to kill me in my cell." (Hamer cited in McLaurin, "Voice of Calm," p. 13) Freedom and imprisonment collapse into an environment constantly threatened by unpredictable violence from jail to roadside to home. "Every day of my life I pay with the misery of that beatin'," she said. Hamer cited in Egerton, *A Mind to Stay Here*, p. 100.

42. "Verbatim transcript of interview by phone by Jack Minnis with Mrs. Fannie Lou Hamer," March 17, 1964, SNCC Papers.

43. Hamer cited in Mills, *This Little Light of Mine*, p. 22.

44. June Johnson, "Broken Barriers and Billy Stickes," *Sojourners* 11:11 (December 1982), 17.

45. Hamer cited in Raines, *My Soul Is Rested*, p. 254.

46. Hamer, "Affidavit."

47. Scarry, *The Body in Pain*, p. 49.

48. "Verbatim Transcript of Interview by Phone by Jack Minnis."

49. Bob Moses, "Mississippi: 1961–1962," *Liberation*, January 1970, p. 14.

50. Fannie Lou Hamer, cited in Mills, *This Little Light of Mine*, p. 69.

51. "Fannie Lou Hamer conversation with SNCC worker, Dale Grunemeier, Ruleville, Mississippi, 1964," Tracy Sugarman taped interview, private collection.

52. Cone, *My Soul Looks Back*, p. 14.

53. Johnson cited in Mills, *This Little Light of Mine*, pp. 60–61.

54. Hamer cited in McLaurin, "Voice of Calm," p. 13.

55. G. H. C. Macgregor, "Acts: Text, Exegesis and Exposition," *The Interpreter's Bible* (New York and Nashville: Abingdon-Cokesbury Press, 1954), vol. 9, p. 23.

56. "Verbatim transcript of interview by phone by Jack Minnis."

57. Ibid.

58. Hamer cited in Mills, *This Little Light of Mine*, p. 65.

59. Ibid., p. 70.

60. Hamer cited in Egerton, *A Mind to Stay Here*, p. 100.

61. Athanasius, *The Life of Antony*, translated by Robert C. Gregg (New York: Paulist Press, 1980), p. 42. Dorothy Cotton reports of Mrs. Hamer's demeanor: "When we got there, I remember the jailer standing around saying pleasantries to me. Then Mrs. Hamer and Annell came out of cell and Mrs. Hamer pointed to him as the same one that had beaten her. I felt intense anger—I could have

done real harm to him, and he had been standing there talking friendly to me." Mrs. Hamer, however, spoke of the weather. Kay Mills, *This Little Light of Mine*, p. 67.

62. Hamer, "To Praise Our Bridges," p. 326.

63. Hamer cited in McLaurin, "Voice of Calm," p. 16.

64. Mills, *This Little Light of Mine*, p. 79.

65. Charles M. Payne, *I've Got the Light of Freedom*, p. 258.

66. Fannie Lou Hamer in *Freedom on My Mind*, documentary film produced and directed by Connie Field and Marilyn Mulford (Berkeley, Cal.: Clarity Educational Productions, 1994).

67. Hamer, "To Praise Our Bridges," p. 327.

68. John Dittmer, letter to the author, June 11, 1996.

69. Hamer cited in Payne, *I've Got the Light of Freedom*, p. 259.

70. Ibid.

71. Ibid., p. 260.

72. Hamer cited in McLaurin, "Voice of Calm," p. 15.

73. Payne, *I've Got the Light of Freedom*, p. 260.

74. John Lewis cited in Richard Lischer, *The Preacher King*, p. 244.

75. Ibid., p. 245. See also Stanley Hauerwas, "Remembering Martin Luther King, Jr., Remembering," *Journal of Religious Ethics* 23:1 (Spring 1995), 141.

76. Mills, *This Little Light of Mine*, p. 78.

77. "Initiation Ceremony of the White Knights of the Ku Klux Klan of Mississippi," in Chet Dillard, *Clearburning*, p. 121.

78. Hamer, interview with Neil McMillen, p. 11.

79. Mills, *This Little Light of Mine*, p. 82.

80. John Dittmer, letter to the author, June 11, 1996.

81. Lawrence Guyot and Mike Thelwell, "The Politics of Necessity and Survival in Mississippi," *Freedomways* 6 (Spring 1966), 132.

82. See William H. Chafe, *Never Stop Running: Allard Lowenstein and the Struggle to Save American Liberalism*, pp. 187–210.

83. Cited in Dittmer, *Local People*, p. 209.

84. Willie Peacock cited ibid., p. 210.

85. John Lewis, interview with the author.

86. These sometimes disputed numbers are based on the statistics of the *Congressional Quarterly*, week ending July 5, 1963, pp. 1,091–93.

87. John Lewis, interview with the author.

88. Bob Moses cited in Eric R. Burner, *And Gently He Shall Lead Them: Robert Parris Moses and Civil Rights in Mississippi* (New York: New York University Press, 1994), p. 129.

89. Ibid; Clayborne Carson, *In Struggle: SNCC and the Black Awakening of the 1960s*, p. 99.

90. Moses cited in Carson, *In Struggle*, p. 101. Richard Lischer points out that King's phrase, with its clear Hegelian resonances, was borrowed from the Ameri-

can philosopher Josiah Royce "to evoke the period of brotherhood that would follow the current social struggle" (Lischer, *The Preacher King*, p. 234). Yet King placed less emphasis on the specific details of the ideal, less emphasis on techniques of engineering the beloved community, than on the character of life required to foster the coming of a new order. King was a preacher, not an economist or political theorist. Importantly, Lischer shows that as his rhetoric became tempered by a keener understanding of social realities, King's use of the phrase was eventually replaced by specific reference to the Kingdom of God. The former phrase, "the beloved community," carries overtones of utopian idealism; the latter, Lischer says, acknowledges "God's claim upon all human achievement." However, one should add that to many local people in the movement, the "beloved community" itself acknowledged the prevenience of divine grace inasmuch as it represented, in one activist's words, a "tiny taste of the Kingdom to come."

91. Hamer cited in Carson, *In Struggle*, p. 99. Clayborne Carson claims that most of the supporters of the proposed Summer Project were veteran SNCC volunteers. In her study, *A Case of Black and White: Northern Volunteers and the Southern Freedom Summers, 1964–1965*, Mary Aickin Rothschild adds, "Fannie Lou Hamer believed that the 'bridge' built between white volunteers and black children was one of the greatest achievements of the summers. Never again would southern blacks be so separated from the white community. Likewise, the white community simply could not continue to maintain many of the myths about the 'necessity' of separation of the races, which, of course, had never existed anyway when there was work to be done" (Westport, Conn.: Greenwood Press, 1982), p. 172.

92. James Forman cited in Clayborne Carson, *In Struggle*, p. 99.

93. Cleveland Sellers with Robert Terrell, *The River of No Return: The Autobiography of a Black Militant and the Life and Death of SNCC*, p. 56.

94. Sally Belfrage, "Freedom Summer," manuscript on microfilm, Armistad.

95. Ibid., p. 3.

96. Certainly the backgrounds of the students were diverse, and in some cases, not religious at all. In his book *Freedom Summer*, Doug McAdam offers a precise and fascinating account of the biographical roots of the student activists; see especially pages 35–65.

97. Hamer, "To Praise Our Bridges," p. 326.

98. Curtis Hayes interviewed in *Freedom on My Mind* (film). Vicki Crawford writes, "Mrs. Hamer was a large influence on young and old; many younger women such as Unita Blackwell were personal friends and proteges whom she encouraged and guided. Blackwell, the daughter of sharecroppers, would later expand upon her activist role to assume political leadership as the first black woman mayor in Mississippi, elected in 1976. She recalled the close personal relationship with Mrs. Hamer and how her deep faith and understanding of human injustice instructed others, especially angry youth, of the need to use anger and indignation

in creative ways that would be empowering rather than debilitating. 'She would make you laugh and make you cry,' said Blackwell, 'and when she told the story she would say. "But you have to love [whites], for they know not what they do. And you had better get this anger out of you. And organize your people." ' " Vicki Crawford, "Race, Class, Gender and Culture: Black Women's Activism in the Mississippi Civil Rights Movement," *Journal of Mississippi History* 58:1 (1996), 17.

99. Hamer cited in Sugarman, *Stranger at the Gates*, p. 113.

100. Ibid., p. 117.

101. Ibid., p. 121.

102. Fannie Lou Hamer, "Foreword," to ibid., p. vii.

103. Fannie Lou Hamer cited in Edwin King, "Go Tell It on the Mountain," *Sojourners* 11:11 (December 1982), 87.

104. Hamer, "Foreword," *Stranger at the Gates*, p. xi.

105. Bob Moses cited in Dittmer, *Local People*, p. 272.

106. Sellers, *The River of No Return*, pp. 108–9.

107. Cited in *Letters from Mississippi*, edited by Elizabeth Sutherland, pp. 214–15.

108. Dittmer, *Local People*, pp. 282–83.

109. Edwin King, "The White Church in Mississippi," manuscript, Edwin King Private Papers.

110. Sellers, *The River of No Return*, p. 108. On the Klan's campaign against the Jews in Mississippi, see Jack Nelson, *Terror in the Night: The Klan's Campaign against the Jews*, and the cagey memoir by Thomas A. Tarrants III, *The Conversion of a Klansman: The Story of a Former Ku Klux Klan Terrorist* (Garden City, N.Y.: Doubleday, 1979).

111. Mills, *This Little Light of Mine*, p. 115.

112. McAdam, *Freedom Summer*, pp. 118–19.

113. Johnson cited in Mills, *This Little Light of Mine*, p. 112.

114. Aaron Henry cited in Mills, *This Little Light of Mine*, p. 117.

115. Letter from John Dittmer to the author, June 11, 1996.

116. Edwin King cited in Mills, *This Little Light of Mine*, p. 118.

117. Fannie Lou Hamer, "Credentials Committee Transcript," Edwin King Papers.

118. Ibid.

119. Sellers, *The River of No Return*, p. 109.

120. Holt, *The Summer That Didn't End: The Story of the Mississippi Civil Rights Project of 1964*, p. 169.

121. Joseph Rauh, in *Freedom on My Mind* (film).

122. Holt, *The Summer That Didn't End*, p. 169; Edwin King, "Freedom Summer," manuscript, Edwin King Private Papers.

123. Irving Bernstein, *Guns or Butter: The Presidency of Lyndon Johnson* (New York: Oxford University Press, 1996), p. 139.

124. Dittmer, *Local People*, pp. 292, 294.

125. "Credentials Committee Report on Mississippi," cited in Holt, *The Summer That Didn't End*, p. 173.

126. Cited in Dittmer, *Local People*, p. 294.

127. Hamer, "Foreword" in *Stranger at the Gates*, p. vii. As William Strickland, the executive director of the Northern Student Movement, would write, "What does the MFDP challenge, then, really mean? It means more than threatening the solid South and more than the ouster of a group of Dixiecrats who have voted consistently, and with great arrogance, against the civil rights bill, the poverty bill, medicare, and all progressive social legislation which has come before Congress. The MFDP is, I think, the first emergence of a new politics in American—a politics of idealism and truth. It means that the people we have never heard from before have taken a part in this struggle, and that is the most hopeful sign of all." "The Movement in Mississippi," *Freedomways* 5:2 (Spring 1965), 312–13.

128. Hamer cited in King, "Go Tell It on The Mountain," p. 19.

129. Kay Mills, *This Little Light of Mine*, p. 125.

130. King, "Go Tell It on the Mountain," p. 20.

131. Edwin King, interview with the author.

132. Holt, *The Summer That Didn't End*, p. 171.

133. Courtland Cox cited in *Voices of Freedom: An Oral History of the Civil Rights Movement From the 1950s through the 1980s* (New York: Bantam Books, 1990), p. 199.

134. Dittmer, *Local People*, p. 297.

135. Ibid., p. 299.

136. Hamer, "Sick and Tired of Being Sick and Tired," p. 23.

137. Victoria Gray cited in *Voices of Freedom*, p. 203.

138. Hamer cited in Mills, *This Little Light of Mine*, p. 132.

139. Marshall Ganz in *Freedom on My Mind* (film).

140. Willie Peacock, ibid.

141. Sellers, *The River of No Return*, p. 111.

142. Ed Brown, "Interview with Tom Dent," Dent Collection, Amistad.

143. See Sara Evans, *Personal Politics: The Roots of Women's Liberation in the Civil Rights Movement and the New Left*, pp. 90–94.

144. Bob Moses, in *Freedom on My Mind* (film).

145. Bob Moses cited in Burner, *And Gently He Shall Lead Them*, p. 213; Dittmer, *Local People*, p. 326.

146. Hamer, "To Praise Our Bridges," pp. 326–27.

147. King, "Go Tell It on the Mountain," p. 87.

148. Sally Belfrage, "Freedom Summer," pp. 245–46.

149. Sellers, *The River of No Return*, p. 110.

150. Leslie Burl McLemore, "The Mississippi Freedom Democratic Party: A Case Study of Grass-Roots Politics," p. 128.

151. See Polly Greenberg's moving account of the Child Development Group of Mississippi, *The Devil Has Slippery Shoes* (London: Macmillan, 1969).

152. Danny Collum, "Stepping out into Freedom: The Life of Fannie Lou Hamer," *Sojourners* 11:11 (December 1982), 15.

153. Hamer cited in Kay Mills, *This Little Light of Mine*, p. 307.

154. Hamer, "Sick and Tired of Being Sick and Tired," p. 25.

155. Hamer, "Foreword," in *Stranger at the Gates*, p. vii. On the religious motives of the summer volunteers, see McAdam, *Freedom Summer*, pp. 46–49; 62–65.

156. Curtis Hayes in *Freedom on My Mind* (film).

157. Fannie Lou Hamer, "Songs My Mother Taught Me," tape produced by Bernice Johnson Reagon, 1980.

158. The subversive and polyvalent dimension of slave spirituals has been analyzed in a wide range of literature. Some examples are John W. Blassingame, *The Slave Community: Plantation Life in the Antebellum South* (New York: Oxford University Press, 1972), pp. 137–48; Joseph R. Washington, Jr., *Black Religion: The Negro and Christianity in the United States* (Boston: Beacon Press, 1964), pp. 206–20; C. Eric Lincoln and Lawrence H. Mamiya, *The Black Church in the African American Experience* (Durham: Duke University Press, 1990); James H. Cone, *The Spirituals and the Blues: An Interpretation* (New York: Seabury Press, 1972); Theophus H. Smith, *Conjuring Culture: Biblical Formations of Black America* (New York: Oxford University Press, 1994), pp. 115–39.

159. Conversations with Ed King, as well as his theological reflection on the life of Mrs. Hamer in *Sojourners* magazine, are my primary inspiration for this reading of the spirituals.

160. As Michael Walzer writes, "God's promise generates a sense of possibility (it would be rash, given the fearfulness of the Israelite slaves, to say that it generates a sense of confidence): the world is not all Egypt. Without that sense of possibility, oppression would be experienced as an inescapable condition, a matter of personal or collective bad luck, a stroke of fate." *Exodus and Revolution*, pp. 21–22.

161. In his excellent book, *Civil Rights and the Idea of Freedom*, Richard King explains, "The centrality to black theology of the Exodus story meant that slavery/freedom was understood on a figural-spiritual level by many black Christians. Thus slavery and freedom referred to more than 'just' a secular experience or status, for they were also spiritual or sacred experiences of a people whose experience was part of God's purpose and plan. Freedom, according to this spiritual interpretation, was a destination in sacred history as well as a goal of action within secular history; it was a future condition implying a fundamental transformation in individual and group life" (p. 29).

162. Because this dialectic was so exuberantly at play in Mrs. Hamer's theology, she did not need to replace the first person singular pronoun "I" with the plural "we." Lincoln and Mamiya's claim would not hold in her case, that "the creators of the civil rights songs always used the first person plural pronouns—'we' and

'our,'" in order to foster a sense of solidarity, of acting together as one consolidated body" (*The Black Church in the African American Experience*, p. 370). For Mrs. Hamer, the "I" included both the individual self and the beloved community; as the writer Zora Neale Hurston once said of the ritual of "shouting," it is both "absolutely individualistic" and "a community thing." Cited in Joseph M. Murphy, *Working the Spirit: Ceremonies of the African Diaspora* (Boston: Beacon Press, 1994), p. 173.

163. Bob Moses in *Freedom on My Mind* (film).

Chapter Two

High Priest: Sam Bowers

1. Sam Bowers, interview with the author.

2. Cited in William H. McIlhany II, *Klandestine*, p. 113.

3. Wyn Craig Wade, *The Fiery Cross: The Ku Klux Klan in America* (New York: Simon and Schuster, 1987), p. 334.

4. Jack Nelson, *Terror in the Night: The Klan's Campaign against the Jews*, p. 62.

5. "Eaton J. Bowers," obituary. Mississippi Department of Archives and History.

6. Cited in Don Whitehead, *Attack on Terror: The FBI against the Ku Klux Klan in Mississippi*, p. 4.

7. The claim is Bowers's own. Although historical records indicate that Sallie Lee Dinkins, daughter of Eliza and Robert Dinkins (of Madison County, Mississippi, originally from Charlotte, North Carolina) married Eaton Jackson Bowers, the great-grandfather of Sam Holloway Bowers, Jr., and that Adelaide Dinkins married Dr. Charles Betts Galloway, the father of Bishop Galloway, whether the two Dinkinses were sisters cannot be established. Mississippi Department of Archives and History

8. Eaton J. Bowers, "Autobiography," Mississippi Department of Archives and History.

9. Sam Bowers, interview with the author.

10. *Jackson City Directory*, 1945 and 1948, Mississippi Department of Archives and History.

11. Sam Bowers, interview with the author.

12. Ibid.

13. Ibid.

14. Ibid.

15. Cf. Ralph E. Luker, *The Social Gospel in Black and White: American Racial Reform, 1885–1912*, pp. 289–301, and also Maxwell Bloomfield, "Dixon's *The Leopard's Spots*: A Study in Popular Racism," in Charles E. Wynes, ed., *The Negro in the South since 1865* (Tuscaloosa: University of Alabama Press, 1965), pp. 83–102.

16. Patsy Sims, *The Klan* (New York: Stein and Day, 1978), p. 259. During his

murder trials two decades later, newspaper writers often referred to his stylish attire: "Nattily dressed in a tan sports coat, khaki-colored trousers but without his usual sunglasses, Bowers balked at being handcuffed when taken from the FBI office to the U.S. commissioner"; "Bowers, a neat, sandy-haired man who appears younger than his years;" "the dapper Laurel vending machine company owner."

17. Cited in McIlhany, *Klandestine*, p. 39.

18. Nelson, *Terror in the Night*, p. 26.

19. Sam Bowers, interview with the author.

20. Ibid.

21. Ibid.

22. Ibid.

23. "Initiation Ceremony of the White Knights of the Ku Klux Klan of Mississippi," in W. O. "Chet" Dillard, *Clearburning*, p. 121.

24. "Executive Lecture of March 1, 1964," McIlhany, *Klandestine*, p. 123.

25. Ibid., p. 135.

26. Ibid.

27. Thomas A. Tarrants III and John Perkins, with David Wimbish, *He's My Brother: A Black Activist and a Former Klansman Tell Their Stories*, p. 75.

28. Letter from Burke Marshall to Dan H. Shell, July 15, 1964; Statement of Donald T. Appell, Chief Investigator, Committee on Un-American Activities, October 19, 1965, McCain Library and Archives, University of Southern Mississippi.

29. Tarrants and Perkins, *He's My Brother*, p. 75.

30. Nelson, *Terror in the Night*, p. 27.

31. In his excellent book *Baptized in Blood: The Religion of the Lost Cause, 1865–1920*, Charles Reagan Wilson argues that in the 1820s "the dream of Southern nationalism" came largely from indigenous sources, although it resembled the ideas of Romantic nationalism that were flourishing on European soil. But then, in the 1850s, Wilson claims, "Southern leaders began more consciously drawing from European ideas. Southerners came to believe in 'cultural nationalism,' the longing of a homogenous people (of the same blood and lineage, and possessing common artifacts, customs, and institutions) for national political existence" (p. 3).

32. The newspaper did not inform readers that the July 1964 clash erupted only after whites attacked an interracial group of civil rights activists seeking to place their orders at the front window, rather than at the usual "colored line" in the back.

33. *Activities of Ku Klux Klan Organizations in the United States: Hearings before the Committee on Un-American Activities, House of Representatives, February 1–4 and 7–11, 1966*, p. 2,938. See also Walker Percy's novel *Love in the Ruins* (New York: Ivy Books, 1989).

34. Nelson, *Terror in the Night*, p. 27.

35. Bowers cited in McIlhany, *Klandestine*, p. 31; "Executive Lecture of March 1, 1964," ibid., p. 133.

36. Norman Cohn's historical analysis of these theories needs to be kept clearly

in view. Cohn writes, "Hatred of the Jews has so often been attributed to their role as money-lenders that it is worth emphasizing how slight the connection really was. The phantasy of the demonic Jew existed before the reality of the Jewish money-lender, whom indeed it helped to produce. As, in the age of the crusades, religious intolerance became more and more intense, the economic situation of the Jews rapidly deteriorated. At the Lateran Council of 1215 it was ruled that Jews should be debarred from all civil and military functions and from owning land; and these decisions were incorporated into Canon Law. As merchants too the Jews were at an even greater disadvantage, for they could no longer travel without risk of being murdered. Besides, Christians themselves began to turn to commerce and they very quickly outstripped the Jews, who were debarred from the Hanseatic League and who could of course not compete with the Italian and Flemish cities." Norman Cohn, *The Pursuit of the Millennium: Revolutionary Millennarians and Mystical Anarchists of the Middle Ages* (New York: Oxford University Press, 1970), p. 79. See also Ephraim Radner's article on the Jewish conspiracy theories promulgated by television evangelist Pat Robertson, "New World Order, Old World Anti-Semitism," *The Christian Century* 112:26 (September 13–20, 1995), 844–47.

37. Sam Bowers, interview with the author.

38. 1 Kings 18:21, 41.

39. Gerhard von Rad, *Old Testament Theology*, vol. 2, translated by D. M. G. Stalker (New York: Harper & Row, 1965), p. 17.

40. Sam Bowers, interview with the author.

41. Theodore H. Robinson, *A History of Israel*, vol. 1, *From the Exodus to the Fall of Jerusalem, 586 B.C.* (Oxford: Clarendon Press, 1932), p. 167.

42. Exodus 22:20; von Rad, *Old Testament Theology*, 2:18.

43. Bowers quoted in Tarrants and Perkins, *He's My Brother*, p. 78.

44. Sam Bowers, interview with the author.

45. 1 Corinthians 15:13–14, 20, 22–25.

46. Sam Bowers, letter to the author, September 12, 1993.

47. Ken Dean, interview with the author.

48. Sam Bowers, letter to the author, September 12, 1993.

49. Sam Bowers, interview with the author.

50. Whitehead, *Attack on Terror*, p. 4.

51. Ibid.

52. "Imperial Executive Order" cited in ibid., pp. 5–8.

53. Bowers cited in Seth Cagin and Philip Dray, *We Are Not Afraid: The Story of Goodman, Schwerner, and Chaney and the Civil Rights Campaign for Mississippi*, p. 266.

54. Ibid. William Bradford Huie describes Schwerner's exuberant humanism: "Perhaps he believed so tenaciously in Man because he did not believe in God. He insisted that he was an atheist; that he believed in All Men rather than in One God. . . . He didn't believe in original sin but in original innocence. Because he held no hope of heaven, he held extravagant hopes for the earth. Because he had no God to love, he loved God's creatures all the more." *Three Lives for Mississippi*, p. 49.

55. John Dittmer, *Local People*, p. 247.

56. Michael F. Starr, "Affidavit," *Mississippi Black Paper* (New York: Random House, 1965), p. 64.

57. Mr. and Mrs. Roosevelt Cole, interview with the author.

58. Starr, "Affidavit," p. 65.

59. Ed King, "Testimony from Mt. Zion," in "Freedom Summer," manuscript, Edwin King Private Papers; Mrs. Roosevelt Cole, interview with the author.

60. Starr, "Affidavit," p. 66.

61. Cagin and Dray, *We Are Not Afraid*, p. 295.

62. Doyle Barnette's testimony cited in Whitehead, *Attack on Terror*, p. 183.

63. Bowers cited in McIhleny, *Klandestine*, p. 209.

64. Bowers cited in Wade, *The Fiery Cross*, p. 340.

65. Unnamed man and woman cited in "Freedom on My Mind" (film); Huie, *Three Lives for Mississippi*, p. 169.

66. Shelton cited in W. C. Shoemaker, "Probers Disclose 12-Hour Time Gap," *Jackson Clarion Ledger*, June 26, 1964, p. 14.

67. Florence Mars, *Witness in Philadelphia*, p. 106.

68. Cited in ibid., pp. 108–9. The pamphlet exposes Bowers's awareness that Mississippi moderates, after a summer of extensive FBI investigation, wanted no further Klan violence. He protests too much: "We are absolutely opposed to street riots and public demonstrations of all kinds. Our work is largely educational in nature. We make every effort that sober, responsible, Christian Americans can make to awaken and persuade atheists and traitors to turn from their un-Godly ways. We are under oath to preserve Christian Civilization at all costs. All of our work is carried on in a dignified and reverent manner. We operate solely from a position of self-defense for our homes, our families, our Nation and Christian Civilization. We are never motivated by malice nor by vengeance. It is the incumbent duty of every American to defend the Spiritual Ideals and Principles upon which this Nation was founded, even at the cost of his life. We are all *Americans* in the White Knights of the Ku Klux Klan of Mississippi" (cited ibid., p. 109).

69. Vernon Dahmer cited in *Hattiesburg American* 71:8 (January 10, 1966), "Negro's Home and Store Burned by Nightriders; 3 Hurt," 1.

70. Charles Pickering, interview with the author.

71. Cited in Arlie Schardt, "A Mississippi Mayor Fights the Klan," *The Reporter*, January 27, 1966, Joan Trumpauer Mulholland Papers. Bucklew roared, "Can you imagine a loving, merciful, forgiving God blessing the act of any creep who would burn a home or a house of worship? Those who create such acts of violence are not only Godless, they are traitors. These mob fiends who are infecting our city and state are actually demanding that the Federal government move in and take over every phase of our existence" (p. 40).

72. See Don Whitehead's account in *Attack on Terror*. See also my article, "Rendezvous with the Wizard," *The Oxford American*, October/November 1996, 22–32.

73. Cohn, *The Pursuit of the Millennium*, p. 84. Cohn explains, "In his relation to human beings . . . Antichrist is a father scarcely to be distinguished from Satan himself; a protecting father to his devilish brood, but to the Saints an atrocious fa-

ther, deceitful, masking evil intentions with fair words, a cunning tyrant who when crossed becomes a cruel and murderous persecutor" (p. 86).

74. *The Klan Ledger*, cited in McIlhany, *Klandestine*, p. 187.

75. Ibid., pp. 189, 190.

76. For an excellent analysis of racist theologies, see Alan Davies, *Infected Christianity: A Study of Modern Racism*; see also Cornel West, "The Genealogy of Modern Racism," in *Prophesy Deliverance! An Afro-American Revolutionary Christianity*, pp. 47–65.

77. For helpful studies of anti-Jewish theologies in the German Christian Church, see Robert P. Erickson, *Theologians under Hitler: Gerhard Kittel, Paul Althaus, and Emmanuel Hirsch* (New Haven: Yale University Press, 1985); Victoria Barnett, *For the Soul of My People: Protestant Protest against Hitler* (New York: Oxford University Press, 1992); and Doris L. Bergen, *Twisted Cross: The German Christian Movement in the Third Reich* (Chapel Hill: University of North Carolina Press, 1996).

78. *The Klan Ledger*, cited in McIhleny, *Klandestine*, p. 191.

79. Bowers cited ibid., p. 191.

80. Sam Bowers, interview with the author.

81. "The Present Day Ku Klux Klan Movement," in McIlheny, *Klandestine*, p. 191.

82. Ibid.

83. Alan Davies, *Infected Christianity*, pp. 37–38.

84. Sam Bowers, interview with the author.

85. Ibid.

86. Bowers cited in Jack Nelson, *Terror in the Night*, p. 12.

87. Although popular fundamentalist writers like David Wilkerson, author of the bestselling autobiography *The Cross and the Switchblade*, do make such claims as "God . . . set America in a good land and blessed its founding fathers," their optimism can quickly turn to harsh judgments of America's sinfulness and moral degeneracy. As Wilkerson put it, "America today is one great holocaust party, with millions drunk, high, shaking their fist at God, daring him to send the bombs." See Paul Boyer, *When Time Shall Be No More: Prophecy Belief in Modern American Culture*, pp. 239, 234.

88. My thanks to Michael Franz for historical clarification of the following ideas. For further discussion of what Franz calls the "pneuma-pathological consciousness," a scheme by which authority is justified by appeal to a stream of enormous historical events, see his *Eric Voegelin and the Politics of Spiritual Revolt: The Roots of Modern Identity* (Baton Rouge: Louisiana State University Press, 1992).

89. Sam Bowers, interview with the author.

90. In his open letter "To the Christian Nobility," Luther explained his idea in terms of the demolition of three idols. The first is the barrier that exists between spiritual power and temporal duties. Spiritual authority no longer resides simply in ecclesiastical offices, but diversifies itself in new forms and in unexpected

places. Any believer can be a priest, fully equal in authority to the Roman Catholic clergy. Second, the idolatry surrounding scriptural interpretation is the presumption that there is a privileged elite of authoritative interpreters of Scripture. This presumption—this idol—must be destroyed. Luther protests: inasmuch as the Word of God is free, and bound by no authority, so is the believer free to interpret Scripture, unconstrained by dogma or official canon. Finally, the idols of papal authority come crashing down with the demolition of the first two; dissent against an intrusive outside establishment—the church hierarchy—is given holy sanction. Martin Luther, *Selected Political Writings*, pp. 37–51.

91. Sam Bowers, interview with the author.

92. Ibid.

93. Ibid.

94. Bowers's point calls to mind Klan theology of an earlier era. In 1925, in his *Message of the Emperor*, the Grand Dragon of Georgia wrote, "*The Constitution of the United States is based upon the Holy Bible and the Christian religion, and an attack upon one is an attack upon the other*" (italics in original). See Nancy MacLean's book, *Behind the Mask of Chivalry: The Making of the Second Ku Klux Klan*, p. 92.

95. Sam Bowers, interview with the author.

96. Ibid.

97. Ibid.

98. Ibid.

99. Sam Bowers, "Executive Lecture of March 1, 1964," cited in McIhleny, *Klandestine*, p. 123.

100. Sam Bowers, interview with the author.

101. Ibid.

102. Cohn, *The Pursuit of the Millennium*, pp. 75, 86.

103. The historical resonances of the assault were loud and clear. Monroe Billington explains, "When the great sectional crisis reached its climax, the South defended its way of life with fervor imbued with religious convictions. From the southern point of view, the Civil War was a fight between right and wrong, a religious crusade, a holy war, a defense of a beloved Zion. Southerners who died for the cause saw themselves as being like the religious warriors of an earlier era who had defended the Holy Land from the attack of the infidels." Monroe Billington, "South as Zion," in *Encyclopedia of Southern Culture*, Volume 4, edited by Charles Reagan Wilson and William Ferris (New York: Anchor Books, 1989), p. 81.

104. Bowers's current views are difficult to fathom, as a scene from one of our conversations in the summer of 1994 illustrates:

Bowers sits with his back to me, reading a newspaper. There is no one else in the room. He turns around to greet me as I approach the table. He nods his head and tells me to have a seat.

He is wearing a navy pin-strip suit, a blue pin-striped shirt, a blue and red striped tie, and white suspenders. He also wears a wide brown belt with a large buckle in the shape of Mickey Mouse. He wears white pearl cuff links with reliefs of the waving Mickey in the center. He wears a Mickey Mouse watch. On the lapel of his jacket is a small silver fish—*agape*—the symbol of the risen Jesus.

A copy of the *Jackson Clarion Ledger* rests in his lap. Days earlier the paper ran a front-page story on Bowers, making the strong case that he should be brought back to trial for the Vernon Dahmer killing. The Jackson paper has already been instrumental in winning a new trial for the murderer of civil rights leader Medgar Evers. Still, the highly celebrated conviction of Byron de la Beckwith—a mean, stupid man, who always tried a little too hard to impress his mentor Sam Bowers—would look like a sideshow were the Imperial Wizard himself retried.

I tell Bowers that my grandfather, who covered Mississippi politics in the 1960s for an out-of-state paper, always referred to the Jackson press as the "Glaring Error." He smiles and asks me if I'd like some iced tea.

A man wearing a baseball cap opens a swinging door and appears with two glasses on a tray. Bowers introduces me as a "theologian from Maryland." I shake hands with the man and the two of us stare at each other in silence.

"I've agreed to talk to you about this work you're doing even though I still cannot understand it. But the first thing you should know is that I have total hatred for the academy and the pagan media. I hope and pray that both implode on the force of their own corruption and stagnation. I have always hoped and prayed for this to happen."

I make a mental note of the exit door several tables behind me and start to ask a question, but he interrupts.

"You seem to take quite a lot of interest in the 1960s. Well, today, just like then, we need people who will offer their physical lives in opposition to these idols, to attack the establishment at the very center of its power and prestige. We need to implement concrete actions which enable us to once again see America as the fulfillment of the Abrahamic promise."

I ask him who is doing this kind of work today.

He mentions a number of right-wing groups like the National Alliance and Passe Commitatis; he mentions Andrew Macdonald and his dark novel, *The Turner Diaries* (which seems to turn up in the mountain huts and fallout shelters of every bomb and militia fanatic in the nation).

Bowers assumes a professorial demeanor. "Macdonald's book proposes that a covert system of enclaves be established for the purpose of training and coordinating an invisible underground army to attack and destroy all remnants of our constitutional government. They would have us launch nuclear missiles on the Russians so that we in turn would be annihilated."

Then: "I surely do not feel compelled to avoid personal injury for the sake of attacking the false gods."

Then: "But unlike the *Turner Diaries*, I want to see the Constitution preserved. In fact, you may know I began my own literary work twenty-five years ago after I observed Richard Nixon's impeachment. I had a guilty conscience watching Nixon get torn to pieces by anarchists, communists, and the demagogues of the Democratic party. These reprobates were ripping him to shreds. I thought I should get off of my stinking ass and put my gifts to work, and if I pursued the task well, I could emasculate these guys.

"My writing was stimulated, I should say, by my mother's high standards for learning. My mother was a very educated and disciplined person; she would not allow an ungrammatical word to pass from my mouth without punishment."

His eyes narrow.

"So much has been said about me that's that untrue."

He seems agitated now. He stirs in his chair and grimaces toward the ceiling in defiance of some invisible enemy.

"By the age of fifteen I was deeply suspicious of everyone in authority. I'm not sure why, but I felt the degeneracy of the adult world with great intensity. I was a hyper child. I didn't want to grow up. It always seemed like those in authority were bent on making impositions on me, and I despised them for it."

But now his anger vanishes, giving way to a loud belly laugh—his whole face spreads into a comically wide country grin—and his shrieking voice changes to a friendly, expansive sort of hillbilly twang.

"I love to see children throw tantrums," Bowers says. "I was recently having dinner with a friend of mine whose granddaughter started to feel ignored. So she sassed her grandmom, and was quickly reproved by a slap on the hand. That little girl turned beet red with anger, and ran over to a wall and began pounding and kicking it with all her might."

Bowers demonstrates this by getting out of his chair and slapping his hands against the flimsy masonite paneling.

"I just loved watching that," he says, as his eyes slowly grow sorrowful and distant.

"You know, Jesus prefers the little ones, which is why we should go slow on beating children."

His thoughts drift. "I've got tapes going on in my head that are forty or fifty years old. Maybe that's just senility. I sometimes forget certain periods of my life, and remember others with total clarity."

He talks until late Sunday night, while I pause from my writing only to ask questions. He speaks eloquently of his grandfather, E. J. Bowers, a U.S. congressmen from Mississippi, whom he worshiped. He opines on the doctrine of predestination: "I am a stern believer in the notion. People are not simply spiritually but also genetically predetermined." He talks about his impressions after leaving prison in 1976: "My first experience was that the outside world was full of filth. In prison, we never had any problem with garbage, but outside was a different story."

"Did your views change at McNeil Island?" I ask.

"The only thing that happened to me at McNeil Island was that information was gained and then applied to my theological and political ideas. I've been about this task for a long time."

He rubs his forehead with the tips of his fingers. "Let me tell you a story," he says, "and then I must turn in for the night.

"I've always asked myself the question, 'Who am I? What am I doing here? What is the world all about? What is my position within in it?' On Easter Sunday 1972, I had an experience at McNeil Island that put that question into a new perspective for me. At the time, I was in my second year of prison. As I had done every Easter season since my baptism, I was preparing myself for resurrection Sunday with calculated devotion and seriousness. Although I felt myself to be spiritually inadequate much of the year, Easter always inspired me towards a time of earnestness and tranquility.

"On Good Friday of that year I sat at my desk in the prison's education department reading through some back issues of a news magazine. An article about a theological controversy caught my attention. The focus of the piece was the decision of a Christian college to fire one of its faculty members who had declared atheist ideas in the classroom. The heretic had petitioned the American Association of University Professors to have the school discredited institutionally, claiming that his civil liberties were being violated by the institution. The magazine seemed predictably biased in favor of the plaintiff's complaints. Shortly after finishing the story, I was taken back to my cell for afternoon lock-up. Resting in my bunk before supper, my mind began to reel as I thought about the situation: here was the church—my church—seeking to purify itself from heretical filth but instead finding itself under attack by an atheist and the heathen media. I began to be filled with rage. Rage, rage, rage. And I thought: 'Look at me, I'm locked up in this place, powerless to do anything; my church is being assaulted by this wicked man, when it should be the other way around. The heretic should be suffering, not the body of Christ.' I wanted to retaliate, to strike back, but, of course, I was confined in prison. I felt tormented and full of confusion.

"On Easter morning, while several of my friends got up early to gather for a season of anguished prayer, I remained in my cell, restless, and burdened with mental anguish. In this frame of mind, I entered the chapel with the rest of the inmates for the Easter service at 10 o'clock. As we began to find seats in the crowded chapel, I saw my friend Alton Wayne Roberts [also convicted for his role in the murders of Chaney, Goodman, and Schwerner] and the two of us took a seat next to each other in the pew. I immediately noticed that we were surrounded by some real degenerate types: dope dealers making transactions, homosexuals seeking dalliances, all kinds of perverted, disreputable characters. There were also two or three bad niggers sitting directly behind us, saying all sorts of crazy things, insults and slurs.

"But Wayne Roberts was a man with a justifiable reputation as a physical militant, and he began talking to me in a loud voice, obviously hoping to pick a fight with the black guys. I felt torn between allegiances. Had I been alone in the chapel, I would have ignored the situation because I was determined to keep a clean prison record. But there was a bond between the two of us. I felt like I should back Roberts up—whatever he did. We were all on the verge of physical violence when the minister appeared at the front of the chapel—not in the pulpit but in the space just beneath it. His arms were raised in celebration. He spoke with an excited voice, wishing the blessing of the resurrected Christ on all of us. I noticed tears in his eyes. He wanted us to know that God was real and full of majesty.

"In a semicircle behind him stood a racially mixed choir of reprobates that had been assembled for the occasion. When the minister concluded his invocation, the choir began to sway back and forth, singing 'The Battle Hymn of the Republic.' As suddenly as the singing began, another choir, this time invisible and angelic, surrounded the prison choir with a deep, thundering sound. Their singing swelled up from the chapel front and flowed over the congregation. I don't fully understand what happened next. I was jolted—swept away—by the music. I began to shake. My heartbeat accelerated. I felt disoriented and dizzy. It was a moment of pure ecstasy, like a lightening flash. Then the choir concluded the anthem, and we all sat down and the service proceeded. But I remained transformed. My mental anguish was gone. My restless thoughts were calmed. God had spoken deep inside my soul: 'Be not afraid, the Lord your God is God.'

"When we got to the mess hall after the service, I sat down at a table next to a notorious racist, who was always a little deferential towards me. When the fellow saw me, he leaned over at the table and asked: 'What in the world was going on in chapel?' I turned to him and smiled, 'That, my friend, was the Holy Spirit.' 'Man, I've never felt anything like that before in my life,' said the man. 'No, and you may never again,' I replied.

"You see, God visited us that Easter Sunday. He came to us as an experience of the actual undeserved imposition of the Holy Spirit on our depraved human consciousness. My anger was gone; and with it, my murderous desire for the heretic. There was a quick change of black and white to technicolor; a change that was immediate—instantaneous. I returned to my cell that afternoon, feeling certain that I could never again condemn heresy from the standpoint of rage, but from a vigorous orthodoxy, from reason, as best I can."

As we leave the restaurant by the back door, Bowers hands me a document he has recently written: "Glossary: The 9 Insights of the *Celestine Prophecy*." He has mentioned the best-selling novel several times throughout the evening.

Insight number 5 reads: "There is an universal, transcendent, continuing and humanly inexhaustible supply of supernatural energy which is potentially capable of imposing itself upon an individual human proprietor: as a mystical experience, which, potentially, enables the individual to live in a delicate state of interactive human community, without: (1) having to steal life force energy from others, (2) without having his own life force energy stolen into a condition of exhausted depletion by and through his interaction with others in the human community."

Chapter Three

Douglas Hudgins: Theologian

1. Quoted in Edwin King, "The White Church in Mississippi."

2. Ibid.

3. Ibid.

4. Calvin Trillin, "State Secrets," *New Yorker*, May 29, 1995, p. 55.

5. John Dittmer, *Local People: The Struggle for Civil Rights in Mississippi*, p. 58.

6. "O Sovereignty," *The Rabble Underground* 1:1 (March 1964), Joan Trumpauer Mulholland Papers.

7. John Dittmer, *Local People*, p. 46; Neil McMillen, *The Citizens' Council: Organized Resistance to the Second Reconstruction, 1954–1964*, p. 27; *Racial Facts* cited ibid., p. 180.

8. Cited in Stephen J. Whitfield, *A Death in the Delta: The Story of Emmett Till*, p. 9.

9. Tom P. Brady, *Black Monday*, p. 64.

10. Ibid., p. 45.

11. Other factors certainly influenced the fear of miscegenation. As Anthony Walton has written, "What is intriguing about the larger battle over miscegenation is that so many of its constituent struggles end up being about neither sex nor race, but about property. In a circuitous manner, miscegenation laws ensured white supremacy. By barring black-white marriage, whites kept blacks, who already had been deprived of property rights by slavery, from gaining property through marriage or inheritance. This constant exclusion of blacks had also the effect of circumscribing the lives of white females, reducing them too, to de facto status as property, as they were limited by law and mores to white men, while privileged men essentially did as they pleased." Anthony Walton, *Mississippi*, p. 132.

12. The Citizens' Council primer for third and fourth graders explains this concept: "God wanted the white people to live alone. And He wanted colored people to live alone. The white man built America for you. White men built America so they could make the rules. George Washington was a brave and honest white man. . . . The white man has always been kind to the Negro. . . . Negro people like to live by themselves. Negroes use their own bathrooms. They do not use white people's bathrooms. . . . This is called our Southern Way of Life." Cited in Nicholas von Hoffman, *Mississippi Notebook*, p. 46.

13. Mississippi State Sovereignty Commission Charter, Johnson Family Papers.

14. Wilson F. Minor, interview with the author. The NKVD (Naródnyĭ Komissariat Vnútrennikh Del), the People's Commissariat of Internal Affairs from 1934 until 1946, was the Soviet government's secret service organization, which operated to protect communist orthodoxy from internal dissent.

15. Cited in Trillin, "State Secrets," p. 55.

16. Cited in Dittmer, *Local People*, p. 60.

17. Adam Nossiter, *Of Long Memory: Mississippi and the Murder of Medgar Evers*, p. 99.

18. Erle Johnston, Jr., in Mississippi State Sovereignty Commission files, December 12, 1963, McCain Library, University of Southern Mississippi, Hattiesburg. (emphasis mine).

19. Dittmer, *Local People*, p. 58.

20. James Silver, *Mississippi: The Closed Society*, p. 6.

21. David Donald, cited in Dittmer, *Local People*, p. 59.

22. William Faulkner cited in Whitfield, *A Death in the Delta*, p. 68.

23. Walker Percy, "Mississippi: The Fallen Paradise," pp. 43–44.

24. Cited in Dittmer, *Local People*, p. 139.

25. Cited in Kathy Lally, "A Journey from Racism to Reason," *Baltimore Sun*, January 5, 1997.

26. "Mister Baptist," cited in Anne Washburn McWilliams, "W. Douglas Hudgins: Man for This Hour," *Baptist Record*, January 30, 1969.

27. Ken Dean, interview with the author.

28. The voice of civil religion: "The worth of a youth inheres in what he is, rather than what he can do. Rugged Americanism, often longed for by many, is an emphasis on truth, honesty, purity, virtue, loyalty, domestic fidelity and the unalloyed fear and love of Almighty God. Herein lies the great function and value of the churches of America" ("Dangers Facing Youth in a Post-War World," an address delivered by Hudgins at the regular meeting of the Downtown Kiwanis Club of Houston, February 7, 1945), p. 5, Douglas Hudgins Papers.

29. Cited in *The Jackson Daily News*, "A Great Television Sermon by Dr. W. Douglas Hudgins," n.d., Douglas Hudgins Papers.

30. Douglas Hudgins, "Baptists and the Bible," sermon, First Baptist Church, Jackson, Mississippi, January 26, 1947, Douglas Hudgins Papers.

31. Harold Bloom, *The American Religion: The Emergence of the Post-Christian Nation*, p. 203.

32. Gladys Carroll, "Pulpit Profiles," *Houston Post*, July 23, 1944.

33. "William Douglas Hudgins 20th Anniversary," First Baptist Church, Douglas Hudgins Papers.

34. Arthur Laro, "Profiles," n.p., n.d., Douglas Hudgins Papers.

35. McWilliams, "W. Douglas Hudgins," p. 5.

36. Ted Ownby, *Subduing Satan: Religion, Recreation and Manhood in the Rural South, 1865–1920*, p. 118.

37. Kenneth L. Bailey, *Southern White Protestantism in the Twentieth Century*, pp. 4, 18.

38. Cited ibid., p. 2.

39. John W. Porter, "Dress and Licentiousness," cited ibid., p. 46.

40. Cited in Ownby, *Subduing Satan*, p. 199. In 1962 Hudgins would shout from the Jackson pulpit, "Look at our current novels, or plays, or motion pictures! To read through the popular novel you have to wade through the sewer and the

cesspool in company with social tramps and admired libertines. On the stage homosexuality and perversion are paraded in brash verbiage that should embarrass even a male audience. On the screen the perfidies of a sinuous harlot are portrayed in the atmosphere of angelic adoration and the morally positive individual is held up to ridicule and scorn." W. Douglas Hudgins, "One Nation, under God," sermon, April 11, 1962, Jackson, Mississippi, Douglas Hudgins Papers.

41. John W. Porter cited in Bailey, *Southern White Protestantism*, p. 47.

42. Ted Ownby, *Subduing Satan*, p. 119.

43. Cited in Bailey, *Southern White Protestantism*, p. 46.

44. Cited ibid., p. 17.

45. Southern Baptist Convention, *Annual*, 1921, p. 28, cited ibid., p. 48.

46. Cited ibid., 112.

47. W. Douglas Hudgins, sermon, October 24, 1943, Douglas Hudgins Papers.

48. Cf. Clyde T. Francisco, "The Curse on Canaan," *Christianity Today*, April 24, 1964.

49. George M. Fredrickson, *The Black Image in the White Mind: The Debate on Afro-American Character and Destiny, 1817–1914*, p. 88.

50. Cited in Foy Dan Valentine, *A Historical Study of Southern Baptists and Race Relations: 1917–1947* (New York: Arno Press, 1980), pp. 28, 129.

51. Ibid., p. 129.

52. Cited in I. A. Newby, *Jim Crow's Defense: Anti-Negro Thought in America, 1900–1930*, p. 100.

53. Lipsey and Johnson cited in Valentine, *A Historical Study*, p. 68.

54. McWilliams, "W. Douglas Hudgins," p. 5.

55. Ibid.

56. Ibid.

57. Gladys Carroll, "Pulpit Profiles."

58. James P. Boyce cited in Henlee Hulix Barnette, "The Southern Baptist Theological Seminary and the Civil Rights Movement: From 1859–1952." *Review and Expositor* (Louisville, Ky.) 90 (Fall 1993), 531.

59. Charles Spurgeon Gardner cited ibid., 534.

60. Ibid., 543.

61. William A. Mueller, *A History of Southern Baptist Theological Seminary* (Nashville: Broadman Press, 1959), p. 212.

62. Cooper Waters, "A Testimony to W. Douglas Hudgins," Douglas Hudgins Papers.

63. "Dr. W. Douglas Hudgins," *The History of First Baptist Church*, Houston, p. 40, Douglas Hudgins Papers.

64. Clayton Sullivan, interview with the author.

65. Clayton Sullivan, *Called to Preach, Condemned to Survive: The Education of Clayton Sullivan* (Macon, Ga.: Mercer University Press, 1985), p. 51.

66. Arthur Laro, "Profiles," n.p., n.d., Douglas Hudgins Papers.

67. McWilliams, "W. Douglas Hudgins."

68. W. Douglas Hudgins, "Furnishing the Pulpit," *The Baptist Program*, August 1957, p. 26, Douglas Hudgins Papers. Emphasis added.

69. "Proceedings of the 1954 Southern Baptist Convention," p. 56.

70. Audiotape collection, Historical Commission of the Southern Baptist Convention, Nashville, Tenn.

71. Ibid.

72. Hudgins cited in "Jackson Pastor Clarifies Convention Segregation Act," *Jackson Daily News*, n.d., Douglas Hudgins Papers. Hudgins had earlier made a similar remark, calling the Brown decision "a school question or a political question, and not a religious question" (cited in Dittmer, *Local People*, p. 63). Alex McKeigney, Sr., the superintendent of the Sunday school at First Baptist, was less inclined to invoke Hudgins's distinction, finding comfort instead in the familiar rhetoric of white supremacy: "The facts of history make it plain that the development of civilization and of Christianity itself has rested in the hands of the white race." School desegregation, McKeigney continued, "is a direct contribution to the efforts of those groups advocating intermarriage between the races" (ibid.).

73. Tom Ethridge, *The Clarion Ledger*, March 31, 1966. Elizabeth Marsh Papers.

74. *Jackson Daily News*, n.d., Elizabeth Marsh Papers.

75. "Is It More Than Just Coincidence?" *The Jackson Daily News*, May 28, 1963.

76. "1964—The Hottest Summer in History," Elizabeth Marsh Papers.

77. Richard Aubrey McLemore and Nannie Pitts McLemore, *The History of First Baptist Church* (Jackson: Hederman Brothers, 1976), p. 226.

78. Cited ibid., p. 262.

79. Ibid., p. 55.

80. Minutes of the Deacons' meeting, June 11, 1963, microfilm, Mississippi Department of Archives and History.

81. "Financial Report for the Year 1964, First Baptist Church, Jackson, Mississippi," microfilm, Mississippi Department of Archives and History.

82. Falwell cited in Randall Balmer, "American Fundamentalism: The Ideal of Femininity," in *Fundamentalism and Gender*, edited by John S. Hawley (New York: Oxford University Press, 1994), p. 56. See also Shelley Baranowski, "Jerry Falwell," *Twentieth Century Shapers of American Popular Religion*, edited by Charles H. Lippy (New York: Greenwood Press, 1989), pp. 131–39.

83. *San Francisco Chronicle*, July 28, 1964, p. 6.

84. Jane Stembridge, interview with the author.

85. Ibid.

86. *San Francisco Chronicle*, July 28, 1964, p. 6.

87. Edwin King, interview with the author.

88. *San Francisco Chronicle*, July 28, 1964, p. 6.

89. Hudgins and other Mississippi Southern Baptist pastors received numerous chiding letters from Baptist missionaries overseas, most of whom appealed to the evangelistic hypocrisies of the Christian segregationists. One missionary wrote,

"What you do and say in America today is speaking so loud our people around the world are finding it more difficult to hear what we say. Our people listen to the radio. They read the newspaper. And some even have television. They know what is happening today. It is impossible to explain why a black person can't worship in a Baptist church in America when you send us out here to tell them that Jesus loves them." From a pamphlet, "Your Missionaries Speak," Historical Commission of the Southern Baptist Convention, Nashville, Tenn.

90. Jack Nelson, *Terror in the Night*, pp. 68, 71.

91. Dean was a member of First Baptist Church, though shortly after he had joined the church in 1965 his affiliation with the pro-civil rights Mississippi Council was discovered, and he became a pariah among the congregation. Kenneth Dean, interview with the author.

92. Cited in Nelson, *Terror in the Night*, p. 71.

93. Lucian A. Harvey, "Nomination of Douglas Hudgins to the Golden Deeds Award Committee," January 12, 1968, Douglas Hudgins Papers.

94. Nelson, *Terror in the Night*, pp. 71, 72, 76.

95. Hudgins cited ibid., p. 76.

96. Lillian Smith, *Killers of the Dream*, p. 85.

97. E. Y. Mullins cited in Bloom, *The American Religion*, pp. 200–201.

98. William Douglas Hudgins, "Distinctive Principles of Baptists," sermon, First Baptist Church, Jackson, Mississippi, June 8, 1947, Douglas Hudgins Papers.

99. Mullins cited in Bloom, *The American Religion*, p. 227. The Baptist theologian Fisher Humphreys adds, "[Mullins] formally assented to the importance of Christian community, but his mind turned instinctively and inevitably to the private experiences of conversion and moral transformation. He was intoxicated by personal freedom, even by personal rights—a category which owes more to the Enlightenment than to the New Testament—even to the loss of the indispensability of society and social relationships of personal life." Fisher Humphreys, "E. Y. Mullins," in *Baptist Theologians*, edited by Timothy George and David S. Dockery (Nashville: Broadman Books, 1990), p. 346.

100. Hudgins, "Distinctive Principles of Baptists."

101. W. D. Hudgins, "Observing the Ordinances." *Arkansas Baptist*, n.d., Douglas Hudgins Papers.

102. Hudgins, "Distinctive Principles of Baptists."

103. Hudgins, "Baptists and the Bible."

104. Hudgins, "Distinctive Principles of Baptists."

105. Bloom, *The American Religion*, pp. 205–6.

106. Hudgins, "Distinctive Principles of Baptists."

107. W. Douglas Hudgins, "The Decade of Destiny: The 1960s," sermon, Douglas Hudgins Papers.

108. In the 1940s Hudgins's sermons contained frequent polemics against alcohol and "moral decay." He preached, "The church in our day must proclaim unhesitatingly, a standard of morality and righteousness as high as that of its

Founder. There should never be any question as to where a church or its members should stand on a moral issue. Conventionality, public opinion, politics, expediency, economic advantage, or personal pleasure, should not tempt the individual or the church to compromise or complacency. If and when the church in our day sets its face against moral wrong and national evil there will be no possibility, for example, of a national lottery, as is now being urged by many nefarious forces. Graft, black marketing, gambling, vice, alcoholism, Sunday desecration, and such things, would be greatly weakened if the church itself would speak in positive tones and its members would live in keeping with its ideals." Hudgins, "The Church in Our Day," *A Souvenir of the Baptist Hour*, First Baptist Church, Jackson, Mississippi, July 21, 1946, pp. 13–14, Douglas Hudgins Papers.

109. Hodding Carter, *Where Main Street Meets the River* (New York: Rinehart, 1952), p. 281.

110. W. D. Hudgins, "The Agent's Obligation," *Life Association News*, n.d., p. 574, Douglas Hudgins Papers.

111. Hudgins, "The Decade of Destiny."

112. Douglas Hudgins, "Christ Our Hope," annual sermon to the Southern Baptist Convention at Houston, June 4, 1968, Douglas Hudgins Papers.

113. Hudgins, "Baptists and the Bible."

114. W. D. Hudgins, "Our Future Is Now," sermon, Columbia Church of the Air, December 6, 1953, Douglas Hudgins Papers.

115. W. D. Hudgins, "The Perils of Progressive Paganism," president's address, Mississippi Baptist Convention, November 13, 1962, Douglas Hudgins Papers. Ephesians 6:12.

116. Hudgins, "Our Future Is Now."

117. Ibid. The joke that Baptists don't make love standing up because it might lead to dancing ought not obscure the serious business of the body's startling contretemps.

118. Hudgins would write with uncharacteristic hostility of the Christian Life Commission in a letter to denominational leader Porter Routh: "I know you and I do not see social patterns in the same light, but if our Christian Life Commission continues to assume to speak for all our churches, we are going to have a 'knockdown-drag-out' on the Convention floor one of these days—and this is the last thing I would want to happen." Correspondence, March 26, 1965, Executive Committee Records, Historical Commission of the Southern Baptist Convention. Nashville, Tenn.

119. Hudgins, "The Decade of Destiny."

120. Hudgins, "The Decade of Destiny."

121. W. Douglas Hudgins, "Good Tidings," sermon, October 24, 1943, Douglas Hudgins Papers.

122. Hudgins, "The Decade of Destiny."

123. W. Douglas Hudgins, "One Nation under God," sermon, April 1962, n.p., Douglas Hudgins Papers.

124. Hudgins was in good company among Mississippi white conservative Protestant clergy. Reverend G. T. Gillespie, president emeritus of Belhaven College at the time, had written an influential pamphlet, *A Christian View on Segregation*, which the Citizens' Council published in 1954 and distributed widely. Gillespie offered theological and biblical justifications of segregation and argued that although the apostle Paul described the unity of all believers in Christ as "a spiritual relationship resulting from the mystical union of each believer with Christ," Paul did not have in mind the unity of Christians "in external relations and the wiping out of all distinctions of race, nationality, social status, sex or cultural heritage." G. T. Gillespie, *A Christian View on Segregation* (Winona, Miss.: Association of Citizens' Councils of Mississippi, 1954), p. 12. Gillespie invoked the "mark of Cain," "the promiscuous intermarriage" in the Old Testament of the descendants of Seth, and "the Confusion of Tongues" in the story of Babel (to name just a few of his biblical sources) as evidence that segregation was one of God's and nature's universal laws. Gillespie's views, shared (for example) by the Reverend Reid Miller, longtime pastor of the affluent First Presbyterian Church in Jackson, earned the two men reputations as the "patron saints of the Citizens' Council." Wilson Minor, interview with the author.

Chapter Four

Ed King's Church Visits

1. Lillian Smith, *Killers of the Dream*, pp. 16, 31. In his 1965 essay "Mississippi: The Fallen Paradise," Walker Percy puts a different twist on the same point, as when he writes, "During the past ten years Mississippi as a society reached a condition which can only be described, in an analogous but exact sense of the word, as insane. The rift in its character between a genuine kindliness and a highly developed individual moral consciousness on the one hand and on the other a purely political and amoral view of states' rights at the expense of human rights led at last to a sundering of its very soul," p. 42.

2. Edwin King, "Growing up in Mississippi in a Time of Change," *Mississippi Writers: Reflections of Childhood and Youth*, Volume 2, edited by Dorothy Abbott (Jackson: University Press of Mississippi, 1986), p. 375.

3. Smith, *Killers of the Dream*, p. 23; King, "Growing up in Mississippi in a Time of Change," p. 375.

4. Smith, *Killers of the Dream*, p. 18.

5. Percy quoted ibid., p. 71.

6. King, "Growing up in Mississippi in a Time of Change," p. 375.

7. Ibid., p. 378.

8. Ibid., p. 380.

9. Ibid., p. 378.

10. Cited in Walter G. Muelder, *Methodism and Society in the Twentieth Century*, p. 235.

11. Ibid.

12. King, "Growing up in Mississippi in a Time of Change," p. 378. King says, "In the national church, we talked about the issues of peace, justice and civil rights, so there was this inner connection between young people." Edwin King, interview with the author.

13. It was one of King's theological teachers, Reinhold Niebuhr, who later said, "Admonitions to be more loving are on the whole irrelevant"; cited in Larry Rasmussen, *Reinhold Niebuhr: Theologian of Public Life* (Minneapolis: Fortress Press, 1988), p. 5.

14. Smith, *Killers of the Dream*, pp. 29, 30.

15. Michael Fuquay, "The Desegregation of Millsaps College through 1965," senior thesis, Millsaps College, 1992, pp. 2–3. In 1955, the faculty and Board of Trustees issued "The Purpose of Millsaps College," affirming the institution's "attitude of continuing intellectual awareness of tolerance, and of unbiased inquiry, without which true education cannot exist" (cited ibid., p. 3). The Citizens' Council had pegged Millsaps College as a sanctuary for subversives and communists since 1954, the year the council was formed to preserve racial segregation, and had kept a close watch on its involvement in the interracial alliance.

16. John Dittmer, *Local People*, p. 62.

17. "Council Head Says Public Concerned," *Jackson State Times*, March 9, 1958.

18. Cited in Dittmer, *Local People*, p. 62.

19. Paul Deats, "Introduction to Boston Personalism," in *The Boston Personalist Tradition in Philosophy, Social Ethics, and Theology*, edited by Paul Deats and Carol Robb, p. 2.

20. Richard Morgan Cameron, *Boston University School of Theology, 1839–1968* (Boston: Boston University School of Theology, 1968), p. 102.

21. On Chalmers's role as head of the Scottsboro Defense Committee, see Dan T. Carter, *Scottsboro: A Tragedy of the American South* (New York: Oxford University Press, 1969), pp. 335–63.

22. Cameron, *Boston University School of Theology*, p. 124.

23. Howard Thurman, *Jesus and the Disinherited*, p. 88. King later called his encounter with Thurman a "personal anointing." Thurman's eloquent meditations on mysticism, prayer, and spiritual discipline were influential in King's decision to retain belief in the miraculous character of Christian faith, guarding it against social and political reductionisms. Edwin King, interview with the author.

24. "France Watching Girl's Trial Here," *Montgomery Advertiser*, May 10, 1960.

25. "20 Post Appeal Bonds in Disorderly Conduct," *Montgomery Advertiser*, April 2, 1960.

26. Edwin King, interview with the author.

27. King conceded in a letter to Ray Jenkins of the *Alabama Journal* that "police state" may not have been the best way for him to describe conditions in Mont-

gomery to the press. Nonetheless, he explained to the white city editor that from the perspective of the capital city's black residents, the description seemed appropriate. He wrote, "The night after our trial was recessed early in May, I was invited to attend a religious meeting of Negro students in a Negro church in your city. The church was being watched by men identified to me as being police. We were in the church only a few minutes before the police dared to enter a House of God while the congregation was singing hymns of the Christian faith. They stood in the back of the church as the Holy Scriptures were read and as we were led in prayer. After a Negro minister had addressed the congregation I was given an opportunity to speak. Both of us had been arrested by the police and therefore could hardly think these police were there as part of a friendly congregation. It is a rare experience for a Christian minister in America to face hostile police as he tries to preach what God would have him preach." Letter of May 30, 1960 from Reverend Edwin King to Mr. Ray Jenkins, Edwin King Private Papers.

28. "Minister Chops Wood, Cuts Grass for City," *The Alabama Journal*, June 9, 1960.

29. King applied for a formal deferral of his course requirements for the spring. He explained, "I would like to request permission [to] have an extension granted on the due date for papers and reading reports. When I returned from Singers' Tour I found I had to go on to Montgomery, Ala. for my trial. . . . Therefore I request an extension date of June 15. I should be able to finish my work by that date—even with trial and perhaps a few more days in jail." Letter to the faculty, May 16, 1960, Edwin King Private Papers.

30. Letter to Ed King from Elroy Embry, June 30, 1960, Edwin King Private Papers.

31. Letter re: Return, Fall, 1962. Edwin King Private Papers.

32. Edwin King, interview with the author.

33. Ibid.

34. King recalls, "The theologians back in Boston were thrilled with this; so far as they could tell, I was the only person who had ever been ordained into the Christian priesthood without being tied to a denomination, at least since Greeks and Romans had split. I did not have 'full orders,' as the Episcopalians would say, but my ordination conjured up all the mystery of the apostolic succession that Methodist clergy claimed for themselves." Interview with the author. In fact, in 1963 King would be stripped by a vote of 89–85 of any appointments to churches or access to their benefits by the Mississippi Methodist annual conference. "Divided Flocks in Jackson," *Christian Century*, November 27, 1963, special report.

35. Edwin King, interview with the author.

36. Ibid.

37. Ed King, "Sixties and Sit-ins," manuscript, p. 16, Edwin King Private Papers.

38. Edwin King, interview with the author.

39. Ibid.

40. See John Salter's memoir of the Jackson movement, 1962–1964: *Jackson, Mississippi: An American Chronicle of Struggle and Schism.*

41. Dittmer, *Local People*, p. 202.

42. Ibid.

43. The central jurisdiction was the black conference of United Methodist Church.

44. Cited in W. J. Cunningham, *Agony at Galloway*, pp. 5–6.

45. Bishops' letter, ibid., pp. 58–59. The seven seminary professors arrested at Capitol Street Methodist Church reached even graver conclusions in their written response in claiming that the exclusion of blacks from the church was a violation of human dignity, an affront to the Christian conscience and heresy. "A Prepared Statement by Van Bogard Dunn, A. Jeffrey Hopper, Paul M. Minus, Jr., and Everett Tylson, April 2, 1964," Ed King Papers, Box 9, Folder 439.

46. Cunningham, *Agony at Galloway*, p. 55.

47. Letter from Brewster Kneen to Ed King, April 1, 1963, Ed King Papers, Box 1, Folder 47.

48. King, "The White Church in Mississippi"; there is no consistent pagination in this manuscript.

49. Ibid.

50. Ibid.

51. Cited in "Church Integration Effort in Mississippi: Pro and Con," *Chicago Daily News*, October 26, 1963; and in "Divided Flocks in Jackson."

52. Letter to King from Cleveland, Ohio, May 31, 1963, Ed King Papers, Box 2.

53. "White Minister Held in Jackson," *New York Times*, May 30, 1963.

54. Ray Holder, *The Mississippi Methodists: 1799–1983: A Moral People "Born of Conviction"* (n.p.: Maverick Prints, 1984), p. 148; "Born of Conviction" quoted in King, "The White Church in Mississippi."

55. Cited in the "No Negro Pews and Empty Pulpit," *New York Herald Tribune*, June 10, 1963.

56. Letter of December 13, 1965, cited in Cunningham, *Agony at Galloway*, p. 115.

57. Ibid., pp. 53–54.

58. Ibid., p. 114.

59. Ibid., pp. 51–52.

60. King, "The White Church in Mississippi."

61. Summary Report on Arrests at Methodist Church in Jackson, Mississippi, October 6, 1963, Ed King Papers, Box 9, Folder 432.

62. While the scenario in Jackson played out, Julie Zaugg's father (a research chemist) was delivering the layman's Sunday sermon at the family's interdenominational church in Lake Bluff, Illinois. He said, "Of all the sins that a Christian can commit, hypocrisy is the most insidiously dangerous. It is in the very nature of hypocrisy to blind the hypocrite to its presence in him. Christ seldom spoke in

anger but when He did it was usually in the face of hypocrisy. He saw no other way to break through to a walled-off conscience being subjected to treacherous erosion from within. Can we really blame Him for preferring the company of repentant thieves and prostitutes to that of the stiff-necked Pharisees who comprised the White Citizens' Council of His day?" Harold E. Zaugg, "Black and White Together," sermon, Union Church, Lake Bluff, Illinois, Ed King Papers, Box 9, Folder 439.

63. "They Went to Chicago," *Chicago Daily News*, October 9, 1963; "Path to Church Leads 3 to Jail," *Mississippi Free Press*, October 12, 1963.

64. Cited in King, "The White Church in Mississippi."

65. Ibid.

66. Ibid.

67. Ibid.

68. Edwin King, interview with the author.

69. "Denies Right to Go to Church," *Christian Century*, October 30, 1963, p. 1,324. King, "The White Church in Mississippi," part four.

70. King, "The White Church in Mississippi."

71. Cited in "Church Integration Effort In Mississippi: Pro and Con," *Chicago Daily News*, October 26, 1963, p. 28. The bishop of Mississippi himself, Dr. Marvin Franklin, had recently declared that "integration is not [to be] forced on any part of our church" and concluded that it was the responsibility of white Methodists to "move on to do the work of the Church, loving mercy, doing justly, and walking humbly before our Lord." Cited in Dittmer, *Local People*, p. 226.

72. "12 Arrested at Churches Here Sunday," *Clarion Ledger*, October 21, 1963.

73. "Divided Flocks in Jackson," *Christian Century*, November 27, 1963, special report.

74. King, "The White Church in Mississippi."

75. "Church Mix Groups Fail in Attempts," *Jackson Clarion Ledger*, July 22, 1963.

76. Edwin King, interview with the author.

77. King, "The White Church in Mississippi."

78. King cited in "Persecution in Mississippi Spreading, Minister Warns," Ed King Papers.

79. King, "The White Church in Mississippi."

80. Ibid.

81. William Bradford Huie, *Three Lives for Mississippi*, p. 43.

82. King, "The White Church in Mississippi."

83. Ibid.

84. Cited in William H. Chafe, *Never Stop Running: Allard Lowenstein and the Struggle to Save American Liberalism*, p. 181.

85. Ed King, "White Church—Beauty for Ashes," manuscript, p. 2, Edwin King Private Papers.

86. King, "The White Church in Mississippi."

87. Ibid.

88. Cited in Joel L. Alvis, Jr., "Racial Turmoil and Religious Reaction: The Rt. Rev. John M. Allin," *Historical Magazine of the Protestant Episcopal Church* 50:1 (March 1981), 84.

89. King, "The White Church in Mississippi."

90. King writes, "White Mississippians had a very proper and traditional role in building—or rebuilding Negro churches. It was still paternalism. Worse, far worse, was the fact that this effort gave these white moderates a great sense of pride and pious relief that their critics could not say they were doing nothing about the racial crisis. This effort allowed them to avoid their real responsibility—stopping the bombing, facing the violence. Of one such project by the interfaith group called 'The Committee of Concern,' " King says, "In the literature put out for fundraising in Mississippi (and for favorable national publicity), this group said it was raising funds for Black churches—but pointedly was vague about the unknown causes for the church burnings" ("The White Church in Mississipppi").

91. James Chaney's body had been buried late that afternoon in a new black cemetery a few miles southwest of Meridian. Memorial services for Mickey Schwerner and Andrew Goodman were held in New York City. The Schwerner family had tried to arrange a burial of their son with James Chaney in Mississippi, but segregation laws prohibited interracial funerals—unless, as William Bradford Huie said, "you bury them at night in a dam" (*Three Lives for Mississippi*, p. 227).

92. This account is taken from Dittmer, *Local People*, p. 284.

93. Dennis quoted ibid., p. 249.

94. David Dennis, Eulogy for James Chaney, August 7, 1964. Audiotape, Edwin King Private Papers.

95. Ibid.

96. Dennis quoted in Dittmer, *Local People*, p. 249.

97. Dennis, Eulogy for James Chaney, August 7, 1964.

98. In an interview more than a decade later with fellow civil rights activist and movement historian Tom Dent, Dennis explained his state of mind and sudden departure from Mississippi after the Atlantic City convention: "My feelings about the movement changed tremendously at the time of the Schwerner, Chaney and Goodman deaths. That was my first time publicly calling people out to take arms. That was blown up nationally . . . because I did it at Chaney's funeral. And from that point on [the movement] never made any sense to me. . . . We went to Atlantic City and after being in Atlantic City for two days, I got out. I didn't do anything but sit around. I went to bars and drank. I didn't want no part of it anymore and I didn't participate with it because all of a sudden, I'm looking at people playing politics. . . . To me, just all of a sudden, just none of it made sense. I didn't want no part of it. I'm talking life and death; I'm talking about a change and every time being asked to take a step back. And from that point on, it just never did make sense to me at all. And then I realized I'd made a tremendous mistake a long time in the movement. I thought the whole nonviolence bit and everything else

was just a mistake. And I did not believe in it anymore, and I didn't believe in the government, the system or anything else anymore. I sort of divorced myself, I guess, from the movement as a whole; I started just moving out. . . . All this crap, with people dying and taking anybody with them was really just a waste of good lives. 'Don't use your guns, nonviolence is the way'—that just went totally out the window from then on."

Dennis's subsequent involvement in New Orleans with the militant Deacons for Defense and Justice seemed to him a more appropriate response to the situation: "They got better jobs and they didn't play. The kids went out on demonstrations and the parents went out there with guns on their shoulders watching. You didn't have any problems then, you know what I mean? . . . White folks respect that. As long as you bend over . . . and get your butt kicked, the Deacons felt you were nothing but a bunch of cowards. But every time you fought back, that's the language they understood. I thought: we should have gone into areas [in Mississippi] to do voter registration and at the same time say, 'We're not taking no shit. We want to do this in a peaceful manner, but if you don't want to do it that way—bring it on!'" David Dennis interview, Tom Dent Oral History Collection, Amistad.

99. Ed King, "Eulogy for James Chaney, August 7, 1964. My emphasis. The German theologian Dietrich Bonhoeffer had said in 1934 of the Confessing Church in Germany that opposed the Ayran laws of the German Christian Church, that if you aren't in it, you aren't a Christian.

100. Ibid.

101. John F. Baggett and Philip M. Dripps, "Christian Unity, the Methodist Church and Jackson," *Behold* (December 1963), p. 5.

102. Karl Barth, *The Word of God and the Word of Man*, pp. 67–68.

103. Christopher Morse, *Not Every Spirit: A Dogmatics of Christian Disbelief* (Valley Forge, Pa.: Trinity Press International, 1994). Morse writes in his luminous book, "[The] call not to credit or give credence to that which is not God is given repeated assertion in the Old Testament injunctions against idols: 'Do not turn to idols or make cast images for yourselves: I am the Lord your God' (Lev. 19:4). In the Hebrew Bible the blessing of God is seen to include the cursing and rejection of that which is not of God. We see this understanding carried over into the New Testament where the Greek word for 'cursed' is *anathema*. Paul, to cite one instance, writes to the Galatians, 'If anyone proclaims to you a gospel contrary to what you received, let that one be accursed (*anathema*)'" (p. 4).

104. Joan Trumpauer Mulholland, interview with the author.

105. Edwin King, interview with the author.

106. On King's involvement in Atlantic City, see Anne Cooke Romaine, "The Mississippi Freedom Democratic Party through August, 1964" (M.A. thesis, University of Virginia, pp. 251–79); Dittmer, *Local People*, pp. 286ff; Chafe, *Never Stop Running*, pp. 196–202; Eric R. Burner, *And Gently He Shall Lead Them: Robert Parris Moses and Civil Rights in Mississippi* (New York: New York University Press, 1994), pp. 169–99.

107. Edwin King, interview with the author.

108. Julie Zaugg, "Minutes, Tougaloo Movement, Fall, 1963," Ed King Papers. SNCC staff member Mary King recalls, "The Reverend Ed King and his wife, Jeannette, at Tougaloo College, made their campus home an oasis for me and everyone else in the movement. Ministers, journalists, foreign visitors, and civil rights workers wandered through their huge residence at all hours of the day and night. Jeannette brewed what I thought of as a magic pot of coffee—it never ran out." *Freedom Song: A Personal Story of the 1960s Civil Rights Movement* (New York: Quill, 1987) p. 424.

109. King, *Freedom Song*, p. 366.

110. Edwin King, interview with the author; King, "The Herrons and the Beloved Community," unpublished paper, p. 4, Edwin King Private Papers.

111. Jane Stembridge, untitled poem, in Ed King Papers.

112. King, "The White Church in Mississippi."

113. Edwin King, interview with the author.

114. King, "The Herrons and the Beloved Community," p. 2.

115. Ibid., p. 5.

116. Smith, *Killers of the Dream*, p. 16.

Chapter Five

Cleveland Sellers's River

1. Jack Bass and Jack Nelson, *The Orangeburg Massacre*, p. 123.

2. Cleveland Sellers, interview with the author. Washington explained in his Atlanta Exposition Address, "Our greatest danger is that in the great leap from slavery to freedom we may overlook the fact that the masses of us are to live by the productions of our hands, and fail to keep in mind that we shall prosper in proportion as we learn to dignity and glorify common labor and put brains and skill into the common occupations of life; shall prosper in proportion as we learn to draw the line between the superficial and the substantial, the ornamental gewgaws of life and the useful. No race can prosper till it learns that there is as much dignity in tilling a field as in writing a poem. It is at the bottom of life we must begin, and not at the top." Cited in *Black Protest: History, Documents, and Analyses*, edited by Joanne Grant (Greenwich, Conn.: Fawcett, 1968), pp. 196–97.

3. Cleveland Sellers with Robert Terrell, *The River of No Return: The Autobiography of a Black Militant and the Life and Death of SNCC*, pp. 4–5, 7.

4. Cleveland Sellers, interview with the author.

5. Sellers, *The River of No Return*, p. 7.

6. Ibid.

7. Robert J. Blanton, *The Story of Voorhees College* (Smithtown, N.Y.: Exposition Press, 1983), pp. 150, 233; "In Memoria, The Reverend Canon Henry L. Grant," Episcopal Diocese of South Carolina, Charleston.

8. Sellers, *The River of No Return*, p. 9.

9. Ibid., pp. 10–11.

10. See Stephen Whitfield, *A Death in the Delta: The Story of Emmett Till*, p. 25.

11. Ibid., p. 42.

12. Sellers, *The River of No Return*, p. 16. The murder of Emmett Till awakened numerous young black southerners to the brutal realities of Jim Crow. In her memoir *Coming of Age in Mississippi*, Ann Moody wrote that after the lynching and the not-guilty verdict, she began to hate for the first time in her life. "I hated the white men who murdered Emmett Till and I hated all the other whites who were responsible for the countless murders Mrs. Rice had told me about and those I vaguely remembered from childhood. But I also hated Negroes. I hated them for not standing up and doing something about the murders. In fact, I think I had a stronger resentment toward Negroes for letting the whites kill them than toward the whites. Anyway, it was at this stage in my life that I began to look upon Negro men as cowards. I could not respect them for smiling in a white man's face, addressing him as Mr. So-and-So, saying yessuh and nossuh when after they were home behind closed doors that same white man was a son of a bitch, a bastard, or any other name more suitable than mister" (p. 129).

13. Sellers, *The River of No Return*, p. 17.

14. Program for the Eleventh Annual Summer School of Religious Education for the Youth of the Fourth Province, Protestant Episcopal Church in the United States, Sunday, June 19–Friday, June 24, 1960, Cleveland Sellers Papers.

15. Cleveland Sellers, interview with the author.

16. *The Church Speaks on Race: Official Statements of the Episcopal Church and the Anglican Communion, 1940–1958* (New York: National Council, 1959), p. 5. Unlike resolutions in the Southern Baptist Convention, the General Convention's resolutions are authoritative for every diocese.

17. See Michael P. G. G. Randolph, *A Faithful Journey: Black Leadership in the Episcopal Church* (Cincinnati: Forward Movement Publications, 1994).

18. Sellers, *The River of No Return*, p. 17.

19. See Miles Wolff, *Lunch at the 5 & 10* (Chicago: Ivan R. Dee, 1990).

20. As the bishop wrote to Sellers on April 5, 1960, "As you know, I am to be at your church next Tuesday. I shall look forward to seeing you there. I shall be very grateful to you if you will make yourself known to me after the service." Cleveland Sellers Papers.

21. Cleveland Sellers, interview with the author.

22. In Charleston, Grant served as a canon in the Episcopal diocese, operated a downtown mission, and later helped create an interracial parish in the city. Blanton, *The Story of Voorhees College*, p. 234.

23. Sellers, *The River of No Return*, p. 29.

24. Cleveland Sellers, "Black Power, 1966–1996," public lecture, Baltimore, April 9, 1996 (videotape, author's collection); Sellers, *The River of No Return*, p. 29.

25. Mary King, *Freedom Song: A Personal Story of the 1960s Civil Rights Movement*, p. 419.

26. Sellers, *The River of No Return*, pp. 58–59.

27. Cleveland Sellers, interview with the author.

28. Dan T. Carter, *The Politics of Rage: George Wallace, The Origins of the New Conservatism, and the Transformation of American Politics* (New York: Simon & Schuster, 1995), p. 213.

29. Gloria Richardson had opposed the charter amendment on public accommodations on the grounds that the right to be served in a public place was inherent in human rights as such and ought not be delineated as in any way exceptional. See Peter B. Levy, "Civil War on Race Street: The Black Freedom Struggle and White Resistance in Cambridge, Maryland, 1960–1964," *Maryland Historical Magazine* 89:3 (Fall 1994), 306.

30. Sellers, *The River of No Return*, pp. 68, 70, 58.

31. Peter S. Szabo, "An Interview with Gloria Richardson Dandridge," *Maryland Historical Magazine* 89:3 (Fall 1994), 348. Paula Giddings, *When and Where I Enter: The Impact of Black Women on Race and Sex in America* (New York: William Morrow, 1984), p. 292. Cleveland Sellers, *The River of No Return*, p. 71.

32. Sellers, *The River of No Return*, p. 71.

33. Danny Lyon, *Memories of the Southern Civil Rights Movement* (Chapel Hill: University of North Carolina Press, 1992), p. 136.

34. Sellers, *The River of No Return*, p. 73.

35. Ibid., p. 75.

36. Seth Cagin and Philip Dray, *We Are Not Afraid: The Story of Goodman, Schwerner, and Chaney and the Civil Rights Campaign for Mississippi*, p. 320.

37. Cleveland Sellers, interview with the author.

38. Sellers, *The River of No Return*, p. 91.

39. Cleveland Sellers, interview with the author.

40. Donaldson cited in Clayborne Carson, *In Struggle: SNCC and the Black Awakening of the 1960s*, p. 116.

41. Cleveland Sellers, interview with the author.

42. Cleveland Sellers, "Field Report," SNCC Papers; King, *Freedom Song*, p. 330.

43. Cleveland Sellers, interview with the author.

44. Had Sellers established some relationship to the Episcopal church in Mississippi, he might have discovered one courageous churchman, the Reverend Duncan Gray, Jr., rector of St. Peter's Church in Oxford and son of the bishop of the state. In the fall of 1962, Gray preached a series of sermons declaring that Christians should accept "the admission of James Meredith to the University," admonishing his parishioners to "pray daily, even hourly, for God's guidance and direction that we may faithfully fulfill this responsibility to the end that God's will may be done." Sermon Preached at St. Peter's Church, Oxford, Mississippi. September 30, 1962; Duncan Gray, personal papers. Sellers might also have learned that the Episcopal Diocese of Mississippi in 1954 had given moderate support to *Brown vs. Board of Education* in a widely distributed pamphlet, *The Church Considers the Supreme Court Decision* (Jackson: Diocese of Mississippi, 1954). The diocese had

even affirmed that all Episcopal services "are open to any Churchman who wishes to attend, without regard for his race or color" (p. 9). However, Sellers did know something of the state's most infamous Episcopalian, namely Byron de la Beckwith, the murderer of Medgar Evers, whose diatribe of March 16, 1956, "Open Letter to All Episcopalians," was aimed directly at Beckwith's old schoolmate, Duncan Gray: "Let's get the race mixers out of the Episcopal Church, for it is rapidly becoming the 'Devil's Workshop'! Because of our luke-warm attitude, we are about to be labeled by other's faith's [sic] as 'The Black Christians.' Let's get red-hot on the subject—if the race mixers don't resign and leave, I say, Thrown [sic] them out bodily, if necessary. These men, disguised in the robes of the clergy, deliberately and maliciously defy the laws of God and drag the sacred name of Jesus Christ through the mud in the attempt to crucify the white race on the black cross of the NAACP." Ed King Papers; Reverend Duncan M. Gray, Jr., interview with the author.

45. Cleveland Sellers, interview with the author. Another summer volunteer compared the experience to the "psychological set of a soldier going to the front lines at a time of rather heavy and personal fighting. . . . You didn't really believe in 'beyond the Project,' just as I suppose you don't really believe in 'beyond the war.'" Cited in Mary Aickin Rothschild, *A Case of Black and White: Northern Volunteers and the Southern Freedom Summers, 1964–1965* (Westport, Conn.: Greenwood Press, 1982), p. 59.

46. Sellers, *The River of No Return*, p. 51.

47. Pauline Sellers, Letter to Cleveland Sellers, Cleveland Sellers Papers.

48. The story is based on Sellers's memoir, *The River of No Return*, pp. 101ff., and interviews.

49. Sellers, *The River of No Return*, p. 103.

50. "SNCC Report on the Death of Yancey and Scales," SNCC Papers, Box 14.

51. Sellers, *The River of No Return*, p. 104.

52. "SNCC Report on the Death of Yancey and Scales."

53. Cleveland Sellers, interview with the author.

54. Sellers, *The River of No Return*, pp. 106–7.

55. Lawrence Guyot and Mike Thelwell, "The Politics of Necessity and Survival in Mississippi," *Freedomways* 6 (Spring 1966), 121. Mary Aickin Rothschild writes, "From this point on, in the southern civil rights movement, the term 'white liberal,' previously used as a neutral or even praiseworthy description of a person's politics, became an epithet." *A Case of Black and White*, p. 71.

56. Cleveland Sellers, interview with the author; Sellers, *The River of No Return*, p. 111.

57. Pauline Sellers, Letter to Cleveland Sellers, November 12, 1964, Cleveland Sellers Papers.

58. Pauline Sellers, Letter to Cleveland Sellers, September 19, 1964, Cleveland Sellers Papers.

59. Pauline Sellers, Card to Cleveland Sellers, Cleveland Sellers Papers.

60. Sellers, *The River of No Return*, p. 112.

61. Ibid., p. 113.

62. Carson, *In Struggle*, p. 133.

63. "Prospectus from the 1964 Waveland Retreat," Charles Sherrod Papers, Box 23.

64. Minutes of November 8, 1964 Staff Meeting, SNCC Papers, Box 7.

65. Sellers, *A River of No Return*, p. 117. See also the discussion in John W. De Gruchy, *Christianity and Democracy: A Theology for a Just World Order*, pp. 13–34, 131–64.

66. See Sara Evans, *Personal Politics: The Roots of Women's Liberation in the Civil Rights Movement and the New Left*; Carson, *In Struggle*, p. 144.

67. Carson, *In Struggle*, p. 152.

68. Ibid., p. 154.

69. Cleveland Sellers, interview with the author; Sellers, *The River of No Return*, p. 131. Sara Evans added, "The position they represented was an exaggerated version of 'Let the people lead themselves,' focusing on individual freedom, reacting against the least suggestion of authority, and romanticizing the local people. . . . They were frequently the people who challenged any decision not made by the whole group or reached by consensus, who were continually suspicious of anyone they perceived as powerful." *Personal Politics*, pp. 94–95.

70. David Burner, *Making Peace with the 60s*, p. 50.

71. Sellers, *The River of No Return*, pp. 131–32. One anonymous staff member in a prospectus paper for the November 1964 Waveland conference described the problem in similar terms: "SNCC leaders have an unwillingness to set priority on certain things that must be dealt with. Instead they let them drift until a solution evolves (which is not always the best one) or until the situation becomes so demanding that it has to be dealt with." Introduction: Self-Introspective," Charles Sherrod Papers, File 23.

72. Carson, *In Struggle*, p. 155.

73. Cleveland Sellers, interview with the author; Cleveland Sellers to SNCC staff members, July 20, 1964, SNCC Papers, Box 104.

74. Cleveland Sellers, interview with the author; Julian Bond, "Fannie Lou Hamer," *Ebony* (August 1977), p. 140.

75. Sellers, *The River of No Return*, p. 133.

76. John L. Kater, Jr., "Experiment in Freedom: The Episcopal Church and the Black Power Movement," *Historical Magazine of the Protestant Episcopal Church* 48 (March 1979), 71.

77. Cleveland Sellers, interview with the author.

78. Sellers, *The River of No Return*, p. 135.

79. Cleveland Sellers, interview with the author.

80. Sellers, *The River of No Return*, p. 134.

81. Cleveland Sellers, interview with the author.

82. Ibid. Malcom X in James Cone, *Martin and Malcolm: A Dream of a Nightmare* (New York: Orbis Books, 1992), p. 107.

83. Cleveland Sellers, interview with the author.

84. John Lewis, "SNCC Executive Committee Meeting," April 12–14, 1965, Holly Springs Mississippi, SNCC Papers.

85. "Program Review," SNCC Papers, Box 6A.

86. Sellers, *The River of No Return*, p. 144.

87. Ibid., p. 145.

88. "Statement on Vietnam, January 6, 1966, Student Nonviolent Coordinating Committee," SNCC Papers, Box 5.

89. Clayborne Carson writes, "These urban efforts strained SNCC's capabilities and made the staff painfully aware of their meager resources and lack of long-range programs to confront urban problems. For some staff members, organizing among urban blacks was a way of escaping the responsibilities they had faced in the deep South or, in some northern cities, of abandoning fund-raising obligations. Most of the urban offices floundered during 1965, although Donaldson had some success in helping to establish a 'community foundation' in Columbus that made small grants for local projects approved by a democratically-elected community board" (*In Struggle*, p. 168).

90. Hugh Pearson, *The Shadow of the Panther: Huey Newton and the Price of Black Power in America*, p. 83.

91. Carson, *In Struggle*, p. 166.

92. John Hulett, "The Lowndes County Freedom Party," in *Black Protest: History, Documents and Analyses, 1619 to the Present*, edited by Joanne Grant (Greenwich, Conn.: Fawcett Premier Book, 1968), pp. 403–7.

93. Cited in Carson, *In Struggle*, p. 166.

94. It also bears mentioning that photographs of black panthers that Bob Zellner had taken at the Atlanta zoo (at the request of Sellers) were used by his wife Dottie Zellner as models for sketching the Lowndes County emblem (Bob Zellner, interview with the author).

95. Pearson, *The Shadow of the Panther*, p. 83.

96. Sellers, *The River of No Return*, p. 156.

97. James Meredith cited in William L. Van Deburg, *New Day in Babylon: The Black Power Movement and American Culture, 1965–1975* (Chicago: University of Chicago Press, 1992), p. 32. In 1988, James Meredith would support former klansman David Duke for governor of Louisiana.

98. David J. Garrow, *Bearing the Cross: Martin Luther King, Jr., and the Southern Christian Leadership Conference*, pp. 476–77.

99. Sellers, *The River of No Return*, p. 163.

100. Reed Massengill explains, "Had King's movements during the Meredith March been less erratic and better publicized, it is likely he might have met his fatal bullet earlier. While they had most often focused their hatred on targets in their home state of Mississippi, the White Knights reviled King and his ability to use the media to his advantage. King was, after all, doing a far better job than the Klan of swaying public opinion. Former Klan Titan Delmar Dennis remembered a

1965 planning session at which he was asked by Imperial Wizard Sam Bowers whether or not he could find a volunteer sniper to assassinate King as he traveled through Mississippi on a trip unrelated to the Meredith March. Bowers had learned that King would be using a highway between Philadelphia and Meridian, and planned what would have become his most ambitious Project Four. Snipers were to be placed at either end of a bridge along King's route, and would be armed and ready to fire high-powered rifles as his car approached or withdrew. Beneath the bridge, dynamite would be planted as a safeguard, in case the snipers missed their mark. Dennis reported the plan to his FBI contacts, and they made sure King changed his travel route, thwarting the White Knights' attempt on Dr. Martin Luther King, Jr.'s life." *Portrait of a Racist: The Man Who Killed Medgar Evers*, p. 241.

101. Garrow, *Bearing the Cross*, p. 481. SNCC member Willie Ricks had tried out the "Black Power" slogan during the Greenwood march before Carmichael brought it to national attention in his own inimitable way. Ricks, also known as "The Reverend" for his homiletical flair, warned in his speech at the Yazoo City fairgrounds of "white blood flowing" and of a new black militancy. After Ricks received enthusiastic ovations for his radical sentiments, Carmichael took center stage and made the speech that would change the course of the movement. See Gene Roberts, "The Story of Snick," in *Black Protest in the Sixties*, edited by August Meier and Elliot Rudwick (Chicago: Quadrangle Books, 1970), p. 139.

102. "Letter from Birmingham City Jail," *A Testament of Hope: The Essential Writings of Martin Luther King, Jr.*, edited by James Melvin Washington, p. 297.

103. Cited in Garrow, *Bearing the Cross*, p. 485.

104. Martin Luther King, Jr., *Where Do We Go From Here: Chaos or Community?* (New York: Bantam Books, 1967), p. 43.

105. Cited in Garrow, *Bearing the Cross*, pp. 485, 488.

106. Richard Lischer, *The Preacher King*, p. 108.

107. Sellers, *The River of No Return*, p. 168.

108. Ibid., p. 165.

109. Ibid., p. 173.

110. Martin Luther King, *Strength to Love* (Cleveland: William Collins and World, 1963), p. 50.

111. James Forman, *The Making of Black Revolutionaries*, p. 476. Mrs. Hamer was saddened by the new separatism even though she continued publicly to describe Stokely Carmichael as one of the kindest persons she'd ever known (Kay Mills, *This Little Light of Mine*, p. 365).

112. John Lewis, interview with the author. See also Sean Wilentz, "The Last Integrationist," *The New Republic*, July 1, 1996, pp. 19–26.

113. Jack Minnis cited in Carson, *In Struggle*, p. 203; John Lewis, interview with the author.

114. Cleveland Sellers, "Memo, August 23, 1966," SNCC Papers, Box 104.

115. James Peck, "Black Racism," *Liberation* (October 1966), p. 31.

116. Joyce Ladner, "What 'Black Power' Means to Negroes in Mississippi," *Trans-action* 5 (November 1967), 202.

117. Ralph McGill cited in Carson, *In Struggle*, p. 226.

118. Cited in John L. Kater, Jr., "Experiment in Freedom: The Episcopal Church and the Black Power Movement," *Historical Magazine of the Protestant Episcopal Church* 48 (March 1979), 72.

119. Lewis cited in Jack Nelson, "*Los Angeles Times* Report" July 29, 1966, SNCC Papers, Box 6.

120. Cleveland Sellers, interview with the author.

121. Evelyn Marshall, secretary to Mr. Carmichael, Letter to Mr. Dick Janson, December 21, 1966, SNCC Files, Box 24.

122. See David Burner's discussion of Black Power's contribution to cultural identity in *Making Peace with the 60s*, pp. 49–83.

123. Franz Fanon, *The Wretched of the Earth*, translated by Constance Farrington (New York: Grove Press, 1963), pp. 35, 316.

124. Roberts, "The Story of Snick," p. 143.

125. Cleveland Sellers, interview with the author.

126. Olisanwuche P. Esedebe cited in Josiah Ulysses Young III, *A Pan-African Theology: Providence and the Legacies of the Ancestors* (Trenton, N.J.: Africa World Press, 1992), p. 15.

127. Cleveland Sellers, interview with the author. Importantly, this dimension of Black Power did not go unnoticed in the black religious community. The National Committee of Negro Churchman—only three weeks after the Greenwood speech in July 1966—met informally to offer a theological affirmation of Black Power. In a statement first published in the *New York Times* (July 31, 1966), the committee asserted: "For . . . interaction to take place, all people need power, whether black or white. We regard as sheer hypocrisy or as a blind and dangerous illusion the view that opposes love to power. . . . What love opposes is precisely the misuse and abuse of power, not power itself" (cited in Kater, "Experiment in Freedom, p. 71). The committee's statement was commendable for its willingness to think theologically alongside the discourse of black self-determination, as well as to point out that a conviction of black power had (to some extent) long shaped black religious and social identity. The Committee applauded Black Power for its visceral reminder that the church must vigorously preach the reign of God in this world and in this time, thus redressing its sometimes "distorted and complacent view of an otherworldly conception of God's power," even though its blessings on Black Power betrayed, at the same time, the restrictions of such a task: "From the point of view of the Christian faith, there is nothing necessarily wrong with concern for power. At the heart of the Protestant Reformation is the belief that ultimate power belongs to God alone and that men become most inhuman when concentrations of power lead to the conviction . . . that any nation, race or organization can rival God in this regard." Cited in "Statement by the National Committee of Negro Churchman," in James H. Cone and Gayraud S. Wilmore, *Black*

Theology: A Documentary History, 1966–1979 (Maryknoll, N.Y.: Orbis Books, 1982), p. 27. The dialectical impulse described in the passage, the protest against any identification of God with human powers and institutions, was far from SNCC's intent. Sellers vigorously defended the notion that there was nothing wrong with the concentration of power in the black race and in the black community. As such, the "Protestant principle" invoked by the ministers (as the theologian Paul Tillich termed the anti-idolatrous impulse of the Reformation) and its concern about concentration of power in particular nations, races, or organizations, might be appropriate for people who have power and have come to feel guilty about it, but not for people whose access has been systematically denied.

128. Roberts, "The Story of Snick," p. 148.

129. A staff member wrote in a prospectus for the November 1964 Waveland conference, "We have been only dealing with the surface issues and unwilling to attack the problem at its roots." "Introduction: Semi-Introspective," SNCC Conferences, Charles Sherrod Papers, File 23. The issue was raised in December of 1966, during the meeting at the New York resort owned by black comedian Peg Leg Bates. Discussions about white involvement reached "a new level of intensity," as James Forman recalls. The staff passed a resolution (19 for, 18 against, 24 abstaining) that whites could not be members of the Coordinating Committee, although they could work for SNCC (*The Making of Black Revolutionaries*, p. 475).

130. Bob Zellner, interview with the author.

131. Zellner cited in "Central Committee Meeting Notes and Decisions of May, 1967," SNCC Papers, Box 7.

132. Ibid.

133. See Bob Zellner, "Notes of a Native Son," *Southern Exposure* 9:1 (Spring 1981), 48. Zellner writes, "It is not that I never knew only Southern white people before. I grew up in Alabama. My uncle was a sharecropper. I have relatives who used to be in the Ku Klux Klan, and some still are. But I left this world and went into another one. I left because I knew I could not live in a world filled with racism and hate. I had to change that world. I left because I saw no hope of any of the people I had grown up with changing the world—and I saw that black people were going to change it" (p. 48).

134. Sellers, *The River of No Return*, p. 194.

135. "Central Committee Meeting Notes and Decisions of May, 1967."

136. Ibid.

137. Bob Zellner, interview with the author.

138. Cleveland Sellers, interview with the author.

139. Stokely Carmichael cited in George M. Fredrickson, *Black Liberation: A Comparative History of Black Ideologies in the United States and South Africa* (New York: Oxford University Press, 1995), p. 295.

140. Cleveland Sellers, interview with the author.

141. Sellers, *The River of No Return*, pp. 188, 202.

142. He responded at a court hearing by stating that "the central question for

us is not whether we allow ourselves to be drafted, for we have resolved that this shall not happen by any means. The central question for us is how do we stop the exploitation of our brothers' territories and goods by a wealthy, hungry nation such as this." Ibid., p. 191.

143. In the wake of urban riots the previous year, FBI Director J. Edgar Hoover expanded the bureau's operations against the Black Power movement. In September 1967, Attorney General Ramsey Clark instructed Hoover to "use the maximum resources, investigative and intelligence, to collect and report all facts bearing upon the question as whether there has been or is a scheme or conspiracy by any group of whatever size, effectiveness or affiliation, to plan, promote, or aggravate riot activity." Cited in Richard Gid Powers, *Secrecy and Power: The Life of J. Edgar Hoover* (New York: Free Press, 1987), p. 424.

144. Cleveland Sellers, interview with the author.

145. Cited in Bass and Nelson, *The Orangeburg Massacre*, p. 52.

146. Sellers, *The River of No Return*, p. 217.

147. Bass and Nelson, *The Orangeburg Massacre*, p. 65.

148. Sellers, *The River of No Return*, p. 218.

149. Bass and Nelson, *The Orangeburg Massacre*, pp. 77, 111, 73.

150. Cleveland Sellers, interview with the author; Kenneth O'Reilly, *Racial Matters: The FBI's Secret File on Black America, 1960–1972*, p. 257.

151. Bass and Nelson, *The Orangeburg Massacre*, p. 177. Carmichael told his Cuban audience, "We greet you as comrades because it becomes increasingly clear to us each day that we share with you a common struggle; we have a common enemy. Our enemy is white western imperialist society. (Note that we use the term white western society as opposed to white western civilization. The west has never been civilized. It has no right to speak of itself as a civilization.) Our struggle is to overthrow this system which feeds itself and expands itself through the economic and cultural exploitation of non-white, non-western peoples—the THIRD WORLD." "Speech by Carmichael in Cuba," SNCC Papers, Box 24.

152. Bass and Nelson, *The Orangeburg Massacre*, p. 83.

153. Kenneth O'Reilly, *Racial Matters*, p. 257. Harry Ashmore of the Center for the Study of Democratic Institutions and a Pulitzer Prize-winning editor wrote, "The saddest dispatch that I have read lately from my native state was not the one that reported the senseless slaughter of Negro students at Orangeburg, but the report that followed a day or so later proclaiming that high officials had concluded that the student unrest was the work of important black militants. For television purposes, the investigators finally were able to dig up one black man with bushy hair and an African costume to explain why unarmed Negro youths were found dead with police bullets in their backs and in the soles of their feet" (Bass and Nelson, *The Orangeburg Massacre*, p. 125).

154. Sellers cited in Nelson and Bass, *The Orangeburg Massacre*, p. 126.

155. Cleveland Sellers, interview with the author.

156. Sellers, *The River of No Return*, p. 244.

157. Carson, *In Struggle*, p. 305.

158. Jack Bass, "Justice Finally Comes in the Orangeburg Massacre," *Los Angeles Times*, August 22, 1993; Bass and Nelson, *The Orangeburg Massacre*, pp. 209–10; O'Reilly, *Racial Matters*, p. 257.

159. Cited in Bass and Nelson, *The Orangeburg Massacre*, p. 210.

160. Cited in O'Reilly, *Racial Matters*, p. 257.

161. Cited in Bass and Nelson, *The Orangeburg Massacre*, p. 210; "Mother Defends Sellers," newspaper article, n.d., Cleveland Sellers Papers.

162. Tollie L. Caution, Letter to Pauline Sellers, February 16, 1968, Cleveland Sellers Papers.

163. Sellers, *The River of No Return*, pp. 266–67.

164. Richard King, *Civil Rights and the Idea of Freedom*, pp. 138–71.

165. James Cone, *Black Theology and Black Power*, p. 41. See also Cone's *A Black Theology of Liberation* (Philadelphia: Lippincott, 1970); Albert B. Cleage, Jr., *The Black Messiah* (New York: Sheed and Ward, 1969); and Vincent Harding, "Black Power and the American Christ."

166. Cleveland Sellers, interview with the author. Sellers's rendering has echoes of writer Richard Wright's reflections on "black power" in his 1954 open letter to Kwame Nkrumah, then prime minister of the Gold Coast: "Be on top of theory; don't let theory be on top of you. In short be *free*, be a living embodiment of what you want to give your people." Richard Wright, *Black Power: A Record of Reactions in a Land of Pathos* (San Francisco: Harper Perennial, 1995), p. 392.

167. "The Student Nonviolent Coordinating Committee (as revised in conference, April 29, 1962)," Charles Sherrod Papers, File 24.

168. Cleveland Sellers, interview with the author.

169. Cited in King, *Civil Rights and the Idea of Freedom*, p. 166.

170. Václav Havel, *Living in Truth*, p. 32.

171. Consider the defining passage of Carmichael's Cuban speech on Black Power. "Black Power attacks this [white western racist] brain-washing by saying, WE WILL DEFINE OURSELVES. We will no longer accept the white man's definition of ourselves as ugly, ignorant and uncultured. We will recognize our own beauty and our own culture and will no longer be ashamed of ourselves, for a people ashamed of themselves cannot be free." "Speech by Carmichael in Cuba," SNCC Papers, Box 24.

172. King, *Civil Rights and Idea of Freedom*, pp. 160–61.

173. Cited in Anne Cooke Romaine, "The Mississippi Freedom Democratic Party through August, 1964."

174. King, *Civil Rights and the Idea of Freedom*, p. 161.

175. Victor Anderson, *Beyond Ontological Blackness: An Essay on African American Religious and Cultural Criticism* (New York: Continuum, 1995). Anderson criticizes Black Power and its theological formations on the ground that self-identity is bound and determined by, and ultimately dependent upon, white racist structures and "their perdurance in time." He explains, "Ontological blackness is a phi-

losophy of racial consciousness. It is governed by dialectical matrices that existentially structure African Americans' self-conscious perceptions of black life. Under ontological blackness, the conscious lives of blacks are experienced as bound by unresolved binary dialectics of slavery and freedom, negro and citizen, insider and outsider, black and white, struggle and survival. However, such binary polarities admit no possibility of transcendence or mediation" (p. 14).

176. Like white Mississippi's own extremists, the closed society of SNCC turned defensive and full of suspicion toward outsiders. Matters of personal and organizational security were heightened to a near paranoid level. One SNCC document cautioned, "EVERY BODY IN THIS ORGANIZATION HAS TO LEARN TO KEEP HIS MOUTH SHUT ABOUT CERTAIN MATTERS AND TO LEARN HOW NOT TO TALK TOO MUCH ON THE PHONE . . . ANYTHING YOU ARE WORRIED ABOUT KEEPING SECRET, DO NOT DISCUSS IN OUR OFFICES . . . SCRAMBLERS FOR OUR PHONES SHOULD BE BOUGHT . . . DUPLICATES FOR IMPORTANT INFORMATION SHOULD BE MADE AND STORED . . . DO NOT TALK TOO MUCH IN CERTAIN CARS. WE MUST ASSUME THAT DEVICES CAN BE PLANTED THERE . . . REFERENCES OF PEOPLE WHO CLAIM TO BE FRIENDLY SHOULD BE CHECKED OUT." "Conclusions and Recommendations," SNCC Papers, Box 6.

Conclusion

Clearburning

1. Quoted in Jack Nelson, *Terror in the Night*, p. 113.

2. Douglas Hudgins, "What Do We Believe about God?" sermon, First Baptist Church, n.d., Douglas Hudgins Papers.

3. Dietrich Bonhoeffer had written from a concentration camp shortly before his execution by the Nazis: "Here and there people flee from public altercation into the sanctuary of private *virtuousness*. But anyone who does this must shut his mouth and his eyes to the injustice around him. Only at the cost of self-deception can he keep himself pure from the contamination arising from responsible action." Bonhoeffer, *Letters and Papers from Prison*, p. 5.

4. Michael Waltzer, *Exodus and Revolution*, p. 98.

5. Cited in Edwin King, "Go Tell It on the Mountain: A Prophet from the Delta," *Sojourner* (December 1982), 18.

6. Fannie Lou Hamer, tape interview, Tracy Sugarman private collection.

7. Sally Belfrage, *Freedom Summer*, pp. 78–79.

8. Fannie Lou Hamer, "Songs My Mother Taught Me," produced by Bernie Johnson Reagon, 1980.

9. Eberhard Jüngel, *God as the Mystery of the World*, p. 395.

10. See Karl Barth, *Church Dogmatics*, vol. 4, part 3, translated by G. W. Bromiley (Edinburgh: T & T Clark, 1961), p. 148.

11. In the terms of a more formal discourse, the theological fact of God's own

mercy and goodness enlivens the anthropological responsibility toward justice. As the theologian Peter Hodgson writes, "[We] are empowered by God to shape earthly communities of freedom and solidarity—finite, fragile, fragmentary—that image in their very plurality the heavenly kingdom of freedom." Hodgson argues that God is present in history "in the myriad shapes freedom," intimated in "praxis of a particular sort, namely, free, liberating, emancipatory, transfigurative praxis" (p. 44). "Movement" signifies at once the metaphor and form of the process, wherein the "divine gestalt" or "figure" (Gestalt) takes "the shape of love-in-freedom" (p. 194). Hodgson writes eloquently, "God is present in specific shapes or patterns of praxis that have a configuring, transformative power within [the] historical process, moving the process in a determinate direction, that of the creative unification of multiplicities of elements into new wholes, into creative syntheses that build human solidarity, enhance freedom, break systematic oppression, heal the injured and broken, and care for the natural." Peter Hodgson, *God in History: Shapes of Freedom*, p. 205. Similarly, but with closer attention to the American South, James Cone posed the question, "How could both black and white churches be Christian if they took opposite stands and both claimed Christ and the Bible as the basis of their views?" James Cone, *My Soul Looks Back*, p. 27. This question Cone regards "as important theologically as those that spurred the Protestant Reformation in Europe." Toward the end of a more responsible church, Cone claims that the Christian church "must be an instrument of freedom's revelation in the world." Ibid., p. 68.

12. Victoria Gray Adams, interview with the author.

13. John Lewis, interview with the author. He explained further, "I really believe that I had been called by God to enter the struggle. I had to learn to turn myself over and follow; to be consistent and follow, and somehow trust that it's all going to be taken care of; it's all going to work out. My faith in God was at the heart of what I did. I grew up being taught in Sunday school about Jesus; I heard the minister preaching, saying that if I believed in Jesus, then my hands and my feet must become the hands and feet of other men and women. I knew that if I was going to be a follower, I must do the work of the movement."

14. Cleveland Sellers, interview with the author.

15. Victoria Gray Adams, interview with the author.

16. Curtis Hayes in "Freedom on My Mind" (film).

Afterword

1. King explains the significance of his 5 percent white vote: "The chaplain of Rusk College, who was also a Methodist minister, ran for Senate against Jim Eastland when I ran for Congress. So all of our posters had a black man and a white man side by side. This is the first vote the year after the Voter Registration Act of 1965, with everyone like Mrs. Hamer and Larry Guyot thinking it was very im-

portant that in one district we have a black and a white candidate. This was a way of saying we were getting beyond race; although I did not campaign in white neighborhoods." Edwin King, interview with the author.

2. For a fascinating account of the campaign, see William H. Chafe, *Never Stop Running: Allard Lowenstein and the Struggle to Save American Liberalism*, pp. 262–75.

3. In 1972 King represented the Mississippi Loyalists delegation as a supporter of George McGovern.

4. Rosellen Brown, *Civil Wars* (New York: Knopf, 1984), p. 370.

5. Hamer cited in Kay Mills, *This Little Light of Mine*, p. 274.

6. "Beatnik missionaries," cited in *The Commercial Appeal*, June 22, 1964, microfilm, Memphis Public Library.

7. Edwin King, interview with the author.

8. Sansing cited in Jerry Mitchell, "'Mississippi is 'Free at Last' with Conviction," *Jackson Clarion Ledger*, February 7, 1994; Edwin King, Letter to author, February 25, 1994.

9. Calvin Trillin, "State Secrets," *The New Yorker*, May 29, 1995, p. 58.

10. Ibid., p. 59.

11. Edwin King, interview with the author.

12. Since 1989, the McCain Library at the University of Southern Mississippi has housed portions of the Sovereignty Commission files, which are available to researchers.

13. Fred Hiatt, "Mississippi's Secret," *Washington Post*, April 14, 1996. See also Ed King, "Sovereignty Commission Victims Must Act Soon," *Jackson Clarion Ledger*, January 27, 1997, p. 15.

14. John Salter, Letter to Mary Margaret Bowers, December 28, 1994, author's collection.

15. Edwin King, interview with the author.

16. Dietrich Bonhoeffer, *Letters and Papers from Prison*, p. 229.

17. Protestant theologians of an earlier era spoke often of the requirements of "realism" and "honesty." Reinhold Niebuhr built his reputation as a public theologian on his clarion call to Christians to separate genuine faith from cultural and national self-confidence, though no one wrote more eloquently of theology's bold task than Walter Marshall Horton: "[The] word 'realism' suggests to me, above all, a resolute determination to face all the facts of life candidly, beginning preferably with the most stubborn, perplexing, and disheartening ones, so that any lingering romantic illusions may be dispelled at the start; and then, *through* these facts and not in spite of them, to pierce as deep as one may into the solid structure of reality, until one finds whatever ground of courage, hope, and faith is *actually* there, independent of human preferences and desires, and so casts anchor in that ground." Cited in Robin W. Lovin, *Reinhold Niebuhr and Christian Realism*, 1995, p. 47.

18. Cleveland Sellers, *The River of No Return*, pp. 273, 277. As Medgar Evers had earlier declared of his native Mississippi, "There's land here, where a man can

raise cattle, and I'm going to do that someday. There are lakes where a man can sink a hook and fight bass." Cited in Adam Nossiter, *Of Long Memory*, p. 37.

19. Cleveland Sellers, interview with the author.

20. Ibid.

21. Ibid. See Harold T. Lewis, *Yet With a Steady Beat: The African American Struggle for Recognition in the Episcopal Church*; *The Church Speaks on Race: Official Statements of the Episcopal Church and the Anglican Communion, 1940–1958* (New York: National Council, 1959); David L. Holmes, *A Brief History of the Episcopal Church* (Valley Forge, Pa.: Trinity Press International, 1993), pp. 162–67; Robert W. Prichard, *A History of the Episcopal Church* (Harrisburg, Pa.: Morehouse Publishing, 1991), pp. 242–44.

22. Carlton Morales, interview with the author.

23. "Carlton Owen Morales," *Episcopal Clerical Directory* (New York: Church Hymnal Corporation, 1995), p. 583.

24. Cleveland Sellers, "Black Power, 1966–1996," public lecture, Baltimore, April 9, 1996, videotape, author's collection.

25. Carlton Morales, interview with the author.

26. Cleveland Sellers, interview with the author.

27. Ibid.

28. Cited in Jack Bass, "Justice Finally Comes to the Orangeburg Massacre," *Los Angeles Times*, August 8, 1993.

29. Cleveland Sellers in Ron Chepisiuk, *Sixties Radicals, Then and Now* (Jefferson, N.C.: McFarland, 1995), p. 55.

30. Cleveland Sellers, interview with the author.

31. Ibid.

32. Ibid. He says, "There was a time when, say, if I saw something was happening in Arkansas, I would jump in my car and go there to help out. Today, I would send a contribution, but I'm not going to go to Arkansas." Cleveland Sellers in Chepisiuk, *Sixties Radicals, Then and Now*, p. 49.

ACKNOWLEDGMENTS

A 1965 PHOTO of my grandfather hangs over my desk. He is finger-pecking a story on his typewriter somewhere in the Mississippi Delta. He stands behind the trunk of an automobile, on which the typewriter is placed, a study in concentration, the smoke from his cigar circling into the hot day.

My grandfather, Kenneth Toler, covered Mississippi politics for more than thirty years as a newspaper man for the *Memphis Commercial Appeal*. His offices in Jackson were in the King Edward Hotel and the state capitol, and he lived with his wife and four daughters a few blocks away, near Belhaven College. A large section of his notes and newspaper articles were kept in a file cabinet in the sleeping porch of their home, and remained there after he died in the fall of 1966. I was eight years old at the time. Over the years I have read sections of his writings and notes; his interests in the 1940s and 1950s varied widely, from prohibition to the crazed Governor Bilbo, to the state's chilling mental health practices (for which his courageous reporting should have received wide acclaim). From the early 1960s and until his untimely death his stories focused almost exclusively on civil rights and massive white resistance. I don't remember him talking about this much—I *was* just a kid—but I do remember how tired he seemed in the late afternoons, sitting in his reading chair, working over the *New York Times* crossword puzzle with the cigar in his mouth.

At family gatherings there wasn't much talk about civil rights either, but among the sons-in-law and daughters and grandchildren there was a lot of talk about God. My grandfather mainly kept silent.

That silence got me thinking over the years. Honesty required great carefulness with one's subject matter. "DeDe" knew this well, always writing even-handedly of the people and events colliding in Mississippi in the last years of his life. How to make sense of the colliding images of God was another matter. In any case, my grandfather, a man of deliberate but reserved piety, who wanted only the hymn "O God Our Help in Ages Past" sung at his funeral, was not going to add to the confusion.

But as a trained theologian, born in Alabama and raised in Mississippi, I come to the subject matter with a different responsibility. I have been haunted all my life by the perplexing Christian world of my childhood. In this manner, I have come to understand my task as that of bringing the same honesty to theological material that my grandfather brought to the more expressly political.

I owe a great debt to many colleagues for reading and commenting on part or all of the book: Jim Buckley, Karen Wright Marsh, Larry Rasmussen, Ed King, Taylor Branch, and the members of the Leadership Seminar for Younger Scholars at Duke University. John Dittmer, in a remarkable gesture of academic collegiality, offered detailed comments on the entire manuscript and vastly improved the book as a result. Of course, I am responsible for errors of fact that may appear in the manuscript. Many other people offered helpful suggestions and comments: Joan Trumpauer Mulholland, David Garrow, Neil McMillen, Tracy Sugarman, Jack Nelson, Greg Jones, Craig Dykstra, Clayborne Carson, Victoria Gray Adams, John Findlay, Clayton Sullivan, Betty Robinson, Claire Mathews, Matthew Galman, Cheryl Sanders, Robin Lovin, Andrew Young, Jerry Thornberry, John Lewis, James Deotis Roberts, Fisher Humphreys, Tommy King, Cleveland Payne, John Perkins, Spencer Perkins, Chris Rice, Bob Zellner, Will D. Campbell, and Duncan Gray, Jr. Many thanks also to my tenacious and spirited research assistants: Carlene Bauer, Christian Wright, Susan Fields, Janet Chwalibog, Amanda Walker, and Brian Wabler.

I take great pleasure in thanking the numerous fellowship programs and foundations that have supported the research and writing of this book: the Evangelical Scholars Program of the Pew Charitable Trusts; the Loyola College Junior Faculty Sabbatical Program; the Louisville Institute for the Study of the Protestantism and American Culture; and the J. Mack Robinson Foundation of Atlanta.

In addition to all the people who granted me interviews and corresponded with me, thanks are due to the archivists and librarians at the Amistad Research Center at Tulane University; the Archives of the Episcopal Diocese of Maryland; the Martin Luther King, Jr., Library and Archives; the University of California at Los Angeles; the Morland Springarn Research Center at Howard University; the Mississippi Baptist Historical Commission; the Lauren Rogers Museum and Library in Laurel, Mississippi; the McCain Library and Archives at the University of Southern Mississippi; the Jackson State University Library; the State Historical Society of South Carolina; the Episcopal Diocese of Charleston; Voorhees College in Denmark, South Carolina; the City Library of New Orleans; First Baptist Church, Jackson, Mississippi; First Baptist Church, Houston, Texas; Broadway Baptist Church, Ft. Worth, Texas; the State Historical Society of Wisconsin; the Library of Congress; and the Loyola College Library and Interlibrary Loan Department. Mattie Sink, Director of the Special Collection at the Mississippi State University, Clarence Hunter at Coleman Library, Tougaloo College, and Bill Sumner at the Historical Commission of the

Southern Baptist Convention in Nashville went beyond the call of duty to help find documents and materials. I was also fortunate enough to see portions of the private papers of Edwin King, Nan Toler, Elizabeth Marsh, Cleveland Sellers, and Joan Trumpauer Mulholland.

I wish to make a special mention of all those people who offered steady encouragement toward the writing of the book: James Davison Hunter, Wolfgang Huber, Jean Bethke Elshtain, Robert Coles, Wilson Minor, Alan Jacobs, David Roswell, Tom Scheye, and my agent, Carol Mann. Ann Wald, my editor at Princeton University Press, was always supportive, always reassuring. Thanks also to her editorial assistant Helen Hsu and to my extraordinary copy editor, Margaret Case, for the invaluable help they provided. My colleagues in the Theology Department at Loyola College never ceased to inspire me with their kindness and intellectual comradery. Van Gardner, the Dean of the Episcopal Cathedral of the Incarnation in Baltimore, allowed me the use of a sunny office in a semi-hidden room behind the organ pipes (which only occasionally sent me to the library). I am grateful to Van and his colleagues Fran Brown, Bess Garrett, and Mary Grace Dudley for their big-hearted friendship. My fellow travelers in Theological Horizons always believed in the importance of this work and were always the most gracious hosts on my frequent trips to the South. I am deeply grateful for their continued patronage of my work: Kamal and Cleo Mansour, David and Donna Allman, Sonny and Marion Ellis, David and Laura McDaniel, Jerry and Catherine Capps, Judy and Marion King, Isabelle and Andrew Robinson, Jim and Jenny Ewing and Lee Burge, among others. Many of my neighbors in Baltimore proved to be wonderful conversation partners in this project, sometimes even sharing with me their own movement memories: Sid and Esther Levin, Mike, Susan and Rachel Morrison, Abe and Rita Genecin, and Aleine Cohen.

I also wish to call attention to the hospitality of many Mississippians: to Chryssy Wilson, publicity director for the Mississippi Department of Archives and History, who presides over the coolest front porch in Jackson, and to Kathleen Warnock and Paige and Rick Dunkerton for their many acts of kindness during our stay in Laurel. Charles and Margaret Ann Pickering introduced my two city boys to all the same wonderful mysteries of farm life they had shown me three decades ago. I am especially grateful to Joy Roberts, who saw to it that my family was always well fed and well dressed. Many thanks to Paul and Jo Helen Schneider for the generous use of their home during the summer of 1995. My grandmother, Nan Toler, has inspired me in many ways; her vigorous intellect and her well-honed powers of debate, always best displayed around her unbeatable cooking, have given to me time and again a parable of God's own welcoming table. My loving parents, Bob and Myra Marsh, were a never-ending source of encouragement and support. My father's eloquent sermons, especially ones like "Amazing Grace for Every Race," and his long-standing commitment to racial justice, continue to give strength to my own modest efforts to fight the good fight.

I am deeply blessed to have a family that not only endured my writing and frequent trips to the deep South but was always eager to talk about the characters and events, and often even willing to accompany me on my travels just for the fun of it. My wife, Karen Wright Marsh, with her irrepressible energy, joined me in the adventure of this book: I am certain it would not have been written without her own many creative contributions along the way. My love and respect for her are difficult to express adequately here; but I will say of Karen, and of our sons, Henry and Will, that they are my greatest delight, my abiding joy.

In 1967, my family moved to Laurel, Mississippi, where my father became pastor of the First Baptist Church. After three years of a wretched Jim Crow school system, integration finally came. On a sweltering morning in late August, my mother drove me to the brown stone fortress that would serve as the new seventh grade. I had no conception at all of the significance of the morning. None of the white kids did as far as I knew. As I stood outside the school doors waiting for textbooks, my mind was on other things: a new pair of blue jeans, for example, which were sticking to my legs like fly paper, stinking like wet hay. I do not remember taking much notice of the African American children standing with me in line, even though blacks made up half the class. The school year unfolded without drama, full of little successes, pleasures, and embarrassments. Only much later did I realize the resolute and unreflective courage of our being together as black and white children in a common school building in the state of Mississippi. I am so glad I was there, and happy that my friends and I—white and, in time, black—had the good sense not to think too much about it. I dedicate this book to all my classmates in Laurel, but especially to Joe Porter, Jerome Johnson, Terry Caves, Walter Chandler, and Joey Roberts.

SELECTED BIBLIOGRAPHY

Archives

Personal papers and some archival collections are not organized in such a way that locations of individual records can be given in the notes.

Amistad Research Center, Tulane University, New Orleans

Charles Sherrod Papers, State Historical Society of Wisconsin, Madison, Wisconsin

Cleveland Sellers Papers, private collection

Douglas Hudgins Papers, First Baptist Church, Jackson, Mississippi

Edwin King Private Papers, private collection

Ed King Papers, Coleman Library, Tougaloo College, Tougaloo, Mississippi

Elizabeth Marsh Papers, private collection

Historical Commission of the Southern Baptist Convention, Nashville, Tennessee

Joan Trumpauer Mulholland Papers, private collection

Johnson Family Papers, McCain Library and Archives, University of Southern Mississippi, Hattiesburg

Lauren Rogers Museum and Library, Laurel, Mississippi

Mississippi Baptist Historical Commission, Jackson, Mississippi

Mississippi Department of Archives and History, Jackson

Mississippi Oral History Program, McCain Library and Archives, University of Southern Mississippi, Hattiesburg

Mississippi State University, Special Collection, Starkville, Mississippi

SNCC Papers, Martin Luther King, Jr., Center, Atlanta, Georgia

Tracy Sugarman, Oral History Archives, private collection

Books and Articles

Activities of Ku Klux Klan Organizations in the United States: Hearings before the Committee on Un-American Activities, House of Representatives, February 1–4 and 7–11, 1966 (Washington, D.C.: U.S. Government Printing Office, 1966).

Anderson, Victor. *Beyond Ontological Blackness: An Essay on African American Religious and Cultural Criticism.* New York: Continuum, 1995.

Bailey, Kenneth L. *Southern White Protestantism in the Twentieth Century.* New York: Harper & Row, 1964.

Baldwin, James. *The Fire Next Time.* New York: Vintage Books, 1993.

Barth, Karl. *The Word of God and the Word of Man*, translated by Douglas Horton. Gloucester, Mass.: Peter Smith, 1978.

Bass, Jack, and Jack Nelson. *The Orangeburg Massacre*. Macon, Ga.: Mercer University Press, 1984.

Belfrage, Sally. *Freedom Summer*. New York: Viking Press, 1965.

Bloom, Harold. *The American Religion: The Emergence of the Post-Christian Nation*. New York: Simon and Schuster, 1992.

Bonhoeffer, Dietrich. *Letters and Papers from Prison*. New York: Macmillan, 1972.

Boyer, Paul. *When Time Shall Be No More: Prophecy Belief in Modern American Culture*. Cambridge: Harvard University Press, 1992.

Brady, Tom P. *Black Monday: Segregation or Amalgamation . . . America Has Its Choice*. Winona, Miss.: Association of Citizens' Councils of Mississippi, 1955.

Buber, Martin. *I and Thou*, translated by Walter Kaufmann. New York: Charles Scribner's Sons, 1970.

Burner, David. *Making Peace with the 60s*. Princeton: Princeton University Press, 1996.

Cagin, Seth, and Philip Dray. *We Are Not Afraid: The Story of Goodman, Schwerner, and Chaney and the Civil Rights Campaign for Mississippi*. New York: Macmillan, 1988.

Campbell, Will D. *Brother to a Dragonfly*. New York: Seabury, 1977.

————. *Race and the Renewal of the Church*. Philadelphia: Westminster Press, 1962.

Carmichael, Stokely, and Charles V. Hamilton. *Black Power: The Politics of Liberation in America*. New York: Random House, 1967.

Carson, Clayborne. *In Struggle: SNCC and the Black Awakening of the 1960s*. Cambridge: Harvard University Press, 1981.

Chafe, William H. *Never Stop Running: Allard Lowenstein and the Struggle to Save American Liberalism*. New York: Basic Books, 1993.

Cobb, James C. *The Most Southern Place on Earth: The Mississippi Delta and the Roots of Regional Identity*. New York: Oxford University Press, 1992.

Cohn, Norman. *The Pursuit of the Millennium: Revolutionary Millenarians and Mystical Anarchists of the Middle Ages*. New York: Oxford University Press, 1970.

Coles, Robert. *Children of Crisis: A Study of Courage and Fear*. New York: Dell, 1966.

Cone, James H. *Black Theology and Black Power*. San Francisco: Harper & Row, 1969.

————. *My Soul Looks Back*. Nashville, Tenn.: Abingdon Press, 1982.

Cruse, Harold. *The Crisis of the Negro Intellectual: A Historical Analysis of the Failure of Black Leadership*. New York: Quill, 1984.

Cunningham, W. J. *Agony at Galloway: One Church's Struggle with Social Change*. Jackson: University Press of Mississippi, 1980.

Davies, Alan. *Infected Christianity: A Study of Modern Racism*. Kingston: McGill-Queen's University Press, 1988.

Deats, Paul, and Carol Robb. eds. *The Boston Personalist Tradition in Philosophy, Social Ethics, and Theology*. Macon, Ga.: Mercer University Press, 1986.

De Gruchy, John W. *Christianity and Democracy: A Theology for a Just World Order*. Cambridge: Cambridge University Press, 1995.

Dent, Tom. *Southern Journey: A Return to the Civil Rights Movement.* New York: William Morrow, 1997.

Dillard, W. O. "Chet." *Clearburning: For Felonies Compounded by the FBI, Et Cetera.* Jackson, Miss.: Lawyer's Publishing Press, 1992.

Dittmer, John. *Local People: The Struggle for Civil Rights in Mississippi.* Urbana and Chicago: University of Illinois Press, 1994.

Douglas, Mary. *Purity and Danger: An Analysis of the Concepts of Pollution and Taboo.* London: Routledge & Kegan Paul, 1966.

Egerton, John. *A Mind to Stay Here: Profiles from the South.* New York: Macmillan, 1970.

Eighmy, John Lee. *Churches in Cultural Captivity: A History of the Social Attitudes of Southern Baptists.* Knoxville: University of Tennessee Press, 1976.

Evans, James H., Jr. *We Have Been Believers: An African American Systematic Theology.* Minneapolis: Fortress Press, 1992.

Evans, Sara. *Personal Politics: The Roots of Women's Liberation in the Civil Rights Movement and the New Left.* New York: Vintage Books, 1979.

Findlay, James F., Jr. *Church People in the Struggle: The National Council of Churches and the Black Freedom Movement, 1950–1970.* New York: Oxford University Press, 1993.

Forman, James. *The Making of Black Revolutionaries.* Seattle: Open Hand Publishing, 1985.

Fredrickson, George M. *The Black Image in the White Mind: The Debate on Afro-American Character and Destiny 1817–1914.* Hanover, N.H.: Wesleyan University Press, 1987.

Garrow, J. David. *Bearing the Cross: Martin Luther King, Jr. and the Southern Christian Leadership Conference.* New York: Vintage Books, 1988.

Hampton, Henry, and Steve Fayer. *Voices of Freedom: An Oral History of the Civil Rights Movement from the 1950s Through the 1980s.* New York: Bantam Books, 1990.

Harding, Vincent. "Black Power and the American Christ," in *Black Theology: A Documentary History, 1966–1979,* edited by Gayroud S. Wilmore and James H. Cone (Maryknoll, N.Y.: Orbis Books, 1979), pp. 35–42.

Havel, Václav. *Living in Truth.* London: Faber and Faber, 1987.

Hegel, G. W. F. *Introduction to the Philosophy of History,* translated by Leo Rauch. Indianapolis: Hackett, 1988.

Hodgson, Peter C. *God in History: Shapes of Freedom.* Nashville, Tenn.: Abingdon Press, 1989.

Hollifield, E. Brooks. *The Gentlemen Theologians: American Theology in Southern Culture 1795–1860.* Durham: Duke University Press, 1978.

Holt, Len. *The Summer That Didn't End: The Story of the Mississippi Civil Rights Project of 1964.* New York: Da Capo Press, 1992.

Huie, William Bradford. *Three Lives for Mississippi.* New York: WCC Books, 1965.

Johnson, Erle. *Mississippi's Defiant Years, 1953–1973.* Forest, Miss.: Lake Harbor Publishers, 1990.

Jordon, Winthrop D. *The White Man's Burden: Historical Origins of Racism in the United States.* New York: Oxford University Press, 1974.

Jüngel, Eberhard. *God as the Mystery of the World,* translated by Darrell L. Guder. Grand Rapids, Mich.: Eerdmans, 1983.

King, Edwin. "The White Church in Mississippi." Manuscript, Edwin King Private Papers.

King, Mary. *Freedom Song: A Personal Story of the 1960s Civil Rights Movement.* New York: Quill, 1987.

King, Richard, *Civil Rights and the Idea of Freedom.* New York: Oxford University Press, 1992.

Lawson, Steven F. "Freedom Then, Freedom Now: The Historiography of the Civil Rights Movement." *American Historical Review* 96:2 (April 2, 1991), 456–71.

Lewis, Harold T. *Yet with a Steady Beat: The African American Struggle for Recognition in the Episcopal Church.* Valley Forge, Pa.: Trinity Press International, 1995.

Lischer, Richard. *The Preacher King: Martin Luther King, Jr. and the Word That Moved America.* New York: Oxford University Press, 1995.

Lovin, Robin W. *Reinhold Niebuhr and Christian Realism.* Cambridge: Cambridge University Press, 1995.

Luker, Ralph E. *The Social Gospel in Black and White: American Racial Reform, 1885–1912.* Chapel Hill: University of North Carolina Press, 1991.

Luther, Martin. *Selected Political Writings,* edited by J. M. Porter. Philadelphia: Fortress Press, 1974.

MacLean, Nancy. *Behind the Mask of Chivalry: The Making of the Second Ku Klux Klan.* New York: Oxford University Press, 1994).

Manis, Andrew Michael. *Southern Civil Religions in Conflict: Black and White Baptists and Civil Rights, 1947–1957.* Athens: University of Georgia Press, 1987.

Mars, Florence. *Witness in Philadelphia.* Baton Rouge: Louisiana State University Press, 1977.

Marsden, George M. *Fundamentalism and American Culture: The Shaping of Twentieth-Century Evangelicalism, 1870–1925.* New York: Oxford University Press, 1980.

Massengill, Reed. *Portrait of a Racist: The Man Who Killed Medgar Evers.* New York: St. Martin's Press, 1994.

McAdam, Doug. *Freedom Summer.* New York: Oxford University Press, 1988.

McClendon, James Wm., Jr. *Biography as Theology: How Life Stories Can Remake Today's Theology.* Nashville, Tenn.: Abingdon, 1974.

McIlhany, William H., II. *Klandestine: The Untold Story of Delmer Dennis and His Role in the FBI's War against the Ku Klux Klan.* New Rochelle, N.Y.: Arlington House Publishers, 1975

McLemore, Leslie Burl. "The Mississippi Freedom Democratic Party: A Case Study of Grass-Roots Politics." Ph.D. dissertation, University of Massachusetts, Amherst, 1971.

McMillen, Neil R. *The Citizens' Council: Organized Resistance to the Second Reconstruction, 1954–1964*. Urbana: University of Illinois Press, 1971.

———. *Dark Journey: Black Mississippians in the Age of Jim Crow*. Urbana: University of Illinois Press, 1989.

Meier, August. *A White Scholar and the Black Community, 1945–1965*. Amherst: University of Massachusetts, 1992.

Mills, Kay. *This Little Light of Mine: The Life of Fannie Lou Hamer*. New York: Dutton, 1993.

Mills, Nicolaus. *Like a Holy Crusade: Mississippi 1964—The Turning of the Civil Rights Movement in America*. Chicago: Ivan R. Dee, 1992.

Mississippi Black Paper: Fifty-seven Negro and White Citizens' Testimony of Police Brutality, the Breakdown of Law and Order and the Corruption of Justice in Mississippi. New York: Random House, 1965.

Moody, Anne. *Coming of Age in Mississippi*. New York: Doubleday, 1968.

Muelder, Walter G. *Methodism and Society in the Twentieth Century*. New York: Abingdon, 1961.

Nelson, Jack. *Terror in the Night: The Klan's Campaign against the Jews*. New York: Simon and Schuster, 1993.

Newby, Idus A. *Jim Crow's Defense: Anti-Negro Thought in America, 1900–1930*. Baton Rouge: Louisiana State University Press, 1965.

———. *The Development of Segregationist Thought*. Homewood, Ill.: Dorsey Press, 1968.

Newton, Michael, and Judy Ann Newton. *The Ku Klux Klan: An Encyclopedia*. New York: Garland Publishing, 1991.

Niebuhr, Reinhold. *The Self and the Dramas of History*. New York: Charles Scribner's Sons, 1955.

Nossiter, Adam. *Of Long Memory: Mississippi and the Murder of Medgar Evers*. New York: Addison-Wesley, 1994.

O'Connor, Flannery. *Mystery and Manners*. New York: Farrar, Straus and Giroux, 1969.

O'Reilly, Kenneth. *Racial Matters: The FBI's Secret File on Black America, 1960–1972*. New York: Free Press, 1989.

Ownby, Ted. *Subduing Satan: Religion, Recreation and Manhood in the Rural South, 1865–1920*. Chapel Hill: University of North Carolina Press, 1990.

Payne, Charles M. *I've Got the Light of Freedom: The Organizing Tradition and the Mississippi Freedom Struggle*. Berkeley and Los Angeles: University of California Press, 1995.

Pearson, Hugh. *The Shadow of the Panther: Huey Newton and the Price of Black Power in America*. Reading, Mass.: Addison-Wesley, 1994.

Percy, Walker. "Mississippi: The Fallen Paradise," in *Signposts in a Strange Land*, edited by Patrick Samway. New York: Farrar, Straus and Giroux, 1991, 39–52.

Percy, William Alexander. *Lanterns on the Levee: Recollections of a Planter's Son*. Baton Rouge: Louisiana State University Press, 1973.

Raboteau, Albert J. *Slave Religion: The "Invisible Institution" in the Antebellum South.* Oxford: Oxford University Press, 1978.

Raines, Howell. *My Soul Is Rested: Movement Days in the Deep South Remembered.* New York: Penguin, 1983.

Rasmussen, Larry. *Reinhold Niebuhr: Theologian of Public Life.* Minneapolis: Fortress Press, 1988.

Rauschenbusch, Walter. *A Theology for the Social Gospel.* Nashville, Tenn.: Abingdon, 1978.

Roberts, J. Deotis. *Liberation and Reconciliation: A Black Theology.* Philadelphia: Westminster, 1971.

Romaine, Anne Cooke. "The Mississippi Freedom Democratic Party through August, 1964." Master's thesis, University of Virginia, 1970.

Rorty, Richard. *Contingency, Irony and Solidarity.* Cambridge: Cambridge University Press, 1987.

Salter, John. *Jackson, Mississippi: An American Chronicle of Struggle and Schism.* Malabar, Fla.: Robert E. Krieger, 1979.

Scarry, Elaine. *The Body in Pain: The Making and Unmaking of the World.* New York: Oxford University Press, 1985.

Sellers, Cleveland, with Robert Terrell. *The River of No Return: The Autobiography of a Black Militant and the Life and Death of SNCC.* Jackson: University Press of Mississippi, 1990.

Silver, James. *Mississippi: The Closed Society.* New York: Harcourt, Brace and World, 1964.

Smith, Hilrie Shelton. *In His Image, But: Racism and Southern Religion, 1780–1910.* Durham: Duke University Press, 1972.

Smith, John David, ed. *The Biblical and "Scientific" Defense of Slavery.* New York: Garland, 1993.

Smith, Lillian. *Killers of the Dream.* New York: W. W. Norton, 1949.

Smith, Theophus H. *Conjuring Culture: Biblical Formations of Black America.* New York: Oxford University Press, 1994.

Stoper, Emily. *The Student Nonviolent Coordinating Committee: The Growth of Radicalism in a Civil Rights Organization.* New York: Carlson, 1989.

Sugarman, Tracy. *Stranger at the Gates.* New York: Hill and Wang, 1966.

Sutherland, Elizabeth, ed., *Letters from Mississippi.* New York: McGraw-Hill, 1965.

Tanner, Kathryn. *The Politics of God: Christian Theologies and Social Justice.* Minneapolis: Fortress Press, 1992.

Tarrants, Thomas A., III, *The Conversion of a Klansman: The Story of a Former Ku Klux Klan Terrorist.* Garden City, N.Y.: Doubleday, 1979.

—— and John Perkins, with David Wimbish. *He's My Brother: A Black Activist and a Former Klansman Tell Their Stories.* Grand Rapids, Mich.: Chosen Books, 1994.

Taylor, Charles. *Hegel and Modern Society.* Cambridge: Cambridge University Press, 1979.

Thurman, Howard. *Jesus and the Disinherited*. Richmond, Ind.: Friends United Press, 1981.

———. *With Head and Heart: The Autobiography of Howard Thurman*. New York: Harcourt Brace Jovanovich, 1979.

Tillich, Paul. *The New Being*. New York: Charles Scribner's Sons, 1955.

Von Hoffman, Nicholas. *Mississippi Notebook*. New York: David White, 1964.

Walton, Anthony. *Mississippi*. New York: Alfred A. Knopf, 1996.

Walzer, Michael. *Exodus and Revolution*. New York: Basic Books, 1985.

Warren, Robert Penn. *Segregation*. New York: Random House, 1956.

Washington, James Melvin, ed. *A Testament of Hope: The Essential Writings of Martin Luther, King, Jr.* San Francisco: Harper Collins, 1986.

West, Cornel. *Prophesy Deliverance! An Afro-American Revolutionary Christianity*. Philadelphia: Westminster, 1982.

Whitehead, Don. *Attack on Terror: The FBI against the Ku Klux Klan in Mississippi*. New York: Funk & Wagnalls, 1970.

Whitfield, Stephen J. *A Death in the Delta: The Story of Emmett Till*. Baltimore: Johns Hopkins University Press, 1988.

Wilson, Charles R. *Baptized in Blood: The Religion of the Lost Cause, 1865–1920*. Athens: University of Georgia Press, 1980.

Wind, James P., and James W. Lewis. *American Congregations: Volume 1: Portraits of Twelve Religious Communities*. Chicago: University of Chicago Press, 1994.

Woodward, C. Vann. *The Strange Career of Jim Crow*. New York: Oxford University Press, 1974.

Wright, Richard. *Black Boy: A Record of Childhood and Youth*. New York: Harper, 1945.

INTERVIEWS

Victoria Gray Adams, Petersburg, Virginia, April 6, 1995

Marion Barry, Washington, D.C., February 1994

Sam Bowers, Laurel, Mississippi, July 30, 31, August 3, 1994

Will D. Campbell, Mt. Joliet, Tennessee, July 6, 1993

Roosevelt and Beatrice ("Bud" and "Biddie") Cole, Philadelphia, Mississippi, August 7, 1994

Ken Dean, Hattiesburg, Mississippi, July 2, 1994; (telephone), July 4, September 10, 1994

Mrs. Annie Devine (telephone), June 22, 1995

Duncan Gray, Jr., Jackson, Mississippi, July 25, 1993

Fisher Humphreys, Birmingham, Alabama, July 14, 1994

Mrs. Allen Johnson (telephone), July 15, 1994

Edith Jones, Baltimore, Maryland, October 28, 1996

Edwin King, Jackson, Mississippi, July 10, 1993, June 11, July 13, August 7, 1994, May 5, June 10, July 13, September 23, 24, 1995; Alexandria, Virginia, January 4, 1995

Thomas King, Hattiesburg, Mississippi, July 25, 1994

John Lewis, Washington, D.C., April 4, 1994

Florence Mars, Philadelphia, Mississippi, August 7, 1994

Wilson Minor, Jackson, Mississippi, August 2, 1994, May 10, 1995

Carlton Owen Morales (telephone), June 15, 1996

Joan Trumpauer Mulholland, Arlington, Virginia, September 10, 11, 1994, February 10, 1995

Jack Nelson (telephone), September 10, 1993

Devours Nix (telephone), September 8, 1993

Cleveland Payne, Laurel, Mississippi, July 22, 1994

Spencer Perkins, Jackson, Mississippi, July 23, 1994; Baltimore, Maryland, September 6, 1995

Charles Pickering, Hebron, Mississippi, July 24, 1994

Betty Robinson, Baltimore, Maryland, April 9, 1996

Cleveland Sellers, Denmark, South Carolina, July 29, August 1, 1995; Baltimore, Maryland, April 8, 9, 1996

Jane Stembridge (telephone), March 19, 1995

Clayton Sullivan (telephone), March 20, 1995
Wilson Terrell, Laurel, Mississippi, August 1, 1994
Andrew Young, Baltimore, Maryland, March 23, 1993
Bob Zellner, New Orleans, March 5, 6, 1995; Baltimore, Maryland, November 6, 1995

INDEX

abortion, 196
American Civil Liberties Union, 122, 198
American Friends Service Committee, 122
Anderson, Victor, 191, 249–250n175
Athanasius, 24

Baker, Ella, 34–35
Baldwin, James, 9
Baptist Record, The, 70
Barbour, William H., 197–198
Barnett, Ross, 46, 51; as Sunday School
    teacher at First Baptist Church, Jackson,
    Mississippi, 89
Barth, Karl, 3, 122
Bass, Jack, 202
Bates, Daisy, 156
Batiste, John, 161
Beck, Harold, 121
Beckwith, Byron de la, 177, 196–197,
    242n44
Belafonte, Harry, 44
Belfrage, Sally, 30, 43, 193
beloved community, 6, 8, 29, 148,
    149–151, 166, 170, 174, 178, 196, 204
Bergmark, Robert, 120
Bertocci, Peter, 121
Bevel, James, 10, 12, 13, 175
Billington, Monroe, 221n103
Black Panther party, 176, 187
black power, 7, 189, 246–247n127,
    249n166,171; and Christianity,
    189–190; and organizing in the South,
    181–182; origins in the 1966 Meredith
    March Against Fear, 176–179. *See also*
    Carmichael, Stokely; Sellers, Cleveland
Blackwell, Unita, 212–213n98
Bloom, Harold, 109–110
Bogue Chitto Swamp, 69
Bonhoeffer, Dietrich, 122, 198, 250n3
Borinski, Ernst, 120, 126

"Born of Conviction," 132
Bowers, Eaton Jackson (grandfather of
    Samuel Holloway Bowers, Jr.), 50, 51
Bowers, Eaton Jackson, Sr. (great-grand-
    father of Samuel Holloway Bowers, Jr.),
    50
Bowers, Evangeline Peyton (mother of
    Samuel Holloway Bowers, Jr.), 50, 51,
    51–52
Bowers, Samuel Holloway (father of
    Samuel Holloway Bowers, Jr.), 51, 52
Bowers, Samuel Holloway, Jr., 5, 112, 192,
    193; against "adult authorities," 52; anti-
    Jewish theology of 60, 73–74, 192; bib-
    lical influences of, 60–64; on "black
    soviets," 79–80, 81; childhood of,
    50–53, 223; current views of, 221–225;
    on the desecration of Mississippi, 49,
    60; education of, 52; 53; on eliminating
    the heretics, 5, 49, 78–79; father of, 51,
    52; on the "Five Tiered Crystallized
    Logos of Western Civilization," 75–78;
    on harassment, 57; hobbies of, 53–54;
    as Imperial Wizard of the White Knights
    of the Ku Klux Klan of Mississippi, 27,
    56–57, 58–59; incarceration of, 73, 192,
    222–225; intellectual influences of, 53;
    mother of, 50, 51, 51–52; and the mur-
    der of Dahmer, 71, 192, 222; and the
    murder of Martin Luther King, Jr.,
    244–245n100; and the murders of
    Schwerner, Chaney, and Goodman, 49,
    64–69, 71; psychology of, 72; religious
    self-understanding and development of,
    5, 52–55, 78–80, 223; on the resurrec-
    tion of Jesus Christ, 63, 75–76, 77; on
    the Summer Project, 65–66, 113; terror-
    ism of, 49; trials of, 72
Boyce, James P., 95
Brady, Tom P., 85